THIS
HOLY PLACE

THIS HOLY PLACE

On the Sanctity of the Synagogue during the Greco-Roman Period

Steven Fine

WIPF & STOCK · Eugene, Oregon

Wipf and Stock Publishers
199 W 8th Ave, Suite 3
Eugene, OR 97401

This Holy Place
On the Sanctity of the Synagogue During the Greco-Roman Period
By Fine, Steven
Copyright©1997 by Fine, Steven
ISBN 13: 978-1-5326-0926-8
Publication date 10/17/2016
Previously published by The University of Notre Dame Press, 1997

Contents

Preface　vii
Introduction　1

CHAPTER ONE
"Sacred Places That They Call Synagogues"　25
The Roots of Synagogue Holiness during the Second Temple Period

CHAPTER TWO
"They Are Sacred Even When Destroyed"　35
The Holiness of Synagogues in Tannaitic Literature

CHAPTER THREE
"The Sanctity of the Synagogue"　61
The Holiness of Synagogues in Amoraic and Post-Amoraic Literature from the Land of Israel

CHAPTER FOUR
"May Peace Be unto All Those Who Gave Charity
in *This Holy Place*"　95
Archaeological Evidence for the Holiness of Late Antique Synagogues in the Land of Israel

CHAPTER FIVE
"You Believe the Place Is Holy Because the Torah and Prophets
Are There. . . ."　127
Synagogue Holiness in the Diaspora during Late Antiquity

Conclusion　159
Postscript　163
Notes　173
Bibliography　241
Photo Credits　279
Index of Ancient Literary Sources　281

Preface

This study has its origins in a field trip to ancient synagogue remains in the Galilee that I led in the spring of 1989. My busload of American and European students and I arrived at our last stop of the day just as the shadows were beginning to descend on the Sea of Galilee. In the golden light of that afternoon the colors of the synagogue mosaic of Hammath Tiberias were particularly brilliant. Stepping down onto the late antique pavement, I proceeded to explain to my students the most intelligible element of the mosaic, the numerous dedicatory inscriptions in Greek and Aramaic. I then proceeded to the visual images, discussing the panel containing a Torah shrine flanked by seven-branched *menorot* and then the magnificent zodiac wheel. Enroute back to Jerusalem I continued to think about the relationship between the inscriptions and the images that appear in this mosaic. The parallel that immediately came to my mind was Picasso's *Guernica*.[1] A person who sees this modern icon but does not know its title cannot possibly understand the intention of the artist. In modern art, the title, or the lack of a title, is important. Perhaps some element of the synagogue inscriptions might serve as a "title" for the Hammath Tiberias mosaic, and hence as an interpretive key to unlocking the religious history of the ancient synagogue. The "title" of the Hammath Tiberias synagogue mosaic was immediately apparent to me. The synagogue building is referred to as a "holy place" in two of its mosaic pavement inscriptions. In a Greek inscription the building is referred to as a *hagios topos* and in Aramaic as *hadain atra qadisha* "this holy place." This is the only name for the synagogue in the dedicatory inscriptions from Hammath Tiberias. The community that tread upon this mosaic pavement thought of their synagogue as a "holy place." What did they mean?

I devoted the next seven years to answering this question. Before presenting the results of this research it is my pleasant duty to thank those individuals and institutions who helped me along the way. I am grateful, first of all, for the financial support that made this research possible. This was generously provided by the

The synagogue mosaic of Hammath Tiberias B, 2a.

Jewish Community Foundation of the Jewish Federation Council of Greater Los Angeles (1987–1988), the Interuniversity Fellowship Program in Jewish Studies (1987–1990), the Lady Davis Fellowship Trust (1989–1990), the National Foundation for Jewish Culture (1991–1992), and the Finkelstein Fellowship of the University of Judaism (1991–1993).

"This Holy Place" is a revised version of my doctoral dissertation, which was written in the Department of Jewish History of the Hebrew University of Jerusalem, under the direction of Professor Lee I. Levine and Professor Lawrence H. Schiffman.[2] Professors Levine and Schiffman guided me through my years of doctoral study. I thank both for their many acts of kindness, their mentorship, and for their continued friendship.

I benefited from the wisdom and generosity of numerous friends and teachers in the process of researching and writing this book, many more than space permits me to mention. Still, I would like to thank the following individuals for their special contributions: Professor Isaiah Gafni (Hebrew University of Jerusalem), Professor Rachel Hachlili (University of Haifa), Rabbi Daniel Landes (Pardes Institute, Jerusalem), Professor Eric M. Meyers (Duke University), Professor Avigdor Shinan (Hebrew University of Jerusalem), Professor Elieser Slomovic (University of Judaism), Rabbi Dr. Aryeh Strikovsky (Pardes Institute, Jerusalem), Ms. Rhoda Terry (Yeshiva University Museum), Professor Joseph Yahalom (Hebrew University of Jerusalem), Professor Ziony Zevit (University of Judaism), and the late Professor Amos Funkenstein (University of California, Los Angeles).

My research for *This Holy Place* was the basis of a related project, *Sacred Realm: The Emergence of the Synagogue in the Ancient World*, an exhibition organized by Yeshiva University Museum in New York (February–December 1996).[3] Through *Sacred Realm* I developed new insights into the history of the ancient synagogue that I in turn integrated into the present book. I thank Mrs. Sylvia Herskowitz, director of Yeshiva University Museum, for championing the idea of *Sacred Realm* and for supporting my research in every way. I will always be appreciative of the many donors, first among them the National Endowment for the Humanities, who made *Sacred Realm* a reality.

Many of the costs of preparing this manuscript for publication were covered by the faculty publications fund of Baltimore Hebrew University. I thank Professor Robert O. Freedman, president, my colleagues and the professional staff of Baltimore Hebrew University for showing me every possible consideration. Sidney Vidaver of the University of Toronto was a great help in the final proofreading. I also thank Professor Gregory Sterling, and the people of the University of Notre Dame Press, for bringing this project to fruition in such a happy way. Finally, I owe much to Carole Roos, who served as editor for the press and saved me from many an unfortunate blunder. Naturally, any remaining errors are mine alone.

On a personal level, I thank my parents, Jane and Leonard Fine, for nurturing my love of Jewish history and of Jewish art from the very beginning. Mr. Yearl E. Schwartz, my first teacher of Judaism, facilitated my first visit to Israel in 1975. All that I do professionally can be traced to that summer. Finally, my wife Leah Bierman Fine has stood at my side throughout this exploration. The completion of this study is a tribute to her wisdom and caring. Our son Elisha Nir has done "great things"[4] from the moment of his birth, many of which have shaped the course of this project. This study is dedicated to Leah, and to Elisha on his sixth birthday.

Introduction

JERUSALEM

On the road to Bethlehem I live.
And in Emeq Refa'im a friend of mine
bakes small cookies, sprinkles sugar
in the German Colony. Amazing

how the old is joined to the new
like sewer pipes on an old wall
in this Jerusalem, as if on canvas
the artist adds here a flower, there an oak—

And here I am with a detective book,
and there an old woman, and here the rails of the train,
and a church, and an Abyssinian priest.

And a man who for his messiah waits
and a hand that on a wall writes:
Holy place, it is forbidden here to urinate.[1]

In this poem Moshe Ha-Na'ami reflects upon the sights and sounds of his Jerusalem as he routinely experienced them during the early 1960s. Any visitor to Jerusalem who sets out, even today, to see the remnants of pre-1967 Jerusalem can immediately recognize the images recounted by the author. That is, except for one: "Holy place, it is forbidden here to urinate." Until recently these words were part of every Jerusalemite's cultural baggage. Painted on the back of a synagogue by a pious Jew "who for his messiah waits," this strange admonition was roughly written on the outer wall of a Sephardi synagogue in Mamilla, a district that was

"Holy Place, it is Forbidden Here to Urinate," synagogue exterior, formerly in Jerusalem's Mamilla Quarter.

razed as part of a recent urban redevelopment project. The person who painted this caution was intent upon protecting the holiness of his synagogue from unknowing irreverence by passers-by. To him, as for all practitioners of Judaism, the synagogue is a holy place deserving of vigilant protection against desecration.[2]

The ascription of holiness to synagogues is, in fact, the result of a long and creative historical process. This study will reach back to the earliest history of the synagogue, over two thousand years ago, to explore how this institution first came to be perceived as a "holy place."[3] Literary and archaeological sources dating to the Greco-Roman period,[4] from the Land of Israel and the Diaspora, all call the synagogue a "holy place."[5] These range from dedicatory inscriptions in Greek, Aramaic, Hebrew, and Latin to Second Temple period authors like Philo of Alexandria and Josephus, Talmudic sources, Patristic literature, Roman law, and synagogue art and architecture. We will show that the idea that synagogues were somehow holy was essential to the ideological development of the synagogue and is indicative of important trends in the history of Judaism during the Greco-Roman period.

In *This Holy Place* we will trace the development of synagogue holiness from source to source, period to period, and place to place. We will argue that the biblical scrolls that were read, studied, and stored within synagogues were the most essential source of synagogue sanctity in the minds of the ancients. The "Sacred Scriptures" developed as the "cult objects" or "relics" of the ancient synagogue, the physical manifestation of the Divine within local congregations. This sanctity was often expressed in terms derived from the Temple, though the synagogue was never a "competitor" with or "replacement" for the eternal Temple of Jerusalem.

In chapter one we will explore the earliest history of synagogue holiness. We will interpret papyri and inscriptions from Ptolemaic Egypt, the writings of Philo of Alexandria and Josephus Flavius, traditions preserved in a Dead Sea text, and the earliest synagogues yet uncovered by archaeologists. We will show that by the first century C.E., while the Temple yet stood, most synagogues were meeting houses where Scripture was read and studied communally. Meeting houses that served groups on the margins of Second Temple period Judaism were apparently attributed with sanctity, though there is little indication that others were. The synagogues belonging to one sect were explicitly called "holy places."

In chapter two we will discuss the role that the synagogue played in the Rabbinic reformulation of Judaism between 70 C.E. and the early third century C.E. Beginning with the Tannaitic Sages at Yavneh, south of modern Tel Aviv, the synagogue took on new significance, becoming an important locus for the early Rabbinic reformulation of Judaism. Through a careful reading of Tannaitic literature we will explore the ways that the synagogue became the premiere institution of what the Sages called *zeman ha-zeh* (literally "this time"), the period between the destruction of the Temple in 70 C.E. and its expected messianic rebuilding. The sanctity of the biblical scrolls, the application of Temple motifs to synagogues, and the development of public prayer were the building blocks of this developing conception of the synagogue as a holy place.

Chapter three treats the development of synagogue sanctity in the Land of Israel from the early third century of the Common Era through the close of antiquity, as this tentative holy place of the Tannaim becomes a full-fledged holy place and focal point of Jewish religious consciousness. Our sources will include the Palestinian and Babylonian Talmudim, midrash, targum, liturgy (including liturgical poetry, *piyyut*) and post-Talmudic legal literature.[6] By the third and fourth centuries the Sages of the Palestinian Talmud conceived of the interior of the synagogue building as being divided into realms of holiness, based upon proximity to the sacred books; the "sanctity of the ark" being greater than the "sanctity of the synagogue" as a whole. At the same time the Rabbinic study house (*beit ha-midrash*) was becoming increasingly important. The success of the synagogue is expressed in the fact that study houses were construed to be holy on the model of synagogue sanctity. The study house was even considered by some Amoraic Sages to be more holy than the synagogue. Both institutions were increasingly conceptualized using terms and categories derived from the Jerusalem Temple, each being called a "small sanctuary" (*miqdash me'at*). The attitudes toward synagogue and study house sanctity that appear in Amoraic sources were further developed in later literature, where synagogues and study houses were called "holy place" (*maqom qadosh*) and "holy house" (*beit qudsha*). Liturgical development was particularly significant to this process. Synagogues and study houses became the undisputed "holy places" of *zeman ha-zeh*. Their significance was so great that they were woven into the fabric of sacred time. They were projected into the messianic future, the biblical past, and the heavenly realm. Indicative of the synagogue's significance is the fact that the biblical Tabernacle itself came to be conceptualized as a synagogue, with a Torah shrine as its focal point.

Chapter four examines archaeological evidence for synagogue sanctity in the Land of Israel from the third century C.E. through the Islamic conquest of Palestine during the seventh century. The large number of synagogue remains in Israel from this period provide considerable evidence for the history of this institution that is external to the Rabbinic corpus. The phrase "holy place" first appeared archaeologically in the Land of Israel in the fourth-century synagogue mosaic of Hammath Tiberias B. This designation is somewhat common in dedicatory inscriptions dating to the fifth and sixth centuries. Archaeological remains reflect the increasing significance of the sacred scrolls within the meeting house, along with the clearly secondary use of Temple motifs. As in literary sources, archaeological remains suggest that prayer was an important element of synagogue life.

Our last chapter, chapter five, explores the concept of synagogue sanctity in the Diaspora during late antiquity. Though the Babylonian Talmud's descriptions of synagogues and synagogue holiness in Sassanian Babylonia (modern Iraq) generally parallel Palestinian sources, a unique phenomenon in Babylonia was what we call the "extra-holy" synagogue. The attribution of greater sanctity to the synagogues of *Shaf ve-Yatev* in Nehardea and of *Hutsal* reflects a desire for concrete focal points for local religious patriotism. Our knowledge of synagogues in the Roman empire during late antiquity is based almost entirely upon the often stunningly beautiful archaeological remains of synagogues and the writings of non-Jews. Roman law and Patristic literature provide important sources for the history of the synagogue. In the western Diaspora notions of synagogue holiness parallel trends that we have identified in Babylonia and Palestine. Considerable local variation is evident, as in the most extreme example, "Synagogue of the Maccabean Martyrs" in Antioch on the Orontes, whose holiness was derived from the human relics that were stored there.

On Our Use of Historical Sources

Over the past century numerous scholars have written about aspects of the ancient synagogue, to the point that synagogue studies almost constitute a subdiscipline of academic research. The development of this field has been fueled by the lightning pace (by the standards of ancient history) by which new archaeological and literary sources have come to light. Archaeological excavations in Israel and throughout the Mediterranean world turn up "new" synagogue remains on a regular basis. Similarly, literary sources are being identified from the Cairo Genizah collections at almost the same speed. With this, the first and last full-scale study of the ancient synagogue to utilize all of the varieties of evidence was the monumental *Synagogale Altertümer*, published by the eminent Hungarian scholar Samuel Krauss in 1922.[7] The vastness of this corpus, more than one hundred years after Solomon Schechter visited the Cairo Genizah and ninety years after the first modern synagogue excavations in Palestine by Heinrich Kohl and Carl Watzinger,[8] has required new and interdisciplinary ways of looking at the early history of the synagogue.[9]

Since the mid-1950s historical studies on ancient synagogues have focused in one way or another on questions raised by Erwin R. Goodenough in his *Jewish Symbols in the Greco-Roman Period*[10] Appearing over a fifteen-year period, between 1953 and 1968, *Jewish Symbols* caused a profound paradigm shift. Goodenough's influence is attested in the vast number of reviews of *Jewish Symbols* that were published during the 1950s and 1960s and continue to appear. As Morton Smith noted, "Informed opinion of ancient Judaism can never, henceforth, be the same as if they were before he published."[11]

Throughout the first half of this century it was generally assumed that Judaism during the Greco-Roman period was a monolithic Rabbinic religion, ruled over by the Sages of the Talmud. This model is usually associated with the work of George F. Moore and his notion of "normative Judaism."[12] Remains of ancient synagogues were read as physical remnants of a Rabbinically dominated society.[13] In response to "normative Judaism" Goodenough developed his counterhistory. He believed that over against a limited and self-limiting island of Rabbinic religion there flourished a popular empire-wide Jewish mystery religion. He argued that this Hellenized Judaism is reflected in Hellenistic Jewish writers (mainly Philo of Alexandria) and in archaeological finds. Through the interpretation of visual "symbols" Goodenough believed that he had discovered this ancient "mystery religion." Goodenough's stilted image of the Rabbinic Sages, his "mystery religion," and his method of interpreting "symbols," have largely been discredited by scholars.[14] This said, his radical bifurcation between Rabbinic sources and the archaeological record has stimulated scholars to confront more directly than ever before the differences in perspective and practice that existed among ancient Jews from period to period, from place to place, and from source to source.

Each genre of evidence that we will survey in this study has its own particular interpretive problems and issues. These need to be overcome before a synthetic history can be written. While art historical methods are most important for the interpretation of the archaeological sources,[15] careful literary analysis is necessary for textual material. Saul Lieberman's often quoted maxim in regard to Rabbinic literature is equally applicable to other literatures and to archaeological sources: "Every single passage of Talmudic literature must be investigated both in light of the whole context and as a separate unit in regard to its correct meaning, time and place."[16]

Rabbinic sources pose a particular problem for the historian. Scholarship over the last three decades, much of it associated with Jacob Neusner and his students, has shown the near impossibility of writing biography and political history based upon this most collective of literatures.[17] What may be written, however, is the history of issues that were central to Rabbinic concerns. These are generally social and cultural histories.[18] Among the most influential scholar of this school, other than Neusner himself, was the late Baruch M. Bokser.[19] Bokser's study of the Passover *seder* and its development is a model for such scholarship.[20] Our study is strongly indebted to Bokser's scholarship, particularly on the Rabbinic transformation of the notion of "sacred space," in our attempt to trace a central feature of Rabbinic religion from the Second Temple period through late antiquity.

Each variety of Rabbinic literature requires differing, though related, exegetical tools. Sources that reflect synagogue life are scattered far and wide throughout the collections that make up the Tannaitic, Amoraic, and post-Amoraic corpora. All traditions must be assembled and analyzed utilizing careful historical-philological methods developed by scholars over the last century.[21]

"Tannaitic" sources (*baraitot*) that appear in Amoraic collections and purportedly Palestinian traditions that appear in the Babylonian Talmud pose particular challenges. Scholarship has shown that Tannaitic sources that appear in later collections are not always Tannaitic at all, or have been reformulated to suit the interests of later tradents.[22] Similarly, traditions that appear to be of Palestinian origin in the Babylonian Talmud often reflect Babylonian and not Palestinian concerns.[23] Great care is thus necessary in using these sources. The rule of thumb that we have adopted is that *baraitot* in Amoraic collections and Palestinian sources in the Babylonian Talmud will be used only when they reflect trends or issues that are clearly present in less problematic sources.

For our purposes it is ultimately immaterial whether sage so-and-so made a particular statement or whether an event mentioned ever actually happened. What is important is the fact that the author or editor approached a particular issue at all, how it is presented in the literature, and the ramifications of that text for the understanding of Jewish culture during late antiquity. The construction of the idea of synagogue holiness within the Rabbinic community (which includes the editors of the discrete collections) is our object as we study this literature.

It has by now become a scholarly commonplace that Rabbinic sources must be unpacked from a literary perspective before historical analysis can begin.[24] A number of scholars have shown the value of studying sources within the literary contexts of their individual collections.[25] While this literary approach is an important tool for interpreting each source, it is not conducive to the writing of a readable synthetic history. We will thus use it sparingly, and only when such analysis yields significant historical data. In general we will read each source within the context of contemporaneous literature. E. P. Sanders' comments in regard to Tannaitic literature are appropriate to Amoraic and post-Amoraic literatures as well: "It is my contention . . . that with regard to the question of how religion and the religious life worked, and how the religion functioned (how one gets in and stays in) a common pattern can be discerned which underlies otherwise disparate parts of Tannaitic literature. . . ."[26] Throughout this study I have attempted to balance the need for careful (often laborious) analysis of sources with the rhetorical requirement of a clear narrative.

A related issue is the problem of balancing literary and archaeological sources such that neither becomes subservient to the other. This has often been the case with Jewish literary remains, which are used only as proof texts for pre-conceived conclusions about visual evidence. The overemphasis in modern scholarship on the messianic content of Jewish symbols is the most pervasive example of this phenomenon.[27] For this reason we will discuss the various corpora in relative isolation from one another and comparison will be undertaken only once the material has been explored in its own right. We will attempt to treat archaeological and literary forms of expression on an equal basis, without, in the words of Sabine Mac Cormack, "one aspect insensibly sinking into the inferior position of merely providing illustrative footnotes for the other."[28]

The sanctity of the ancient synagogue has never been discussed in an exhaustive manner by modern scholars. A subcategory of this issue, the ideological relationship between the Temple of Jerusalem and the synagogue, has been addressed on numerous occasions.[29] Most authors have argued that after 70 C.E. the synagogue became a Temple-like "replacement" for the lost Jerusalem Temple. The synagogue acquired, in A. T. Kraabel's words, "some of its functions, characteristics and aura."[30] In 1984 Shaye J. D. Cohen,[31] modified the replacement hypothesis, arguing that the synagogue had little cultic resemblance to the Temple, and, so, to his mind, little sanctity at all:[32]

> The little sanctity which the synagogue has derives from two sources: from the fact that is a pale imitation of the temple, and the fact that sacred activities are conducted in its precincts.

While Cohen is correct in modifying the replacement hypothesis, he underestimates other sources of holiness, particularly the importance of Scripture in the sanctification of the synagogue. If the synagogue in fact had minimal holiness, it is unlikely that so many literary and archaeological sources, including Rabbinic sources, would call it a "holy place"! In a brief treatment that discusses the synagogue within the context of contemporary Christianity, also in 1984, Jack N. Lightstone reached conclusions regarding the Temple/synagogue relationship that are similar to Cohen's. He went on to suggest, however, that the Torah scroll was treated as a "sacred relic," within certain Diaspora synagogues, and thus was an important source of synagogue sanctity.[33] Lightstone's insight, expressed in schematic terms, is applicable to synagogues in the Land of Israel as well, as our study will show.[34]

Interest in synagogue holiness has been so great during the 1990s that Martin Goodman, Lee I. Levine, and Ze'ev Safrai all discussed this subject and thereby enriched my own study. While Goodman stressed the notion of synagogue sanctity in the Diaspora, Safrai explored this idea in Rabbinic sources, particularly Byzantine period texts. Levine discussed the notion of synagogue holiness in the Land of Israel and in the Diaspora using Rabbinic sources, archaeology, and the Christian context, suggesting that one of the sources for the development of synagogue holiness may have been the "rise of Christianity and its penetration into fourth-century Palestine, with emphasis on the sanctity of church buildings and other religious sites."[35] Christian influence was surely important during the Byzantine period, with that, it is not unlikely that Jewish concepts of synagogue sanctity influenced Christians during this period of cross-fertilization across religious boundaries. The best example of this may be found in the homilies against the Jews by John Chrysostom.

The works of three contemporary scholars have been particularly important for my understanding of Judaism and ultimately of the synagogue during the later Greco-Roman period. These are E. P. Sanders, Jonathan Z. Smith, and Peter Brown. Sanders' work on the early Christian movement within its Jewish matrix stresses that which was common to the various elements of Jewish society during the later Second Temple period. Responding directly to Goodenough and his contemporary followers, Sanders' scholarship explores the "broad agreement" among Jews in Palestine and the western Diaspora during the Second Temple period on basic issues of theology and praxis.[36] He has accomplished this without slighting the diversity of opinions and religious praxis within Second Temple period Judaism. Sanders describes the shared religion as "common Judaism."[37] In this study I will argue for the existence of a "common Judaism" throughout the Greco-Roman world in the centuries after the Temple's destruction. This "common denominator" is reflected in Jewish literature, in archaeological remains, and in non-Jewish sources on Jews and Judaism. The wealth of sources available for the study of synagogues and of synagogue sanctity provides a unique opportunity to examine the religious experience of the far-flung Jewish communities of late antiquity. The "common Judaism" that we will explore in this book parallels the "Mediterranean" or "Christian" "koine" that Peter Brown suggests united the strongly divergent brands of Christianity throughout the Roman world.[38]

Jonathan Z. Smith and Peter Brown have both discussed issues of sacrality in ways that have been important for this study. Smith rejects the idealist approach to "sacred space" within the history of religions school, most prominently Mircea Eliade's ahistorical notion of the *axis mundi* with its implicitly Durkheimian dichotomy between the sacred and the profane.[39] He argues that the sacrality of a place is not static and metahistorical, but rather is determined by the society that construes it to be holy. Sacrality is not eternal and fixed, as Eliade thought, but a dynamic social construct.[40] In dealing with our period, Smith has shown that sacrality became "movable" during the Hellenistic period and was no longer dependent upon the great temples that dominated the ancient cityscape.[41] He suggests that the locus of sanctity was increasingly the holy man.

Peter Brown argues that concern for the sacred, whether the sacred person, object, or place, was a central issue within late antique culture.[42] His historical study of the cult of the saints includes the liturgical context of late antique Christianity, the church.[43] Brown has shown that churches were often sanctified through the presence of the relics of the saints of the church.[44] Contact with these relics provided an opening to the heavenly realm, a notion that was further developed in the cult of icons.[45] In a brief essay, Brown has discussed the significance of art and architecture in the construction of Christian sacred space:[46]

> In a Late Antique church, the processional movements, the heavy silver of the sacred vessels and the binding of the gospel books as they flashed by on their way to the altar, the mysterious opacity of the curtains shrouding the

entrance (even if the curtain itself might have been woven with frankly secular scenes), these things in themselves were the visual "triggers" of a Late Antique worshipper's sense of majesty. Indeed, it is in such terms that Late Antique sources describe their churches. . . . They are *ho topos*, the "place" where it was possible to share for a moment in the eternal repose of the saints in paradise.

His focus on the interrelatedness of text, artifact, and ritual for the articulation of the Christian *topos* is essential for our understanding of the synagogue and its developing holiness. Brown's emphasis upon sanctity as a primary category in late antique Christianity, and particularly the expression of this sanctity within the liturgical realm, sets a challenge for us in our study of the ancient synagogue.

Sanctity in Ancient Judaism

The concept of holiness in biblical, Second Temple period, and Rabbinic thought have not been exhaustively researched.[47] Such a study is well beyond the scope of the present research, particularly as regarding the biblical concept. It is nevertheless important to set out some of the basic categories of holiness in Second Temple and particularly in Rabbinic sources as a prelude to our study of synagogue sanctity.

Arthur Marmorstein and Max Kadushin collected the Rabbinic sources, Kadushin considering sanctity to be a central "value concept" of Rabbinic Judaism. Neither sufficiently differentiated Rabbinic sources chronologically nor geographically, though Marmorstein's study is somewhat more nuanced.[48] Since Kadushin, over thirty years ago, the only scholar to discuss sanctity in Rabbinic thought in a sustained manner is Lawrence A. Hoffman. Hoffman presents a model of sanctity in Rabbinic sources that builds upon Mary Douglas's structuralist interpretation of sanctity in the book of Leviticus.[49] Simply put, for Douglas "purity" and "sanctity" are an expression of order in the Levitical "holiness code." Impurity is disorder, what Douglas calls "dirt."[50] Hoffman corrects one significant element of Douglas's program: ". . . she confused the system [of the biblical holiness system], with its parts, for purity explained by holiness does not mean that purity is holiness. Purity is the desired end of the system; holiness is a quality to be sought in its parts."[51] According to Hoffman, "the holy . . . is a category of things, the binary opposite of unholy. Impurity occurs when these two categories—the holy and the opposite—are mixed."[52] He argues that "true to Douglas' model whereby purity is order, and true also to Israel's essence of being a holy People charged with not profaning (that is, polluting) the holy with the everyday, rabbinic Jews take great care not to mix categories." Hoffman's approach is broad and systemic. In this discussion I will present a general overview of the Rabbinic approach that generally agrees with his, though we will see that holiness (*qedushah*) and purity (*tehorah*) are sometimes more closely related as a "category of things" than Hoffman allows for. I will emphasize the chronological development of specific conceptions within the Rabbinic corpus that will be important for our study of synagogue sanctity.

Rabbinic discussions of sanctity follow directly upon biblical conceptions particularly as expressed in the Pentateuch. Biblical notions of sanctity include the holiness of the Tabernacle/Temple and its service,[53] Jerusalem and the Land of Israel,[54] the Sabbath, festivals, new moons, sabbatical years and jubilees,[55] Israel, the priests and the Levites,[56] the firstborn,[57] nazarites,[58] and God, His host and His heavenly abode.[59] These categories were taken for granted and further elaborated by the Sages. Sanctity is expressed through differentiation. The reciprocal of *qodesh* in Rabbinic thought is generally *ḥol*. This follows on biblical models. In Leviticus 10:10 we find that Aaron and his sons are charged not to drink wine that could impair their primary responsibility "to differentiate between *qodesh* and *ḥol*, between *tameh* (defiled) and *tahor* (pure)."[60] The borders differentiating *qodesh* and *tahor*, *ḥol* and *tameh* are sometimes loose in Rabbinic conceptions, as they are in biblical sources (which, incidentally, helps to explain Douglas's conflation of the sacred and the pure).[61] *Qodesh* and *ḥol* is the primary binary structure of holiness in Rabbinic thought, with everything in Creation being closer to either absolute *qodesh* (that is, God) or to *ḥol*.[62] *Ḥol* is best defined in most cases as that which is not holy, though it need not bear the negative charge of "profane" as it is used in contemporary parlance.[63] It is religiously inert, "mundane" or "ordinary," with no negative dynamic quality.[64]

The Rabbinic "separation" (*havdalah*) blessing recited at the conclusion of the Sabbath and festivals poignantly reflects the dichotomy between *qodesh* and *ḥol* as it was understood by the Sages. An early version of this blessing appears anonymously in *b. Pesahim* 104a. It praises God as the one who:

> differentiates between *qodesh* and *ḥol*, between Israel and the nations,[65] between the seventh day and the six days of action, between defiled (*tameh*) and pure (*tahor*), between the sea and the dry land, between the upper waters and the lower waters, and between the Priests, Levites and Israelites. . . .[66]

While the gulf between *qodesh* and *ḥol* seems to be absolute in this text, the reality is that the Sages, again following biblical models, posited a gradient of hues between these extremes. We see this in the "separation" recited at the conclusion of the Sabbath when a festival follows on Saturday night. One Tannaitic Sage praises God as "(He who) differentiates between greater holiness (*qodesh ḥamur*) of the Sabbath and lesser holiness (*le-qodesh ha-qal*) of the festival."[67] The intermediate semi-festival days of the Passover and *Sukkot* festivals are called *ḥulo shel moed*, "the secular (days) of the festival" in Tannaitic sources.[68] This term reflects a search for terminology that reflects varying degrees of sanctity, not unlike the terms used to distinguish the *qodesh*, the "Holy," from the *qodesh ha-qedoshim*, the "Holy of Holies," in biblical (and Rabbinic) terminology. The liminal borders between *qodesh* and *ḥol* occasioned definition and ritual distinction in Rabbinic thought. This is particularly true in the construction of time, where the beginning and conclusion of the Sabbath and festivals and transitions of social status were of special interest to the Sages. Both a new month and a marriage commence, for example, only after they are "sanctified."[69]

Graded hierarchies that are implicit in Scripture were systematized and made explicit by the Sages.[70] An example of this is the spatial "map" of sacred space that is set out in *m. Kelim* 1:6–9. As in Scripture, the closer one came to the Temple and the deeper one penetrated into it, "the greater the sanctity and the greater the restrictions on those who may enter and the greater the degree of purity required."[71] According to *m. Kelim* 1:6–9 the Holy of Holies of the Jerusalem Temple is the most sacred spot, standing at the spiritual center of the Earth.[72] It is followed in descending order by nine lesser realms of sanctity: The Temple sanctuary (*hekhal*), the area between the porch (*ulam*) of the Temple and the altar, the courtyard of the priests, the courtyard of the Israelite (Men), the courtyard of the (Israelite) Women, the barrier (*ḥael*) surrounding the Temple and its courtyards within which non-Jews were not permitted to enter, the Temple Mount, the walled city of Jerusalem, other walled cities in Palestine, and the Land of Israel. Greater holiness is occasioned by ever more restricted cultic activities at each step. So, for example, no one could enter the Holy of Holies except the high priest during the Day of Atonement service.[73] Though the sanctity of the Land of Israel is nowhere stated explicitly in Scripture, *m. Kelim* rightly understands that this sanctity is implied.[74] The Land of Israel is assigned the lowest level of holiness on *m. Kelim*'s hierarchy:[75]

> The Land of Israel is holier than all (other) lands.
> What is its (distinctive) holiness?

That they bring from it (to the Temple) the barley offering (*omer*), the first fruits and the two loaves of bread.[76]
These are not brought from any other lands.

The revaluation and application of sanctity to new contexts is reflected in Rabbinic sources. This is most apparent in the ways that holiness was applied to the biblical scrolls, to communal groups, and to individuals. As we shall see, the sanctification of synagogues was part of this trend.

The "Sacred Scripture"

The primary focal point of Rabbinic religion was the Divinely ordained Scriptures, particularly the Pentateuch. In fact, the Sacred Scripture was arguably more central to Rabbinic conceptions than the Tabernacle/Temple.[77] This revaluation has Second Temple period antecedents.[78] From an early date the Tannaim viewed even the Temple and its service through the refracting lens of Scripture. This is reflected, for example, in the biblicized Temple dimensions presented in *m. Middot*.[79] Scripture was seen to have transcended the destruction of the Temple.[80] It stood above all other institutions as the source of continuing communion with the Divine. This factor is essential for the interpretation of Rabbinic Judaism, and of the Rabbinic conception of the synagogue.

It is not surprising, therefore, that in Second Temple and Rabbinic sources the scrolls within which Scripture was written came to be considered holy. This is a major shift from earlier biblical literature, where scrolls of Scripture are not presented as being sacred. The sanctification of biblical scrolls was part of the larger shift from direct Divine revelation to textual interpretation during the Second Temple period. The priestly *urim* and *tummim* oracles gone (Neh. 7:65), and direct prophesy on the wane, the scroll came to be treated as an oracular document from which God's will could be discerned.[81] This shift is first expressed in Nehemiah 8:1–8, during the covenant renewal ceremony convened by Ezra in Jerusalem. In the literature of the latter Second Temple period inspired Scriptures were often called holy books.[82] This first appears in 1 Maccabees 12:9 (after 63 B.C.E.), where we hear of *ta biblia ta hagia* (the holy books), *ha-sefarim ha-qedoshim* or *sifre qodesh* in the original Hebrew text.[83] Josephus during the latter first century refers to the Torah as *ton hieron nomon . . . to biblion* ("The sacred law . . . the book") and as *tous Mouseos nomous* ("of the laws of Moses").[84] The Letter of Aristeas' portrayal of Ptolemy II prostrating himself before scrolls containing a Greek translation of the Torah[85] and his insistence that these books be carefully stored may reflect the sanctification of biblical scrolls in the Hellenistic Diaspora.[86] The biblical scrolls were considered to be holy during the latter Second Temple period and were treated by Jews and gentiles alike as objects of veneration.[87]

During the latter Second Temple period, at the latest, biblical scrolls were written according to precise traditions and handled and stored with great care.[88] This is clear from texts uncovered at Qumran and the manner in which many of these scrolls were stored.[89] Non-canonical and sectarian documents from Qumran and Masada use scribal forms that are most likely derived from biblical scrolls. This usage suggests an attempt to cloak these documents in the mantle of the holy books.[90] The mode of writing "holy books," the *sifre qodesh*, described in Tannaitic literature parallels that which appears in many of the Qumran scrolls and reflects continuity between the later Second Temple period and the Tannaitic period.[91]

From the latter Second Temple period onward the developing canon of the Hebrew Scriptures was divided into a graded hierarchy of three parts. The Pentateuch was ascribed with the highest level of sanctity, followed by the Prophets and the Writings (called in Greek the Hagiographa, "Holy Writings").[92] Scholars have generally suggested that inclusion of a text in the canon was the equivalent to ascribing it with sanctity.[93] S. Z. Leiman has argued, however, that for the Rabbinic Sages the attribution of sanctity to a biblical book was quite separate from the question of its inclusion in Scripture. According to Leiman, a canonical book was ascribed with holiness only when it was determined to be Divinely inspired.[94] The Song of Songs, Ecclesiastes, and other books were declared to be Divinely inspired and thus holy centuries after their inclusion in the biblical canon.[95]

The practical expression of the sanctity of biblical books in Tannaitic literature is the notion that touching these parchments "defiles the hands." This taboo limits contact with the holy books, protecting the scrolls while stressing their holiness. "Defilement of the hands," a form of Rabbinically ordained impurity, is a manifestation of the scroll's holiness. The possibility of being defiled by contact with the scrolls regulated the manner in which the "holy books" themselves were handled. Note that the scroll's ability to defile is a measure of its sanctity, differentiating the biblical scroll from ordinary objects. The application of purity laws to the sacred scrolls is part of a larger trend that began during the later Second Temple period and which was developed significantly by the Rabbis. Gedaliah Alon notes that this includes the extension of the laws of defilement to "sacred objects" that "are not included in the sanctity of the Temple and its sacred objects."[96] The earliest named authority to use the notion of hand defilement is

Rabban Yoḥanan son of Zakkai.[97] "Defilement of the hands" was often coupled with "holiness" in Tannaitic discussions. The claim attributed to Rabbi Aqiva that "no Israelite disputed that the Song of Songs defiles the hands . . . for all of the writings are holy, and the Song of Songs is Holy of Holies" reflects the close relationship between the sanctity of the scroll and its ability to cause defilement.[98]

Amoraic literature follows the lead of the Tannaim regarding the sanctity of Scripture. The concept of "defilement of the hands" is not stressed in Amoraic literature. It appears only once, in a position cited by the Palestinian Talmud's editor in support of rescuing books of the Hagiographa from fire on the Sabbath.[99] The Amoraic Sages promoted reverential handling of the sacred scrolls. Rabbi Yohanan is recorded in the Babylonian Talmud, for example, as warning that "he who holds a Torah scroll (when it is) naked (not holding it with a cloth wrapper) will be buried naked."[100] Proper decorum in reading and storing sacred books was of particular interest.[101] One tradition insists that one must stand in the presence of a Torah scroll, a practice derived from the manner in which one shows deference to a Sage.[102] Similarly, a Sage who has forgotten his learning through no fault of his own is to be treated with the "sanctity of the ark."[103] He is to be treated with the same honor as a Torah shrine whose Torah scroll has been removed. These traditions suggest a close relationship between the oral learning of a Sage and the written revelation, between the oral and the written Torah. In a sense, the scroll is personified and the Sage is treated as a scroll.[104]

Post-Amoraic sources show increased attention to the Scriptural scrolls. Regard for the sanctity of the biblical scrolls was expressed through increased regulation of the manner in which they were handled within private and public contexts. The *Tractate Sofrim* ("Scribes"), which is in large part a guide for the copying of biblical scrolls, their careful use and liturgical reading in public, reflects this trend.[105] This interest may have partially been caused by the fact that copying on scrolls was declining as the preferred manner of producing books during this period, in favor of the codex. The scroll form was becoming ever more anachronistic, eventually being used only for the writing of biblical books and liturgical texts that were read ceremonially. The uniqueness of this form and its localization within synagogues afforded it even greater holiness.[106]

Hebrew, the language of most of the Scriptural books, is first referred to as sacred in a text uncovered in the Qumran library.[107] It is called *leshon ha-qodesh*, which might correctly be translated as the "holy language" or the "language of God." This usage is unique among the literature of the Second Temple period. Esther Eshel and Michael Stone, the editors of this text, suggest that the documents claim that at the end of days the universal language will be Hebrew, "the holy tongue," "may indicate why the members of the sect, who believed that they were living in the end of days, insisted on writing their sectarian compositions in Hebrew."[108] That the Qumran sectarian documents were written in "the holy tongue" suggests an attempt to make them as Scripture-like as possible. This parallels the scribal practices that we have noted. The Qumran document's interest in Hebrew reflects the realization that Palestine was a multi-lingual country, where Hebrew, God's language, was "unnaturally" less influential as a spoken language than either Greek or Aramaic.[109]

This terminology next appears in Tannaitic sources.[110] The use of Hebrew for the composition of Tannaitic literature seems to have been ideological as well, intended to impart traditional authority upon this body of literature. This phenomenon was concurrent with the decline of Hebrew as a spoken language.[111] By the second and third centuries C.E. the use of Hebrew was increasingly restricted to Torah reading, prayer, academic discourse, and to small pockets of speakers (including the household of Rabbi Judah the Prince).[112]

The process whereby Hebrew was localized in ritual and academic settings continued throughout antiquity. The language was sanctified by virtue of its distance from ordinary speech. In Amoraic and post-Amoraic sources, as in the Dead Sea scroll fragment, Hebrew is God's language, the language of Scripture through which the world was created. It is the universal tongue of the messianic future.[113] By the later part of our period Aramaic-speaking Jews referred to Hebrew as the "language of the holy house." "Holy house" apparently refers to the synagogue. Hebrew had become fully associated with the institution where it was still a living entity, the synagogue.

"The Holy One" and His Holy People

In Amoraic and post-Amoraic sources God is commonly referred to in Hebrew as *ha-Qodesh* "The Holy (One)" and *ha-Qadosh Barukh Hu*, "The Holy (One), Blessed be He" (Aramaic: *Qudsha berikh hu*).[114] "The Holy (One)" has strong precedents in Greek sources of the Second Temple period, which follow on biblical sources.[115] Oddly, these Hebrew terms are rare in Tannaitic literature, where *Maqom* ("Place") is the most common epithet for God.[116] The reason for the Amoraic preference for *ha-Qodesh* and *ha-Qadosh Barukh Hu* is not clear. It is possible that preference for this Divine name in Amoraic literature is related to the broader attribution of sanctity, particularly to individuals, that we will show to be characteristic of this literature. God stands above the hierarchy of *qedushah*, and Himself is described in terms of His own sanctity.[117]

The sanctity of God is emphasized liturgically through the recitation of Isaiah 6:3, "Holy, Holy, Holy is the Lord of Hosts the universe is full of his glory." Its recitation by Rabbinic prayer assemblies is in conscious imitation of the heavenly host.[118] While the recitation of this verse is evidenced in Second Temple, Tannaitic, and Amoraic sources,[119] it came into its own in the liturgical poetry of the Byzantine period. In the liturgical poetry of Yannai, dating to about the sixth century C.E.,[120] we find endless plays on this verse and reflections on holiness, especially the sanctity of God.[121] These often appear in the ninth and final section of the *qedushta* poem, where the poet reaches his crescendo.[122] While the subject of the piyyut changes with the Sabbath or festival Scriptural reading, an overriding theme is that God's holiness towers above that of His creation. We will cite just two of the numerous extant examples. After reciting Isaiah 6:3, Yannai comments on the sons of Noah (Gen. 9:18):[123]

> Holy, Holy, Holy is the Lord of Hosts the universe is full of his glory.
> Holier than the masters of fame (*Shem*) and deed,
> Holier than the speakers of a beautiful language (Jafeth),
> Holier than those who receive good recompense (Ham).
> Holy, Holy, Holy is the Lord of Hosts the universe is full of his glory.
> Holier than Shem, who stands with *tzitzit* (ritual fringes) in fame (*shem*) and deed,
> Holier than Jafeth who set up the translators of Torah in a beautiful language (Greek),
> Holier than Ham, who set up wise (proselytes), committed and blessed. . . .

The literary structure of this text is determined by the tripartite "Holy, Holy, Holy" of Isaiah 6:3. This standard form in Yannai appears in a *qedushta* in which the poet praises the angels who protected the patriarch Jacob on his way to and from the Holy Land:[124]

> Their beautiful song is directed to Jacob/ They sanctify you, O Holy One of Jacob/ and respond and say:
> Holy, Holy, Holy is the Lord of Hosts the universe is full of his glory.
> Holy are the angels of mercy/ Holy are the angels of peace/ Holy are the ministering angels.
> Holy, Holy, Holy is the Lord of Hosts the universe is full of his glory.
> Holy are the angels of mercy who escorted Jacob as he departed (the Land of Israel),

Holy are the angels of peace who guarded the place where he slept,
Holy are the ministering angels who were revealed to him in his dream,
Holy, Holy, Holy is the Lord of Hosts the universe is full of his glory. . . .

Within God's "holy people" the biblical distinction between priests, Levites, and Israelites was maintained by the Rabbinic sages, though the prerogatives of the priests were essentially not. The Sages asserted their own priority over that of the priesthood, while theoretically maintaining the biblical caste hierarchy.[125] The priesthood was upstaged by a Rabbinic scholarly elite that increasingly applied Temple categories to itself and its institutions.[126] A number of sources point to the priority of the Sage over the priest, even the high priest.[127] Rabbis become the "priests" of the post-Temple era. In Tannaitic literature early Sages are portrayed dining together in cultic purity, a type of fellowship that was taken over from the priests.[128] The usurpation of priestly prerogative is also expressed in Amoraic sources. For example: Rabbis demand that tithes previously reserved for priests and Levites be redirected to their use.[129]

The holiness of the Jewish people was expressed most profoundly by the Sages in the often repeated blessing formula: "Blessed are You, Lord our God, King of the universe, who has sanctified us by His commandments and has commanded us to. . . ."[130] Sanctification through fulfillment of Divine commandments, as mediated by the Sages, is basic to the Rabbinic concept of a holy people.[131] This separateness is also expressed in the "sanctity" of one who abstains from idolatrous or foreign practices, like attendance in the circuses or even gentile hairstyles.[132] A life of sanctity, understood as separatism (*perishut*), was basic to Rabbinic self-understanding.[133] This is reflected in the Tannaitic commentary to Leviticus 19:2: "Be *qadosh* for I, the Lord your God, am *qadosh*." The *Sifra* interprets: "be *qedoshim*, be *perushim* (separate or separatists)."[134] Separatism is portrayed here as a method by which one can attain "sanctity," whose purpose, according to Leviticus 19:2, is imitation of the Divine.[135] *Pereshut* thus becomes the functional equivalent of *qedushah*.

The opposite of separatist *qedushah* has negative connotations that are not always expressed in the notion of *ḥol*, the "everyday." The opposite of separatist *qedushah* in one tradition is explicitly stated to be *tumah*, defilement. This notion is expressed in *b. Yoma* 39a, where, based upon the proximity of the biblical injunction against defilement through contact with a lizard with the command to "sanctify yourselves" in Leviticus 11:43–44, *qedushah* is interpreted to be synonymous with ritual purity. The sanctity and the defilement read by Sages into this verse, however, is pietistic rather than cultic:

Our Sages taught: Do not be defiled by them (Lev. 11:43).
If a person defiles himself a little, they defile him a lot.
(If a person defiles himself a little) below, they defile him a lot above.
In this world: they defile him in the world to come.

Our Sages taught: Sanctify yourselves and be holy (Lev. 11:44).
If a person sanctifies himself a little, they sanctify him a lot.
(If a person sanctifies himself a little) below, they sanctify him above.
In this world: They sanctify him in the world to come.

This text, and other sources that are less explicit, breaks down any systemic distinction between the "holy" and the "pure." Holiness here is "purity," the opposite of defilement.

The explicit application of "sanctity" to the Sages is rare in Rabbinic literature, the first instances appearing in Amoraic sources. A number of traditions in the Babylonian Talmud speak of the late first- or second-century "holy congregation of Jerusalem."[136] It is unclear from these texts whether the holiness of this community reflects a high level of asceticism, if it is a result of their communal organization and collective halakhic authority,[137] or is because the "holy congregation of Jerusalem" resided in the holy city.[138] Later sources attributed this holiness to a pietistic daily routine.[139]

In Amoraic literature from the Land of Israel sanctity is attributed to selected Tannaim and to one early Amora.[140] No Amoraic sage beyond the first Palestinian generation is called *qadosh,* and no Babylonian sage is so designated. "Holiness" is said to have been an attribute of the Tannaitic sage Rabbi Meir, who is praised by a contemporary in y. *Berakhot* 2:7, 5b, as "a great man, a holy man, a modest man."[141] Two Sages who flourished toward the beginning of the third century are called holy by the Palestinian Talmud, Rabbi Judah the Prince and the first generation Palestinian *amora* Rabbi Nahum son of Simai.[142] Rabbi Nahum son of Simai is called "Nahum of the Holy of Holies" in the Palestinian Talmud. This title was purportedly coined "because he never looked upon the (idolatrous) image on a coin." Similarly, the Palestinian Talmud interprets Rabbi Judah the Prince's title, "Our Holy Teacher" (*Rabbenu ha-Qodesh*), to mean that "he never looked upon his circumcision." This type of sexual asceticism[143] is retrojected to the prophet Elisha, the "holy man of God" (*ish Elohim qadosh*) of 2 Kings 4:9. Amoraic Sages pondered what specific behavior occasioned this appellation:[144]

> . . . Said Rabbi Abun: He never (*mi-yamav*) looked upon her (the Shunamite).

Our Masters of Caesarea said: He never saw a drop of seminal pollution (*qeri*) on his garment....[145]

Sexual self-control was considered to be a sign of holiness even for non-virtuosos. So, for example, "whoever abstains from (*poresh mi'*) prohibited consanguineous relations is called holy."[146] To a much greater extent than in Rabbinic Judaism, however,[147] sanctity deriving from bodily abstinence was a hallmark of the Christian religious virtuoso.[148]

The small number of people designated as *qedoshim*, ("holy ones" or "saints") in Rabbinic circles is striking when compared with the ubiquitousness of this designation among late antique Christians.[149] This disparity was apparently also sensed by the author of a tradition preserved in *Midrash Tehillim*, a collection that has been dated to the late Byzantine or early Islamic period. This text attempts to explain the scarcity of this terminology in Jewish circles:[150]

> The Holy One, Blessed Be He, does not call a righteous person (*tzadiq*) *qadosh* until he is laid in the earth.
> Why?
> Because the evil inclination inclines him (the living person to sin), and he is not believed in this world until the day of his death....
> Thus it is said of the *qedoshim* that are in the earth. And even the fathers of the universe were not called *qedoshim* until they were laid in the soil....
> Said Rabbi Pinhas: If the fathers of the universe had asked (in their lifetimes) to be taken up above they could have been. Even so, they were not called holy until they died and the tomb was sealed and closed before them.

Two points within this text are of immediate importance for us. First, saintliness (*qadosh*) is defined in terms of control of one's "evil inclination." This reflects the ascetic path to sanctity that we have seen throughout this discussion. The second point has to do with Jewish relations with holy men. Ze'ev Safrai has collected ample evidence for a Jewish cult of the saints as well as Jewish reactions to the Christian cult.[151] Jewish veneration of the "fathers of eternity," Abraham, Isaac, and Jacob, in the Cave of Makhpelah in Hebron during late antiquity is known from a number of sources.[152] A late antique poetic formulation that is preserved in the medieval circumcision rite takes a different tact. It suggests that one of the patriarchs, probably Abraham, was "sanctified in the womb" for his future role, a status that is reserved in Scripture for the prophet Jeremiah.[153] In apparent response to Christian "holy men," who populated Palestine in large numbers during the Byzantine period,[154] our *Midrash Tehillim* tradition declares that while the biblical patriarchs could have been "taken up" to the Divine realm at their will, even they were not declared to be *qedoshim* until they (together with their "evil inclinations") were dead and entombed. This high standard explains for our author why Jewish *qedoshim* were so rare.

The language of sanctity appeared with increasing regularity in Jewish contexts as late antiquity proceeded, as it did in Christian sources.[155] *Le-qedushat* so-and-so was a salutation formula in correspondence at least from the Amoraic period.[156] It appears in Geonic letters[157] and is paralleled by a dedicatory inscription from the sixth-century Khirbet Susiya synagogue.[158] Synagogue communities were called "holy" in liturgical texts from the Gaonic period and in synagogue inscriptions, though interestingly, not in earlier Rabbinic sources.[159]

Sanctity and Periodization

The Sages never explicitly speak of holiness in terms of historical periods or epochs, except in terms of the biblically ordained sabbatical years and jubilees. Nevertheless, this notion permeates Rabbinic thought and is important for understanding Rabbinic notions of synagogue sanctity. The Sages conceived of time in binary terms. In general, time is divided between the period when the Temple exists and the time when it does not ("this time") on the one hand and between "this world" and the afterlife. In truth, it is often difficult to untangle these notions in Rabbinic sources, where they and the terminology used to describe them are often thoroughly intertwined. Rabbinic articulation of chronology directly parallels the Christian division between this unredeemed world and the second coming and between this world and paradise after death.[160]

Rabbinic concepts of the afterlife have been analyzed by modern scholars, and so need not detain us here.[161] This is not the case of the chronological division of time into periods when the Temple exists and when it does not.[162] This notion first appears in the Mishnah in its legal discussions of priestly agricultural gifts and their disposition when the Temple does not exist, "at this time" (*ba-zeman ha-zeh*).[163] A *baraita* in y. *Terumot* 4:4, 42a makes this distinction explicit, differentiating between "the time of the Miqdash" (*sha'at ha-Miqdash*) and "this time," *zeman ha-zeh*.[164] Similarly, *baraitot* and anonymous discussions (though not named scholars) throughout the Babylonian Talmud differentiate "the time when the Temple exists" from "the time when the Temple does not exist."[165] In the

Land of Israel (as opposed to Babylonia) some Jews during late antiquity counted years beginning from the destruction of the Temple, in this way differentiating the era before the destruction from that which followed. This practice appears in synagogue inscriptions from Palestine and in documents from the Cairo Genizah. Counting years from the destruction reflects continuing awareness of the Temple's loss in Palestinian Jewish culture, at a time when counting from creation was also widespread.[166]

The Sages construed the destruction of the Jerusalem Temple as a temporary interruption of the Temple cult, and so prepared for its resumption. Rabbinic perceptions and institutions were projected into sacred time, both into the period of the rebuilt Temple and the pre-destruction Temple. This is particularly so of the Amoraim, who, by the third century, possessed a sense that communal life without the increasingly distant Temple was viable.[167] Synagogues are a case in point. For one Amoraic tradition King Solomon not only built the Temple, but frequented Jerusalem synagogues as well. In the other direction, synagogues await the pious "in the world to come."[168] Again, the intertwining of conceptions about the future make it hard to know whether this projection describes Temple time, an otherworldly paradise, or both. Yosef H. Yerushalmi well summarizes the Rabbinic notion of chronology:

> In the interval between destruction and redemption the primary Jewish task was to respond finally and fully to the biblical challenge of becoming a holy people. And for them (the Sages) that meant the study and fulfillment of the written and oral law, the establishment of a Jewish society based fully on its precepts and ideals, and, where the future was concerned, trust, patience and prayer. . . . Compared to these firm foundations contemporary history must have seemed a realm of shifting sands. The biblical past was known, the messianic future insured; the in-between-time was obscure.[169]

For the Sages the interplay between past, present and future was often seamless. They applied categories drawn from sacred time to *zeman ha-zeh*, while projecting their world onto time before the Temple's destruction and onto the eschatological future(s). In chapters two, three, and five we will show that to the Sages the synagogue was fundamentally an institution of "this time," having undergone its major development after the destruction of the Temple. It was a "holy place" within the limitations of unholy or inert time. This said, the synagogue became so significant in the lives of some late antique Jews that it was projected into the sacred time, becoming part of the weave of the Jewish past, present, and future.

Summary

For the Rabbinic Sages, *qedushah* generally involved the differentiation of realms of higher religious significance from those of lower significance. *Qodesh* is generally in opposition to *hol*, the religiously inert and ordinary, though it is sometimes conflated with the notion of purity. The Sages inherited from the latter part of the Second Temple period the notion that biblical scrolls were holy and thus deserving of separate treatment. This concept increased in significance as antiquity drew to a close, as the scroll form became an anachronistic object of the synagogue ritual. Notions of holy peoplehood were also taken over from biblical sources, and in this area as well we see major development. The Tannaim usurped the biblically favored authority of the priests, declaring a life of sanctity, defined as "separatism," to be the path to holiness. In Amoraic sources we hear of another type of sanctity, a life of virtuoso separatism attributed to specific early Sages. This virtuoso separatism parallels, but is not equivalent to the development of the Christian "holy man." Sanctity through sexual restraint was a Rabbinic goal for all Jews. We have seen that toward the end of our period sanctity was attributed to many varied areas of Jewish life. Finally, we noted that the sanctity in time is particularly important for understanding Rabbinic literature as a whole and the Rabbinic concept of synagogue sanctity in particular. With these basic definitional tools in hand, we can now turn to the specific sanctity of synagogues.

CHAPTER ONE

"Sacred Places That They Call Synagogues"

The Roots of Synagogue Holiness during the Second Temple Period

The earliest history of the synagogue cannot be recovered, though the best scholars of both ancient Judaism and early Christianity have certainly tried.[1] It is probably unrecoverable, because the synagogue did not develop in a revolutionary manner. No "theses" were ever posted on the door of the Temple harbingering the advent of the synagogue as Luther did for Protestant Christianity at Wittenberg Cathedral. Rather, at a certain point during the Second Temple period, probably near the Maccabean revolt,[2] Jews in the Land of Israel began to come together in synagogues for communal religious experience, while remaining fully committed to the Jerusalem cult. The distinguishing feature of synagogues during the Second Temple period seems to have been the reading of Scripture within them. Josephus and the author of the Acts of the Apostles considered this characteristic so basic that they ascribed the institution of public Torah reading back to Moses himself.[3]

Jonathan Z. Smith's discussion of the "mobility" of Greco-Roman religion is particularly important for the early history of the synagogue. He suggests that religion appropriated imagery derived from temple culture while asserting (whether intentionally or unintentionally) its independence from temples.[4] It is likely that the early development of the synagogue is related to larger trends in Greco-Roman religion, particularly the development of religious communities that were not temple-based. The development of collegia and "private cults" beginning during the Hellenistic period[5] seems to be particularly important as Jews came together in ways that were not directly in competition with their allegiance to the

Jerusalem Temple. Smith's suggestion that "rather than a sacred place, the new center and chief means of access to divinity will be the Divine man..." does not bespeak the religious experience of the synagogue. Rather, the Sacred Scripture became the locus of sanctity within ancient synagogues.[6] While some scholars have attributed the rise of synagogues to the Pharisaic stress on Scripture, hence to the second-century B.C.E., this phenomenon seems to have been broader than just the Pharisaic community.[7] What we can say with certainty is that Scripture-centered Jewish meeting houses (often called synagogues) crossed sectarian and even national bounds by the first century C.E. at the latest. Hints that these synagogues, or at least activities within them, were ascribed with sanctity can be found in sources from both the Diaspora and the Land of Israel.

A group of Greek inscriptions from Egypt, dating as early as the third century B.C.E., are often considered to be the earliest evidence of synagogues. These sources suggest that Jewish "prayer places," existed in Ptolemaic Egypt.[8] The association between the *proseuchē* and the synagogue was made by the first century C.E.[9] By this time the term *proseuchē* was essentially a synonym for "synagogue" in many areas of the Greco-Roman Diaspora (including Egypt). The most important activity of both was the same: the public reading and study of Scripture. The title *proseuchē* suggests that at least in its origins the most important feature of the "prayer place" was prayer. It is possible, however, that some other sort of worship (perhaps even sacrifice) occurred in "prayer places." We know virtually nothing about this institution during the over two centuries before Philo wrote about it during the first half of the first century C.E., other than the fact that it shows great similarity to contemporaneous polytheistic temples and associations in Egypt.[10] Prayer, for example, was an important feature of polytheistic temple service.[11]

Papyri and inscriptions from Egypt describe Jewish "prayer places" as holy, using the Greek verb *hieros*. This word refers to temple contexts in Greek literature, in Egypt and elsewhere.[12] Like non-Jewish religious institutions, at least one Jewish "prayer place" in Ptolemaic Egypt was built on "holy land" (*hiera gē*)[13] and another was built within a "holy compound."[14] A dedicatory inscription from a *proseuchē* in Xenephyris (Kom el Akhdar) commemorates the benefaction of "the pylon (*ton pulona*) of the *proseuchē*."[15] This "pylon" seems to represent a particularly Egyptian element, drawn from the architecture of native temples.[16] Like contemporaneous temples, the Jewish "prayer place" was often dedicated to the Ptolemaic ruler.[17] They were treated with special protection under Ptolemaic law that was generally reserved for temples. Like Egyptian sanctuaries, for example, at least one "prayer place" in Ptolemaic Egypt is known to have been a place of asylum.[18] In addition, synagogue officials "sometimes bore titles very similar to those of their pagan counterparts."[19] The epigraphic remains suggest that the "sanctity" of the Ptolemaic *proseuchē* was adapted from the temple culture of Ptolemaic Egypt. This evidence is admittedly limited, and provides only one angle from which to view this institution. What was actually done there religiously is beyond our grasp. Nevertheless, it is clear that the sanctity of the Ptolemaic *proseuchē* is expressed in local terms.[20]

Our image of the "prayer place" in Roman Egypt is considerably clearer. Philo of Alexandria provides considerable evidence for "prayer places" and their sanctity in Roman Egypt of the first century. In *Flaccus*, a work written shortly after the anti-Jewish Alexandrian riots of 37 C.E. in order to denounce the perpetrators to the Roman authorities,[21] Philo mentions the sanctity of "prayer places." He describes the dedication of Alexandrian Jewry to "their prayer places (*tas proseuchas*) and to their ancestral customs"[22] in the face of Greek rioting and the resulting destruction of synagogues. Philo explains the ramifications for his community of losing the "prayer places":[23]

> . . . because they are the only people under the sun who by losing their prayer places were losing also what they would have valued as worth dying many thousand deaths, namely, their means of showing reverence to their benefactors, since they no longer had the sacred compounds (*hierous peribolous*) where they could set forth their thankfulness.

This text is clearly apologetic in its claim that "showing reverence" to the "benefactors" of the Augustian house (line 49: *ton Sebaston oikon*) was the central purpose of the synagogue. Philo expands upon this notion:[24]

> . . . everywhere in the habitable world the religious veneration of the Jews for the Augustian house has its basis as all may see in the *proseuchai*, and if we have these destroyed no place, no method is left to us for paying homage.

This text is significant in light of the rise of the emperor cult at this time. The "prayer place" is portrayed as an institution not unlike a temple to the emperor in purpose. According to Philo's *Embassy to Gaius*[25] the "prayer places" were virtually covered with dedicatory inscriptions to the emperor:

> I say nothing of the tributes to the emperors that were pulled down at the same time (that Alexandrian mobs ravaged and demolished prayer places), the shields and gilded crowns and the slabs and inscriptions. . . .

This parallels extant dedications to the Ptolemaic rulers which appear in *proseuchē* inscriptions.[26] Philo describes the "prayer places" as sacred compounds (*hierous peribolous*). The same term is used in a dedicatory inscription that we have seen which speaks of the "holy compound" (. . . t]on hieron peribolon) of a "prayer place."[27]

More importantly, in two separate texts Philo describes the religious activities that took place within Alexandrian "prayer places," of which "there are many in each section of the city":

> And . . . you sit in your convecticles and assemble your regular company and read in security your holy books, expounding any obscure point and in leisurely comfort discussing at length your ancestral philosophy.[28]

> . . . the Jews every seventh day occupy themselves with their ancestral philosophy, dedicating that time to acquiring knowledge and the study of the truths of nature. For what are our prayer places throughout the cities but schools of prudence and bravery and control and justice, as well as of piety and holiness and virtue as a whole, by which one comes to recognize and perform what is due to men and God?[29]

These passages describe the religious service of the *proseuchē* in an essentially uniform manner. For Philo, the *proseuchē* is dedicated to weekly instruction in the "ancestral philosophy." What is surprisingly missing from Philo's writings is any mention of prayer in the "prayer place." This could be because study was a uniquely Jewish cult act, while prayer was conducted by other religious communities. One wonders, however, if this ancient title for Egyptian synagogues still reflected the most significant element of the religious experience of the *proseuchē* during the first century. It is possible that at a certain point study became the central function of Alexandrian "prayer places." Perhaps the name "prayer place" was used residually to describe these meeting places, even after their central feature had become study rather than prayer.

Josephus describes two Jewish meeting places that apparently had characteristics of temples; the one in Antioch, the other in Sardis. He preserves a Roman decree which gave the Jews of Sardis the right to come together in a "place" (*topos*) of their own to "offer their ancestral prayers and sacrifices to God."[30] It is unclear whether the permission to offer sacrifices reflects a misunderstanding of the synagogue ritual by polytheists, is a deliberate attempt by the Jewish community to describe its liturgy using a term that was comprehensible to its neighbors, or perhaps simply that Jews in Sardis offered sacrifice. As Lee Levine notes, the significance of this privilege "remains elusive to this day."[31] Sardis is the only community, however, that is presented as possibly having performed sacrifices.

Josephus used the term *hieron*, "temple," to denote a number of synagogues.[32] Of particular interest in this regard is a "synagogue" in Antioch on the Orontes, the capitol of Seleucid Syria. Josephus describes the dispersal of treasures from the Jerusalem Temple by Antiochus IV and how some of them came to be housed in this synagogue:[33]

> For, although Antiochus surnamed Epiphanes sacked Jerusalem and plundered the Temple, his successors on the throne restored to the Jews of Antioch all such votive offerings that were made of brass (*chalka*), to be laid up in the synagogue (*tan sunagogan*) and, moreover, granted them citizenship rights on equality with the Greeks. Continuing to receive similar treatment from later monarchs, the Jewish colony grew in numbers, and their richly designed and costly offerings formed a costly ornament to the temple (*to hieron*).

According to this source, the "successors" to Antiochus IV treated the Jews on a par with their Greek subjects. This included the "restoration" of property taken from the Jerusalem Temple to the Jewish community of Antioch and its deposition in their synagogue. As we will see, the donation of "costly offerings" to synagogues parallels Greco-Roman benefaction to temples, and later to churches.[34] It is significant that Josephus calls this building both a "synagogue" and a "temple." Our author describes this synagogue as having been seen as a "temple" by Greek and Jew alike. "Synagogue" and "temple" are treated as virtual synonyms.[35] It is perhaps significant that Josephus sees nothing strange or unusual about this. The synagogue of Antioch, like the "prayer places" of Egypt and perhaps the *topos* of Sardis Jewry, was seen by non-Jews and apparently by Jews alike as a local temple. The religious significance of this ascription is not clear, though this categorization was clearly important for the position of this institution within society.

The first tentative evidence for the sanctity of synagogue buildings in the Land of Israel does not appear in contexts which reflect the mainstream of "common Judaism" during this period.[36] Rather, sanctity is expressed in sources that stem from the margins of Jewish society: the rebel's meeting house on Masada, a statement in the *Damascus Covenant* that was discovered in the Cairo Genizah and among the Qumran scrolls, and in Philo of Alexandria's description of the Essenes. This holiness seems to be derived from two sources: the sanctity of the biblical scrolls and the application of Temple motifs.

During this period, the books of the Bible were seen by both Jews and gentiles as the cult objects of the synagogue.[37] Synagogue buildings in Palestine were most essentially places where communities came together to read and study the "holy books."[38] The centrality of Scriptural reading and study is mentioned explicitly in the Theodotos inscription from the City of David in Jerusalem:[39]

> Theodotos, son of Vettenos the priest and synagogue leader (*archisynagogos*), son of a synagogue leader and grandson of a synagogue leader, built the synagogue for the reading of the Torah and studying of the commandments, and as a hostel with chambers and water installations to provide for the needs of itinerants from abroad, which his fathers, the elders and Simonides founded.

This synagogue, meters away from the Temple itself, was clearly not in competition with the Temple. One can imagine Jews moving seamlessly from the communal study of "the commandments" in this synagogue, to the Temple for a particular rite or sacrifice, and back for more study.

The architecture of the rebel's meeting house on Masada (66–74 C.E.),[40] reflects the centrality of the Holy Scripture and its public reading.[41] According to our definition, then, it is certainly a synagogue.[42] Benches with four tiers on three sides of the room direct attention toward the center of the hall, where Scripture was most likely read.[43] The interior measurements of the hall are 12.5 × 10.5 meters. On the fourth side, at the northwestern end of the building, a large protruding room (measuring 3.6 × 5.5 meters)[44] was constructed within which biblical scrolls were buried "while the synagogue was still in use." Fragments of Deuteronomy and Ezekiel were discovered in two pits excavated there.[45] It is likely that this major obstruction on the northwestern wall served to house the biblical books of the synagogue, and was not merely a repository for worn scrolls, a Genizah. Most ancient documents that were discovered on Masada were found within close proximity to the synagogue.

The corner room was built opposite the entry way of the synagogue, and served as a visual focal point.[46] This room was surely built in this obtrusive position by design. It could easily have been built on the southwestern wall on either side of the door, and thus to have been much less obtrusive.[47] The wall of the cell was visibly differentiated from the others. A single bench was installed on it, while the other walls bore four tiers of benches. Perhaps this single bench was for dignitaries who sat with their backs to the cell, facing the community.[48] It is unclear whether the cell was aligned with Jerusalem by design, or, as Ehud Netzer suggests,[49] by coincidence.

The Masada Synagogue.

Philo describes the Sabbath study of the "Essenes" as having taken place in "synagogues" that were considered to be sacred:[50]

> For that day has been set apart to be kept holy and on it they abstain from all other work and proceed to sacred places (*hierous . . . topous*) that they call synagogues (*sunagogai*). There, arranged in rows according to their ages, the younger below the elder, they sit decorously as befits the occasion with attentive ears. Then one takes the books (*biblous*) and reads aloud and another of especial proficiency comes forward and expounds what is not understood. . . .

The source of this synagogue sanctity is unclear, though it clearly parallels Philo's description of the Egyptian "prayer places" as sacred compounds (*hierous peribolous*). The texts that were studied on the Sabbath were in all likelihood biblical. The "sacred places" called "synagogues" were not as unique to the Essenes as Philo thought. As we have seen, in the Theodotos inscription, *sunagogē* was the usual word for synagogue buildings in the land of Israel.[51] The arrangement of the assembly "in rows . . . the younger below the elder" parallels nicely the bleacher-type seating of the Masada synagogue and the Gamla synagogue.[52]

Lee Levine and Ezra Fleischer have both argued that communal prayer during the later Second Temple period took place both within the bounds of the Temple Mount and to a limited extent outside the Temple.[53] Literary and epigraphic sources, they suggest, do not explicitly mention communal prayer as a behavior that took place in Palestinian synagogues before 70 C.E. It is possible, as perhaps in Philonic Alexandria, that the numerous sources that do not mention prayer stress that element of Jewish liturgy that is uniquely Jewish, taking for granted the element that was shared with other religious groups, communal prayer.[54] Be it as it may, the overwhelming impression gained from extant sources is that early synagogues were places of communal Scripture reading and instruction.

Some evidence for communal prayer within meeting houses may be adduced from the literature of the latter Second Temple period.[55] An important text in this regard was found at Qumran, the *Songs of the Sabbath Sacrifice*. It was also found in close proximity to the Masada synagogue. If the *Songs of the Sabbath Sacrifice* was a liturgical text, as its editor Carol Newsom believes,[56] this may suggest that prayer was recited in the Masada synagogue.[57]

The *Damascus Covenant*, a source discovered both in the Cairo Genizah and in the Qumran library suggests that the sectarians gathered together for prayer:[58]

> And all who enter the house of prostration, let him not come in a state of defilement requiring washing. . . .

Prostration, most likely prayer in general,[59] in a specific place seems to have been essential to the ritual life of this community. Lawrence H. Schiffman notes that "this text seems to indicate that sectarians who were scattered in the towns and cities of Palestine established permanent places of sanctity for the conduct of sacred services."[60] Prostration in a state of purity was required,[61] just as purity was required for entry to the Temple.[62] The "house of prostration" was thus given Temple attributes. This process was the result of the sect's perception that the Hasmonean/Herodian Temple was profaned and so an unsuitable cultic setting. This spiritual distancing led to the "templization" of the Qumran community itself.

Summary

The origins of the synagogue, steeped in mystery as they are, will probably never be known. This is no doubt because this institution began as a "still, small voice," appearing in a form that we can recognize only during the last century of the Temple's existence. While sanctity was ascribed to the Egyptian *proseuchē*, the source of that sanctity is difficult to determine. It seems to have been a local phenomenon, related the sanctity ascribed to temples in Ptolemaic culture. What "prayer" took place there is hard to say. By the first century, however, "prayer places" in Egypt seem to have been places where Scripture was read and studied in public. This activity may have bestowed some holiness on the *proseuchē*, though whether it was actually conceived in this way is unknown.

The two possible sources of synagogue holiness in latter Second Temple period Palestinian synagogues were the sanctity of the Sacred Scripture and the application of Temple forms to communal worship. The extant evidence stems from marginal groups within Jewish society of the time, the defenders of Masada, the Qumran sectarians, and Philo's Essenes. There is no evidence to suggest that these phenomena were prevalent among wider segments of Jewish society, though that may be a factor of our sources and not representative of the historical reality. Both the sanctity of Scripture and Temple imagery were, however, central to the Tannaim after 70 C.E., for whom a conception that holiness was movable was essential if they were to weather the Temple's destruction.

CHAPTER TWO

"They Are Sacred Even When Destroyed"

The Holiness of Synagogues in Tannaitic Literature

The traumas associated with the destruction of the Jerusalem Temple and the loss of the sacred center were met by the earliest Rabbinic Sages with an affirmation of those elements of Judaism that were still in place. Sacred Scripture stood at the center of this process, serving as the vehicle for the Rabbinic reconstruction of Judaism. Study and interpretation of the "Sacred Scripture" were thought to provide access to the Divine that was unaltered by the loss of the Temple. Its very mobility made the synagogue the ideal vehicle for the Tannaim. Baruch Bokser, more that any other recent scholar, explored the ways that this reconstruction led to a new construction of what it meant to be Jewish. Bokser has shown how those elements of Jewish practice that were not lost in 70 C.E. were emphasized by the Sages, while those that were gone were both memorialized and subtly de-emphasized.[1] In this way, for example, the cult meal described in biblical and Second Temple period literature as having taken place on Passover eve was replaced with the Seder.[2] The synagogue, a legacy of the "common Judaism" of the latter Second Temple Period, served the Sages as the institutional locus for the Tannaitic reconstruction of Judaism.

The place where Torah had been read and studied for generations was transformed in subtle and less subtle ways by the Tannaim. As in synagogues before 70 C.E., the centrality of Scripture within synagogues was stressed by the Sages, who ascribed a small amount of holiness to the synagogue because of this relationship. This sanctity was enveloped in metaphors derived from the Temple. This strategy was common to the Tannaitic approach. An active memory of the lost Temple was perpetuated and became central to the religion of *zeman ha-zeh*.

The "templization" of synagogues was strengthened by the localization there of daily liturgy modeled loosely upon the Temple service. As in the Temple, the assembly could meet the Divine through communal liturgy in synagogues.

In an age when temple-based religion was essential to Greco-Roman conceptions, the Tannaim were careful that synagogues not become replacements for the Jerusalem Temple. Sacrality was attributed to synagogues in the present, this holiness having little or no cosmic significance. The Tannaitic synagogue is a good example of Smith's concept of "movable holiness" in Greco-Roman religion. With the Temple gone, the immediate focus of communal activity was within the synagogue. Synagogues and their sanctification were important for the Tannaitic reconstruction of Judaism after the Temple's destruction, the synagogue becoming the institutional locus for this transformation.

Tannaitic writings present Torah reading and study as the synagogue's most significant functions.[3] Secondary functions that do not appear in Second Temple period synagogues also appear for the first time.[4] The appearance of new synagogue functions represents a veritable explosion in its use and, consequently, of its significance to its community. The most important of these "new" functions was communal prayer. Prayer became a significant synagogue activity during the Tannaitic period, though it is eclipsed in our literature by Torah study.[5] This increase in functions was paralleled by the developing notion that synagogues were in some way holy. In Tannaitic sources, this sanctity is derived from the biblical scrolls that were read in synagogues and through the application of Temple imagery to this institution. A leitmotif of these texts is that holiness is bestowed upon the synagogue by the community that gathers within it.

The Synagogue: The Realm of Torah

The Mishnah and the Tosefta describe the synagogue as a ritual space that was fundamentally the domain of Torah and Torah study. Proper behaviors within the synagogue are delineated in t. *Megillah* 2:18. This text attempts to ensure that the synagogue environment be conducive to Torah study:

> Synagogues:
> They do not behave frivolously within them,
> one does not go into them on a hot day because of the heat,
> or on a cold day because of the cold,
> nor on a rainy day because of the rain.
> They do not eat in them
> nor do they sleep in them,

nor do they take a stroll in them,
nor do they derive benefit from them,[6]
but they read (Scripture) in them and repeat (traditions) in them
and expound (lessons) in them.
A public eulogy is eulogized in them.

Inappropriate behavior is forbidden inside a synagogue, while the reading, recitation, and exposition of Torah are supported. Reading Scripture, recitation and explication of traditions, and public eulogies are permitted in this carefully controlled environment. Eulogies may already have included biblical exegesis at this time, though this practice is first attested only in Amoraic literature.[7]

The Tannaitic synagogue was the place where God's Scriptures were studied. The language of the synagogue was a factor that differentiated this environment from others which the late antique Jew met. We have already noted that Tannaitic sources reflect the sanctification of the "holy tongue" as it was increasingly relegated to the religious sphere.[8] The need for Aramaic[9] and Greek[10] translation of the Torah in Tannaitic period synagogues points to Rabbinic acceptance of the reality of Hebrew's decline as a spoken language. Hebrew may not have been completely understood by all.[11] Like Latin in a pre-Vatican II French-speaking church, Hebrew was recognizable to Aramaic-speaking Jews, though it was not a language with which most were fully comfortable.[12] The use of Hebrew, the "holy tongue," in synagogues (as well as study houses) contributed to the differentiation and sanctification of this place.

The interior space of the synagogue was also differentiated from other environments. Tosefta *Megillah* 3:21 is suggestive of the manner in which synagogue interiors were arrayed. This text suggests that the entire congregation was arranged before the Torah chest.[13] Other sources provide further details. Dedicatory inscriptions within synagogues are mentioned in Tannaitic sources,[14] lamps (*nerot*), lampstands (*menorot*),[15] cloth wrappers, the casing for books (*tiq*) and the chest (*teva*) to house the holy books.[16] In some synagogues the Torah chest was topped with an arched lid[17] and rested upon a stand or a carpet.[18] The scrolls were read upon a specially designated table, the *angalin shel sefer*.[19] They were wrapped in fine embroidered (*mezuyarot*) cloths[20] that were adorned with bells that "make noise."[21] The bells, together with any liturgical music and the cantillation of the biblical readings, differentiated the sounds experienced within the synagogue from those of other environments. Similarly, *t. Sukkah* 4:6 suggests that the reading of Scripture in the Alexandria synagogue took place on a raised platform. The folkloristic lavishness of this synagogue is most likely a projection of attitudes toward synagogues in late antique Palestine.[22] Diaspora communities before 70 also differentiated the synagogue environment by means of decoration.

The Sanctity of Synagogues: Holiness through Hierarchy

In traditions preserved in the Mishnah and the Tosefta the sanctity of the synagogue is shown to be derivative of the holy books that were read and apparently stored there. This is stated through case law in m. *Megillah* 3:1, which sets the conditions under which the people of a town[23] might sell their communal religious properties:[24]

> The people of a town who sold their town square:
> They must buy a synagogue with its proceeds;
> If they sell a synagogue, they must acquire a (scroll) chest.
> If they sell a (scroll) chest, they must acquire cloths (to wrap sacred scrolls).
> If they sell cloths, they must acquire (biblical) books.[25]
> If they sell books, they must acquire a Pentateuch (scroll).[26]
> But, if they sell a Pentateuch, they may not acquire (biblical) books.
> And if they sell books, they may not acquire cloths.
> And if they sell cloths, they may not acquire a chest,
> And if they sell a chest, they may not acquire a synagogue.
> And if they sell a synagogue, they may not acquire town square.
> So too, with the left-over (money).
> They may not sell public property to an individual, because they are lowering its holiness, so Rabbi Meir.[27]
> They said to him: If so, then they cannot sell from a larger town to a smaller town.

In this passage the primacy of the Pentateuch scroll is set out in a form that might be visualized as a stepped pyramid, the scroll of the Pentateuch at the apex:

<pre>
                    Torah Scroll
                         *
        Other biblical Books +   – Other biblical Books
            Cloth Wrappers +   – Cloth Wrappers
                Chest +   – Chest
            Synagogue +   – Synagogue
        Town Square +   – Town Square
</pre>

The structure of this text is maintained through the formulaic repetition of "if they sell Y, they must acquire Z" and "if they sell Y, they may not acquire X." This conception is made explicit by the support offered by the second-century sage, Rabbi Meir, for his rebuffed argument, "because they are lowering its holiness." The basis of Rabbi Meir's approach is a conception of hierarchical holiness that the Mishnah applies to the Temple context:

> Thirteen tables were in the Temple . . . and two in the entrance hall, inside: one of marble and one of gold. On the marble (table) is put the showbread when it is brought in, and on the golden (table) when it is removed, for (the bread is) increased in holiness, and not decreased.[28]

Mishnah *Megillah* 3:1 spells out the principle that "(objects are) increased in holiness, and not decreased" in an architectonic manner. Much of the content of this tradition (if not its literary structure) predates c. 150 C.E. when it was subjected to sustained discussion by scholars of the Usha generation.[29] Our Mishnah text ascribes holiness to synagogue buildings, deriving this sanctity from the presence of Sacred Scripture within them. The hierarchical division of Scripture, here the Pentateuch and less holy books of the Prophets and Writings, is extended beyond the biblical canon to objects and places that came in contact with the biblical scrolls. The principle that "objects are increased in holiness, and not decreased" is applied in the Tosefta to the hierarchical stacking of scrolls within the "chest." Torah scrolls may be laid on top of scrolls containing individual books of the Pentateuch, which in turn may be stacked on top of prophetic books.[30] Scrolls were generally laid horizontally for storage during this period.[31]

Tannaitic traditions suggest that sanctity is transferred from the Torah scroll to its appurtenances through physical contact with the scroll. This sacrality is expressed as hand defilement in *t. Yadaim* 2:12:

> The casing for books (*tiq*)[32] and wrappers, and the book chest, when they are pure defile the hands.[33]

Appurtenances of the Torah that had only occasional contact with biblical scrolls did not defile. Thus *m. Kelim* 16:7 legislates that the table upon which the scroll is read, the *angalin shel sefer*,[34] is not subject to defilement. This is because the book was placed upon the table only when it was being read and therefore had no permanent contact with the table. Similarly, then, the synagogue building has no capacity to defile. This tradition expresses an important distinction between the scrolls and their immediate implements: the sanctity of the synagogue devolves from the more holy and ultimately defiling higher order holy objects.[35]

The sanctity of the synagogue is expressed in *m. Megillah* 3:1 through the magnificently structured stepped hierarchy of holiness. The Scrolls, their cabinet, and their cloth wrappers are described as being more holy than the synagogue. This sanctity is protected from impious use by the taboo of hand defilement.

Community Prerogative: Selling Holy Property

The Tannaitic discussion of the sale of sacred property explores the meaning of sacred possessions, particularly synagogues, in the period after the Temple's destruction. That such objects could be sold at all shows that on some level they were looked upon as economic assets. Even still, the Sages looked negatively upon the sale of holy objects, particularly of Torah scrolls.[36] In m. Megillah 3:1 Rabbi Meir attempts to limit who may buy communally owned holy objects: "They may not sell public property to an individual, because they are lowering its holiness." This tradition assumes that a community has more holiness than an individual, and that individuals sometimes bought holy objects. Rabbi Meir's position is reduced *ad absurdum* by his contemporaries; "They said to him: If so, then they cannot sell from a larger town to a smaller town." It is assumed that this limitation would stymie sales. Clearly the subject is movable property and not synagogues or town squares, otherwise the response of the Sages makes no sense.

The Mishnah then turns to the disposition of a synagogue building. Three scholars of the Usha generation (c. 150 C.E.) present increasingly liberal conditions under which a community may relinquish a synagogue building and dedicate the structure for non-sacral uses. In m. Megillah 3:2–3 we read:

> A synagogue may be sold only on condition that if they (the sellers) wish, they (the purchasers) will return it, the words of Rabbi Meir.
> The Sages say: They sell it in perpetuity, except for four purposes: as a bath house, as a tannery, as a ritual bath and as a urinal.
> Rabbi Judah says: They sell it as a courtyard (i.e., without stipulations) and the purchaser may do with it as he will.

Synagogue buildings were permanent architectural features on the town landscape. Buildings, especially public buildings, often retain their original designations long after they are discarded or reused for another purpose. They were qualitatively different from the town square, which could be sold and built upon, and thus forgotten. They were also different from movable objects which, while not losing their sanctity, might be sold and forgotten.[37] This phenomenon stands behind t. Megillah 2:12's restriction upon Rabbi Lazar son of Rabbi Zadok's reuse of the Alexandrian synagogue in Jerusalem that is presented in the name of Rabbi Judah:

> Said Rabbi Judah: It happened that Rabbi Lazar son of Rabbi Zadok acquired the synagogue of the Alexandrians that were in Jerusalem, and did with it as he wished.
> They only forbade (such utilization of the building) while it was called by its original name (that is, the "Synagogue of the Alexandrians").[38]

In m. Megillah 3:2 three Tannaim address the question of how (not if) one might "lower the holiness" of a synagogue building to facilitate its transfer to secular usage. The Ushan scholars of m. Megillah 3:1–2 suggest a range of attitudes toward the sale of a synagogue. These range from Rabbi Meir, who suggests a sort of long-term leasing system,[39] to the Sages, who favor sale with stipulations against unseemly reuse, to Rabbi Judah, who asserts that a synagogue which is sold for another purpose is no longer to be treated as a synagogue.[40] According to the Sages, synagogue buildings may not be reused as bath houses, tanneries, immersion pools, and water closets.[41] These places were the antitype of synagogues, being settings into which Sacred Writings were not to be brought and where Torah study was forbidden.[42]

Rabbi Judah's position appears to be the most radical of the three. He asserts that the significance of a synagogue building is determined by the community's attitude toward it. If the community no longer esteems the synagogue building, its significance diminishes. In t. Megillah 2:12, cited above, Rabbi Judah claims that his position has precedent reaching back to the latter Second Temple period.[43] If this tradition accurately reflects the last years before 70 (as the Tannaim believed it did), Rabbi Meir and the Sages were clearly innovators in ascribing residual holiness to discarded synagogue buildings. No text that can serve as a precedent for their positions appears in writings that claim to predate them.

The positions attributed to Rabbi Meir, the Sages and to Rabbi Judah reflect radically different attitudes toward the disposition of a synagogue. The tension involved in the disposition of a synagogue building reflects the developing significance of this institution that is expressed through the notion of holiness.

Imitatio Templi: Temple Imagery in the Sanctification of the Synagogue

In m. Megillah 3:3 Rabbi Judah forges an explicit connection between synagogues and the Temple:[44]

Additionally, Rabbi Judah said:
A synagogue that was destroyed:
eulogies are not said in it,
ropes are not twisted in it,
nets are not stretched in it,
fruit is not spread on its roof (to dry).
It is not used as a shortcut, for it is written:
"I will destroy your sanctuaries"—
they are sacred even when destroyed.
Grasses grow within them:
They must not be picked (so as to provoke) sadness.

The proof text for this position, Leviticus 26:31, utilizes the term *miqdash*, a word derived from the root *q-d-sh*, "holy." The intent of *miqdasheihem* "your temple(s)" is interpreted as follows: "I, God, have destroyed YOUR synagogues." A related exegesis of this verse appears in the *Sifra*, a somewhat later work, many of the anonymous traditions of which scholars generally ascribe to Rabbi Judah son of Ilai.[45] This text reads both synagogues and study houses into Leviticus 26:31, "I will destroy your temples":[46]

Temple, my temple, your temples—
to include synagogues and study houses.

The word *miqdasheihem*, "your temples," provides the stimulus for this midrash. In Leviticus 26:31 *miqdasheihem* refers to "your (local, illicit) temples."[47] Tannaitic exegetes attempted to reconcile the fact that *miqdash*, "temple," appears elsewhere in the Pentateuch only regarding the ordained Temple of God, yet appears in a plural form in this verse.[48] They found referents for the plural form among the institutions of their own time.[49] The *Sifra* text projects synagogues and study houses back into the mythic reality ordained by the Torah itself. They are set on the same level as the Temple itself. This device was often used in Tannaitic sources to legitimize contemporary institutions.[50] Tannaitic Sages believed that both a synagogue and a study house existed on the Temple Mount. Whether or not this belief corresponds with historical reality,[51] it legitimized both contemporary institutions in the eyes of the Tannaitic Sages.[52]

Perhaps significantly, this is the only Tannaitic source to touch on the holiness of study houses.[53] No Tannaitic sources explore the disposition of a study house building, or the sanctification of study house appurtenances. This may be because, as Lee Levine suggests, permanent institutionalized study houses developed in Palestine only during the third century.⁵⁴ It is likely that the building housing this new and increasingly significant institution was not venerated until the period of the Amoraim.

In m. *Megillah* 3:3 the interpretation of Leviticus 26:31 garbs the synagogue in the aura of the Temple and suggests a relationship between this institution and the synagogue. On a more subtle level, Rabbi Judah's prohibition against using the destroyed synagogue as a shortcut⁵⁵ parallels an anonymous Tannaitic prohibition against using the Temple Mount as a shortcut.⁵⁶ Similarly, the prohibition of frivolity in active synagogues in t. *Megillah* 2:18, which predates Rabbi Judah's comments there, parallels m. *Berakhot* 9:5's prohibition of frivolity "opposite the eastern gate of the Temple."⁵⁷ The Tannaim believed these prohibitions to have been taken over from the Temple to the synagogue. Whether synagogue decorum is here read back into the Temple, or memory of proper behavior in the Temple before 70 C.E. is incorporated into the synagogue cannot be determined.⁵⁸ The mediating concept bridging the gulf between the Temple and synagogues is expressed most explicitly by the anonymous *Sifra*'s interpretation of Leviticus 26:31, synagogues are your temples even when the Jerusalem Temple does not exist.⁵⁹

The special treatment that Rabbi Judah prescribes for a destroyed synagogue is intended to maintain the attachment of the community to the synagogue building. He allows the building to be enveloped in weeds in the hope of causing "anguish." Rashi correctly interpreted Rabbi Judah's intent:⁶⁰

> Weeds are left in the synagogue ruin so that those who see the building will be saddened and remember the days when the synagogue building was standing and how they used to congregate inside it, and request mercy from God that it be rebuilt as it once was.

It is likely that the special treatment given to a ruined synagogue and the acute interest in its reconstruction are colored by the strong Rabbinic interest in the rebuilding of the Jerusalem Temple.

In t. *Sukkah* 4:5 Rabbi Joshua son of Ḥaninah describes an idealized schedule that he and his compatriots followed in the Temple during the intermediate days of *Sukkot* that included visits to the Temple synagogue and the Temple study house. Having mentioned the Temple synagogue, the editor of the Tosefta injects a discussion of the great synagogue of Alexandria. The Alexandrian synagogue building is described in t. *Sukkah* 4:6 as having had many elements in common with buildings on the Temple Mount. This probably suggested to him the redactional placement of this tradition within the Tosefta:

Said Rabbi Judah: Whosoever has never seen the double colonnade of Alexandria[61] of Egypt has never seen the great glory of Israel in his entire life.
It was a kind of large basilica, one colonnade within another.
Sometimes twice as many (people) as those who went out of Egypt were within it.
There were seventy-one thrones there, one for each of the seventy-one elders, each one made of twenty-five talents, with a wooden platform (bema) in the center.
The leader of the assembly (ḥazan ha-knesset) stands upon it at its horn, with flags in his hand.
When one begins to read,[62] the other would wave flags so (the people) would answer "amen" for each and every blessing.
Then that one would wave the flags and they would answer "amen."
They did not sit in a jumble, but the goldsmiths sit by themselves, the silversmiths by themselves, the common weavers by themselves, the Tarsian (that is, fine) weavers[63] by themselves, and the blacksmiths by themselves. . . .[64]

The Torah reading sequence in Alexandria is most probably modeled upon Nehemiah 8:3–6.[65] Another model (or perhaps, a parallel) is the Tannaitic description of the wooden podium used during the public reading of the Torah by the king on the first day of *Sukkot* after the Sabbatical year in the Temple (*haqhel*).[66] In both the Alexandrian synagogue and the *hakhel* ceremony the officiant in charge is the *ḥazan ha-knesset*.[67] This title is used elsewhere in Tannaitic literature to refer to a Temple functionary[68] and to the synagogue leader.[69] By using the same title in both the synagogue and in the Temple, Tannaitic literature forges a continuity between these functionaries.[70] Both the Alexandrian synagogue and the Temple Mount are described as being constructed as a "stoa within a stoa."[71] In the Babylonian Talmud this tradition is ascribed to none other than Rabbi Judah.[72] These descriptions of the Temple Mount and the Alexandrian synagogue, attributed to the same scholar, forge a relationship between the two "double-stoas."[73] The number of thrones upon which the elders of the Alexandrian synagogue sat, seventy-one, parallels the number of Sages in the Great Sanhedrin that met in the Chamber of Hewn Stones on the Temple Mount. The Babylonian Talmud makes this connection explicit: "There were seventy-one thrones of gold, corresponding to the seventy-one (members) of the Great Sanhedrin."[74] The description of the thrones of the elders, "each one made of twenty-five talents" of gold is clearly *aggadic*.[75] Finely decorated synagogues are, however, recorded during the later Second Temple period.[76] We have seen that Philo describes a synagogue in Alexandria that was hung with shields, gilt crowns, and stone slabs bearing inscriptions.[77] Josephus similarly relates that the synagogue of Antioch was beautifully adorned.[78] Perhaps beautifully furnished synagogues existed in Palestine as well both before and after 70 C.E. Interestingly, the author of our tradition does not mention the Torah shrine, but focuses upon the Torah reading. The *teva* was evidently not the focal point of the synagogue. It was certainly not of interest to our author. The waving of a flag is reminiscent of the role of the assistant priest in the Mishnah's portrayal of the rituals surrounding the *Tamid* sacrifice. This is particularly true in the Erfurt manuscript's version that we have quoted, where the *ḥazzan ha-knesset* stands at the "horn," the corner, of the *bema*. "Horn" is a clear reference to the "horn" of the Temple altar. According to the tradition preserved in the Erfurt manuscript, the synagogue bema is like the Temple altar. In *m. Tamid* 7:3 the assistant priest is described standing on the horn of the altar with flags in his hands that he waved to alert the Levites to begin their song.[79]

We cannot know whether the author of this tradition had any firsthand or even secondhand knowledge of the Alexandrian synagogue.[80] We can say, however, that the text that stands before us has been molded by Tannaitic conceptions, reflecting aggadic and halakhic motifs that are well documented in Tannaitic literature.[81] The Tannaim used Temple motifs in "constructing" this fantastic description of the Alexandrian synagogue. The immediate purpose of this text is to exemplify the "glory" of Alexandrian Jewry and its synagogue.[82] The use of Temple forms in this text was undoubtedly stimulated by the developing use of Temple imagery within their own synagogues.[83]

Another text that applies Temple architecture to synagogues is *t. Megillah* 3:21–23. This anonymous Tannaitic tradition projects several architectonic elements that were to be taken over from the Tabernacle/Temple to post-70 C.E. synagogues. The centrality of Torah reading and alignment toward Jerusalem is also stressed:[84]

> . . . The Community leader (*ḥazan ha-knesset*) arises to read, someone stands until the time when he reads.
> How do the elders sit? Facing the people, their backs to the *qodesh*.
> When they set down the (Scroll) chest—its front is toward the people, its back to the *qodesh*.
> The *ḥazan ha-knesset* faces the *qodesh*.

All the people face the *qodesh*.
For it is said: "and the congregation was assembled at the door of the tent of meeting (Lev. 8:4)."

The doors of the synagogue are built on the eastern side, for thus we find in the Tabernacle, for it is said: "Before the Tabernacle toward the east, before the tent of meeting eastward (Num. 3:38)."

It is only built at the highest point of the town, for it is written: "Above the bustling (streets) she (wisdom, i.e., Torah)[85] calls out (Prov. 1:21)."

Here, the architecture of the synagogue, its location in the town, and its internal arrangement are articulated through reference to the biblical Tabernacle and the Temple of Jerusalem. As in the Alexandrian synagogue, the *hazan ha-knesset* reads Torah ceremonially. *t. Megillah* 3:23 adds a biblical nuance to the role of the *hazan ha-knesset*. The synagogue leader is explicitly cast in the mold of Moses. In Leviticus 8:4–5 Moses assembles and addresses the community before the gate of the Tabernacle and relates to them God's command. In our tradition, the synagogue leader reads the Torah of Moses before his own assembly.

Like the Tabernacle and the Temple, synagogue doors in this idealized conception are to open toward the east.[86] Similarly, like many Greco-Roman temples (most important among them, the Jerusalem Temple), synagogues are to be built on the "highest ground" of the city.[87] From there Torah will "call out" to the faithful. The interior space of the synagogue hall is arranged to focus upon the *qodesh*.[88] That is, toward the Temple of Jerusalem.[89]

The elders sit with their backs to the *qodesh*. Their attention is focused upon the center of the hall, where, as in Alexandria, Torah reading presumably took place. The internal alignment of the hall was toward the Torah chest, resting with its "back to the *qodesh*." The Torah chest in our tradition is clearly set in the place of the Ark of the Covenant, though no explicit lexical connection is made between it and the biblical *aron*. The community aligned itself toward the Torah shrine, and through it, toward Jerusalem. This arrangement assumes the Tannaitic spatial "map" of holy realms in *m. Kelim* 1:6–9. This map was also manifested, as we will see, through alignment toward Jerusalem during the recitation of the *Tefillah*.[90] As we have noted, these traditions may well represent patterns of synagogue design that are first evidenced in the Masada synagogue.

The synagogue furnishings that we have discussed thus far have been mainly centered on the Torah scroll, its storage, beautification, and reading. Tannaitic sources mention one category of synagogue appurtenances that were not directly connected to the Torah, yet were vital to the synagogue service: lamps (*nerot*) and lampstands (*Menorot*).⁹¹ In Tannaitic literature, lampstand, *menorah* in Hebrew, refers to both secular lighting appliances and to branched *menorot* modeled the Temple *menorah*. In *t. Megillah* 2:14 donation of a *menorah* inscribed with a dedicatory inscription to a synagogue is described:⁹²

> He who makes (or donates) a *menorah* or a lamp for a synagogue, until the name of the owners is removed from them, it is impermissible to use them for another purpose. Once the name of the owners is removed, it is permissible to use them for another purpose.

The use of the term *menorah* in this tradition is significant to Joshua Brand,⁹³ followed by Lee Levine,⁹⁴ who see this *menorah* as a branched *menorah* modeled on that of the Temple. Donation of lamps to the Temple is reflected in *m. Yoma* 3:10, which reports that Queen Helena of Adiabene donated a *nivreshet*, a gold lamp, which hung "at the gate of the Sanctuary."⁹⁵ Palestinian Amoraim differed as to the type of lamp donated by Helena, one suggesting that it was a *menarta* (*menorah*), the other a conch-shaped hanging lamp.⁹⁶ The identification of the "*menorot*" with the Temple *menorah* in the traditions that we have discussed is far from certain. *m. Sukkah* 5:2 describes, for example, "four golden *menorot*" that illuminated the Court of the Women during the "Water Drawing" festivities during the festival of *Sukkot*. These lampstands are said to have each supported four large golden lamps (*sefalim*), not seven lamps as on the Temple *menorah*, and to have been ascended by four "ladders" (*sulamot*) to service each lamp. There is no reason to assume that these lampstands bore any resemblance to the Temple *menorah*.

Fortunately, other sources are extant that may shed light on this ambiguity. Two ostensibly Tannaitic sources that appear in the *Midrash ha-Gadol* to Exodus 20:20 forbid the construction of *menorot* that look like the Temple *menorah*.⁹⁷ In the first of these traditions we read:

> "You shall not make with Me gods of silver, neither shall you make for yourselves gods of gold, (You shall not make for yourselves)" (Ex. 20:20).
>
> That no one may make an altar like the altar, a table in the form of the table, a *menorah* like the *menorah*, so the words of Rabbi Meir.

Unfortunately, this tradition does not appear in any of the extant Tannaitic collections, and so its authenticity may be questioned.⁹⁸

The second, anonymous tradition is based upon a text which appears in the b. Rosh ha-Shanah 24a–b (and parallels):[99]

> Our Rabbis taught: No one may make a building (*bayit*) in the form of the Shrine
> (*Hekhal*), an exedra[100] in place of the entrance hall (*ulam*),
> a courtyard (*haṣer*) in place of the court (*azarah*),
> a table in place of the table (of the bread of the Presence),
> a *menorah* in place of the *menorah*,
> but one may make (a *menorah*) with five, six or eight (branches).
> Even of other metals (you shall not make a *menorah*).

The list of artifacts that may not be replicated is much longer here than in our tradition attributed to Rabbi Meir. The specific concern for the *menorah* in this tradition is of particular interest since it is the only Temple appurtenance that this text discusses in detail.

The interest that these texts show in the *menorah* may reflect the living reality of second-century synagogues, the prohibition against other Temple elements being somewhat more academic. While the *menorah* does not appear on the Bar Kokhba coins,[101] it does appear on two ossuaries that L. Y. Rahmani dates to between the first and second Jewish revolts against Rome (late first to mid-second centuries C.E.).[102] One of these *menorot* has five branches.[103] The other two branches were added to a five branched *menorah* to total seven.[104] The *menorah* is a relatively common motif decorating southern Judean oil lamps that have been dated between the first and second Jewish revolts against Rome. Six lamps bearing *menorot* appear in the corpus published by Varda Sussman.[105] Of these, all but one[106] have more than seven branches. Perhaps the preponderance of lamps with eight or more branches in this admittedly small sample suggests a reticence among some Jews to create even images of seven-branched *menorot*.[107]

Ludwig Blau is convinced that these literary traditions show that Jews in Tannaitic Palestine made three-dimensional *menorot* (whether with seven branches or otherwise): "He (Rabbi Meir) must have been trying to oppose a deeply rooted custom, but without success. . . . From these prohibitions it may actually be deduced with great probability that these things actually took place. The Halachic negation is a historical affirmation."[108]

Further evidence for the existence of branched *menorot* in second-century Palestine is found in *m. Kelim* 11:7. Tractate *Kelim* describes the ritual purity of everyday items in Tannaitic Palestine. It is thus significant that this text lists individual elements of a branched *menorah*:

So, too, the branches of a *menorah* are not susceptible to defilement, but the cups and the base are susceptible; and when they are joined together the whole is susceptible.

The terminology used in this text parallels biblical and Targumic descriptions of the Temple *menorah*. This lampstand has "branches," and not a single stem like a Roman candelabrum.[109] "Branches" and "flower" are both terms used in the Exodus descriptions of the *menorah*.[110] "Base" may parallel the Targumic translation of "its stalk" (*yarkhah*) in Exodus 25:31 and 37:17.[111] Mishnah *Kelim* 11:7 describes a *menorah* that has parts like that of the Temple *menorah*, suggesting that branched *menorot* were manufactured in Tannaitic Palestine.

The question then remains, why would the synagogue lampstand be explicitly "templized" as a *menorah*, while the Torah chest, and other synagogue appurtenances were not so explicitly templized? The answer perhaps lies in the fact that the Torah appurtenances were wholly conceptualized in terms of their relationship to the Torah scroll, with no need or interest in assigning to them a Temple component. The synagogue building, however, was conceptualized in terms of the Temple. According to *t. Megillah* 3:21–23 synagogues were to be aligned toward both Jerusalem, and toward the rising sun. The Alexandrian synagogue was "built" on the model of the Jerusalem Temple. The lampstand was an element of the synagogue interior that was unrelated to the Torah scroll. It was seen, therefore, as a neutral element of the synagogue decor. As the once-neutral building became identified with the Temple during this period, the lampstand too attained Temple attributes. In this way the lampstand became a branched *menorah*.

Synagogue Liturgy, the Temple, and the Sanctification of Synagogues

The development of formalized communal liturgy and its eventual localization within synagogues was an important factor in the sanctification of this institution. We have seen that prayer in the "house of prostration" existed already at Qumran. The development of prayer modeled upon the Temple service among the Qumran sectarians reflected their belief that the late Second Temple was profane. The Pharisees too distanced themselves somewhat from the earthly Temple, applying temple motifs to their community.[112] For the Tannaim, who saw the Pharisees as their forerunners, the harsh reality of the Temple's destruction and the ever-increasing chronological gap separating them from God's house led to the use of Temple motifs in the formation of the synagogue and its liturgy.[113]

Tannaitic literature suggests that elements of the synagogue ritual were modeled upon the Temple ritual. We have already seen this in the case of the Alexandrian synagogue, which, like the Tannaitic description of Torah reading on the first day of *Sukkot* after the Sabbatical year (*hakhel*), takes place atop a wooden platform. We have also seen that synagogue and Temple officiants were called *rosh ha-knesset* and *ḥazan ha-knesset*.[114] Torah blessings are said to have been recited by the high priest in the Temple on *Yom Kippur*,[115] "like those that are said in the synagogue."[116] Tosefta *Sukkah* 2:10 relates that on the festival of *Sukkot*, *lulavim* were used ritually and that the priestly blessing was pronounced in Jerusalem synagogues.[117] We cannot know which institution is the model for which of these traditions, whether the synagogue was modeled upon the Temple, or perhaps the rite of the synagogue retrojected to the destroyed (and future) Temple.[118] All of these tendencies may be at play.

Soon after 70 C.E. rituals which the Tannaim understood to have had their roots in the Temple cult were adapted to synagogues. The Mishnah traces this process to an enactment of Rabban Yoḥanan son of Zakkai.[119]

> At first the *lulav* was taken up in the Temple seven (days) and in the countryside (*medinah*) one. When the Temple was destroyed, Rabban Yoḥanan son of Zakkai decreed that the *lulav* be taken up in the countryside seven (days) in memory of the Temple.

Rabban Yoḥanan son of Zakkai used the custom with roots in Second Temple period Jerusalem to take up *lulavim* in synagogues during *Sukkot* as a basis for the *takkanah* that he enacted in Yavneh after the destruction of the Temple...."[120] According to this conception, a behavior that was somewhat limited before 70 C.E. was significantly broadened in scope by the early Tannaitic Sages.[121] The taking up of *lulavim* is to be enacted "in the countryside," apparently in the synagogues.

The "taking up" of the *lulav* outside of Jerusalem is the only enactment of Rabban Yoḥanan son of Zakkai for which an explicit rationale is provided: "in memory of the Temple."[122] The ritual context of Rabbi Yoḥanan's *lulav* enactment is specified in the Mishnah's anonymous explanation of how this *takkanah* is to be enacted:

> The first festival day of *Sukkot* that falls on the Sabbath, all the people bring their *lulavim* to the synagogue (in advance)....[123]

The Mishnah's anonymous application of the edict attributed to Rabban Yoḥanan son of Zakkai reflects an expansion of the function and the ideological significance of the synagogue. Synagogues were no longer presented exclusively as places of "reading and studying Torah," as they are in most later Second Temple period sources. They had become the context for a ritual with roots in the Temple. This ritual was adapted for the specific purpose of "remembering the Temple." Similarly, *shofar* blowing,[124] the recitation of the *Hallel* psalms,[125] the priestly blessing,[126] the organization of prayer at the times when it took place in the Temple,[127] and the recitation of blessings at the reading of the Torah[128] became synagogue functions.[129]

Among the innovations of the scholars at Yavneh was the implementation of regimented communal prayer,[130] often (though not necessarily) within synagogues.[131] Tannaitic prayer was recited in Hebrew that had biblicized elements.[132] The model of Daniel, a Jew who was believed to have lived in Babylonia while the first Temple lay in ruins, was significant in the development of the Tannaitic *Tefillah*.[133] Thrice daily prayer directed toward Jerusalem is evidenced as early as Daniel 6:11. The times when the Tannaitic *Tefillah* was recited were coordinated with the Temple sacrifices. Since the latter Second Temple period these were considered to be a "particularly efficacious time for prayer."[134] This coordination is made explicit in the Tosefta, which asks rhetorically: "Why did they say 'the morning prayer (may be recited) until noon'?" The answer follows: "For so the morning *Tamid* was sacrificed until noon." This text continues with similar presentations of the afternoon and evening prayers.[135] The daily sacrificial "clock" was used by the Mishnah in describing the times for the *Shema*.[136] This model was applied to the *Tefillah*.[137] Prayer came to be perceived as *avodah* (sacrificial service), during this period, a term that had "previously been used to denote the sacrificial service in the Temple."[138] Study too took on this characteristic.[139]

Though Temple models were applied to prayer during this period, Tannaitic prayer was not conceived as a replacement for the Temple service.[140] This new way of relating to the Divine took on characteristics of the Temple service precisely because Temple sacrifice was known to have had Divine sanction. Sources indicate that during the latter years of the Second Temple, prayer had become an important precursor to the Temple sacrifice.[141] With the destruction of the Temple, sacrifices were discontinued and prayer took on central prominence. This phenomenon reflects an attempt to maintain continuity between Temple times and *zeman ha-zeh*.

Alignment in prayer toward the Jerusalem Temple is formulated in *t. Berakhot* 3:15 16, building upon the concentric rings of holiness that we have seen expressed in *m. Kelim* 1:6–9:

> Those who stand outside the Land turn toward the Land of Israel, as it is said: "And pray toward the land" (2 Chron. 6:38).

> Those who stand in the Land of Israel turn toward Jerusalem, as it is said: "and pray toward the city which you have chosen" (2 Chron. 6:34).
> Those who stand in Jerusalem turn toward the Temple, as it says: "When he comes and prays toward this house" (2 Chron. 6:32).
> Those who stand in the Temple turn toward the Holy of Holies and pray, as it says: "When you pray toward this place" (1 Kings 8:30).
> Those stand in the north face south, those in the south face north, those in the east face west, those in the west face east.
> For thus all Israel pray toward one place.

Alignment in prayer was among the most effective ways to preserve the sense of alignment toward the Temple and the unity of the people available to the Tannaim after 70 C.E.[142] This alignment does not represent mere antiquarian nostalgia for a place where God once resided, nor does it reflect non-theological interest in communal survival. Baruch Bokser correctly argues that this text "asserts that God's presence resides on the Temple Mount, irrespective of the Temple itself; the presence was there before the Temple was built, and can remain there without the Temple."[143]

Though the text of the *Tefillah* was in flux for centuries after the period of the Tannaim, its general contours were set during this period.[144] The *Tefillah*'s interest in the messianic redemption culminating in the rebuilding of the Jerusalem and its Temple certainly congealed during the Tannaitic period. Joseph Heinemann notes that "the central motif" of Rabbinic prayer "is unquestionably the belief in the redemption, and the longing for its realization."[145] The benediction(s) for the rebuilding of Jerusalem and the restoration of Davidic kingship are mentioned in *t. Berakhot* 3:25:[146]

> The eighteen benedictions that the Sages recited (*amru*) correspond to the invocations of the Tetragrammaton in "Ascribe to the Lord, O you mighty" (Ps. 29:1).[147]
> One inserts (the benediction) for the sectarians (*minim*) in (the benediction) for the heretics (*perushin*),
> and (the benediction) for the proselytes in (the benediction) for the elders,
> and (the benediction for) David in (the benediction that concludes) "Builder of Jerusalem."
> If one recited them separately (as separate benedictions), he has fulfilled his obligation.

The significance of Jerusalem in the *Tefillah* gives ideological expression to prayer alignment toward the "Holy" city. The blessing(s) for the restoration of Jerusalem and the Davidic line set the spiritual sights of the supplicant directly toward Zion, wherever he himself might be.

Another liturgical factor in the sanctification of synagogues was the recitation of the *Qedushah*, the "sanctification" in communal prayer. The "description of the sanctification of God by the ministering angels on high, which has its roots in the theophanies of Isaiah and Ezekiel,"[148] brought the language of holiness into the realm of liturgy. It set the angelic litanies of Isaiah 6:3 and Ezekiel 3:12 into the mouths of Israel below as they recited either the *Tefillah* or the *Yoṣer* prayers.[149] This holiness was different from that derived from the Torah scroll or the Temple. The invocation of the angelic litany appears in the *Apostolic Constitutions*, early Christian prayers that may be based upon Jewish prayers, where the community as a whole recites Isaiah 6:3 and Ezekiel 3:12.[150]

Little is known of the Tannaitic *qedushah*, other than the fact of its existence. Only one source mentions it at all. In *t. Berakhot* 1:9 we read:

> Rabbi Judah would answer with the one who was blessing: "Holy, Holy, Holy etc. (Isa. 6:3)" and "Blessed etc. (Ez. 3:12)."
> All of these Rabbi Judah would pronounce with the one who was blessing.[151]

Verbal recitation of the *qedushah* together with the officiant was apparently an unknown (or at least rare) behavior among the Sages at Usha, worthy of note by our Tosefta tradition.

Another prayer that uses the language of holiness was the *Qaddish*, elements of which closely parallel the New Testament "Our Father" prayer. J. Heinemann believes that the *Qaddish* existed in "skeletal form" during the Tannaitic period, having been recited at the conclusion of a public sermon.[152] Discussing the *qedushah* and the *Qaddish*, Lawrence Hoffman notes the obvious relationship between these two prayer forms, as well as the thematic similarities. Both, he notes, "praise God and his ultimate kingdom."[153]

The *Mekhilta of Rabbi Ishmael*[154] reflects the development of prayer within synagogues, and attempts provide conceptual underpinnings to this process. By stringing together Tannaitic traditions that are known from other Tannaitic collections, the editor relates the assembly of Jews in synagogues to their assembly the Temple:

> In every place (where I cause My name to be remembered I will come to you and I will bless you) (Ex. 20:21) where I reveal Myself to you—in the Temple.
> From here they said: The Tetragrammaton may not be pronounced in the outlying areas (*ba-gevulin*).
>
> Rabbi Eliezer son of Jacob says: If you will come to my house I will come to yours. To the place that my heart loves my feet will lead me.
> From here they said: Whenever ten people congregate in the synagogue the Divine presence is with them, for it is written, "God (*Elohim*) stands in the congregation of God (*El*)" (Ps. 82:1)....[155]

This text is bound together exegetically by the twice recurring phrase: "From here they said." The first half of the midrash limits "every place" in Exodus 20:21. The only place where the Tetragrammaton may be pronounced is the Temple. Its pronunciation is explicitly forbidden *ba-gevulin*, "in the outlying areas." For our editor, "outlying areas refers specifically to synagogues."[156] This is made clear in the second half of this midrash.

The second half of the midrash asserts in the name of Rabbi Eliezer son of Jacob that the Divine may be encountered. God may be encountered when Jews assemble with the intention of "coming to my house." In parallels to this tradition "my house" clearly refers to the Temple.[157] Here, however, the identification of "my house" is intentionally left vague. It refers both to the Temple, the *Beit ha-Miqdash,* and to the synagogue, the *beit ha-knesset.* This is made clear in the tradition cited to support Rabbi Eliezer son of Jacob's assertion: "Whenever ten people congregate in the synagogue the Divine presence is with them," followed by a prooftext. The word "synagogue" does not appear in the parallels to this tradition in m. *Avot* 3:6.[158] The phrase "in synagogues" binds together this entire composition, making explicit the denotations of *gevulin* and of "my house." Synagogues are like the Temple in that both are "my house" and that God "blesses" Israel in each when He is called upon. It is this assembly and the "remembering" of "My name" that occurs in each that connects the two institutions. The equation is limited, however, by the fact that the Tetragrammaton is pronounced in the Temple service, while it may not be said in the synagogue. For our editor, the synagogue was the place for late antique Jews to gather as a community, and as a community to encounter the Divine. This unique text promises that God will be present to all synagogue communities that call upon him, as he was once accessible to all Israel in the Temple. It parallels traditions that appear in Amoraic literature, which was being composed at the very time that this text was being redacted.[159] Assuming that it is a Tannaitic source, and was not implanted in the *Mekhilta* at a later date, this text serves as a bridge between the Tannaitic period and the Amoraim that followed.

Tannaitic Limits on *Imitatio Templi*

We have traced the process by which the Tannaim applied Temple motifs to synagogues. This "templization" took place during a period when "temple culture" was still quite strong. A temple setting was generally seen as the natural context for religious rites.[160] As at Qumran and within early Christian and polytheistic contexts,[161] temple terminology was used by the Tannaim to describe and define non-temple ritual settings. As Jonathan Z. Smith notes, religion at this time both asserted its independence from great shrines and appropriated imagery derived from temple culture.[162] The Tannaim thus needed to balance between their inclination and that of their followers to participate in this temple culture, and their desire to maintain the uniqueness of the Jerusalem Temple. To do otherwise would violate the Deuteronomic prohibition that the Sages held to be cardinal against temples other than the Temple of Jerusalem.[163] A number of Tannaitic sources set controls upon the process of templization.

Restrictions on the templization of synagogues are reflected subtly in *t. Megillah* 2:13 and 16. The type of sanctity that was applied to the synagogue is here said to be manifestly different from that which emanated from the Temple. Regarding appurtenances that were made specifically for a sacred book, *t. Megillah* 2:13 states:

> Until they are used for a sacred (*gavoha*) purpose, they may be used for a mundane (*hedyot*) purpose. But if a person lent his wrapping cloth (to be used with a holy) book, he may return and take it back.[164]

In *t. Megillah* 2:16 the same notion is applied to objects destined for the Temple, though with different consequences:[165]

> Sacred (*gavoha*) appurtenances:
> Until they are used for a sacred (*gavoha*) purpose they may be used for a mundane purpose.
> Once they are used for a sacred purpose, they may not be used for a mundane purpose.
>
> Stones and beams that were originally carved for a synagogue:
> It is not permissible to use them on the Temple Mount . . . .

The difference between sacred and mundane usage is expressed in a hierarchical fashion in these traditions as "high" (*gavoha*) and "mundane" (*hedyot*). This terminology reflects the notion of ascent in holiness. These terms are used in these traditions regarding objects dedicated for use with a holy book and to those dedicated to the Temple Mount. Reflecting upon this usage, Lieberman notes that:

> At times (the Tosefta) calls "high" sacred objects that are used for "mundane" purposes, and sometimes it refers to objects that are truly "high," i.e., the Temple and its appurtenances. All depends upon the context.[166]

The hierarchy of holiness associated with a sacred book was on a much lower level than Temple sanctity. According to *t. Megillah* 2:13, one may lend his "mundane" wrapping cloth to be used with a sacred book, and take it back at will. No such provision exists for objects donated to the Temple where objects that were made for a "mundane" purpose cannot be used.[167] In illustration of this principle, *t. Megillah* 2:16 disallows the transfer of carved stones that have been intended for use in constructing a synagogue to the Temple. The synagogue and the Temple shared an architectural identity, carved stones and beams were used in both. We have suggested that this identity led to the application of Temple notions to the synagogue building. This tradition teaches that despite these similarities and the use of Temple terminology to describe synagogues, the synagogue is "mundane" in comparison to the Holy Temple.

Other traditions reflect concern that the synagogue building and its appurtenances not look too much like the Temple. In the *Mekhilta of Rabbi Ishmael* we read:

> "(You shall not make with me gods of silver and gods of gold,) You shall not make for yourselves" (Ex. 20:20):

> Lest you say: Since the Torah has given permission to make (it/them) in the Temple, I am going to make them in the synagogues and study houses, Scripture says: "You shall not make unto yourselves."[168]

What is it that existed in the Temple that cannot be made for the synagogues and study houses? Rashi, Rabbi Solomon son of Isaac,[169] suggests that the referent is the cherubim described in the just previous *Mekhilta* pericope.[170] The advantage of this interpretation is editorial. It applies the referent of the previous *Mekhilta* tradition to ours (and possibly to the one that follows),[171] smoothing out the narrative of our redacted *Mekhilta* text.[172] The use of "synagogues and study houses" in our text provides a plural referent to match the plural forms that appear throughout this verse, and parallels the two cherubim.[173] Like the *Sifra*[174] (and some versions of the *t. Sukkah* 4:5), the *Mekhilta of Rabbi Ishmael* is concerned with the sanctification of study houses. This is accomplished through their inclusion in traditions that compare "synagogues and study houses" to the Temple. By comparison, the Mishnah does not ascribe any sanctity to study houses.

It is unlikely that Jews in late antique Palestine would have constructed cherubim for their synagogues and study houses, since even in the Second Temple there had been none.[175] Sectarian temples still existed, however, within the "living" memory of Rabbinic literature, namely the Samaritan temple on Mt. Gerizim[176] and the temple of Onias in Egypt.[177] The memory that Jews had turned to forbidden temples even while the Jerusalem Temple stood might have sensitized the Sages to the possibility that synagogues "at this time" could be transformed into illicit cult centers.[178]

Other scholars[179] suggest that the referent of our *Mekhilta* tradition is found in parallel, ostensibly Tannaitic, sources from the *Midrash ha-Gadol* that we have cited earlier.[180] We have seen that branched *menorot* existed in Tannaitic Palestine. Portrayals of synagogue architecture in literary sources provide a context for Tannaitic concern that synagogue might look too much like the Temple. Both *t. Megillah* 3:21–23's synagogue designs and the Alexandrian synagogue use Temple elements. Perhaps some circles found even this small amount of borrowing to be unacceptable. Whether Rashi is correct that our *Mekhilta* tradition forbids cherubim, or whether Blau is correct in interpreting it in terms of the *Midrash ha-Gadol* source, the *Mekhilta* text certainly attempts to limit the templization of the synagogues and study houses. Controls on templization are pronounced in the liturgical sphere. While Tannaitic sources suggest that the priestly blessing was part of synagogue ritual before 70,[181] the prescribed costume which priests were required to wear in the Temple was no longer "permitted" by the Tannaim. This is reflected in the Mishnah's instructions on how to handle priestly malcontents during the synagogue liturgy:[182]

> He who says: I will not pass before (the Torah cabinet to perform the blessing) in colored clothing, even in whites may not pass.
>
> I will not pass before (the Torah cabinet to perform the blessing) in sandals, even barefooted may not pass.

Apparently, some priests did not agree to this popularization of their ceremony and its particular traditions.[183] The blessing was deemed essential by the Tannaitic legislators, the garment unimportant. A *baraita* that appears only in Amoraic sources, and must therefore be used with great caution, provides a biblical basis for this desire to maintain the blessing. This text hints at priestly objection to some aspect to this ceremony:

> ... Any priest who stands in a synagogue and does not lift up his hands (in the priestly blessing) transgresses a positive biblical commandment (to bless Israel).[184]

The cause of this refusal cannot be determined. Was it because the priests did not like how the blessing was pronounced? Were these priests against the whole idea of pronouncing the priestly blessing in synagogues? Or perhaps some priests simply did not know what was expected of them by the Tannaitic Sages?

M. *Ta'anit* 2:5 mentions one who "passed before the (Torah) chest"[185] on a fast and carried out the ritual as it had been performed in the Jerusalem Temple before 70 C.E.:

> It happened in the days of Rabbi Ḥalafta and in the days of Rabbi Ḥananiah son of Teradyon that one passed before the (Torah) chest and concluded the entire benediction.
> They responded after him:
> "Amen"
> "Sound priests sound! May he who answered Abraham on Mt. Moriah answer you and hear the sound of your cries this day."
> "Sound sons of Aaron, sound! May he who answered your fathers at the Sea of Reeds answer you and hear the sound of your cry this day."
> When the matter was brought before the Sages, they said:
> "Such was the practice only at the Eastern Gates (of the Temple)."[186]

The Mishnah records that this post-Temple ritual occurred under the auspices of two Sages of the Yavneh generation.[187] The Tosefta is more specific, reporting that this fast day ritual was led independently by Rabbi Ḥalafta in Sepphoris and by Rabbi Ḥananyah son of Teradyon at Sikhnin.[188] Both communities are located in the lower Galilee.[189] Was this a local custom, performed by Tannaim and therefore brought to the attention of the "Sages"? During this age of intensive ritual development the unidentified (Yavnean?) Sages reserved elements of this ritual for the Temple alone.

We have noted that Daniel 6:11—"Daniel ... knelt on his knees three times a day, and prayed, and gave thanks before his God"—served as a model for the

Tefillah. Gerald Blidstein perceptively notes that one element of this verse was not taken over into the synagogue; the Tannaitic sources that we have discussed quietly pass over the fact that Daniel "kneeled upon his knees." Blidstein notes that "prostration, as a response to the presence of God, was restricted to the now ruined Temple,"[190] having been limited to the Temple by Tannaitic interpretation of Leviticus 26:1.[191] While the Tannaitic liturgy was structured upon Temple models, this text reflects "the fear that synagogues may go too far in the imitation of structures proper to the Temple."[192]

Summary

Notions of sanctity that we noted in latter Second Temple period synagogues were expanded upon by the Tannaitic Sages after 70 C.E. The Tannaim considered whatever sanctity was ascribed to synagogues to derive from the sacred books that were stored and studied in synagogues. This sanctity was still quite tentative and not addressed directly, thus the need for careful examination of Tannaitic case law. For the Tannaim, the implementation of this sanctity was completely dependent upon the will of each community, which (according to Rabbi Judah) could sell its synagogue and nullify its sanctity at will. Sanctity was expressed through categories and motifs derived from the Temple. The localization of liturgy, which itself was modeled loosely upon the Temple service, within synagogues was important to this process. Like the Temple, the late antique synagogue became a place where communities could encounter the Divine.

The Tannaim were careful that synagogues not become replacements for the Temple. While sanctity within the synagogue was now an established fact, this holiness was to be "ordinary" in comparison to that of the Temple. Synagogues were becoming the sacred institution of profane time, providing the institutional context in which the Tannaitic reconstruction of Judaism was carried out after 70 C.E. The meeting house of latter Second Temple times was transformed, as we have seen in the *Mekhilta of Rabbi Ishmael*, into a place where "God (*Elohim*) stands in the congregation of God (*El*)" (Ps. 82:1). . . ."[193]

CHAPTER THREE

"The Sanctity of the Synagogue"

The Holiness of Synagogues in Amoraic and Post-Amoraic Literature from the Land of Israel

The synagogue, together with the notion of synagogue holiness, reached its full form during the period between the mid-third century and the close of antiquity. In Tannaitic sources the notion of synagogue holiness is still somewhat tentative and generally inexplicit. If Tannaitic literature reflects the working out of the mobility of sanctity within the synagogue, later Rabbinic literature reflects a trend toward firmly establishing this institution, toward making it less mobile. In Amoraic literature from the Land of Israel, by contrast, "the sanctity of the synagogue" became an explicit halakhic category. The synagogue becomes a "small temple" where God could be encountered. The Amoraim of the third and early fourth centuries C.E. generally built upon conceptions that were developed in Tannaitic literature: the sanctity of the biblical scrolls and the application of Temple motifs to synagogues. Indicative of these developments was the transformation of the Torah shrine from the scrolls "chest" (*teva*) of Tannaitic literature into an "ark" (*arona*), a name that reverberates with memories of the Ark of the Covenant. At the same time the study house, an up and coming institution, was endowed with holiness on the model of the synagogue. Some Sages even considered study houses to be more holy than synagogues. Both were projected into sacred time by Amoraic Sages, rooting them in the eternal cosmic order.

Sources that date from the late Byzantine and early Islamic periods, which we call collectively post-Amoraic literature, expand upon the foundations set in Amoraic literature. The diversity of this literature, which includes Halakhic collections, *midrashim*, liturgical texts (including Hebrew and Aramaic poetry, *piyyut*), Aramaic paraphrases of Scripture (*targum*), and magical texts, provides a broader view of synagogue holiness than we have seen previously. Many of these works were unknown to previous generations, having come to light among the documents of the Cairo Genizah.¹ The sanctity of the biblical scrolls was translated into increased ritualization of public Torah reading, and the Torah shrine became a place of magical power. In addition, the notion that synagogues and study houses bore a relationship to the Temple became both a legal principle and a widespread conception. So much so that in one text the Temple was seen as a kind of big synagogue! One marginal group went so far as to apply strict laws of purity that were derived from the Temple to synagogues and study houses. The expansion of *imitatio templi* during this period was balanced by an understanding that synagogues and study houses were not replacements for the Temple. They were at best "second to the Temple."² This position of number two, however, granted them a status in Jewish life that set the synagogue firmly within sacred time. While the application of Temple imagery was intense, it was selective. The concept of synagogue sanctity was a distinctively Jewish cultural phenomenon during late antiquity. It may have been intensified in some quarters in response to Christian interest in the Palestinian "holy places," a phenomenon whose origins can be traced only to the latter fourth century.³

Sanctity through Prayer and Study in Synagogues

Amoraic literature put new stress upon the importance of prayer and study in the synagogue. The focal point of this discussion is y. *Berakhot* 5:1, 8d–9a. This pericope strongly advocates synagogue attendance, particularly for prayer, describing this institution in the most vivid tones. The pericope opens by quoting the Mishnah's report of the extended prayer of the "early pious ones," who would tarry (*shoheh*) for an hour before prayer and one hour afterwards so that they might "direct their hearts toward the Omnipresent (*Maqom*)."⁴ The anonymous Palestinian Talmud asks practical questions of this text: "When did they study Torah? When did they work?" A solution was found: Rabbi Isaac son of Rabbi Eleazar said "since they were pious ones and a blessing was given to their Torah, a blessing was given to their work."⁵ This exemplary piety in regard to public prayer and the "blessing" that comes with it serves the Palestinian Talmud as an introduction to a series of statements designed to bolster synagogue attendance:

> Huna said: He who prays behind the synagogue is called evil, for it is said: "The evil will go around (when baseness is exalted among the children of men)" (Ps. 12:9).⁶

Rav Huna said: Anyone who does not enter a synagogue in this world
will not enter a synagogue in the world to come.
What is the (scriptural) basis?
"The evil will go around (when baseness is exalted among the children of
men)" (Ps. 12:9).

Rabbi Yoḥanan said: He who prays at home it is as if he is surrounded by
a wall of iron. . . .

Rabbi Phineas in the name of Rabbi Hoshaya: He who prays in the
synagogue is like one who sacrifices a pure meal offering (*minḥah*).
What is the (scriptural) basis? "God (*Elohim*) stands in the congregation
of God (*El*)" (Ps. 82:1).

Rabbi Jeremiah[7] in the name of Rabbi Abbahu: "Seek out the Lord
where he may be found" (Isa. 55:6).
Where may he be found? In the synagogues and study houses.
"Call upon him when he is near" (ibid.).
Where is He near? (In the synagogues and study houses).[8]

Said Rabbi Isaac son of Rabbi Eleazar: Not only that, but their God
stands behind them.
What is the (scriptural) basis? "God (*Elohim*) stands in the congregation
of God (*El*)" (Ps. 82:1). . . .[9]

It is a firm promise (*berit kerutah*) that he who toils at his study in the
synagogue will not quickly forget it (that is, his learning). . . .

One might imagine most of these statements being used individually within communal contexts to support attendance. The editor(s) of this text brought varied traditions together to speak with a single authoritative voice. This pericope contains specific promises for those who attend synagogues regularly, and a threat for those who do not. God is present in synagogues, and prayer there is akin to Temple sacrifice. The demand that Jews participate in synagogue ritual resulted in the exaggerated claim that prayer is not heard apart from the synagogue context. Within this pericope, Rabbi Yoḥanan's statement is given to mean that communal prayer outside synagogues is ineffectual. Further, participation in synagogue prayer promises one a place in the heavenly synagogue. This is a strong incentive for Huna's "evil ones" and for Rabbi Yoḥanan's home-prayers to change their habits.

Who is the intended audience of this pericope? Is it directed to the general population who might sometimes avoid the synagogue, or more likely, to members of the Rabbinic community who might have eschewed synagogue attendance in favor of their homes or the study house? Rabbi Yoḥanan's promise that study conducted in synagogues "is not quickly forgotten" seems to be directed to scholars who had not yet taken to praying in synagogues. In *b. Berakhot* 8a and 30b we hear of two scholars of the generation following Rabbi Yoḥanan,[10] Rabbi Ami and Rabbi Assi, who refrained from attending any of the "thirteen" synagogues in Tiberias.[11] They chose instead to "pray between the pillars where they were learning" of the study house. The promise that the Divine may be encountered in synagogues is first stated in the *Mekhilta of Rabbi Ishmael's* interpretation of "God stands in the community of God" (Ps. 82:1)."[12] Rabbi Jeremiah in the name of Rabbi Abbahu's application of Isaiah 55:6, "Seek out the Lord where he is to be found," to synagogues and study houses is a further expansion of this notion.

In *y. Berakhot* 9:1, 13a, the synagogue is touted as a place where the Divine and the human realms converge. Having described the vast distances separating the earth from each of the seven heavens and the vast size of the hoofs of the beasts of heaven, the mystery of Divine immanence is asserted:

> See how high above His world He is! Yet a person can go into a synagogue and stand behind a column and pray in a whisper, and the Holy One, Blessed be He, listens to his prayer.
> For it is said: "Hannah was speaking in her heart; only her lips moved, and her voice was not heard" (1 Sam. 1:13).
> Yet the Holy One, Blessed be He, heard her prayer.

Private synagogue prayer is here modeled upon Hannah's private prayer in the "Temple of God"[13] at Shilo. The synagogue is presented as a place where the prayer of a single individual, even of one who hides "behind a column," can traverse the expanses of the Heavens. It is a place to which God himself will reach down to His people and listen to a lone individual. In this sense it is a place like the Temple.

A number of Amoraic traditions promise that God himself is present when Israel assembles in synagogues and in study houses for liturgical rites. These traditions suggest an attempt by the Amoraic sages to solidify the position of the synagogue in Jewish life and particularly of prayer there. Representative of these traditions are three that appear in the *Pesikte de-Rav Kahana*, all in the name of Rabbi Isaac:

> "My beloved is like a gazelle or a young hart" (Cant. 2:9).
> Said Rabbi Isaac: As a gazelle leaps and skips from tree to tree, from thicket to thicket, and from grove to grove, so the Holy One leaps from synagogue to synagogue, from study house to study house.
> Why?
> In order to bless Israel.
> Through whose merit?
> Through the merit of he who sat at the terebinths of Mamre (Abraham)....[14]
>
> Rabbi Judan said in the name of Rabbi Isaac:
> As long as Israel pause together in synagogues and study houses the Holy One pauses together with them.
> What is the proof?
> "Please allow us to detain you that we may make ready a kid for you" (Jud. 13:15).[15]
>
> Rabbi Haggai in the name of Rabbi Isaac:
> Every time that Israel joins together in synagogues and study houses the Holy One, Blessed be He, joins His *Shekhinah* with them.
> What is the proof?
> "I assembled constantly, O Lord and He inclined toward me and heard my cry" (Ps. 40:2).[16]

Each of these traditions argues midrashically for the efficacy of coming together with God through communal liturgy.[17] Synagogues and study houses were clearly seen by at least some Amoraim as essential places where late antique Palestinian Jews should assemble to meet their Creator.

The threat in y. *Berakhot* 5:1 that "anyone who does not enter a synagogue in this world will not enter a synagogue in the world to come" projects synagogues into the heavenly realm. It provides a delayed punishment for the sin of avoiding the earthly synagogue.[18] This text implies a promise to simple Jews and to members of the Rabbinic elite alike: those who attend synagogues will frequent heavenly synagogues.[19] This is stated explicitly in a tradition preserved in a post-Amoraic collection, *Deuteronomy Rabba* 7:1:[20]

> Anyone who enters synagogues and study houses in this world merits to enter synagogues and study houses in the world to come.
> Whence this?
> For it is said: "Happy are those who dwell in your house, they will again praise you, selah" (Ps. 84:6).

The promise of heavenly synagogue and study house attendance is here based on the exegesis of Psalm 84:6: "Those who dwell in your house . . . will again praise you." When will this "again" happen? In the world to come.[21] The possibility of synagogues and study houses in the "world to come" was completely believable to the authors of these traditions and their audience(s).[22]

One might imagine that those who believed that the Divine could be encountered through communal synagogue liturgy would be angry with those who would thwart this encounter. Our Palestinian Talmud pericope is intended to avoid this. In b. Berakhot 6b this anger is projected upwards; God is said to be angry too:

> Said Rabbi Yoḥanan: When the Holy One, Blessed be He, comes to the synagogue and does not find ten there, he immediately becomes angry. For it is said: "Why have I come and there is no man; have I called, and there is no man; have I called, and there is no respondent" (Isa. 50:2).[23]

The importance of the synagogue and of the study house as the central and perhaps transformative "holy places" in this world is taken for granted in a tradition in Ecclesiastes Rabba 8:10:[24] In this text anger is directed not at Jews, but at non-Jews who refrain from converting to Judaism:

> "And then I saw the wicked buried" (Eccl. 8:10). This speaks of
> Said Rabbi Isaac: This is not "vanity"! What is vanity is that they do not enter (the synagogues and study houses to enter the Israelite fold) of their own accord, proselytes who come and repent.
> "And they came from the holy place" (ibid.) Because they went into a "holy place," these are the synagogues and study houses.
> "And they were forgotten in the city" (ibid.). Their evil deeds were forgotten.
> "But they that had done right" (ibid.). The good deeds that they had performed in the city were forgotten.
> "This too is vanity" (ibid.).

Rabbi Bun said: The righteous went to there, and so they entered, as Joseph to Asenath, Joshua to Rahav, Boaz to Ruth, and Moses to Hovav. Said Rabbi Aha: This is not "vanity," but (what is vanity is) that people do not come and become hallowed beneath the wings of the Divine Presence.

"Holy place" in Ecclesiastes 8:10 apparently refers to a burial site, though this verse is difficult to translate.[25] The author of our midrash does not maintain this denotation, choosing "synagogues and study houses" instead. This parallels contemporaneous synagogue inscriptions, which refer to the synagogue as an *atra qadisha*, a "holy place."[26]

While individual traditions within *Ecclesiastes Rabba* cannot be dated with precision, Marc Hirshman dates the collection as a whole to the sixth or seventh centuries C.E.,[27] the period when this terminology was most commonly used in dedicatory inscriptions. Ecclesiastes 8:10 is reread in this midrash as a transformative text, describing the spiritual lot of a convert to Judaism. Those "evil" gentiles that "repent" and convert to Judaism leave behind the spiritual death of polytheistic and Christian life. Their previous sins are "forgotten," their virtues are emphasized, and they are fully accepted into the Jewish community. The matrixes of this transformation and "sanctification" were the "synagogues and study houses," the "holy places."

The "Sanctity of the Synagogue" and the "Sanctity of the Study House"

The Palestinian Talmud's legal discussion of synagogue holiness is centered in y. *Megillah* 3:1–3, 73d–74a. This discussion is premised upon the Tannaitic principle that objects are "increased in holiness, and not decreased." As in m. *Megillah* 3:1–3, the sanctity of the Torah scrolls and the application of Temple imagery to synagogues were the axes of sanctification. Following Tannaitic sources, sanctification and desanctification within the synagogue context depended upon the desires of the community or of the donor. The mechanisms for sanctification and desanctification were of considerable interest to the Palestinian Amoraim. The Amoraic discussion of this issue is composed as a commentary upon the Mishnah. Much of this presentation is constructed around Tannaitic sources, that we have discussed, the anonymous editor constructing a rhetorical framework in which each Tannaitic source responds to a question regarding sanctification.

The status of the town square is first discussed, where it is suggested that the square should have intrinsic holiness due to the occasional presence of the sacred scrolls. This notion is rejected.[28] The second section deals with the disposition of a synagogue. The status of a destroyed synagogue building is discussed, expanding upon Rabbi Judah's position in m. *Megillah* 3:3 that a destroyed synagogue has some residual holiness. The sanctity of the synagogue is then compared to that of the study house through a projection of the situation in Amoraic Palestine back to Jerusalem before its destruction in 70 C.E.:[29]

> What is the law concerning the sale of a synagogue to buy a study house?[30]
> A statement of Rabbi Joshua son of Levi implies that it is permitted to do so, for Rabbi Joshua son of Levi said: "And he burned the house of the Lord and the king's house and all the houses of Jerusalem; every great house he burned down" (2 Kings 25:9).
> "The house of the Lord" refers to the Temple,
> "and the king's house" refers to the palace of Zedekiah,
> "and all the houses of Jerusalem" refers to the four hundred and eighty synagogues that were in Jerusalem.
>
> Rabbi Phineas in the name of Rabbi Hoshaya: There were four hundred and eighty synagogues in Jerusalem, and every one of them had a school house and a study house; a school house for Scripture and a study house for Mishnah, and all of them Vespasian burned.[31]
>
> "Every great house he burned down" refers to the study house of Rabban Yoḥanan son of Zakkai, in which they repeated the great deeds of the Holy One, Blessed be He.
> For example: "Tell me of the great deeds that Elisha has done"
> (2 Kings 8:4).

Moses son of Simeon Margolies correctly interprets this passage: "(From here) we learn that the sanctity of the study house is greater than that of the synagogue and therefore (the sale of a synagogue to buy a study house) is permitted."[32] The Palestinian Talmud here alters the Mishnah's hierarchy of holiness such that study houses become more holy than synagogues. The stepped pyramid that is presented in m. *Megillah* 3:1 has thus been expanded in this text:

Torah Scroll
*

Other biblical Books +	– Other biblical Books
Cloth Wrappers +	– Cloth Wrappers
Chest +	– Chest
Study House +	**– Study House**
Synagogue +	– Synagogue
Town Square +	– Town Square

According to our tradition, greater holiness of the study house is occasioned by the higher level study that went on in the "great" study house of Rabban Yoḥanan son of Zakkai.[33] The development of permanent institutionalized study houses in Palestine during the third century might explain why this claim is made for study houses for the first time here.[34]

Finally, private and public synagogues are contrasted for the purpose of sale. Rabbi Yohanan is said to have forbidden the sale of a public synagogue, while the editor, citing a *baraita*, allows it. This discussion is continued later in the pericope[35] where the prohibition of certain behaviors within destroyed synagogues by *m. Megillah* 3:3 is applied anonymously to destroyed private synagogues and to working (*banui*) public synagogues. They are applied to study houses as well by Rabbi Yoḥanan and in a parallel to *t. Megillah* 2:18.[36] The more stringent regulation of behaviors within working public synagogues (and study houses) suggests that they were more holy than private synagogues.[37]

The third section deals with the sanctification process: "A building that was (originally) constructed for secular use: What is its status?" Following upon this statement, a Tannaitic source on the timing of sanctification of Torah appurtenances is brought. Sanctification of a secular object occurs, says the anonymous Talmud, when it is dedicated through use.[38] Does this refer to first use (as a Tannaitic source cited indicates), or from the time that they are somehow designated to be holy? Temple models and the status of objects that enter the domain of the dead are brought to bear in response to this question, and both positions are supported:[39]

> (Temple) service appurtenances (*klei sharet*):
> When are they sanctified, immediately, or when they are used (for the first time)?
> If you say, "immediately," there are no difficulties.

> If you say, "when they are used" they (simultaneously) sanctify and confer sanctity (upon things deposited in them a difficulty does arise).
> There is no problem regarding those (Tabernacle appurtenances that were made) for Moses. They were sanctified with anointing oil (available then) and with blood.
> But the (Temple appurtenances that were made) for Solomon, did they sanctify and were sanctified all at once?
> When they entered the Land they put (the already consecrated appurtenances) of Moses in with those of Solomon. . . .

This notion of status being transferred through entrance into a domain is next applied to the spatial confines of a synagogue. The pericope divides synagogue furnishings into two categories of holiness: the general "holiness of the synagogue" (*qedushat beit ha-knesset*), and the more restricted and greater holiness of the Torah ark (*qedushat aron*). This mode of categorization parallels Tannaitic traditions that we have discussed, though the Palestinian Talmud seemingly did not have the *baraita* that we have discussed from b. Megillah 26b.[40] As in those sources, closer proximity to the biblical scrolls occasions the greater holiness of the ark:[41]

> All the furnishings of the synagogue are like (in holiness to) the synagogue.
> Its bench (*safsal*) and its couch (*qaltara*) are like (in holiness to) the synagogue.[42]
> The curtain (*kila*)[43] on the ark (*arona*) is like (in holiness) to the ark.
> R. Abbahu put a cloak (*golta*)[44] under the curtain (*bilan*).[45]
> Rav Judah in the name of Samuel: the *bema*[46] and planks (*levahin*)[47] do not have the sanctity of the ark, and do have the sanctity of the synagogue.
> The reading table (*ingalin*)[48] does not have the sanctity of the ark, and does have the sanctity of the synagogue.

Those synagogue fixtures that have the sanctity of the synagogue, but not of the ark, are: the benches, the sofa, the *bema*, the planks, and the reading table. Only those furnishings that are in constant, close proximity to the ark: the curtain and the cloak, have the sanctity of the ark. Our Palestinian Talmud tradition is the earliest text to mention "holiness of the ark" and "holiness of the synagogue" as explicit categories.

The Palestinian Talmud's mode of differentiating realms within the synagogue is reminiscent of that envisioned in *y. Berakhot* 3:5, 6d. In that text similar methods are used to separate and differentiate the scroll from a room where sexual intercourse takes place:[49]

> One may not have sexual relations when a Torah scroll is with him in the house.
> Rabbi Jeremiah in the name of Rabbi Abbahu: If it was wrapped in a cloth or placed in an aperture (ḥalon) at a height of ten cubits, it is permitted.
> Rabbi Joshua son of Levi: Make a curtain.[50]

Rabbi Joshua son of Levi is said to have required a curtain in the aperture in which the Torah was placed two generations before we hear from Rabbi Abbahu that curtains also were hung before Torah arks. This may suggest that the practice of hanging a curtain before the Torah shrine was derived from secular (perhaps domestic) closet curtains.[51]

It is also likely that the Palestinian Talmud's hierarchical structuring of the synagogue interior is influenced by the divisions into areas of ascending sanctity in the Temple. The discussion of realms of holiness within the synagogue continues with a consideration of "ark holiness":

> Rabbi Jeremiah went to Gavlanah.[52] He saw them putting a hammer[53] into the ark (along with the Torah).
> He came and asked Rabbi Immi.
> He (Rabbi Immi) said to him: "They stipulated concerning that object to begin with (that it would be kept in the ark, and hence it is proper to do so)."
> Rabbi Jonah made[54] himself a cabinet and stipulated that the upper (part) would be used for books and the lower part for utensils (or, garments).[55]

The force of communal and individual intention in the designation of sanctity is striking. These traditions add a spatial dimension to the discussion of sanctification; coining of the terms "holiness of the ark" and "holiness of the synagogue" to describe this phenomenon.

The relationship between the Torah scroll and its ark that is expressed in this text is transferred metaphorically in another Palestinian Talmud tradition to a Sage who has lost his knowledge of Torah:[56]

> Rabbi Jacob son of Abaye in the name of Rabbi Aḥa: An elder (zaken)[57] who forgets his learning through no fault of his own is treated with the sanctity of the ark.

The body of the Sage is to be treated as an "ark" for the oral Torah that this scholar has stored in it.

Torah Reading and the Torah Shrine

The public reading of Torah and its interpretation within synagogues continued to develop in Amoraic and post-Amoraic literature. In one tradition the expositor of Torah within the synagogue is likened to Moses, and sat upon a "chair of Moses."[58] Functionaries in synagogue ritual are singled out as needing to behave in an especially respectful manner:[59]

> Rabbi Samuel son of Rabbi Isaac entered a synagogue. He saw one
> man standing and translating (the Torah reading) while leaning on a
> column.
> He said to him: You are forbidden (to do this). Just as it (the Torah) was
> given with awe, you must behave toward it with awe.

The importance of Scripture in the sanctification of synagogues during the Fatamid period was derided in a polemic lodged by the ninth-tenth–century leader of the Karaite Mourners of Zion movement, Daniel son of Moses Al-Qumisi:

> And if one says that in truth they (synagogues) are holy because of the
> Torah scrolls that are in them, he is in error because any building that
> has within it a Torah (scroll) would (according to his reasoning thus) be
> holy! Similarly, if the sanctity is on account of the Torah, the building
> becomes ordinary when the Torah scroll is removed. . . .[60]

Al-Qumisi's complaints well describe contemporaneous Jewish attitudes. Regard for the sanctity of the biblical scrolls was expressed through increased regulation of the manner in which they were handled within both private and public contexts. We have noted earlier that the composition of a "manual" for the writing and treatment of biblical books, as well as the liturgy used for their public reading, *Tractate Sofrim* reflects this trend. The scroll, by now an ancient form that was no longer used for secular purposes, was treated with increasing holiness as antiquity drew to a close.

In our discussion of *t. Megillah* 3:21 we saw the elders described as seated "facing the people, their backs to the *qodesh*." The people, according to this passage, face the *qodesh*, toward Jerusalem. The *teva* is the intermediate focal point within the synagogue hall. The locus of attention was the Torah reading, toward which everyone faced. The Palestinian Talmud version of this tradition makes no reference to the position of the elders, rather, "the ark (*aron*) faces the people, the priests face the people and Israel faces the qodesh."[61] Perhaps this text reflects the relocation of the elders in some synagogues so as to face the shrine. According to one post-Amoraic text, *The Differences in Religious Customs between Babylonian and Palestinian Jewries*, Palestinian elders sat together with the congregation facing the shrine:[62]

> The sons of Babylonia (the elders) turn their faces toward the congregation and their backs toward the holy ark. The sons of the Land of Israel (the elders) turn their faces toward the holy ark.[63]

Following *t. Megillah* 3:21, the Babylonian elders face the community, with their backs to the *qodesh*. Literary sources suggest that this seating arrangement did not catch on in Palestine. Archaeological sources are less conclusive. Remains of stone benches on the Jerusalem-aligned walls of four Palestinian synagogues show that some Jews sat with their backs to Jerusalem.[64] It is impossible to tell, however, who sat on these benches.

The Torah shrine was considered by some to be a place of considerable power, as is evidenced by instructions in an amulet discovered in the Cairo Genizah. For best effect, the amulet is to be buried "under the ark of the synagogue."[65] An archaeological parallel to this text was discovered in the sixth-century synagogue at Maon (Nirim), near Gaza.[66] Nineteen amulets wrapped in cloth were uncovered in the apse of this synagogue among remains of the Torah shrine and other objects.[67] Naveh and Shaked hypothesize reasonably that "some of the amulets were suspended from the wall near or behind the Ark of the Law, or even from the ark itself."[68] The placement of amulets in close proximity to the Torah shrine at Maon and in our Genizah amulet suggests that Jews in late antique Palestine and in Fatamid Egypt considered the synagogue Torah shrine to be a place of power.[69]

The Nirim amulets were clearly themselves "instruments of power."[70] The opened exemplars appeal for healing[71] and Divine protection.[72] The desire to be close to the scrolls, a source of superior power, was surely a motivating factor. This is evidenced by the use of Hebrew biblical formulae within these amulets.[73] Like our synagogue inscriptions, the terminology used in extant amulets often draw upon biblical and liturgical formulations.[74] For example, Amen, amen selah (and related forms), a phrase that does not appear in Scripture, appears in both amulets[75] and in synagogue inscriptions.[76] The formulae of these amulets closely parallel amulets discovered in the Cairo Genizah that were written on perishable materials such as parchment, paper, or cloth.[77] Rabbinic sources note morphological similarities between amulets, sacred Scripture, *mezuzot*, phylacteries, and prayer texts (*berakhot*).[78]

The language of Scripture, and from there much of the liturgy, and of amulets was itself a vehicle of the synagogue's sanctification.[79] "The language of the holy house," *lishon beit qudsha*, is a phrase that appears in the Palestinian Targumim and in an Aramaic poem preserved in the Cairo Genizah. The meaning of this term has been discussed by a number of scholars. An unpublished Aramaic *piyyut* provides additional insight into the meaning of this term.[80] Having described how Jews congregate in synagogues to sing the "hundred and fifty psalms" of David, the poet of our Genizah text continues:

Songs of prophecy	sweet like honey
The meaning they interpret	in the language of the holy house
He loved and made him (David) holy	the holy king
And He gave him his kingdom	and the Divine name.

For this poet, the language used within late antique synagogues to explicate the biblical Psalms was the "language of the holy house." Similarly, in the Targumim we find that in places where the Targumim break into short Hebrew citations, the Hebrew text is often prefaced with "in the language of the holy house (*lishon beit qudsha*)."[81] Etan Levine and Peter Schäfer translate *lishon beit qudsha* as "the language of the Sanctuary," the Jerusalem Temple.[82] Avigdor Shinan does not accept this identification, arguing that other terms for the Temple appear in the *Targumim*.[83] Shinan, suggests, rather, that *beit qudsha* refers to the synagogue.[84] Only in our *piyyut*, however, is "holy house" clearly used to describe the synagogue. In fact, the relationship between Hebrew and the spoken vernacular during late antiquity that we have described can be seen in the inscriptions of synagogue mosaics as well. So, for example, in the Beth Alpha synagogue mosaic pavement the dedicatory inscriptions are in vernacular Greek and Aramaic.[85] The signs of the zodiac, and more pointedly the short biblical citations that label the Binding of Isaac panel are all in Hebrew. One might have expected the Binding of Isaac panel to have been labeled in Aramaic (as is often the case, for example, in the scene of Moses "when he split the sea" at Dura Europos). Rather, Hebrew is used, suggesting a familiarity with the Hebrew of the biblical text that parallels the Targumic break into Hebrew, the "language of the holy house."

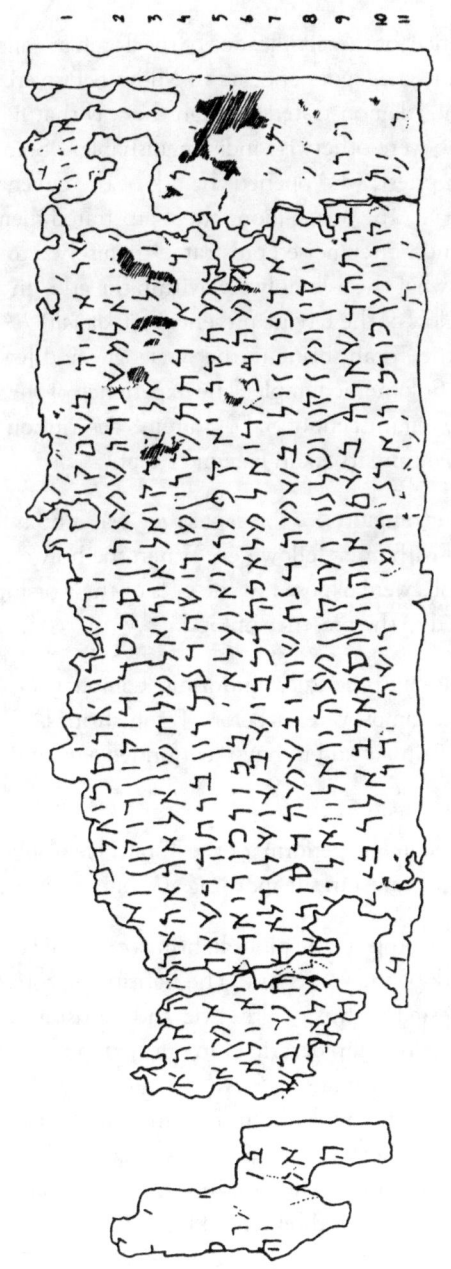

Amulet, Bronze, from the Synagogue at Maon (Nirim).

Further evidence for the significance of the Torah ark and its contents in late antique Palestinian synagogues appears in Midrash Proverbs, chapter 1, where Solomon's wisdom is demonstrated through the way that he differentiated Jews from non-Jews who were otherwise indistinguishable.[86] Solomon is said to have "signaled the high priest, who opened the ark of the covenant." Once opened, the "circumcised," i.e., the Jews, among them prostrated themselves to half their height, while the non-circumcised prostrated themselves to the floor. The midrash then turns to what the assembly saw within the ark: "In addition, their faces were filled by the glow of the Divine presence (*Shekhinah*)." As Lieberman noted, this text projects the Torah shrine in the synagogue and Jewish attitudes to the shrine back to the Solomonic temple. The experience of the Divine described in this text is strongly reminiscent of S. D. Goitein's description of popular attitudes toward the synagogue and its ark in Fatamid Egypt:

> For the popular religion ... the synagogue was a house of meeting both with God and with one's fellowmen. When the holy ark was opened and the Torah scrolls were exposed to the eyes of the worshipper, he felt himself transported to the presence of God. ....[87]

A tradition in the sixth-century midrashic compilation, Canticles Rabba,[88] suggests that votive lamps were lit before Torah shrines.[89] A biblical character, Oved Edom the Gittite, is said to have "performed a great deed (*pe'ulah*) for the Torah":

> What great deed did he perform for the Torah? He would kindle before the *aron* one *ner* (oil lamp) in the morning and one lamp at dusk. ....

This text most likely projects the pious lighting of votive lamps before the Torah ark back to the Ark of the Covenant. The lighting of votive lamps before holy objects is well attested within polytheistic and Christian contexts during late antiquity.[90] The type of lamp described in our text, a *ner*,[91] has been found in a number of synagogue excavations.[92] An oil lamp discovered in Samaria bearing the legend *ner tamid* provides an interesting parallel to our text, particularly considering the many known iconographic similarities between Jewish and Samaritan synagogue remains.[93] The inscription clearly relates this oil lamp to the Temple *menorah*.[94] Biblical and biblicized legends are not unusual in Samaritan inscriptions, particularly on lamps.[95] The suspension of a single glass lamp before the Torah shrine, called an *ashashit* or *qandila* in Rabbinic literature,[96] is common in polytheistic, Christian, and later Moslem contexts. Within the synagogue it reflects the formalization of votive lighting before the Torah shrine.[97]

No ceremony for the removal or return of the Torah scroll to its shrine existed in Amoraic Palestine. A tradition in b. Sotah 39b does, however, require the presence of the community when the scrolls were "removed" at the conclusion of communal reading:

> Said Rabbi Tanḥum, said Rabbi Joshua son of Levi: The prayer leader (shaliah tzibbur) may not uncover the teva in the presence of the community, out of respect for the community.

> Said Rabbi Tanḥum, said Rabbi Joshua son of Levi: The community is not permitted to leave (the synagogue) until the Torah scroll is removed (sheyintal sefer Torah).

In the first tradition Rabbi Joshua son of Levi shows concern that the community not be detained while the prayer leader removes a cover[98] from the Torah chest. Such a delay is seen as an affront to the community's dignity. By contrast, the second tradition is concerned with the dignity of the Torah scroll. Rabbi Joshua son of Levi requires the community to stay in the synagogue while the Torah scroll is "removed." According to the Munich[99] and Vatican[100] manuscripts and most medieval citations of this text the scroll must be "removed" before the community may depart the synagogue.[101] It is unclear to where it is removed. The Oxford manuscript[102] and the Venice edition of 1520–1523 are somewhat more specific, though still quite opaque. According to these texts the Torah must be "set in its place" before anyone may leave.[103] We still do not know, however, where the scroll's "place" was. The Babylonian Talmud seems to suggest that the scroll was "removed" to a storage "place" outside the synagogue. It is not clear whether this interpretation correctly reflects the situation in Palestine or not.[104] The waiting time while the scroll was "removed" created an unarticulated period during which the community was present in the synagogue. This vacuum was later filled with a ritual for the return of the Torah scroll to its shrine.[105]

In post-Amoraic Palestine the removal of the scroll from the Torah shrine and its return there was ritualized.[106] In *The Differences in Religious Customs Between Babylonian and Palestinian Jewries* we find:[107]

> The sons of Babylonia honor the Torah scroll when it is returned to (the Torah shrine)[108] and the sons of the Land of Israel pay it honor when it is taken out (of the shrine) and when it is placed in (the shrine) according to the Torah and the law (halakhah), for it is said: "and when he opened it, all the people stood" (Neh. 8:5).

This text assumes that the community was seated during the actual Torah reading, for otherwise, the prooftext would make little sense. Like the Tosefta's description of the reading platform of the Alexandria synagogue,[109] this ceremony is modeled upon the circumstances of Ezra's Torah reading described in Nehemiah, chapter 8. *Tractate Sofrim* preserves a complicated liturgy that was to precede the Torah reading.[110] It also mentions the ritual removal of the Torah scroll from its storage place (presumably the Torah shrine) and its return there.[111]

> ... Thereupon the *maftir* approaches, takes the Torah and says:
> "Hear O Israel the Lord our God the Lord is one" (Deut. 6:4) pleasantly, and the people say it after him.
> He responds saying: "One is our God, Great is our Master, Holy;
> One is our God, Merciful is our Master, Holy;
> One is our God, Great is our Master, Holy and awesome is His name."
> (The three exclamations) correspond to the three patriarchs;
> Others say that they correspond to the three *qedushot*.[112]
> "Your righteousness, God, extends to the heavens which you made, the great deeds of God, who is like you? (Ps. 71:19)"
> "Lord, your name is eternal, Lord, your memory is from generation to generation (Ps. 135:13)."
> All, give majesty to our God and give honor to the Torah.
> "Magnify the Lord with me and we will exalt his name together (Ps. 34:4)."
> And he must raise up the Torah at (the recitation of) "Hear O Israel," and at the three declarations of the unity of God (*yiḥudim*) and at "Magnify the Lord with me."[113]

The text continues with a version of the *Qaddish* that contains a confessional statement, then . . .[114]

> After that he raises up the Torah and says: "One is our God, Great is our Master, holy and awesome eternally."
> He begins pleasantly and says: "The Lord is the God" (I Kings 18:39), the Lord is his name (Ex. 15:3).
> The people respond after him as he says it twice, and they respond after him two times.[115]
> Immediately he unrolls the Torah scroll a space of three columns,
> elevates it and shows the surface of its script to the people standing to his right and left.

Then he turns it (the raised scroll) in front and behind him, for it is a precept for all men and women to see the script, to bow (or prostrate themselves) and exclaim: "And this is the Torah which Moses set before the Children of Israel" (Deut. 4:44).
He further exclaims: "The Torah of the Lord is perfect, restoring the soul. . . ."[116]
The *maftir* then passes it to the *ḥazan ha-knesset*, and he . . .[117] for it is not honorable for the Torah to be left alone.
Similarly it is not honorable for the *ḥazan* to stand alone before the *teva*, but (two people) should stand with him, one to his left and one to his right, corresponding to the three patriarchs. . . .[118]
The pure-minded ones of Jerusalem acted in this manner when they would take out and return the Torah. They would follow after it as a mark of respect.[119]

Extended descriptions of synagogue ritual (as opposed to liturgical texts) are extremely rare in ancient Jewish literature.[120] The ritual described here treats the Torah scroll as the representation of the Divine among the congregation. It is the closest a late antique Jew could come to seeing and touching God Himself.[121] The raising of the scroll, bowing (or prostration) of both men and women and the communal recitation of "One is our God" ritually makes this connection. The raising of the open scroll and bowing (or prostration) before it is modeled upon Nehemiah 8:5–6.[122] The author of this tradition considered the Torah procession to be very ancient, attributing it to the "pure-minded ones of Jerusalem."[123] *Tractate Sofrim* preserves the earliest evidence of Torah processions in the Land of Israel.

Imitatio Templi: Temple Imagery in the Sanctification of Synagogues

The application of Temple concepts to synagogues and study houses increased greatly in Amoraic and post-Amoraic sources. Templization of the synagogue first appears in Tannaitic literature. It is expressed in the Palestinian Talmud through the hierarchical division of the synagogue interior into realms of holiness. We have also suggested that the term *arona*, "ark," in *y. Megillah* 3:1, 73d, is indicative of *imitatio templi*. The term *arona* is common in Amoraic literature, generally[124] replacing the Tannaitic *teva* ("chest").[125] *Arona* bears biblical resonances. This term appears in the Targumim translating the Hebrew *aron*.[126] This relationship is made clear in a tradition attributed to Rabbi Huna the

Elder of Sepphoris, who is said to have lamented on the occasion of a public fast that:

> Our fathers covered it (the Ark of the Covenant) with gold, and we cover it (the Torah ark) with ashes.[127]

The Torah shrine is here cast in the mold of the Ark of the Covenant which stood in the Holy of Holies of the Tabernacle and the Solomonic Temple.[128] Significantly, however, the Torah ark is not referred to as the "Ark of the Covenant" or the "Holy Ark" in Palestinian Amoraic or post-Amoraic literature.[129] A differentiation is carefully maintained between the synagogue "ark" and the Temple "ark." Lesser synagogue appurtenances, however, were not so carefully distinguished. The curtain before the ark is called *parokhta* in another tradition, reminiscent of the Temple *parokhet* (curtain).[130] The ark and the *parokhet* thus join the *menorah* as synagogue vessels that bear the names of Temple appurtenances.[131]

There were apparently branched *menorot* reminiscent of the Temple *menorah* in synagogues during this period as well. The varieties of lighting known within synagogue contexts is reflected in the Amoraic interpretation of m. *Yoma* 3:10, which reports that Queen Helena of Adiabene donated a *nivreshet*, a gold lamp, which hung "at the gate of the Sanctuary."[132] Palestinian Amoraim differed as to the type of lamp donated by Helena, one suggesting that it was a *menarta*, a *menorah*, the other a conch-shaped (i.e., hanging), lamp.[133] One particularly interesting tradition in y. *Megillah* 3:2, 74a,[134] records that Antoninus the "Emperor" donated a lampstand to a synagogue in the time of his friend Rabbi Judah the Prince, c. 200 C.E.[135] Such a donation seemed quite plausible to the Amoraic Sages, especially since, to cite Gedaliah Alon, "the rule of the Severii (193–235) was the high water mark in friendly relations between Rome and the Jews."[136] One might see this gift giving within the context of developing relations between the Jews and the Severans. Tannaitic sources had already discussed gentile donation of lighting fixtures and architectural members to synagogues.[137] It is quite possible that Antoninus is portrayed donating a branched *menorah* to the synagogue, and not just an ordinary lampstand. Such official recognition might have influenced the development of the *menorah* as a symbol for the Jewish community.

Templization is expressed in both *halakhic* and *aggadic* texts. For example, in y. *Berakhot* 3:5, 6d, we read:

> Rabbi Joshua son of Levi said: He who spits in a synagogue is like one who spits in the pupil of His (God's) eye.

A parallel tradition in *b. Berakhot* 62b applies this position to the Temple after 70:

> Said Rabbi Bibi said Rabbi Joshua son of Levi: He who spits on the Temple Mount at this time is like one who spits in the pupil of His (God's) eye, for it says: "and my eye and heart will be there for all time" (1 Kings 9:3).

While the Mishnah prohibits spitting on the Temple Mount,[138] Rabbi Joshua son of Levi (in many versions, Rabbi Assi) is said by Rabbi Bibi[139] to have prohibited it "at this time," i.e., after 70 C.E. synagogues, like the destroyed Temple, are "the pupil of God's eye." An equation is thus suggested between proper decorum in synagogues and on the Temple Mount that is derived from Tannaitic law regarding the Temple before 70 C.E.[140]

Individual synagogues in various localities are mentioned in Tannaitic and Amoraic sources. In one Palestinian tradition the synagogue of *Madarta* in Caesarea is singled out for special distinction:[141]

> ... "The Lord is in His holy Temple" (Hab. 2:20):
> This is Rabbi Isaac son of (E)leazar[142] (who adjudicates) in the synagogue of *Madarta* in Caesarea.

The Divine presence is in "His holy Temple," i.e., the synagogue, when this scholar decides points of law there.[143] The application of verses that refer to the Tabernacle/Temple to synagogues and to study houses first appears in Tannaitic literature, and was developed further in later centuries. The "templization" of Palestinian synagogues and study houses attained its classical expression in an apparently Palestinian tradition cited in *b. Megillah* 29a:

> Rabbi Samuel son of Isaac:[144] "I will be unto them a small sanctuary (*miqdash me'at*)" (Ez. 11:16):
> These are synagogues and study houses.[145]

Miqdash me'at may be reasonably translated "small sanctuary"[146] or as "diminished holiness."[147] The author of our tradition chose the first possibility as did the translator of the Septuagint to Ezekiel: *hagiasma mikron*. This fits well with the developing templization of Palestinian synagogues and study houses during this period. Amoraic literature betrays no overt attempts to limit the templization of synagogues and study houses.[148]

The application of Temple terminology and forms increased as late antiquity proceeded. The conceptualization of synagogues as "small temples" achieved its fullest expression during this period. So we find in a late midrash from a Genizah manuscript published by Louis Ginzberg:[149]

> ... As long as the Temple existed, perpetual sacrifices and offerings would atone for the sins of Israel.
> Now synagogues are unto Israel in place of the Temple. As long as Israel prays in them, their prayers are in place of the perpetual sacrifices and offerings.
> (By reciting) prayers at their proper time and directing their hearts, they merit and will see the rebuilding of the Temple and (the re-establishment of) the perpetual sacrifices and offerings, as it is said: "And I will bring them to my holy mountain and I will rejoice in my house of prayer" (Isa. 56:7) their sacrifices and offerings will be received well on my altar, "for my house shall be called a house of prayer for all of the nations" (ibid.).

The remembrance of an idyllic past and anticipation of an ideal future sandwich "this time," when synagogues and synagogue prayer serve as a temporary replacement for the Temple. The Temple expressed here, however, is a "house of prayer" based upon Isaiah 56:7. This element of the synagogue service is emphasized in the text's choice of verses to depict the future Temple.

Targum Jonathan, paralleling Rabbi Isaac's interpretation of *miqdash me'at* "to include synagogues and study houses," translates Ezekiel 11:16 to include only synagogues: "I have given them synagogues, second (only) to My Temple...."[150] In a Genizah document titled *Hilkhot Eretz-Israel*, by its editor, *miqdash me'at*, is used as a legal category in the definition of synagogues:[151]

> "And so the Sages said: One shall not enter the Temple Mount with his staff and shoes" (M. Berakhot 9:5).
> Though by our sins the Temple Mount is not ours, we do have the *miqdash me'at*, and we are obligated to behave (towards it) in sanctity and awe. For it is written: "My Temple, fear" (Lev. 19:30, 26:2).
> Therefore the ancients decreed in all synagogue courtyards that lavers of living water for the sanctification of the hands and feet (be set up).
> If there was a delicate or sick person, unable to remove (his shoes), and he was careful as he walked (not to dirty them), he is not forced to remove (the shoes) ...

This passage suggests that piety toward the synagogue, and particularly ritual ablution of the feet and entry to the synagogue barefooted, was taken over from

Ein Gedi Synagogue, washing installation in the narthex.

the Temple to the *miqdash me'at*. The notion that ritual purity was necessary for entrance into late antique synagogues was first developed in post-Amoraic literature.[152] An interesting parallel to our text is the liturgy of Anan son of David (c. eighth century) who, on the model of the Temple, decreed that worshippers wash their hands and feet before entering into early Karaite synagogues.[153] *Miqvaot* have been discovered in close proximity to perhaps three late antique synagogues, which may suggest that a small number of Jews saw an explicit relationship between ritual purity and synagogue life.[154] A washing installation (*gorna*)[155] in the synagogue compound (forecourt?) is evidenced as early as the Palestinian Talmud.[156] Evidence of ritual ablution is found in synagogue ruins from the Byzantine period. A particularly well-preserved washing installation was discovered in the narthex of the last stage of the Ein Gedi synagogue.[157] Water installations for ablutions were also a common feature of polytheistic and Christian religious buildings. Fredrik van der Meer comments that, "the fountain in the middle of the atrium (of a late antique church) doubtless took on symbolic meaning for Christians, as they washed their hands in the waters before entering the basilica; but this kind of fountain was part of the usual decoration of any of the large inner courts in the ancient world."[158] Naphtali Wieder has demonstrated parallels between Jewish foot washing and Islamic practice, arguing that the Jewish practice throughout the Moslem world was of Islamic origin.[159] It seems likely, however, that this Jewish practice preceded the Moslem custom.[160] Jews shared a mode of piety widely practiced by polytheists, Christians, and later Moslems in preparation for sacred rites in religious buildings.

The *Baraita de-Niddah*, a text that was "probably written in the Land of Israel in the sixth or seventh century,"[161] is particularly concerned with defilement of synagogues and study houses, a form of templization that is unknown from any other text.[162] This pollution was caused by the presence of a woman who has discharged blood, which was by definition defiled and defiling.[163] The exclusion of menstruous women from communal ritual was debated by Christian scholars already during the third century, some of whom invoked Temple imagery.[164] Like other texts that we have discussed from post-Amoraic literature, the community that composed the *Baraita de-Niddah* is unknown to us. It is clear, however, from their various legal positions that its authors were situated on the stringent fringe of Rabbinic society.[165]

In the *Baraita de-Niddah* we hear that women who have given birth are excluded from the synagogues and study houses, on the model of the Temple:[166]

> "And to my Temple she shall not come (until the days of her purification are completed) (Lev. 12:4)":
> She is not permitted to enter study houses and synagogues. . . .[167]

Similarly, according to this text the defilement of a woman who has discharged vaginal blood is transferred to others through the most minor forms of physical contact. Thus, a man who comes in contact with the saliva of a menstruous woman is barred from synagogue attendance:[168]

> Said Rabbi Ḥanina: Even the spittle of a menstruous woman which she spat on the bed and her husband or sons tread upon defiles them for every purpose. They are forbidden to enter the synagogue until they immerse themselves in water.
> Why?
> Because the spittle of a menstruous woman defiles.

Separation from synagogues and study houses of menstruous women is justified biblically in the *Baraita de-Niddah*: "And to my temple she shall not come (until the days of her purification are completed) (Lev. 12:4)." Just as ritually defiled women were barred from the Tabernacle/Temple they are not admitted into the Temple-like synagogue.[169]

The lighting of lamps in synagogues and study houses is supported in one Genizah text through analogy to the Temple:[170]

> . . . The lamps: Whether in the Temple or in the synagogues or in study houses, Israel is required (to light lamps).
> For synagogues and study houses are like the Temple,[171]
> For it is said: "I will be unto them a *miqdash me'at*,"
> And as the verse says: "Command the children of Israel that they take (pure pounded olive) oil (for illumination to raise up the lamp eternally) (Lev. 24:2)"
> Now and for all generations.

Beth Shean B Synagogue, mosaic depicting a menorah with a lamp and an incense burner suspended from its lowest branches.

Ze'ev Safrai is clearly correct in saying that this tradition stresses a relationship between the synagogue lamp and the Temple *menorah*.[172] It is unlikely that this text refers to the lighting of branched *menorot*, since none of the versions explicitly refers to the lighting of a *menorah*.[173] Rather, this passage is intended to support charitable donation of lighting oil to synagogues and study houses. This type of donation goes back to Tannaitic times, where, in m. *Terumot* 11:10,[174] oil that was ritually defiled is permitted to be used to light "synagogues and study houses."

Rabbinite donation of oil to the synagogue was attacked by the Karaite Daniel Al-Qumisi.[175] Al-Qumisi further polemicized against the Rabbinite practice of burning incense in their synagogues. He says that the Rabbinites provide incense and lighting oil because they consider the synagogue to be a *miqdash me'at*.[176] This connection was somewhat natural within a late antique context, where churches were "heavy with incense."[177] The burning of incense in synagogues goes unmentioned in Rabbinic sources from Palestine and Babylonia. Chrysostom notes disparagingly that Jews in fourth-century Antioch did not burn incense (*thumiama*) before the synagogal Torah ark.[178] It is possible that the image of an incense shovel flanking a *menorah* in synagogue mosaics and related minor arts beginning during the fourth century is reminiscent of this practice.[179] More compelling, however, are two artifacts from Beth Shean (Scythopolis). The first is the image of an incense censor suspended from the lowest branch of a *menorah* in the mosaic pavement of Beth Shean B.[180] The second is a bronze censor discovered in a side room of the (Samaritan?) synagogue of Beth Shean A.[181] An incense burner bearing a dedicatory inscription and the image of a *menorah* from fifth-century Egypt has also survived.[182]

The centrality of prayer within the synagogue was expanded during the Amoraic period, prayer becoming equal in significance to Torah study. The relationship between liturgy and the Temple sacrifice was further developed by the

Amoraim and continued in post-Amoraic literature. Where Tannaitic sources use Temple models in the formulation of prayer, y. *Berakhot* 5:1, 8b, attributed to Rabbi Phineas in the name of Rabbi Hoshaya, claims that it was as effective as the sacrifices. Similarly, Rabbi Abbahu is said to have interpreted Hosea 14:3, "We offer the words of our lips instead of calves," as: "What makes up for those calves that we used to sacrifice before you? Our lips, in the prayer that we pray before you."[183] An example of the Amoraic investiture of prayer with ever more Temple elements is an alternative to the Tannaitic formula for leading the community in prayer, "pass/go before the *teva*."[184] Palestinian Amoraim ascribed this tradition to the *Tanna* Menaḥem the Galilean:[185]

> Rabbi Phineas, Rabbi Levi, Rabbi Yoḥanan in the name of Menaḥem the Galilean:[186] He who passes before the (Torah) cabinet, do not say to him: "Come and pray," rather "Come and sacrifice (*qarev*), do our sacrifice, fulfill our needs, fight our wars, appease (God) on our behalf."

This text capitalizes upon the fact that *qarev* has the sense of both "come close" and sacrifice.[187] The invitation to lead prayers intentionally uses cultic language drawn from the Temple. Similarly, a tradition in y. *Berakhot* 1:1, 2c, asserts that one must stand "like a priest" in the recitation of the *qedushah*.[188]

In a similar way, the *Pesiqta de-Rav Kahana* describes an otherwise unknown liturgical context that is related to the sacrificial system of the Temple. This text informs us that on holidays Jews would "do many *Tefillot* and many *Musafin*[189] and many *Qorbanot* (lit. "sacrifices")"[190] within the synagogues and study houses. What were the *Qorbanot*? The commentators are strangely silent as to their identity. Perhaps they involve the recitation of biblical passages dealing with the Temple sacrifices. The word order of this passage suggests that in the holiday liturgy the *qorbanot* took place after the *Tefillot* and *Musafin*. Mention of the Temple sacrifices within the Sabbath and festival prayers and holiday Torah readings dates to the Amoraic and post-Amoraic periods. A number of such instances are reflected in the literature. Rav is reported in y. *Berakhot* 4:6, 8c, for example, with teaching:

> One must say something new in the *Mussaf* prayer. . . .
> Rabbi Zeira asked before Rabbi Jose: What is it to "say something new"? He said to him: Even if one said, 'We will fulfill before you our obligations, daily sacrifice and *Mussaf* sacrifice," he has fulfilled his obligation."[191]

Rabbi Zeira's prayer takes for granted that the *Mussaf* prayer is related to the *Mussaf* sacrifice in the Temple, a connection already assumed by t. *Berakhot* 3:3.

Post-Amoraic literature reflects the increased use of Temple themes in liturgical contexts. *Midrash Tehillim* describes a Temple ritual that developed in Palestinian synagogues, the circumambulations and ritual recitation on *Hoshana Rabba*:[192]

> ... and they take up willows of the valley and encircle seven times, and the *hazan ha-knesset* stands like an angel of God with a Torah scroll in his arm,
> And the people go around him on the model of the altar.
> For thus taught our Rabbis: Each day they would go around the altar and say "O Lord deliver!"
> On the seventh day they would go around seven times, for thus it was explained by David, King of Israel. . . .[193]

This ritual is modeled upon the rite that took place around the Temple altar on this day[194] and infuses *Hoshana Rabba* festivities with Temple content.[195] The recitation of Psalm 118 in the Temple liturgy was apparently taken over to the synagogue, and *piyyutim* (*hoshanot*) were composed in late antique Palestine.[196] This added a verbal dimension to this ritual drama. Synagogue poetry provides rich information regarding the "templization" of synagogues. This is expressed in both Tractate *Sofrim*'s addition of the Psalms that "were said in the Temple" to the daily liturgy[197] and to the composition of new liturgical texts. The use of Temple language in the definition of synagogues is exemplified in a *piyyut* published by Simha Assaf[198] and partially reedited by Mordecai A. Friedman.[199] In this fragmentary text the destruction of Jewish communities and their synagogues during the Byzantine period is lamented.[200] The destruction of synagogues during the fifth and sixth centuries is well documented in literary and archaeological sources.[201] A destroyed synagogue at Huseifa in the Carmel is called *zevuli*, "My (God's) residence." In fact, a synagogue destroyed during the later Byzantine period was uncovered in this village.[202] The synagogue of Kefar Hevrona is called *armon*, "palace," and the synagogue of Ono is called both *ulam*, "entrance hall" and *shikeino*, "his dwelling place." Friedman notes that these nouns refer to the Temple in biblical sources, and are here taken over to refer to the synagogue.[203] We have seen that the use of Temple language in regard to destroyed synagogues was among the first exegetical steps in the "templization" of synagogues.[204] This text follows in that tradition.[205] The subtle references to the Temple reflect the intimate knowledge of this concept that the poet possessed and might have expected of his audience. One wonders if this text was associated with the Ninth of Av, or with the Sabbaths preceding this day of mourning. If so, an intimate liturgical connection would be forged between the two destroyed Temples and the numerous synagogues destroyed by the Byzantine Christians.

The earliest extant attributed *piyyutim* were composed by Yose son of Yose (fifth century), and include three poems that reenact in exquisite detail the service of the high priest in the Temple on the Day of Atonement.[206] Quite naturally, priestly themes appear prominently in those collections of *piyyutim* that follow the order of the weekly Scripture readings, such as those of Yannai and Simon son of Megas the Priest.[207] *Piyyutim* that were recited on Sabbath and festival mornings were called *qerovot*, from the language of sacrifice.[208] In a sense, the *paytan* (liturgical poet) takes on the role of the priest offering the "sacrifice" on behalf of the community through his recitation.[209]

Another common theme in late antique *piyyutim* is the priestly *mishmarot* in the Temple. During the Second Temple period the order of the priestly courses (based upon 2 Chron. 24), were of special interest to Jews.[210] The Tannaim preserved idealized memories of the *mishmarot* and the accompanying *ma'amadot*.[211] The priestly *mishmarot* were of significance to the synagogue liturgies of late antique Jews. Numerous *piyyutim* list the twenty-four *mishmarot* and their homes in the Galilee.[212] Lee Levine notes that "most were located in the Bet Netofa Valley in the Lower Galilee, with an additional concentration in the Tiberias area."[213] Dalia Trifon has recently argued that the localization of the *mishmarot* in the Galilee in the *piyyutim* is a form of "local patriotism" practiced by Galilean priestly communities. Trifon rightly notes that during this period priests lived in other areas of Palestine as well.[214] One poet who dealt with the theme of the *mishmarot* was Phineas the Priest who is said to have lived in Kafra near Tiberias.[215] Synagogue inscriptions listing the *mishmarot* were discovered in synagogues in Caesarea,[216] Ashkelon,[217] Reḥov[218] and apparently in the area of Nazareth in the Lower Galilee.[219] Similarly, priests appear as donors in synagogue inscriptions from Naaran,[220] Eshtemoa[221] and Khirbet Susiya[222] in Judea.

Perhaps the strongest evidence for the pervasive "templization" of synagogues during late antiquity is that the reverse process occurred as well. In our discussion of Tannaitic templization of synagogues we questioned whether *halakhot* and institutions that are presented as originating in the Temple actually did. We raised the possibility that established patterns of behavior within synagogues might have been retrojected to the Temple. While we found no evidence of this in Amoraic sources, examples of the "synagogization" of the Temple have been discussed from post-Amoraic sources.

We have discussed the special piety ascribed to Oved Edom the Gittite in *Canticles Rabba* 2:5.[223] According to this text, Oved Edom the Gittite lit lamps before the Ark of the Covenant morning and night. This behavior is a retrojec-

משמרת ראשונה יהויריב מסרביי מרון
משמרת שניה ידעיה עמוק צפורים
משמרת שלישית חרים מפשטה
משמרת רביעית שערים עיתהלו
משמרת חמשית מלכיה בית לחם
משמרת ששית מימין יודפת
משמרת שביעית הקוץ עילבו
משמרת שמינית אביה כפר עוזיה
משמרת תשיעית ישוע ארבל
משמרת עשירית שכניה חבודת רבול
משמרת אחת עשרה אלישיב כהן קנה
משמרת שתים עשרה יקים פשחור צפת
משמרת שלוש עשרה חופה בית מעון
משמרת ארבע עשרה ישבאב צלמון שיחין
משמרת חמש עשרה בלגה מעריה ביוני[?]ת
משמרת שש עשרה אמר כפר נמרה
משמרת שבע עשרה חזיר מגדל[?]
משמרת שמונה עשרה הפיצץ נצרת
משמרת תשע עשרה פתחיה אכלו[?] ערב
משמרת עשרים יחזקאל מגדל נוניא
משמרת עשרים ואחת יכין כפר יוחנה
משמרת עשרים ושתים גמול בית חביה
משמרת עשרים ושלוש דליה גנתון צלמין
משמרת עשרים וארבע מעזיה חמת אריח

Mishmarot plaque from the Caesarea Synagogue, reconstruction.

tion of late antique piety toward the Torah shrine back to biblical times. Similarly, we have seen how, in *Midrash Proverbs*, the Ark of the Covenant is transformed into a Torah ark. We find this phenomenon also in *Midrash Tanḥuma*, where the Tabernacle and the Ark are remade in the molds of a synagogue hall and Torah shrine:[224]

> When Moses told Bezalel to make the Tabernacle
> Bezalel said: "What is the purpose of the Tabernacle?"
> He said to him: "To cause the Divine presence to dwell there and to teach Israel Torah."
> Said Bezalel: "Where is the Torah put?"
> He said to him: "When we make the Tabernacle, we will make an ark. . . ."

Biblical authors would certainly agree that the *mishkan* was where Divine presence was to take up residence and that the "book of Torah" was to be stored in or near the ark. This placement for the book is stated in Deuteronomy 31:26, "Take the book of the Torah and put it to the side (*mi-tzad*) of the ark of the Lord your God and it will be there as a witness." The stress in our *Tanḥuma* text is on the Tabernacle as a place where Torah is taught and the ark as a cupboard for the scrolls. This tradition clearly retrojects late antique synagogue practice to the biblical shrine. The Tabernacle, like the synagogue, was said to be a place to teach the people Torah. In this text the cultic aspects of the Tabernacle go unmentioned. Like the "ark" of a synagogue, the "ark" of the Tabernacle contained the Torah scroll. No notice is taken in this tradition of the tablets of the Ten Commandments that were kept in the biblical "Ark of the Covenant," even though these were of particular interest to the biblical authors.

Amoraic and post-Amoraic literature often emphasize the entire Torah over the Ten Commandments, in part for polemical reasons.[225] We are told elsewhere in the same chapter of *Midrash Tanḥuma* that the "ark,"[226] apparently both the biblical and the late antique, "is beloved because the Torah is kept in it." The role of the synagogue as a place of Torah reading, and of the ark as the "beloved" storage place of the Torah scrolls, is retrojected in *Midrash Tanḥuma* to the Tabernacle and its ark. A continuous loop is created whereby the synagogue takes on attributes of the Temple and the Temple takes on synagogue forms.

Establishing a parallel sort of loop, *Targum Pseudo-Jonathan* to Leviticus 26:1, ". . . nor shall you place a figured stone in your land to bow down upon it," permits the use of mosaics within the "Temple":

> . . . nor shall you place a figured stone in your land to bow down upon it, but a pavement[227] figured with images and likenesses you may make on the floor of your sanctuary (-ies, *miqdasheikhon*). And do not bow down to it, for I am the Lord your God.

The denotation of *miqdasheikhon* within this Targumic tradition is unclear, owing both to the difficulty in determining whether *miqdasheikhon* is a plural or a singu-

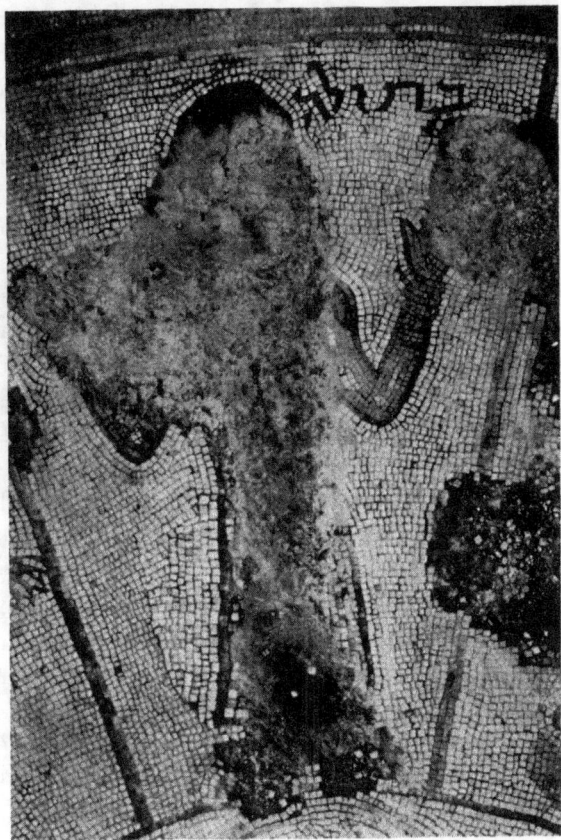

Detail of Virgo from the zodiac wheel of the Naaran Synagogue mosaic.

lar form and due to the complicated redaction history of *Pseudo-Jonathan*.[228] Numerous twentieth-century scholars have read *miqdasheikhon* in the plural, and have suggested that it refers to synagogues.[229] We have seen this approach in Tannaitic sources such as m. *Megillah* 3:1 that interpret *miqdasheihem* in Leviticus 26:31 as a plural noun that thereby refers to synagogues.[230] *Miqdasheikhon* in *Pseudo-Jonathan* to Leviticus 26:1 would then be translated in the plural, "your synagogues." The motivations behind this explanation are Tannaitic interpretations of Leviticus 26:31, the increasing use of Temple language for synagogues, Amoraic and post-Amoraic relaxation of Tannaitic strictures against prostration on mosaics, and most importantly, the discovery of mosaic pavements in ancient synagogues.[231] The *Sitz-im-Leben* of this tradition is said to be the carpet mosaics of late antique Palestinian synagogues, perhaps reacting to the concerns of Jews who were uncomfortable with figured synagogue mosaics. The discovery of iconoclastic defacement in the synagogue mosaic at Naaran and at other sites,[232] and of mosaics without "images and likenesses" at Reḥov, Jericho, and Ein Gedi 2 suggests that at least some Jews disfavored such images.[233] The major problem which argues against this interpretation is that "temple" or "small temple" is never used in Rabbinic literature to refer to synagogues without being paired explicitly with the word "synagogue."

In point of fact, no extant Rabbinic tradition treats "your temple(s)" in Leviticus 26:1 as "your synagogues." Other commentators on our tradition have justifiably read *miqdasheikhon* in the singular and understand it to refer to the Jerusalem Temple.[234] This interpretation follows a Tannaitic interpretation of Leviticus 26:1:[235] while idolatrous "figured stones" are not permissible in "your land," they are permitted in "your Temple." m. *Middot* 1:6 made later Sages aware that the Temple platform was laid with mosaics, "the tops of *pesifasin*."[236] By the third century elaborate carpet mosaics, also called "*pesifasin*," were used to pave synagogue floors.[237] Archaeologically, synagogue floors "figured with images and likenesses" appeared during the fourth century. It is my contention that carpet mosaics, a favorite type of pavement in public buildings (including synagogues, churches, mosques, and palaces) during the Byzantine and early Islamic periods, are retrojected by our Targumic tradition to the *pesifasin* of the Temple.[238] If I am right, the permissible figured carpet mosaics that were thought to have existed in the Temple were used as a precedent by the author of our Pseudo-Jonathan tradition to legitimize the use of carpet mosaics in the increasingly "templized" synagogues. A loop is thus formed between the mosaics of the Temple and late antique synagogue mosaics. This loop parallels the one that we have suggested between the ark and the Ark of the Covenant and between the synagogue lampstand and the Temple *menorah*. This exegesis might have provided a powerful argument in support of mosaics against opinions that were predisposed to forbid and perhaps destroy them: just as mosaics "figured with images and likenesses" were permissible in the *Miqdash*, they now legitimately exist within the *miqdash me'at*.

The Veneer of *Imitatio Templi*

While the Tannaim were concerned that synagogues could become too much like the Temple, the Amoraim and those who followed them were not. This may be attributed to a perception that non-Jewish attachment to temple cults was in decline, to the success of the Rabbinic movement from the late second century onward, and to the ever increasing gulf separating late antique Jews from the ever more heroic Jerusalem Temple.[239] By this time the essential form of the synagogue was set and there was little concern that synagogues might become replacements for the Temple. While the Tannaim loosely modeled prayer on the Temple cult in a tentative way, we have seen that the Amoraic Sages could state that prayer was equivalent to and stood in place of the Temple cult, if only temporarily. It is true that Jewish liturgy took on certain forms from the Temple. The liturgy was, however, a unique creation that was very different from the sacrifice and priesthood-centered Temple service.

The application of Temple motifs within synagogue buildings did not lead to the construction of buildings that resembled the Temple. This may be sensed in one instructive tradition in *Midrash Tanḥuma*:[240]

> Formerly,[241] they would build synagogues at the high point of the town to fulfill that which is written: "(Above the bustling [streets] she calls out,) at the entrances of the gates in the city, you shall pronounce her words" (Prov. 1:21).[242]

Synagogues were not built on especially sacred places, as the Temple of Jerusalem or of Mt. Gerizim were. The very few late antique synagogues built "at the height of the city" were located in villages that themselves were near the tops of hills.[243] Like churches, synagogues during this period were generally built in the city or town center.[244] This location was considered to be most suitable for churches, synagogues, and later mosques, which were first and foremost places where the faithful gathered. The Jewish choice to build synagogues within the town and not on an acropolis clearly does not conform with the Tosefta tradition that like the Temple, synagogues should be built on the high point of the town.[245] Our Tanḥuma tradition suggests that at the time when these buildings were being built some Jews felt it necessary to explain and bridge this discrepancy between the architectural reality and a received literary tradition.

Similarly, the architectural form of late antique synagogues was, as we will see in the next chapter, drawn from the basilica and not from the Temple. The basilica form, with its focus upon accommodating the assembled community, was adapted to synagogues and churches.[246] The interior of the synagogue did not bear any real resemblance to the Temple. The Amoraic Torah "ark" as described in y. *Megillah* 3:1, 73d, was a tall cabinet apparently divided into compartments. This description fits well with images of Torah shrines in synagogue art of the fourth century and later, such as Hammath Tiberias B, Beth Alpha, and Beth Shean A. Even when covered with a *parokhta* reminiscent of the Temple curtain, the Torah "ark" bore no real resemblance to the biblical Ark. This lack of resemblance cannot be attributed to a lack of Rabbinic interest in the construction of the ark. Scholarly discussion of its construction appears prominently, for example in the *Baraita de-Melekhet ha-Mishkan*.[247] Rather, it should be attributed to the use of Temple categories to express the sanctity of the synagogue; not its competition with, or replacement of, the Temple.[248]

Summary

In this chapter we have surveyed literary evidence stretching over five hundred years that reflects the sanctification of synagogues. Despite this long span of time, extant literary sources reflect a remarkable consistency in their portrayals of synagogue holiness. What were the elements that created this powerful religious environment, this "holy place"? The sanctity of synagogues was integrally related to that of the biblical scrolls, the development of liturgy, and the notion of *imitatio templi*. The sanctity of the scrolls spawned an attitude of heightened reverence toward the scrolls and their shrine, which was seen by some as a place of magical power. While Temple imagery was increasingly applied to synagogues and study houses, neither was considered to be a replacement for the Temple in any permanent sense. Their importance increased during this period and is expressed through the projection of synagogues and study houses into biblical and messianic sacred time and the conceptualization of the Temple as a synagogue. The exclusion of menstruous women from the synagogue on the basis of its Temple-like qualities is an extreme manifestation of *imitatio templi*. This development in the relationship between the synagogue and the Temple, however, was only skin deep. Synagogues bore no real physical relationship to the Temple and its furnishings. The process by which synagogues were sanctified had its roots in sectarian sources from the latter Second Temple period, budded under the formative hand of the Tannaim, and reached full bloom in Amoraic and post-Amoraic sources.

CHAPTER FOUR

"May Peace Be unto All Those Who Gave Charity in *This Holy Place*"

Archaeological Evidence for the Holiness of Late Antique Synagogues in the Land of Israel

Remains of over one hundred late antique synagogues have been identified in the Land of Israel.[1] This large corpus, discovered mainly over the last century, provides a well-developed image of the synagogue during this period, reflecting a rich religious culture through a limited repertoire of architectural,[2] artistic, and epigraphic forms. Dedicatory inscriptions that have been discovered in Jewish monumental buildings from late antiquity often call the building a "holy place." What did these ancient Jews mean when they called their synagogue a "holy place"? This term provides the key for understanding the religious significance of synagogue remains in late antique Palestine. In this chapter we will analyze dedicatory inscriptions that shed light upon the sanctity of synagogues. From there we will proceed to architectural and artistic evidence. The focal points of most synagogues that have been discovered were Torah shrines that stood on the Jerusalem-aligned wall. The shrine was often illuminated by seven-branched *menorot*. In one case amulets that may have been suspended from the "ark" were discovered within the synagogue apse. This configuration is reminiscent of motifs that we have discussed in previous chapters. As in literary sources, the sanctity of the biblical scrolls and the application of Temple motifs to synagogues were essential to the articulation of these "holy places." This relationship does not necessarily reflect Rabbinic influence, though the Reḥov synagogue with its twenty-six line mosaic version of a Rabbinic tradition certainly does.[3] Rather, it

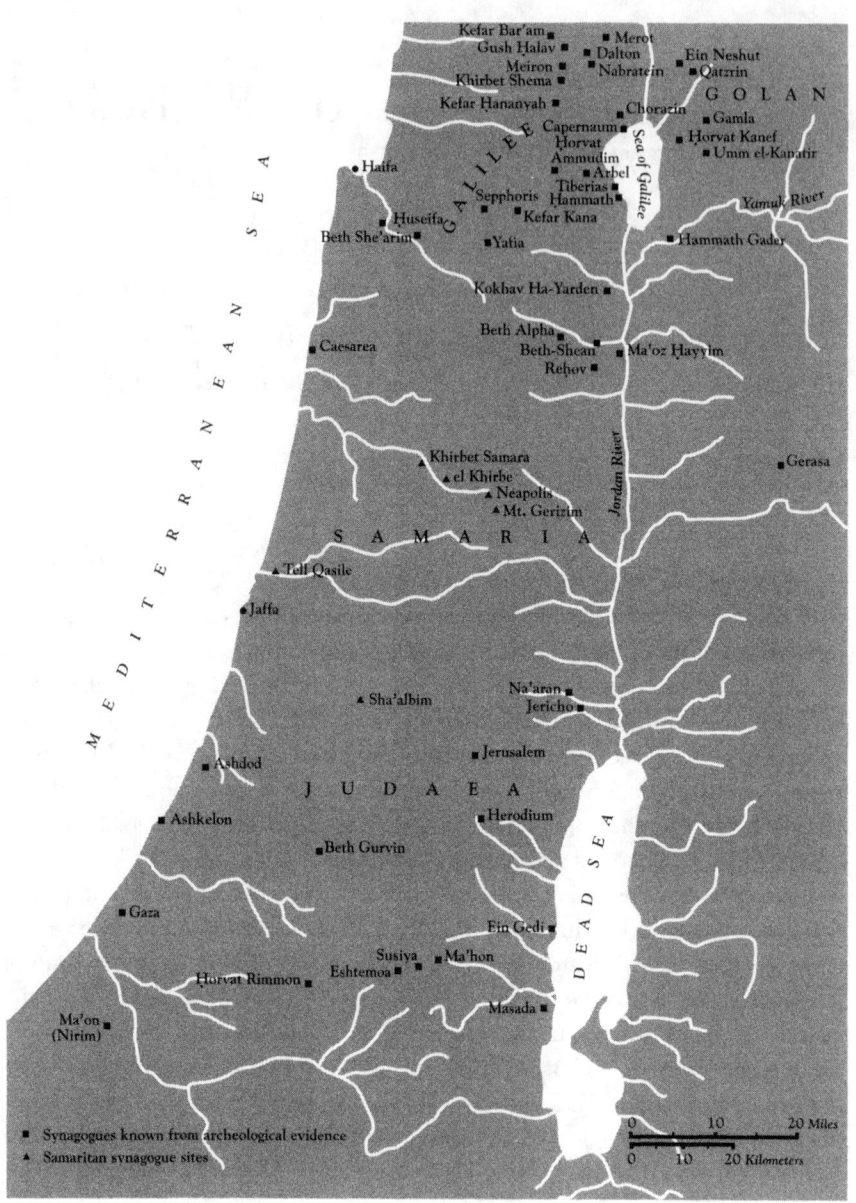

Ancient synagogues in Israel.

reflects a "common Judaism" shared by various groups in late antique Palestine who placed the synagogue as the center of their religious lives, as the "holy place."

Evidence from Dedicatory Inscriptions

Dedicatory inscriptions appear in synagogue remains throughout the Greco-Roman world. These inscriptions generally include mention of the donor(s), the gift, and some sort of blessing or laudatory formula. The earliest extant Palestinian synagogue inscription is the Theodotos inscription from Jerusalem, which is dated either to the end of the first century B.C.E. or the beginning of the first century C.E.[4] Tannaitic[5] and Amoraic sources[6] mention the existence of dedicatory inscriptions which appear in great numbers in synagogue ruins from the later third century onward.[7] Jewish use of public dedicatory inscriptions was part of a general cultural trend during the Greco-Roman period; polytheists, Christians, and Jews all marked their communal or civic giving in this manner.[8] Epigraphic remains parallel Rabbinic sources in suggesting that elements of synagogue buildings and decoration were donated by community members on a subscription basis, and that no individual donated an entire synagogue building.[9] As among Christians, each donor "contributed in a relatively small way" towards the construction of the synagogue or its decoration.[10] Claudine Dauphin[11] aptly describes the rationale behind such donations: "Landowners and rich citizens, both Christians and Jews, vied with each other for attention from the church or the synagogue, and God."

Designations for synagogues in epigraphic sources are similar to those found in literary texts. Synagogues are called "synagogue" (*knisha, sunagogē*), "place" (*atar?, maqom?, atra*), "holy place" (*atra qadisha, hagios topos*), "most holy place" (*hagiotato topo*) and possibly "place of the master of heaven" (*tara de-marei shumyah*).[12] "Place" is modified by the adjective "holy" in a number of exemplars, and at Horvat Ha-Ammudim by the unusual formulation "place of the master of heaven." This inscription marks the donation by two brothers of this "place." It is likely that the "Place of the Master of Heaven" was a particular spot within the synagogue, and not the entire building. The benefaction of an entire synagogue building by so few people is not reflected in literary or epigraphic sources from late antiquity.[13] Besides, one might expect that the donation of an entire synagogue building would have been commemorated by a dedicatory plaque that was more than 29 cm. by 18 cm.[14] Perhaps "Place of the Master of Heaven" refers to the Torah shrine and its surrounding area. "Holy" was also used to describe communities[15] and as an honorific title[16] in synagogue inscriptions.

"Holy place" occurs in Aramaic and Greek inscriptions from all parts of Jewish Palestine, from Transjordan, and from the coastal plain. It appears in Greek and Latin inscriptions from the Hellenistic Diaspora. "Holy place" is first seen at Stobi in Macedonia in 280–281 C.E. and in Palestine soon afterwards at Hammath Tiberias B.[17] "Holy place" does not appear in contemporaneous polytheistic inscriptions,[18] though *atar* appears in Palmyrene[19] inscriptions regarding temples.[20] Yiannis E. Meimaris notes that, "In the Byzantine period, the word Holy, *hagios*, was invariably attributed to everything related to the Christian faith, even to distinguished officials of the Church and State."[21] We hear of the "holy martyria" and the "holy monastery" (*monē*). *Hagios* was used both as an honorific title and to denote a saint.[22] "Holy place" (*hagios topos*) was used by Christians from the later fourth century onward for places that were holy to the church due to their historical associations.[23] This category grew to include the entire "holy land" and its "holy places." Specific "holy places" such as the "Holy Calgary" are often called by their name, together with the adjective "holy."[24]

Only one church in the Palestinian interior is called a "holy place" in an epigraphic context, the fifth-century church at Tabgha, where Jesus was believed to have multiplied the loaves and fishes to feed the multitude.[25] Churches without any apparent historical associations in southern Transjordan,[26] Gaza, and Nessana,[27] regions that served pilgrims as gateways to the holy land, are also called "holy place."[28] This sanctity may express their position at the threshold of the holy land. The use of "holy place" in churches outside Palestine was exceedingly rare. I am aware of only one example, from Assos in Asia Minor.[29] The earliest dated epigraphic evidence for Christian use of this terminology in Palestine is from a tombstone in the martyrium of the north church at Nessana, dated to 475 C.E.[30] Churches were referred to as the "holy church" (*hagia ekklesia*), the "holy prayer hall" (*hagios euktation*), the "holy temple," and the "holy sanctuary" (*hagion thusiastapion*).[31] By the fifth century, these terms, particularly "holy church," were the semantic equivalents to the Jewish "holy place," having been used to denote local religious institutions.[32] Jews and Christians in late antique Palestine shared a vocabulary of holiness in their conceptions of their religious institutions, just as they shared certain architectural forms and furnishings. The Christian "discovery" of the sanctity of place and the long-standing Jewish concept of synagogue sanctity reflect a shared yet unstated late antique religious reality.[33]

"Holy place" appears twice in the fourth-century mosaic pavement of Hammath Tiberias B.[34] The Aramaic and Greek inscriptions are quite similar, employing related phraseology. In the Aramaic we read:

May peace be unto all those who gave charity in this holy place, and who in the future will give charity. May he have His blessing[35] Amen, amen, selah, it is fitting,[36] amen.[37]

We read in the Greek text:

Remembered for good and for blessing Profuturos the elder who made this stoa of the holy place. Blessing upon him, amen, shalom.[38]

The inscriptions are constructed of formulae that are known from extant prayers. The Greek inscription is a literal translation of Aramaic and Hebrew texts.[39]

Lea Roth-Gerson notes that "this inscription, like other Greek inscriptions, reflects . . . the use of blessings that were standard in Hebrew and Aramaic inscriptions and were translated into Greek in a literal manner. . . ."[40] Foerster has pointed out numerous parallels between Aramaic and Greek inscriptions and liturgical formulae. He connects our Aramaic inscription, for example, to the blessing formula at the conclusion of the *Qaddish*: "May there be (great) peace from heaven and life upon us and all Israel" and other Rabbinic prayers for peace.[41] Like liturgical texts and amulets, the language of synagogue inscriptions uses a biblicized vocabulary. This phenomenon may reflect the significance of Torah reading and prayer in synagogues. The originator of this epigraphic formula (or perhaps a liturgical model) sought out a biblicizing formula to apply to the synagogue. Following biblical models, "holy" was appended to "place." "Holy place" may have been chosen in part because it is used for the Tabernacle/Temple in the Scriptures.[42] This term affirms the "templization" of synagogues, while recognizing the gulf separating synagogues from the Temple. It might have been unthinkable to call a synagogue *miqdash*, *miqdash me'at* or *hekhal* even though, as we have seen, all are applied to this institution in exegetical contexts.[43] This might have smacked of violating the Deuteronomic centralization of the cult in Jerusalem.[44] We have seen, moreover, that "holy place" in Ecclesiastes 8:10 has nothing to do with the Temple, yet this text was interpreted by the midrash as referring to "synagogues and study houses." "Holy place" was an appropriate biblical term to apply to synagogues in part because of this ambiguity. It may have been preferable to the Targumic *beit qudsha* due to its biblical pedigree, without infringing upon the uniqueness of the Jerusalem Temple.

From the fifth century on, "holy place" appears in twelve Aramaic and Greek inscriptions from eight sites that have been identified as synagogues. This designation is certainly a continuation of the tradition that is first evidenced at

Hammath Tiberias B Synagogue mosaic, Greek dedicatory inscription to the "Holy Place."

Hammath Tiberias B. The sixth-century synagogue mosaic from Naaran, a Jewish village northwest of Jericho, employs both *atra* and *atra qadisha* to describe the synagogue. The term *atra qadisha* appears four times, while in other synagogues it appears just once in each. Three of these inscriptions appear at the southeastern end of the mosaic, in the register containing Torah shrine imagery. The fourth is on the northwestern side, opposite the entrance. The formulae of the inscriptions are very similar, praising donors to the synagogue for their part in "this holy place." The most expansive of the inscriptions is more specific:

> Remembered for good everyone who donates and contributes, or will (in the future)[45] give in this holy place, whether gold, silver or anything else. Amen. Their portion is in this holy place. Amen.

The placement of three inscriptions near the Torah shrine, and of the fourth inside the main entrance in line with the shrine, is significant. In these locations the inscriptions were most likely to be seen by the community, thus adding to the prestige of the donors. The cramped accumulation of inscriptions in the ark panel of the mosaic may suggest a pious desire to be near the ark, and possibly near the image of Daniel who appears in a prayer position before the ark. At the same time they clearly hoped to gain prominence within the synagogue community.

In the sixth-century carpet mosaic at Beth Shean B[46] the "holy society"[47] and the "holy place" are praised in the same Aramaic inscription:

> Remembered for good all the members of the holy society (*havurta qadisha*) who support the repair of the holy place and its completion. May they have blessing. Amen . . . in abundant peace, covenant love in peace.

In post-Amoraic literature, "holy society" refers to a high-level Rabbinic academy.[48] On a local level, a *piyyut* from the Cairo Genizah that we have discussed in the previous chapter that dates to the Byzantine period[49] laments the murder of *ḥavurat Ono*, the "society of Ono" (a Jewish town near Lod in the Coastal Plain).[50] Simḥa Assaf, editor of this text, identifies the *ḥavurah* of Ono as a "yeshiva."[51] Moshe Beer has shown that *ḥavurah* is a regular designation in Amoraic and post-Amoraic literature for gatherings of Sages and/or their students for the study of Torah. It is "synonymous with '*Bet-Midrash*' and '*Yeshiva*.'"[52] Mordecai A. Friedman, suggests that "*ḥavurah* of Ono" in our text should be understood as "a poetic expression for the '"Sages of Ono."'"[53] It is thus likely that the "*ḥavurah* of Ono" refers to the local assembly of Ono's Sages. Perhaps this is the meaning at Beth Shean B as well. On the model of this *piyyut*, one might conjecture that the "holy society of Beth Shean" could have been known to outsiders simply as "*ḥavurat* Beth Shean." Members of "holy society of Beth Shean" contributed to the renovation of their "holy place."

The "holy place" of this community is a relatively small room, approximately seven meters square.[54] It consisted of one room in a complex containing the "house of Leontis" and a bath, both bearing dedicatory inscriptions.[55] In this it is unique, since extant Palestinian synagogue buildings were all free-standing halls. The walls of this small room were lined with benches, with perhaps the remains of a Torah niche on the southern (Jerusalem) wall.[56] The carpet mosaic is decorated with an inhabited scroll motif, with a *menorah* at its center. There are three inscriptions within this building, all commemorating anonymous benefaction. This is a rare phenomenon. Dedicatory inscriptions were usually the way that individuals were honored by the community for their benefactions. Anonymity sets aside this purpose.[57] Zvi Ilan suggests that the anonymity of the donors in the two Aramaic inscriptions and the "later" Greek inscription[58] at Beth Shean B "is evidence of the communal structure of the community that prayed here."[59] He suggests that this building is the "synagogue of the Sages of Beth Shean."[60] The notion of a "synagogue of Sages" is unknown in Rabbinic literature. In Rabbinic sources a room set aside where Sages congregated, studied, and prayed is called a *beit midrash*. It is not beyond credulity to suggest that this hall could have been a Rabbinic study house, though the evidence is admittedly tenuous.[61]

Unique among synagogue remains is a bronze polycandelon dated to the fifth or sixth century that was discovered in Kefar Maḥer, five kilometers east of Acre. It is dedicated to the "holy place" of Kefar Ḥananyah,[62] a village on the border between the upper and the lower Galilee.[63] The Aramaic inscription engraved on this lamp contains elements that are similar to the dedicatory inscriptions that we have discussed:

Polycandelon from a synagogue in Kefar Hananyah.

This crown . . .[64] to the holy place of Kefar Ḥananyah. . . . May they be remembered for good. Ame(n) selah, shalom, *ptp t*.

Inscriptions on lamps are mentioned in both Tannaitic[65] and Amoraic[66] sources, and commonly appear on contemporaneous church vessels.[67] An unusual feature of this inscription is the formula *ptp t*. Joseph Naveh has compared this formula to magical terminology that appear in an amulet from the Cairo Genizah.[68] The lamp is decorated with two *menorot*, each flanked by a lulav and a shofar. As we will see below, the *menorah* was a symbol of the Jewish *ethnos* within the Empire, a reminder of the Temple, and one of the furnishings of synagogues. These symbols are used to identify the Jewish character of this object, any other connection being secondary. It is impossible to know from the term "holy place" whether this lamp illuminated a synagogue or a study house.

Two Greek inscriptions in which "holy place" occurs have been discovered in the southern coastal plain. One inscription is preserved on a stone slab from a synagogue screen that was discovered in Ashkelon:[69]

> G(od) s(ave)! (We) Mistress Domna the daughter of Ju(lianos) and Master Mari, son of Nonnos in gratitude present. . . . Master . . . the grandson of Helikios (gives) to God and to the ho(ly place a benefaction) for (my) salvation. (I) Master Commodus donate for (my) salvation and life. The year 709 (= 604–605 C.E.).

Similarly, on a plaque found between Jaffa and Gaza we read:[70]

> For the salvation of Jacob, Lazaros, and Mareina (we) donate in thanks (to God and) to the holy place and refurbish the conch together with . . . from the foundations, in the month of March, in the year of the indiction.[71]

The "conch" is of particular interest. Eleazar L. Sukenik suggests, quite reasonably, that the conch refers to "the recess where the Torah shrine rested," "the apse of this holy place."[72]

The synagogue is called the "most holy place" in a dedicatory inscription from the Gaza synagogue:[73]

> Manaamos and Isouos, the sons of the late Isses, wood merchants, as a sign of respect for the most holy place, we have donated this mosaic in the month of Loos, 569 (of the era of Gaza = 508/509 C.E.).

The inscriptions that we have discussed from the southern coastal plain do not follow the Aramaic forms that we examined earlier in this chapter.[74] They are even different from an Aramaic inscription from Maon (Nirim), in the Gaza district, which was composed according to the familiar formulae.[75] Gifts are often presented by the donor in the first person in Greek synagogue inscriptions. The donor's motives for benefaction are often stated, and some inscriptions conclude with the date according to the local chronology.[76] These formulae are common in synagogue inscriptions from the Greco-Roman Diaspora.[77] Church inscriptions also have many of these characteristics. A rather typical inscription dated September 7, 609 C.E. from the east church at Nessana contains formulae that are very similar to those which appear in Jewish inscriptions:[78]

> For the salvation of the benefactors Sergius, ex-assessor and monk, and Pullus his sister and John, the deacon, her son curialis of the metropolitan city of Emesa. In the 5th interdiction, on the 20th of the month of Gorpiaes.

The Gerasa Synagogue mosaic, drawing by Nahman Avigad.

As in the Jewish texts that we have examined, the motive of the benefactors is presented, as is the date of the gift.[79] Despite their religious differences, Jews and Christians donated to synagogues and churches in the hope of gaining "salvation."

A Greek inscription from the Decapolis city of Gerasa in Transjordan also describes the synagogue using the superlative form "most holy place."[80] The inscription surrounds the image of a *menorah*, flanked by a *lulav* and *ethrog*, a *shofar* and an incense shovel:

> ... to the most holy place (*hagio[tato] topo*). Amen, selah.
> Peace to the community (*sunagogai*).

Roth-Gerson is certainly correct that the names of the donors must have appeared in the lost part of the inscription.[81] A Hebrew inscription from the same synagogue closely parallels the Greek text:

> Peace be upon all Israel, Amen amen selah. . . .

The Greek inscription from Gerasa is composed of Hebrew and Greek formulae. "Peace upon the community" is loosely modeled upon the biblical phrase "Peace be upon all Israel" in the Hebrew[82] Psalm 125:5 (and parallels), "Peace be upon all Israel," appears in synagogue inscriptions from Jericho, Ein Gedi, and Ḥuseifa in the Land of Israel and in an inscription on a stone basin from Tarragona in Spain.[83] A similar Greek formula appears in a dedicatory inscription from a synagogue in Apamea in Syria: "Peace and mercy upon all your holy people!"[84] "Amen selah" appears in both inscriptions from Gerasa. "Amen" and "selah" appear in numerous synagogue inscriptions, both from Palestine[85] and from the Greco-Roman Diaspora.[86] "Amen" also appears as the closing formula of Christian dedicatory inscriptions.[87] "Most holy synagogue" clearly derives from Greek formulae. A superlative appears in no Aramaic or Hebrew text, and would be awkward in these languages. This Greek inscription stands on the cusp between Hebrew/Aramaic and Greek models. This mix is quite appropriate in a synagogue that is so close to the Aramaic-speaking Jewish communities of Palestine and the Golan and yet flourished within Greek-speaking Gerasa.

Despite their many formulaic differences, Aramaic and Greek inscriptions from Palestine are united by the rather frequent use of "holy place" to denote synagogues. This is in marked contrast with Christian inscriptions from Palestine proper, where "holy place" seldom occurs. The frequent designation of "holy place" is paralleled in inscriptions from the Greco-Roman Diaspora.

Architecture and Art

Earlier we explored archaeological evidence for ritual ablutions in preparation for entering synagogues and we have just interpreted epigraphic evidence for the sanctity of synagogues. We now turn to the buildings themselves, their architecture, internal arrangement, decoration, and symbolic value in our attempt to determine in what ways the synagogue in late antique Palestine was seen as a "holy place." We will see that synagogue sanctity is expressed through the articulation of the Torah shrine and its area, through orientation toward Jerusalem, and through the use of Temple motifs in synagogue decoration. In addition, secondary liturgical elements that are not in themselves "holy," such as biblical scenes and zodiac wheels, were significant features of synagogues that are labeled as "holy places" in their dedicatory inscriptions.

Sanctity as Reflected in Synagogue Alignment

Synagogues conforming to three main architectural types were constructed by Jews in late antique Palestine: the broadhouse, the "Galilean-type" basilica, and longhouse basilicas, which from the latter fifth or sixth century onward often were apsidal.[88] The basilica form was used by both Jews and Christians beginning around the turn of the fourth century C.E.[89] The basilica was uniquely suited to both the church and synagogue, providing a large, open meeting place for the "community of God."

The interior space of most of these synagogues were aligned toward a permanent Torah shrine,[90] which usually stood on the Jerusalem-aligned side of the

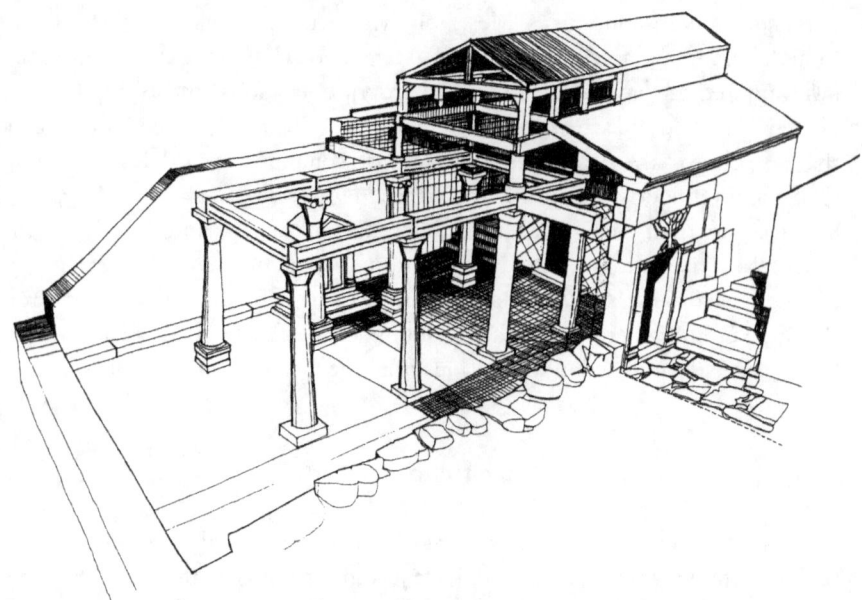

Reconstruction drawing of the Khirbet Shema Synagogue.

synagogue.[91] Alignment of the Torah shrine toward Jerusalem was not absolute during this period and a number of synagogues had their shrines on walls other than the one aligned with Jerusalem. This phenomenon seems to reflect the tension in ancient Judaism that God is in His Temple, yet is everywhere.[92] Instructively, this tension and its architectural ramifications can be sensed in synagogues of the medieval and modern periods. While the standard codes of Jewish law all legislate that the synagogue interior be aligned toward the Torah shrine on the Jerusalem wall of the synagogue, the reality is far more complex even in the most Rabbinically oriented medieval and early modern communities.[93] Alignment toward Jerusalem is an ideal in these sources, though in many cases not an architectural reality.

Interior alignment became more pronounced as our period progressed[94] and closely parallels literary sources that we have surveyed. Archaeological evidence for the existence of permanent Torah shrines in late antique Palestinian synagogues exists from the late third century onward, lagging behind literary evidence for permanent shrines by no more than fifty years.[95] The Torah shrine, the area around it, and alignment toward Jerusalem became the major elements in the sanctification of synagogue buildings during late antiquity. These issues were worked out in somewhat different ways in each of the three major architectural types.

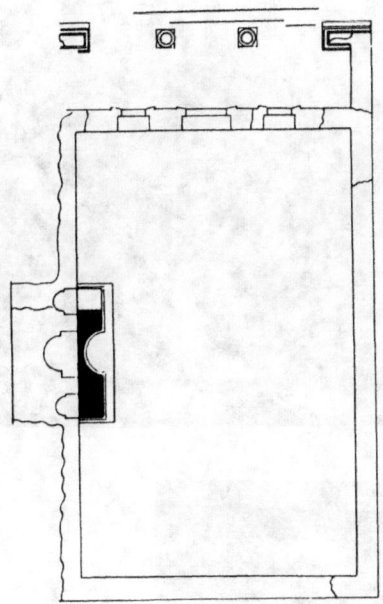

Plan of the Eshtemoa Synagogue.

"Broadhouse-type" synagogues have been discovered at Khirbet Shema in the Upper Galilee, and at Ḥorvat Rimmon 1,[96] Eshtemoa, and Khirbet Susiya in Judea.[97] Benches were built around the interior walls of these synagogues, focusing attention upon the center of the room. Aligned toward the south, the walls of the synagogue at Khirbet Shema (latter fourth century) were lined with benches. A Torah shrine on a stone platform that rose nearly 70 cm. was built sometime after the synagogue's initial construction on the southern (Jerusalem) wall, partially covering the bench.[98]

The broadhouses from the Hebron Hills form a regional type.[99] The entrances of these halls were aligned toward the east.[100] The eastward alignment is perhaps modeled upon the Temple, and parallels t. Megillah 3:23.[101] The interior of the synagogue hall was aligned toward the Torah shrine, which stood on the Jerusalem-aligned wall. The result is a rather awkward double alignment: the facade toward the east, the shrine toward Jerusalem to the north. At Eshtemoa the Torah niche was flanked by two smaller niches. In the third phase at Khirbet Susiya a larger and a smaller platform were constructed on the broad wall.[102] The major *bema* is surrounded by a screen, decorated with images of the *menorah*, the Torah shrine, and floral motifs.[103] A narrative is illustrated on one panel of the Khirbet Susiya partition, of which little is left.[104] Remains of wall decorations that framed the Torah niche flanked by two smaller niches further emphasized the shrine from Khirbet Susiya.[105] In the floor mosaic, before the smaller *bema*, we find

The Synagogue of Kefar Baram.

the image of an enclosed Torah shrine flanked by two *menorot*. The interior arrangement of broadhouses created a less monumental and more intimate environment than that of basilicas.[106]

Galilean-type synagogues are so called because they were all constructed in Galilee. This group includes Capernaum, Chorazin, Meiron, Nabratein and Baram, Umm al-Qanatir, Ḥorvat Ha-Ammudim, and Arbel. Galilean-type synagogues are architecturally related to the narrow gable churches of nearby Syria.[107] Like these churches (and numerous polytheistic temples, including Qadesh in southern Phoenicia), most Galilean-type synagogues were entered through three portals.[108] We do not assume that the use of triple entrances in synagogues had any specific symbolic function,[109] but rather provided immediate access to the nave

Model of the Beth Alpha Synagogue, constructed under the direction of Rachel Wischnitzer.

and two side aisles.[110] They do, however, present a sense of monumentality and the aura of a religious building. A unique feature of these buildings is the arrangement of the interior columns. Columns were constructed on the northern, eastern, and western sides of the hall, creating a "ḥet" shaped arrangement. This served to focus attention on the interior of the southern, Jerusalem wall with its three portals.[111] This arrangement had the effect of drawing the eyes of the congregation (which was seated on benches on the north, east, and west walls) outward toward Jerusalem itself. Some scholars have posited that Torah shrines were constructed between the doors on the Jerusalem wall at Capernaum, Chorazin and Meiron.[112] Such an arrangement was discovered in the Meroth synagogue and at Gush Ḥalav as well.[113] In an instructive parallel, S. D. Goitein notes that in synagogues in Yemen two entrances flank the Torah shrine that stands on the Jerusalem wall, and that this arrangement existed in a Hebron synagogue "during the period of the Cairo Genizah."[114] If this understanding of ancient synagogues is correct, then an intermediate focal point was established within these synagogues. Alignment toward Jerusalem, which epitomizes the interior design of these buildings, was directed past the Torah shrine of the synagogue. In "Galilean-type" synagogues the Torah shrine was not the singular focal point, and was therefore less central than in other basilica and "broadhouse" type synagogues. At

Ma'oz Hayyim Synagogue, apse, third stage.

Chorazin a chair was discovered upon which a prominent member of the community (perhaps the *darshan* who delivered the homily) sat or the Torah scroll rested.[115] Ze'ev Yeivin proposes that the chair at Chorazin rested on a raised platform that was enclosed within an aedicula supported by two columns.[116]

Basilical synagogues were constructed throughout the Land of Israel. In "basilica type" synagogues the visitor might cross the expanse of the atrium, sometimes a narthex,[117] and the nave, to reach the Jerusalem-aligned wall. At the center of this wall was the building's focal point, the Torah shrine, which often stood upon a raised platform. Synagogues from the late fifth century onward[118] often included an apse on the Jerusalem wall that housed the Torah shrine.[119] This feature was borrowed from contemporary churches.[120] The apse both accommodated and promoted the enlargement of the Torah shrine and its compound.[121]

The apse and *bema* were sometimes separated from the nave by a screen (sometimes called a "chancel" screen),[122] as at Ḥamath Gader, Reḥov, Ma'oz Ḥayyim 3, Ein Gedi, Gaza, Ashkelon, and elsewhere.[123] This feature was undoubtedly copied from the church along with the other elements of the basilical plan.[124] The screen served to emphasize and distance the area of the Torah shrine from the assembled community. The Amoraic distinction between the "holiness of the ark" and the "holiness of the synagogue" could have provided some Rabbinically minded Jews with a post facto legitimization for such a physical boundary.[125] What is clear is that the screen served to divide the Torah shrine and at times apparently the Torah reading from the rest of the hall.[126] A synagogue screen seems to be described in the Cairo Genizah version of a text known as *Pereq Mashiaḥ*.[127] As I have recently argued, it is likely that the description of "reed mats made as a partition for the *bema*" in this text refers to synagogue screens:[128]

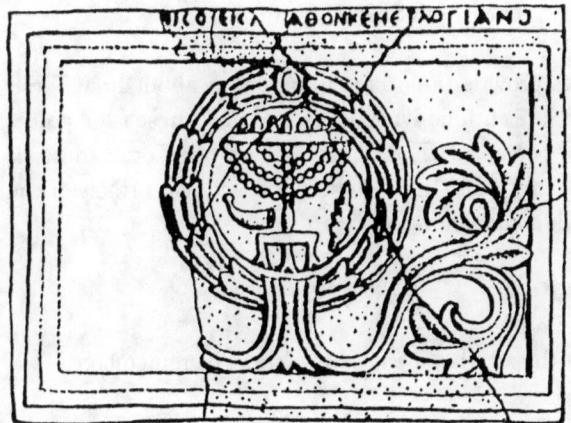

Synagogue screen from Ashdod.

R. Eliezer son of Jacob says: The great study house of the Holy One, Blessed be He, in the future will be eighteen thousand myriad parsangs (in size), for it is written: "Its circumference (will be) 18,000" (Ez. 48:35). The Holy One, Blessed be He, sits on the chair among them, and David sits before him, for it is said: "His chair is like the sun before me" (Ps. 89:37). All the placid women who teach and pay so that their sons may be taught Torah, Scripture and Mishnah, manners, pious sincerity and honesty stand by (or, within) *reed mats made as a partition for the bema* and listen to the voice of Zerubabel son of Shaltiel when he stands as translator (*meturgeman*)....

The ornamentation of stone screens often includes images of *menorot*. The screens from Khirbet Susiya, the most elaborate exemplar preserved, contains images of the Torah shrine, a *menorah*, floral patterns, and a narrative scene in which the hand of God apparently reaches down from a cloud holding a scroll.[129] The Beth Alpha mosaic shows curtains tied back to reveal the shrine complex. The curtains would have effectively closed off the shrine from sight.[130] The development of the shrine area at Ma'oz Ḥayyim is representative of the general expansion of shrine compounds in basilica-type synagogues: a Torah shrine on the Jerusalem wall in the first phase was replaced by a shrine set within an apse in the second phase. A raised platform enclosed by a screen appeared in the third phase.[131]

The Torah Shrine

Archaeological sources provide important information about how Torah shrines were constructed in late antique synagogues, and how these focal points of the synagogue hall were perceived. The significance of the Torah shrine is reflected in two lapidary inscriptions. In the Jebel Druze village of Naveh the donation of a Torah shrine is commemorated:[132]

(... son of) Yudan
(and ...)yh son of his brother
(donated) the house of the ark (*beit arona*). May (they) be remembered (for good).

Beit arona parallels the Rabbinic use of *arona* from the Amoraic period onward. Whether this text suggests that a movable ark was stored here,[133] or whether the shrine itself is the ark, is unclear. An inscription from Dalton reflects a different conception. There the shrine is called *takah raḥmana*, "Receptacle of the Merciful (One)."[134] *Raḥmana*, a Divine appellation, is transferred to the Word of God, Scripture. *Takah raḥmana* suggests reverence toward the shrine as seat of God's revelation, the Torah.[135]

As we might suspect from literary sources, the "ark" did not have the appearance of the "Ark of the Covenant,"[136] but rather of a contemporaneous cabinet or small shrine. Until recently our clearest image of how Palestinian Torah shrines might have looked emerged from illustrations within mosaic panels discovered at Hammath Tiberias B, Sepphoris, Beth Shean A, Beth Alpha, Naaran and Khirbet Susiya and in stone carvings from Chorazin, Capernaum, and other sites.[137] The discovery in 1981 of the pediment of an aedicula from Nabratein, rampart lions on each side, a conch below, and a hole to suspend a lamp at the apex of the conch, provided a three-dimensional structure that is strikingly similar to that illustrated in the Beth Alpha mosaic.[138] Stone Torah shrines and raised platforms (*bemot*) are identifiable at numerous sites.[139] Aediculae were commonly used to house the cult objects of religious communities during late antiquity. As in polytheistic and later Christian shrines, a conch was often used to enclose the cult object. The ribs of the conch converging from the outer edge of the aedicula inward served to focus attention upon the cult object immediately below.[140] Within the synagogue, this object was the Torah scroll.[141] The remains of wooden shrines have been discovered as well.[142] Wooden shrines would not necessarily have been less impressive than those made of stone.[143] A number of shrines are shown with curtains covering their doors. This parallels the usage de-

The Binding of Isaac from the Beth Alpha Synagogue mosaic.

Torah shrine panel from the Beth Alpha Synagogue mosaic.

Pediment of a Torah shrine from the Nabratein Synagogue.

scribed earlier in Amoraic sources, where the ark is covered with a *kila* or a *parokhta*.

The lions resting on top of the gable of the Nabratein aedicula, like the birds of the Beth Alpha pavement, add a sense of power and movement to the Torah shrine.[144] Three-dimensional lions that may have flanked Torah shrines (as represented in the shrine panel from Beth Alpha) convey a similar sense to the entire ark compound.[145] At Khirbet Susiya a large frame that enclosed the main Torah niche and its flanking niches is partially preserved.

Most images of Torah shrines in ancient Jewish art are flanked by *menorot*, or are in close proximity to *menorot*. On a basalt lintel discovered near Belvoir two shrines flank a single *menorah*.[146] Seldom does the image of a shrine appear without a *menorah* being close at hand.[147] It is likely that Torah shrines similar to those represented stood in synagogues, flanked by seven-branched *menorot*, as is represented in numerous contexts.[148]

Seven-branched *menorot* have been discovered at a number of synagogues from the fifth century onward, though they are described in earlier literature. Stone examples from Palestine were found at Hammath Tiberias A,[149] at Eshtemoa,[150] Maon in Judea,[151] and at Khirbet Susiya.[152] The lamps from the Judean Hills region, from Eshtemoa, Maon, and Khirbet Susiya, are quite similar in conception and execution, and may represent a regional type. The cross-bar that connects the burners in many representations is evidence for the existence of metal lamps.[153] This bar is intended to stabilize the otherwise flimsy branches and to keep them from swaying.[154] The "bulb and calyx" motif that articulates the

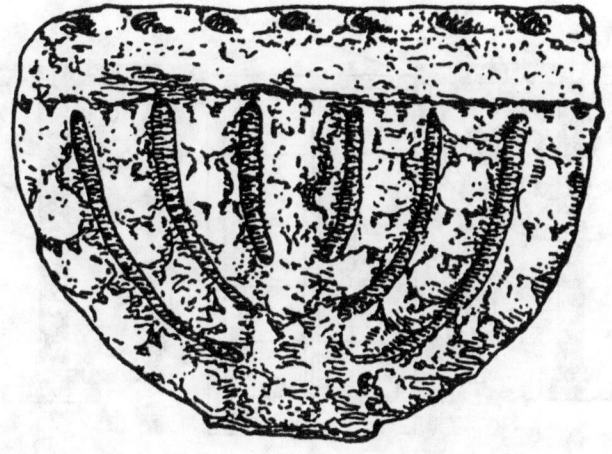

Limestone *menorah* from the Synagogue of Hammath Tiberias A.

branches of many of these *menorot* hearkens back to the biblical description of the *menorah* of the Tabernacle.[155] Similarly, the flames of the *menorot* in the Hammath Tiberias B mosaic are all aligned toward the central flame. This parallels Rabbinic exegesis of Numbers 8:2, "The Lord spoke to Moses, saying: 'Speak to Aaron and say to him: When you mount the lamps, before (*el mul*) the *menorah* the seven lamps will shed their light.'" This verse is interpreted in *Sifre Zutta*:[156]

> Whence (do we know that) all of the lamps were inclined toward the central lamp?
> Learn to say: "toward (*el mul*) the central lamp (Num. 8:2)."
> Similarly (Scripture) says: "He sits up against me (*muli*, Num. 22:5)."
> Said Rabbi Simeon: "When I went to Rome and saw there the *menorah* all of the lamps were inclined toward the central lamp."

A number of images of *menorot* with more or less than seven branches have been uncovered, perhaps reflecting the reticence to produce images with seven branches that we have encountered in Tannaitic sources.[157] The area of the Torah shrine(s) was brightly lit by the *menorot*, which would have served both to emphasize the significance of this focal point and provide additional light for the reading of Scripture. The practice of flanking the shrine with two *menorot* maintained the symmetry of the ark area. This placement of *menorot* beside the "ark" is reminiscent of the Temple arrangement, though it does not copy it. In the Temple one *menorah* stood to the left of the *parokhet*.

Torah shrine panel from the Naaran Synagogue mosaic.

Lamps were sometimes suspended from the branches of the *menorot*, providing additional light.[158] Lamps suspended from the *menorot* appear on the screen from Khirbet Susiya, at Khirbet Kishor, on a tomb door from Kefar Yasif, and in the mosaics at Beth Shean B and Naaran.[159] Within churches, lamps were sometimes suspended from large crosses in a similar manner.[160] A single translucent glass lamp was sometimes suspended immediately before the shrine, which provided a singular focal point for the shrine area and thus for the entire meeting room.[161] In contemporaneous churches the altar that was the focal point of the apse was also brightly lit.[162] The effect would have been a brightly lit focal area within the church or synagogue.[163]

The deposit of holy objects and community property in the area of the Torah shrine reflects the growing importance of this area of the synagogue. This area sometimes served as a repository for the community chest[164] and as a Genizah for spoiled holy books.[165] This is evidenced as early as Hammath Tiberias B, 2a. Moshe Dothan describes a "sunken structure" immediately behind and to the right of the Torah shrine (locus 52) "in which the treasures of the synagogue or at least some of the valuable ritual objects were kept. . . . Coins and broken glass were discovered in this repository."[166] Dothan describes this repository as an *opisthodomos*, "the back chamber common to pagan temples."[167] It is suggestive that the aedicula from the second synagogue at Nabratein was reused in the expansion of the *bema*, apparently after the earthquake of 306 C.E. This stone was not discarded, but reused to pave the area of the shrine. This reuse might suggest that the aedicula had some sanctity, and could not merely be thrown away. It

Image of a cross from a baptistry mosaic in Skira, Tunisia.

might parallel the burial of disused holy books within the apse. This practice serves to emphasize the significance of this area as the home of the Torah scrolls, and may parallel the storage of relics within church apses. At Maon (Nirim) bone furniture joints "possibly for a wooden 'seat of Moses'..., or else from a lectern," carved bone inlay "probably" from the ark, broken glass, bronze suspension rings for lamps, parts of a bronze polycandelon, coins, nineteen amulets (some with signs of having been wrapped in cloth) and other objects were discovered in the synagogue's apse.[168] We have already noted Naveh and Shaked's suggestion that "some of the amulets were suspended from the wall near or behind the Ark of the Law, or even from the ark itself."[169]

The *Menorah* and the Torah Shrine as Visual Symbols

Much has been written about Jewish symbols[170] during this century, the most important work being E. R. Goodenough's *Jewish Symbols in the Greco-Roman Period*.[171] Scholars agree that such images as *menorot*, Torah shrines, and incense shovels are distinctly Jewish symbols. There is lack of agreement, however, on how more secular or even polytheistic imagery within Jewish contexts should be interpreted. Should iconography that was part of the standard repertoire of late antique art, such as geometric forms, nilotic scenes, flora, fauna, and inhabited scrolls be interpreted as specifically Jewish "symbols"? Jews of differing perspectives may or may not have understood these images differently than their neighbors did. This issue is particularly pointed when Jews and Christians commissioned their art from the same craftsmen, as is the case of the extremely similar mosaics discovered in the church of Shellal and the synagogue of Maon (Nirim). Michael Avi-Yonah and most recently Asher Ovadiah speak of a "school of Gaza" that was responsible for both mosaics.[172] It is often impossible to do more than describe the "semantic range" of possible meanings ascribed to each image or composition within a given religious tradition or artistic or literary context. Our concern here, therefore, will be primarily with specifically Jewish iconography that appeared within synagogues.

The most common Jewish symbol in late antique Palestine was the *menorah*. Like the cross in Christian contexts,[173] images of the *menorah* occurred routinely in synagogues, having been used to adorn private homes, tombs, glass vessels, oil lamps, bread stamps, amulets, and personal seals.[174] The distinct form of the *menorah*, based upon the description of the Tabernacle *menorah* in Exodus 25:31–40, 37:17–24,[175] made it a particularly successful visual image.[176] This unique structure is recognized in Rabbinic sources that argue that the biblical description of the *menorah* was difficult for Moses to imagine. Finally, it was drawn for him in fire "by the finger of God."[177] The *menorah* became an internal symbol for the Jewish minority in Palestine (and in the Greco-Roman Diaspora) during late antiquity, and was surely recognized as such by non-Jews as well.[178] We have seen that literary sources already suggest the presence of branched *menorot* in synagogues during the Tannaitic period. The use of the *menorah* as a symbol during late antiquity is surely related to the developing ideology of "remembering the Temple" that we have seen in Rabbinic sources, to the presence of actual *menorot* in synagogues, to the distinctiveness of this image, and (no less importantly) to its appropriateness within the general Greco-Roman setting.[179]

Like other national and religious groups within the Empire,[180] the Jews drew their visual symbols from their cult.[181] They drew from the biblical Tabernacle, the Temple of Jerusalem, and from the furnishings of synagogues.[182] The fact that Jews had a well-known and ancient Temple cult afforded them stature in the eyes of non-Jews before 70 C.E. This status continued even after the cessation of the Temple service in 70 C.E.[183] Jews saw the interruption of the sacrificial cult as temporary, a notion that was reinforced in gentile eyes by Julian the Apostate's attempt to rebuild the Temple.[184] The literary and visual recollection of the cult and its appurtenances was, as we have seen, essential to the Rabbinic attempt to bridge non-holy time, *zeman ha-zeh*.[185]

The Torah shrine served a similar symbolic function, though it was certainly used less frequently than the *menorah*. In literary sources it was related to the Holy Ark of the Temple only during the third century, possibly up to a century

Depiction of a *menorah* from the Torah shrine panel of the Sepphoris Synagogue mosaic.

after the introduction of the synagogue *menorah*. The spread of the Torah shrine as an independent visual symbol may have been impeded by the use of book cabinets in Roman and Byzantine art[186] and of altars and martyria in Byzantine art.[187] The image of the Jewish book cabinet would simply not have been iconographically distinctive enough. In a graffito from Beth She'arim[188] and in images from Sardis and Rome this problem was alleviated by leaving the doors of the shrine open so that the scrolls inside are recognizable. The use of the scroll form for sacred texts was restricted to Jews during the Byzantine period, as Christians took on the codex form.

Representations of Torah shrines flanked by *menorot* were used by Palestinian Jews to make explicit the "Jewishness" of the book cabinet. This usage was surely suggested by the actual furnishings of synagogues, and left no question as to the

Graffito of Torah shrine from the Beth She'arim Necropolis.

Jewishness of the Torah shrine. It also suggests that the shrine had developed associations to the Temple cult beyond its function as a synagogal scroll cabinet. This iconography has clear Christian parallels. Like Torah shrines, Christian martyria were often portrayed flanked by lighting fixtures. The iconographic similarities between Torah shrines and martyria are best seen in contemporaneous mosaic images from the synagogue at Khirbet Susiya and the apse of the Chapel of John the Priest on Mt. Nebo.[189] In the Khirbet Susiya synagogue mosaic the image of the ark flanked by two menorot and enclosed by a prostyle was laid before the "secondary bema."[190] In the Chapel of John the Priest on Mt. Nebo we find a similar image, which Sylvester Saller and Bellarmino Bagatti identify as the image of a funerary monument.[191] Before the altar of this church, a dedicatory inscription flanked with two candelabra was enclosed in a prostyle not unlike that at Khirbet Susiya. In addition, both prostyles are flanked by domesticated animals.

Like the menorah, though to a lesser degree, images of Torah shrines appear as visual symbols outside of synagogue contexts. The symbolic use of the Torah shrine outside of the synagogue context reflects the great significance which this element of synagogue art had for some Jews. Torah shrines are represented within many different settings. Within funerary contexts they appear on the sealing stones of burial kokhim[192] and on a sarcophagus[193] from Beth She'arim. Torah shrines also appear on plaques that were discovered in funerary contexts.[194] The shrine flanked by menorot was used, like the menorah and the shrine alone, to identify the ethnicity of the deceased. One wonders if this imagery was in some way used to symbolize the Temple or the world to come, reading synagogue imagery into the eternal realm. One is reminded of the Rabbinic promise that those who frequent synagogues in this world will also frequent them in the world to come.[195] Images of Torah shrines also appear on a bronze plate from Na'aneh (near Ramle),[196] on a glass plate discovered in Beth She'arim,[197] on a crater from Nabratein,[198] on oil lamps,[199] and apparently on a mirror frame from Shikmona.[200] The Torah shrine was perceived by Jews as an object that was uniquely Jewish. Alone and flanked by *menorot*, the image of the synagogue Torah shrine became a symbol for Jewish identity in late antique Palestine.

The Iconography of Two "Holy Places"

In this section we will interpret the remains of two late antique synagogues that are explicitly called "holy place" in their dedicatory inscriptions, Hammath Tiberias B, 2a (fourth century) and Naaran (sixth century). "Holy place" will be treated as a key to the interpretation of these synagogue environments.

At both Hammath Tiberias B and Naaran the community was aligned toward the Jerusalem wall and the Torah shrine. The shrine panel of the carpet mosaic was laid immediately before the Torah shrine.[201] At Hammath Tiberias B, the earliest example of this arrangement, the base of the Torah shrine is extant. Immediately before it is a mosaic depiction of a Torah shrine flanked by two seven-branched *menorot*. Moshe Dothan, excavator of the Hammath Tiberias B synagogue, reasonably suggests that this mosaic depiction reflects the shrine and lamps of the synagogue itself.[202] Each lamp is in turn flanked by a *lulav* and *ethrog*,[203] a *shofar*[204] and an incense shovel.[205] All of these items were used in the Temple cult. With the possible exception of the incense shovel, all were synagogue appurtenance during late antiquity.[206]

This dual identification may have made them uniquely suitable symbols to accompany the *menorot* and the ark. The *shofar* refers to *Rosh ha-Shanah*, the *lulav* and *ethrog* to *Sukkot*, and the incense shovel apparently refers to *Yom Kippur*. The advantage of the symbols of the fall festivals over the appurtenances of other holidays is that most (if not all) were used in synagogues, and that the formal characteristics of the *shofar*, the *lulav*, and *ethrog* were uniquely Jewish.[207] Most significant, however, is their size: they are small enough to fill the space between the *menorah*'s branches and its base. In contemporaneous depictions, within and without synagogues, single *menorot* are often flanked by these items, their purpose being to fill the void under the branches of the lamps. It is most likely that the artist copied the *menorah*, together with the smaller cult objects, directly from a repertoire of standard patterns. A number of scholars have posited the existence of pattern or sketch books.[208] The clustering of these symbols about the *menorot* and the shrine, seemingly floating on air, does not necessarily reflect their actual position within the synagogue.[209] Together with the flames of the *menorah*, these

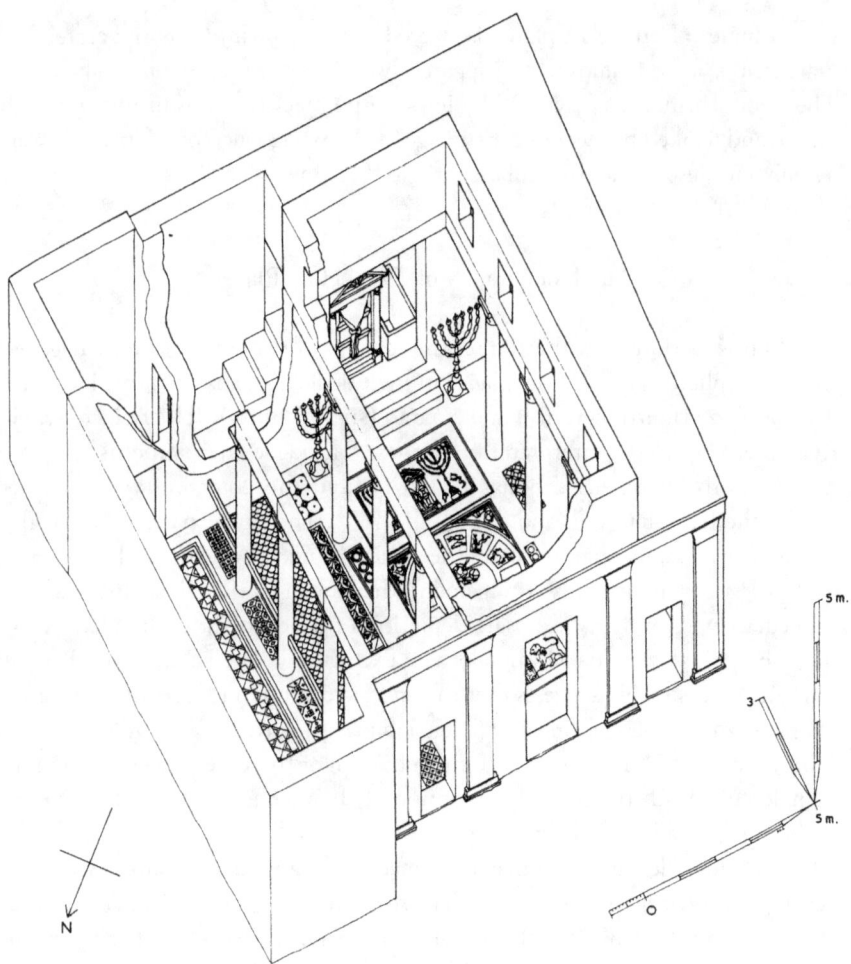

The Hammath Tiberias B Synagogue, reconstruction.

secondary symbols serve to create an almost ethereal environment that contrasts with and compliments the images of the synagogue cult objects. Within the present context the *lulav* and *ethrog*, *shofar*, and incense shovel are formal appendages of the *menorot*. This borrowing, together with the inclined flames at Hammath Tiberias, led to an intentionally imprecise "mirror" image of the synagogue's furnishings. The representation of the Torah shrine and its contents on the floor of the synagogue served to emphasize its central significance within the hall, in much the same way that a reflecting pool does for public buildings today.[210]

Zodiac panel from the Sepphoris Synagogue mosaic.

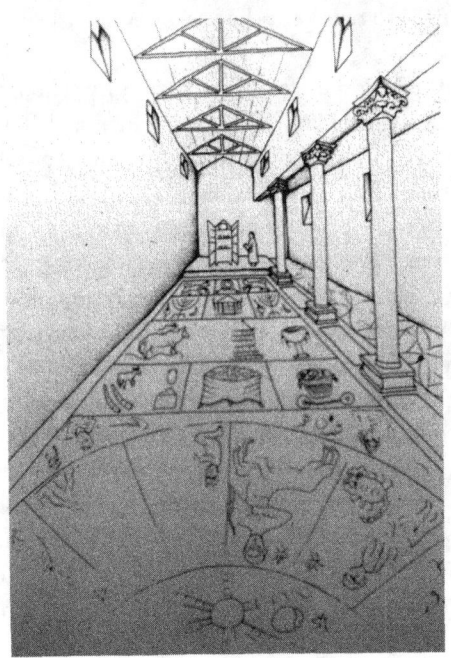

Reconstruction drawing of the Sepphoris Synagogue.

The visual interplay between the floor and the furnishings at Hammath Tiberias B may have created a sense of grandeur and otherness, an effect supported by the zodiac wheel, the "dome of heaven," at the center of the pavement, and the lions flanking the donor plaque opposite the synagogue's entrance.[211] The image of the zodiac, with Helios at its center, was not unique to Jewish art during late antiquity.[212] Its central position within the synagogue nave is nonetheless quite astounding. I can think of no reason why this image in itself is holy, particularly with its uncircumcised image of Libra and of the sun god (even if Helios is simply the standard way that the sun was represented during late antiquity) at its center. The presence of the zodiac within the synagogue was certainly related, as Avi-Yonah suggests, to the lunar cycle of the Jewish year[213] and thus to the liturgy. This connection is driven home by the images of the four seasons in the four corners of the mosaic panel, each accompanied by agricultural products that are representative of that season. The calendrical context of the zodiac image is evidenced archaeologically by juxtaposition of the zodiac signs and the names of the Hebrew months in the recently uncovered zodiac wheel from Sepphoris[214] and in an inscription from Ein Gedi.[215] It is also evidenced by the correspondence between the months and the astrological signs in numerous *piyyutim*.[216] A general Greco-Roman calendar form thus is used to represent the yearly cycle of Jewish sacred time.

The Naaran synagogue was built during the fifth or sixth century. Though the Torah shrine area has been lost, it was most likely enclosed by an apse.[217] The mosaic panel that was situated before the Torah shrine contains the image of the shrine flanked by *menorot*. Hanging from the branches of the *menorot* are lamps, which provide additional light to the sacred precinct. Immediately before the ark image at Naaran, set within the same frame, Daniel appears. As in a relief from En Samsam in the Golan Heights, he is flanked by lions, his arms lifted in a prayerful "orans" position.[218] Images that represent biblical ancestors being saved from danger appear in other Palestinian synagogues, including Noah's ark in a mosaic at Gerasa, and the Binding of Isaac in the Beth Alpha and the visitation of Abraham by the three angels announcing Isaac's birth (Gen. 18) and the Binding of Isaac in the Sepphoris synagogue mosaic.[219] All of these iconographic themes were also used in Christian art from which they were surely drawn.[220] All of these themes are central to Rabbinic conceptions, particularly as reflected in synagogue liturgy. Perhaps the images of biblical characters hearkens broadly to what the Rabbis called *zekhut avot*. This concept suggests that the merits of the biblical ancestors constitute an entitlement, "charged to the account of Israel."[221] Extant prayers emphasize this theme.[222] At Kafr Misr, the names "Abraham" and "Isaac" appear as part of a largely destroyed mosaic inscription,[223] and at Ein Gedi the names of Abraham, Isaac, and Jacob appear together with Daniel's three companions Hananiah, Misha'el, and Azariah.[224] Daniel's prayer gesture is certainly appropriate within the synagogue, by now a place of communal prayer.[225] This liturgical connection also explains the presence of David (as Orpheus) playing his lyre in the synagogue mosaic at Gaza.[226] The Psalms of David were important elements of the synagogue liturgy. In a similar way, the illustration of Aaron performing sacrifices in the Tabernacle, of a table for the show bread, of horns (haṣroṣrot) and of a basket containing first fruits, among others,[227] in the Sepphoris synagogue mosaic bring distinctive sacrificial imagery into the synagogue. This intense visual "recollection of the Temple" is unique in Jewish art from the Land of Israel. It reflects the importance of Temple themes in synagogue life in ways that are anticipated in Amoraic and post-Amoraic literary sources that we have discussed. While illustrations of biblical themes are well known in synagogue mosaics in the Land of Israel, they do not seem to have been considered sacred in themselves. Were this the case, one might expect that Jews would have taken the same course as the Christians and forbidden the placement of biblical images in a possibly denigrating position under foot.[228]

Squeezed in around Daniel and above the *menorot* in the ark panel at Naaran are dedicatory inscriptions to the "holy place." As we have suggested earlier, these donors apparently wanted to be close to the Torah shrine and through it, close to the Temple in Jerusalem. At the same time they clearly hoped to gain prominence within the synagogue community. At the center of the Naaran mosaic is a zodiac panel. At a late date the signs of the zodiac were carefully, if unaesthetically, removed from the mosaic. Toward the close of antiquity Jews in this community considered the presence of this imagery to be inappropriate within the "holy place." In fact, it must have been seen as a kind of sacrilege. Similar iconoclastic attitudes developed among Christians and Moslems. It seems to represent the spirit of an age when images were seen by many to be antithetical to sanctity.[229] It is significant that the nearby synagogue mosaic from Jericho, which dates to the eighth century, lacks such images completely.

Summary

We began this chapter with the suggestion that a title for synagogues found in epigraphic sources, "holy place," might serve as a key for the interpretation of synagogue art and architecture. We have shown that the centrality of the Torah within synagogues was the single most important factor in the articulation of these buildings, followed by the application of Temple motifs. The rites of synagogue Torah reading and prayer melded with late antique artistic and architectural trends to determine the decor of these buildings. During late antiquity the Torah shrine became the defining feature of the Palestinian synagogue. The shrine was set within a delineated precinct, an area that grew and became more elaborate as our period proceeded. The Torah shrine and its precinct drew symbolism from the Temple, toward which the shrine itself was aligned and subservient. The Divine power of the cult object that it housed, the sacred book, was imparted to the shrine and in at least one instance magical power was ascribed to the Torah cabinet. The iconography of the shrine, whether flanked by *menorot*, in proximity to *menorot*, or (rarely) alone, developed a life of its own beyond the synagogue context. Like the *menorah*, it became an internal and external symbol of the Jewish community and a reminder of the indwelling of the Divine presence among the Jews. Architecturally, the Torah shrine and its appurtenances on the Jerusalem-aligned wall were the feature that made Palestinian synagogues "holy places."[230] Other features, including inscriptions, the *menorot*, images of biblical ancestors, and the zodiac were of secondary significance in the articulation of the synagogue hall. These elements were directly related to the liturgical functions of the "holy place." This interpretation takes into account virtually every feature of synagogue and study house architecture, art, and epigraphy. It also corresponds with our reading of contemporaneous literature. Parallels between literary sources that we have discussed and archaeological discoveries are striking evidence of the "common Judaism" shared by the authors of our literary sources and our synagogue builders.

CHAPTER FIVE

"You Believe the Place Is Holy Because the Torah and Prophets Are There. . . ."

Synagogue Holiness in the Diaspora during Late Antiquity

During the Greco-Roman period the Jewish Diasporas of the Mediterranean basin and Babylonia were numerous, powerful, and often wealthy. Synagogues were ubiquitous within the urban landscape, each reflecting the uniqueness of its community and the shared religion that bound all the communities together. In this chapter the sanctity of Diaspora synagogues during late antiquity will be explored and compared to the sanctity of Palestinian synagogues. Late antique synagogues in the Diaspora seem to have been quite similar in function and form to Palestinian synagogues. The Torah scroll was the "cult object" of late antique Diaspora meeting houses, where Temple motifs were common. This is striking evidence of the depth of "common Judaism" during late antiquity. Local variation is, however, apparent.

In our discussion of Palestinian synagogues we had at our disposal a wealth of Jewish sources, both literary and archaeological. No Diaspora community has left behind for us both varieties of sources. Rather, Babylonian synagogues are known almost exclusively from sources preserved in the Babylonian Talmud. This material reflects the interests and perspectives of the Babylonian Sages.[1] Synagogues throughout the Mediterranean basin are known mainly from archaeological remains and the writings of non-Jews. Owing to the vast differences in sources available for the two major lobes of the Jewish Diaspora at this time, we will discuss the synagogues in each Diaspora separately.

Map of Diaspora Synagogues.

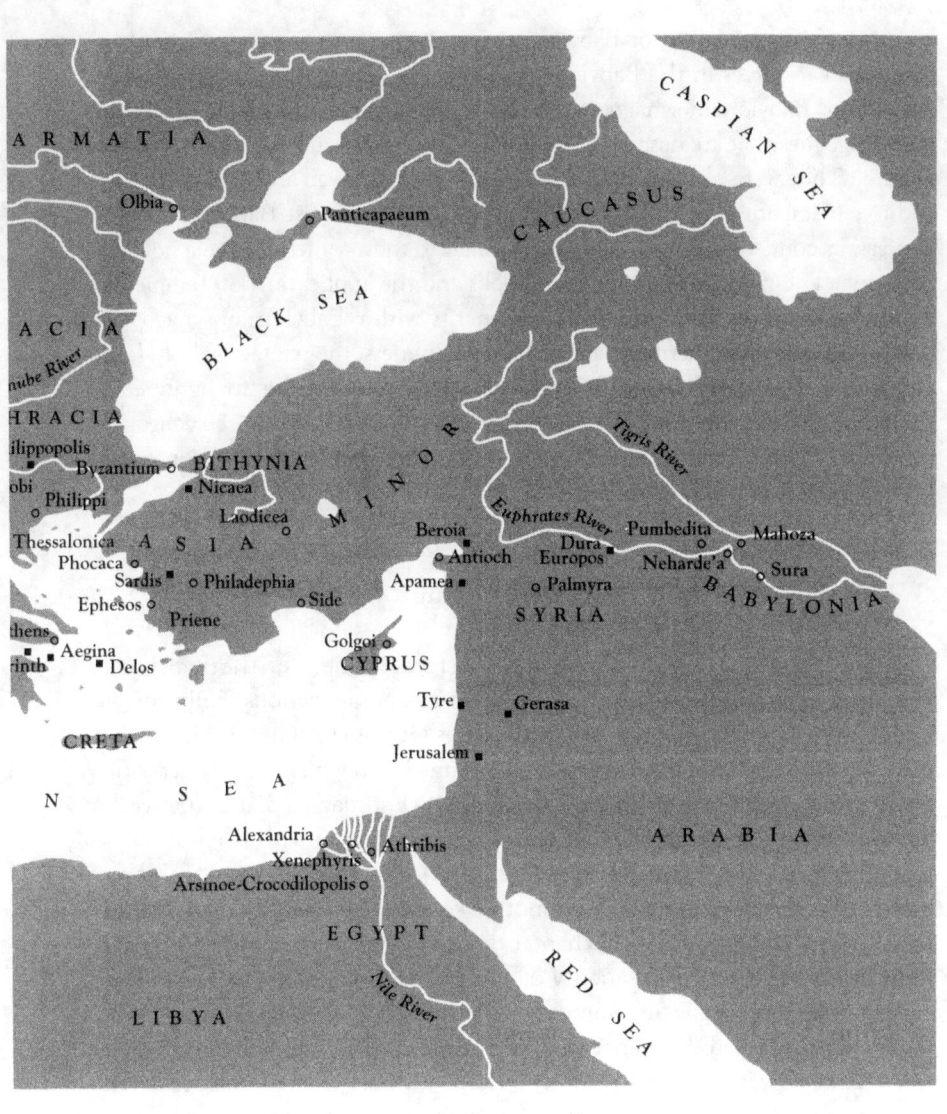

The Sanctity of Babylonian Synagogues

Almost no evidence for Babylonian synagogues is extant before the third century C.E. Sources in the Babylonian Talmud suggest that the overwhelming majority of Babylonian synagogues during the Amoraic period were much like the synagogues that are described in Amoraic and post-Amoraic Palestinian literature.[2] They were places where Jews came together to read and study Scripture and to participate in communal liturgy. The sanctity of most Babylonian synagogues was conceived in ways that were similar to those which we have noted in Palestine. The presence of the sacred books and the application of Temple imagery to synagogues were the sources of sanctity within Babylonian synagogues. Two synagogues were ascribed with additional holiness, the synagogues of *Hutsal* and *Shaf ve-Yatev* in Nehardea.[3] The Divine presence could be encountered in these synagogues with greater intensity than anywhere else. These synagogues became foci of local patriotism. With their heightened status, greater concentration of the Divine within them developed.

The Sacred Scripture

As in Palestine, Torah reading was a central element of the Babylonian synagogue service during the Amoraic and post-Amoraic periods. Following m. *Megillah* 3:1, sanctity within the synagogue was seen as stemming from the holy book. As in Palestine, greater sanctity was attained through closer contact with a Torah scroll. We have seen that an apparently Palestinian *baraita* in b. *Megillah* 26a calls those appurtenances that were in closest contact with the holy books "appurtenances of holiness" (*tashmishei qedushah*). The authors of y. *Megillah* 3:1, 73d, who either did not have or did not make use of this *baraita*, took another path to explore this concept. In chapter three we saw that y. *Megillah* 3:1, 732d, differentiates between the "sanctity of the ark" and the "sanctity of the synagogue." Those synagogue furnishings that were in closest contact with the sacred scrolls in the ark had the "sanctity of the ark" and those which had only occasional contact were attributed with the lesser "sanctity of the synagogue." The opinion of the first generation Babylonian amora Samuel is cited in the Palestinian Talmud tradition:

> Rav Judah in the name of Samuel: the *bema* and planks (*levaḥin*) do not have the sanctity of the ark, and do have the sanctity of the synagogue.

This text suggests that traditions regarding the sanctity of synagogues in early Amoraic Babylonia were applicable to the Palestinian context or at least that Palestinians thought that they were.

In b. Megillah 26b the fourth-generation Babylonian amora Rava explores the implications of "appurtenances of holiness" within the synagogue. This text affords us a glimpse into the furnishings of Babylonian synagogues. The baraita considers "chests for (holy) books" (delusqamei sefarim) and "casing(s) for books" (tiq) to be "appurtenances of holiness." Rava adds two more "appurtenances of holiness" to this list. These are presented in parallel literary formulations:

> Rava said: At first I used to think that the stand (kursaya) (upon which the Torah is placed) is an appurtenance of an appurtenance, and that it is permitted.
> When I saw that the Torah scroll is actually placed upon it, I determined that it is an appurtenance of holiness, and is forbidden (to be used for a lower purpose).
>
> Rava further said: At first I used to think that this textile (peresa)[4] is an appurtenance of an appurtenance, and that it is permitted.
> When I saw that it is folded over and that the Torah scroll is actually placed upon it (alternately: it is spread atop the scroll),[5] I determined that it is an appurtenance of holiness, and it is hidden away.[6]

Rava's notion of second degree "appurtenances of holiness" is an expansion of our baraita, and parallels the Palestinian Talmud's notion of the "sanctity of the synagogue." In these traditions Rava raises the Torah stand and the textile that covered the Torah shrine from the category of "appurtenances of appurtenances of holiness" to be "appurtenances of holiness" themselves. It is significant that the terms for the stand, kursaya, and the textile, peresa, are different from those which appear in Palestinian Talmud traditions.[7] In addition, the Greek loan word deluskama (chest) is translated in the Babylonian Amoraic discussion into the Aramaic parallel of teva, tavuta. These terms seem to reflect the living reality of Babylonian synagogues in the time of Rava, and that Rava is not merely interpreting a Palestinian tradition out of academic interest.

Having raised the stand and the cloth from second to first degree holy objects, Rava then sets them within m. Megillah 3:1's hierarchy of holiness:

> Rava further said: A (Torah) chest (tavuta) that has fallen apart, it is permitted to make it into a smaller (Torah) cabinet, but it is forbidden to make it into a stand (kursaya).[8]

> The stand (*kursaya*) (upon which the Torah is placed) may too be made into a small stand, but it is forbidden to make it into a step (*darga*)[9] for a stand.
>
> Rava further said: When a textile is worn-out, it is permitted to make it into a smaller textile for (biblical) scrolls, but not for a single fifth (of the Torah).

As in Tannaitic sources and in the Palestinian Talmud, the Torah scroll is more holy than scrolls of the Prophets and Writings, which are in turn more holy than individual scrolls of the Pentateuch. The disposal of a worn-out Torah scroll is of particular interest to the authors of our pericope, since the Torah scroll stands at the pinnacle of *m. Megillah* 3:1's hierarchy of holiness. The worn-out Torah scroll cannot be used for any other purpose. Rather, it is to be buried "beside a Sage, or even one who repeats traditions (*shoneh halakhot*)." Worn-out scrolls are to be placed in a clay jar, on the model of Jeremiah 32:14. Following this pattern, Mar Zutra teaches that the textiles used to wrap (holy) books may be used for no lower ritual purpose. Rather, they are to be used as shrouds for bodies that the community is responsible to bury (*met mitzvah*).

Imitatio Templi

The application of Temple imagery to synagogues in Babylonia paralleled directly the situation in Palestine.[10] Following *m. Megillah* 3:3, *b. Baba Bathra* 3b applies categories derived from the Temple context to determine the manner in which a synagogue building may be reconstructed. We have seen that *t. Megillah* 3:23 asserts that synagogues in hilly Palestine be built at the "high point" of the town in a manner similar to the Jerusalem Temple. This position is supported using Proverbs 1:21: "Above the bustling (streets) she (wisdom, i.e., Torah) calls out." In flat Babylonia an Amoraic tradition attributed to the Palestine-trained Rav teaches that the synagogue should be the tallest building in the town:[11]

> Said Rava son of Meḥasyah said Rav Hama son of Guriah said Rav:
> Any town whose roofs are
> higher than the synagogue will in the end be destroyed.
> For it is said: "To raise up the house of our God and to rebuild its ruins" (Ezra 9:9). . . .[12]

This opinion is supported using a proof text drawn from the construction of the Second Temple under Ezra. Nissim son of Reuven Gerondi correctly interprets the proof text:[13]

> Just like one who raises up the house of our God (the Temple), he who does not raise up the house of our God (the synagogue above the other buildings) destroys that which stands.

We have seen that in Palestine the Tosefta's requirement to build synagogues at the "height of the town" seems to have had limited following during late antiquity. In Babylonia a similar tradition was treated with the utmost seriousness by a Sage in fifth-century Matah Meḥesia:[14]

> Said Rav Ashi: I acted (or bequeathed, *avdei*) in Matah Meḥesia (by raising the height of the synagogue higher than every other building)[15] so that it would never be destroyed for this sin.

The concept that synagogue Torah shrines might use the imagery of the Ark of the Covenant may have developed earlier among some Babylonian Jews than in Palestine. In Babylonia the ark was on occasion called "holy ark," an association that was implicit in Palestine but not part of the nomenclature of the Palestinian synagogue. We read in two *baraitot* preserved only in *b. Shabbat* 32a that:

> Our Sages taught: As a result of three sins women die in childbirth. . . . There are those who say: because they call the holy ark *arona*.

> It is taught: Rabbi Ishmael son of Eleazer says: For two sins *amei ha-arasot* (that is, the non-Rabbinic)[16] die. Because they call the holy ark *arona* and because they call the synagogue *beit am* (house of the people).[17]

Arona was apparently considered by the author of this tradition to be an insult to the holiness of the "holy ark." It was the equivalent of calling the ark a closet.[18] The Babylonian Amoraim considered this tradition to be of Palestinian Tannaitic provenance. As Tosafot has already noted, however, no Palestinian Tannaitic tradition uses this terminology.[19] The authors of these traditions did not consider *arona* to be a term parallel to "holy ark." Palestinian Amoraim may not have had these texts, for *arona* is a common term for the ark in the Palestinian Talmud.[20]

The use of "holy ark" to connote the Torah shrine is evidenced in Babylonian literature that does not stem from Rabbinic circles. The fourth-century eastern church father Aphrahat derides the Jews for treating their Torah arks like the "Holy ark" of the Temple.[21] In the liturgy of Anan son of David (c. eighth century), Karaite Torah shrines are also called *aron*.[22] Perhaps this notion was taken over from Rabbinite synagogues. Anan's liturgy shows a stronger interest in *imitatio templi* than do Rabbinic sources.[23]

"Extra-Holy" Synagogues

A pericope in *b. Megillah* 28a–29a explores the sanctity of Babylonian synagogues in some depth. This text represents a forceful retort to a claim cited in the name of the third-generation Palestinian amora Rabbi Assi that the significance of "synagogues in Babylonia is contingent" upon their continued use.[24] According to this apparently Palestinian tradition, the Tannaitic provision of residual sanctity to buildings that had ceased to serve as synagogues[25] is applicable only in the Land of Israel. This claim was taken quite seriously by the authors of our pericope, who respond to this slight to Babylonian synagogues. This pericope reflects the ongoing struggle between Palestinian and Sassanian Jewry for hegemony during late antiquity. It reveals an attitude toward selected synagogues in Babylonia as "extra holy" sites, while providing important sources for the sanctity of Babylonian synagogues that did not share this status. The *aggadic* section of this pericope is of utmost significance for the history of the synagogue in Babylonia, and of synagogue sanctity in particular. It opens with a *baraita* which suggests that the Divine Presence follows Israel into exile:

> It has been taught: Rabbi Simeon son of Yoḥai said:
> Come and see how beloved are Israel in the sight of God, in that in every place to which they were exiled the *Shekhinah* (Divine Presence) went with them. They were exiled to Egypt, the *Shekhinah* went with them, as it says: Did I reveal myself to the house of your father in Egypt
> (1 Sam. 2:27).
> They were exiled to Babylonia, the *Shekhinah* went with them, as it says: "For your sake I was sent to Babylon (Isa. 43:14)."
> It does not say "He will cause to return," but "he will return."
> This teaches that the Holy One, Blessed be He, will return from the exile.[26]

The text then localizes the Divine presence:

> Where is the *Shekhinah* in Babylonia?
> Abaye said: In the synagogue of *Hutsal* and in the synagogue of *Shaf ve-Yatev* in Nehardea. Here and there? Rather it is sometimes in one, and sometimes in the other.

Abaye here asserts that the Divine presence could be encountered in the synagogues of *Hutsal* and *Shaf ve-Yatev*, although the Talmud will provide no support for *Hutsal*'s claim.[27] A variant of this tradition preserved in the *Iggeret Rav Sherira Gaon*[28] citing our pericope, states this position anonymously. This version also suggests that the localization of the Divine within synagogues was a matter of rivalry between *Hutsal* and *Shaf ve-Yatev* from the beginning of the Babylonian Amoraic enterprise:

> The *Shekhinah* was with them, as we say in (tractate) *Megillah*:
> In Babylon where is it?
> Rav said: In the synagogue of *Hutsal*.
> Samuel said: In the synagogue of *Shaf ve-Yatev* in Nehardea. . . .

Abaye is said to have treated *Shaf ve-Yatev* as a sort of pilgrimage site:

> Said Abaye: May I be rewarded because whenever I am within a parsang I go and pray there.

He is willing to walk a parsang (approx. 4.5 km.) to pray at *Shaf ve-Yatev*, despite the fact that the academy had moved from there to Pumpedita in the wake of Nehardea's destruction by the Palmyrenes in 259 C.E.[29] During the mid-fourth century scholars returned to Nehardea, Abaye coming there to pray.[30] No doubt his disciples copied this practice, the synagogue becoming a place of Rabbinic prayer.[31]

Local patriotism of the academy of Pumpedita is a secondary theme within the pericope's general interest in disputing Rav Asi's affront to Babylonian local patriotism.[32] The pericope continues with illustrations of the special qualities of *Shaf ve-Yatev* and the high level of Divine presence there experienced by Rabbinic Sages beginning with the first generation of Babylonian Amoraim:

> The fathers of Samuel and Levi were sitting in the synagogue of *Shaf ve-Yatev* in Nehardea.

The *Shekhinah* came, they heard the tumult and they rose and left.
Rav Sheshet (who was blind)[33] was once sitting in the synagogue of *Shaf ve-Yatev* and the *Shekhinah* came.
He did not leave, and the ministering angels came and threatened him.
He turned to Him and said: Sovereign of the Universe, if one is afflicted and one is not afflicted, who gives way to whom?
God thereupon said to them: leave him.[34]

The pericope continues with a medley of traditions in praise of Babylonian synagogues:

"I have been to them a small sanctuary" (Ez. 11:16).
Rabbi Samuel son of Isaac said: This refers to the synagogues and study houses (which are in Babylonia). . . .[35]
Rava expounded: Why is it written: "Lord you were a habitation (*ma'on*) for us" (Ps. 90:1)?
Rava said: At first I would study at home and pray in the synagogue. Once I heard this which David said: "Lord, I love the habitation (*ma'on*) of your house" (Ps. 26:8) I have studied only in the synagogue.[36]
Rabbi Eleazar ha-Qappar said: In the future the synagogues in Babylonia will be set in place in the Land of Israel. . . .

The collection begins and concludes with traditions that claim Palestinian origin, Rabbi Samuel son of Isaac's comment on Ezekiel 11:16, and Rabbi Eleazar ha-Qappar's apocalyptic statement. Rabbi Samuel son of Isaac's comment is taken to refer specifically to Babylonian institutions. This is clearly reflected in versions of this tradition that conclude with "which are in Babylonia."[37] Rava's two comments interpret a word that refers to the Temple in the biblical sources cited, "habitation" (*ma'on*), to refer to synagogues in general. This was apparently new to this scholar, whose interpretation of a biblical verse legitimized this apparent Rabbinic innovation.[38] The pericope concludes with Rabbi Eleazar son of Qappar's statement of the ultimate apocalyptic placement of Babylonian synagogues in Palestine.

According to our editor, God is in exile in Babylonia, and dwells in Babylonian synagogues. Paramount among these are *Shaf ve-Yatev* and *Hutsal*. This claim is a stunning rebuke to the Palestinian claim that the significance of Babylonian synagogues is conditional upon their continued use. Our pericope claims priority based upon a theology of Divine immanence in Babylonia and, implicitly, Divine disinterest in late antique Palestine. That a tradition based upon the book of Ezekiel appears is no accident, Ezekiel having been the prophet of the Babylonian exile. Even though they exist outside the Land of Israel "at this time," Babylonian synagogues are thus projected into Messianic time.[39] Far from the Temple Mount and the other holy sites of Palestine, Babylonian Jews created a holy site based upon a theology of Divine exile in Babylonia. *Shaf ve-Yatev* and *Hutsal* more than other Babylonian synagogues partially fulfilled the need for Divine immanence within this successful Diaspora.[40]

Sources in the Babylonian Talmud suggest that synagogues in Babylonia were considered to be sacred due to the presence of the holy scrolls within them and the use of Temple motifs within their confines. A unique feature of this Diaspora is the extra-holy synagogues of *Hutsal* and *Shaf ve-Yatev*, which served as focal points for local patriotism.

The Greco-Roman Diaspora

Evidence for the history of the synagogue in the Greco-Roman Diaspora is both varied and sporadic. Information appears in Jewish writings of the Second Temple period, polytheistic authors, patristic sources, and a considerable body of archaeological remains. We have seen that the earliest evidence for the sanctity of communal meeting places is from Ptolemaic Egypt. Synagogue sanctity during late antiquity is generally reflected in archaeological sources and in patristic literature as deriving from the sanctity of the sacred scrolls and the application of Temple motifs. These are the same sources of sanctity that we have isolated in Palestine.

A clear and well-articulated statement on the sanctity of synagogues appears in the writings of the mid-fourth–century Antiochene church father John Chrysostom. Chrysostom polemicized against members of his community who considered synagogues to be "holy places" (*topon hagion*).[41] In John's conception, synagogue holiness was derived from two major factors: from the presence of the holy scrolls within synagogues and from a perceived relationship between synagogues and the Temple. He is the first non-Jewish author to emphasize the significance of the scrolls for the attribution of sanctity to synagogues. He is also the first to discuss at length the late antique synagogue, drawing on a somewhat intimate knowledge of this institution. Chrysostom took to task those who attended synagogues on the Sabbaths and festivals, who considered them to be good places to take oaths, who looked to synagogues as places of healing and magic and were impressed with synagogue ritual. All of these behaviors are known from Palestinian synagogues.[42] John argues strongly against the holiness of synagogues, while trying to convince his listeners that churches are the true holy places.[43]

In two rather long homilies,[44] Chrysostom derides the belief that the presence of biblical books, objects that he too perceives as holy, makes a synagogue holy:

> In short, you believe the place is holy because the Torah (*nomos*) and Prophets are there. . . .[45]

The sanctity of the book makes synagogues holy, reason members of Chrysostom's community, despite the fact that these books belong to Jewish "demons."[46]

Quick to condemn synagogues together with polytheistic temples[47] Chrysostom decries associations that his parishioners made between synagogues and the Jerusalem Temple:[48]

> What sort of ark is it that the Jews now have, where we find no propitiatory, no tablets of the law, no Holy of Holies, no veil, no high priests, no incense, no holocaust, no sacrifice, none of the things that made the ark of old holy and august?

The Jewish practice of calling the Torah cabinet a *kibotos*, "ark" "as if this object is in any way related to the Ark of the Covenant," is particularly loathsome to John. We have seen that this connection was made by Jews in Palestine and Babylonia, in Palestine from the third century onward. In fact, the Torah shrine is called *kibotos* in an inscription from the synagogue at Ostia near Rome as well.[49]

Chrysostom also condemns the leaders of the synagogues, the "patriarchs," who his audience perceives as "priests" on the biblical model:[50]

> Where are the things you held solemn? Where is your high priest, where is his robe, his breastplate, and stones of declaration? Do not talk to me about those patriarchs of yours who are hucksters and merchants and filled with all iniquity. Tell me, what kind of priest is he if the ancient oil for anointing priests no longer exists nor any other ritual of consecration? What kind of a priest is he if there is neither sacrifice nor altar, nor worship? Do you wish me to speak of the laws governing the priesthood and how priests were consecrated in olden times? In this way you would find out that those among you who are called patriarchs are not priests at all. They act the part of priests and are playing a role as if they were on stage, but they cannot carry the role because they are so far removed from both the reality and even the pretense of priesthood.

The attitude reported by John and his antagonism toward it may be intertwined with an issue of legal privilege for synagogue leaders. On 1 December 330 C.E.

Constantine promulgated a law that ordered "that the priests (*hiereis*), the synagogue leaders (*archisynagogis*), fathers of synagogues (*patribus synagogarum*) and others that serve in synagogues shall be free of all corporal liturgy."[51] The exemption of Jewish "priests" is analogous to the exemptions granted by Constantine to polytheistic and Christian "priests."[52] "Priest" is a Roman legal category, into which synagogue functionaries have now been placed.[53] In a similar way, around 370 C.E. Valentinian I declared synagogues to be within the category of "places of religion" (*religionum loca*) and thus exempt from providing hospitality to soldiers.[54] Synagogues were categorized by Roman law as temples that were staffed by priests. John's ire at the status of synagogue "priests" may thus have been reinforced by the tax status granted them by the imperial administration.

Chrystostom's emphasis upon the biblical scrolls and the use of Temple motifs in his community's perception of synagogue sanctity closely parallels Palestinian and Babylonian Jewish sources, as well as archaeological evidence from the Mediterranean Diaspora during late antiquity. Synagogue inscriptions from the Mediterranean Diaspora often call the synagogue a *hagios topos* (sometimes in the superlative). "Holy synagogue" appears in a Latin inscription from Naro in Tunisia, and "most holy synagogue" (*hagiotata sunagoge*) appears in two Greek inscriptions.[55] "Holy place" first appeared in a synagogue context at Stobi in Macedonia (c. 280–281 C.E.), as part of a dedicatory inscription preserved on a column.[56] The relevant sections of this inscription read:[57]

> (The year) 311. (I Claudios) Tiberios Polycharmos, also called Achrios, father of the community of Stobi, having lived all (my) life in accord with Judaism (have) because of a vow (added) to the holy place the buildings as well as the triclinium with the tetrastoon out of my own funds without touching in any way the sacred (funds). . . .

According to this text, the donor, Claudius Tiberias Polycharmos, seems to have separated a section of his personal dwelling to serve as the "holy place" of the Jewish community. The factors that made this synagogue "holy" are unknown to us, and extant elements of this synagogue do not reveal their secret.[58] The fourth-century building, however, may have been aligned toward a Torah shrine that stood on its eastern (Jerusalem) wall.[59]

A Greek inscription from Egypt describes a Jewish communal building, probably a synagogue, as a "holy place," though it provides minimal evidence regarding this "place:"

> . . . og . . . rios son of (?) . . . and to the holy place . . . Israel, God save.

It concludes with the Hebrew *Shalom*.[60] Shalom in Hebrew appears at the conclusion of Greek inscriptions from both Palestinian and Diaspora synagogues.[61] "Most holy synagogue," appears in a Greek inscription from Philadelphia in Lydia, where we hear of the "most holy synagogue of the Hebrews" (*hagiotata sunagogē ton Hebraion*).[62] Again, this text does not reveal what made this synagogue "most holy." An inscription from Side in Pamphylia, which probably dates to the fourth century, provides information that begins to explain how the "most holy first synagogue" was holy:[63]

> [I, Is]aac, administrator of the most holy first synagogue, made successful construction. I both filled in the marble from the raised stage to the *simma* and polished the seven-branched lamp and the two chief capitals [or, columns]. The fifteenth year of the indiction, the fourth month.[64]

This "most holy" synagogue was constructed with a raised stage a *simma*, perhaps an apse, and was decorated and perhaps paved with expensive marble floor. While it is unclear what is meant by the "two chief columns,"[65] the synagogue apparently had metal *menorot* in need of polishing. The lighting of this synagogue with *menorot* is a clear reference to the Temple and its cult.

While no physical evidence of this synagogue has been preserved, many of its attributes appear in the contemporaneous synagogue at Sardis, which we will discuss below. In fact, parallels to all elements except perhaps the columns are extant in the Sardis synagogue. The "most holy first synagogue" was decorated with marble, like Sardis. A raised platform for Torah reading also stood at Sardis, and an apse was constructed on the western end of the Sardis synagogue. An inscription dedicating a "seven-branched lamp," an *heptamyxion*, was found at Sardis, as were fragments of an actual stone *menorah* and a schematic drawing of a *menorah*. An image of a lamp on an ashlar in Nicaea seems to have had a metal *menorah* for its model.[66] No parallel to the "chief capitals or columns" is identified at Sardis or at other synagogues, and it is difficult to interpret the denotation of this term.[67] The "most holy first synagogue" of Side was a focal point for public benefaction by its community. One element of its decor is significant for understanding its sanctity, the presence of a *menorah*. Temple imagery was thus an essential element in the articulation of this synagogue.

Five synagogue buildings from the Greco-Roman Diaspora provide significant evidence for our discussion. These are the synagogue at Naro (Hamman Lif), at Dura Europos, the Priene synagogue, the Sardis synagogue, and the synagogue of Ostia Antica. Of these, "holy synagogue" appears in a Latin inscription from the sixth-century Naro (Hamman Lif) synagogue in Tunisia. Were it not for the dedicatory inscription that calls this sixth-century synagogue a *sancta suna-*

goga⁶⁸ and that it is flanked by two images of seven-branched *menorot*, it would be impossible to identify the mosaic of this building as stemming from a synagogue:⁶⁹

> Your servant Juliana P(?) at her own expense paved with mosaic the holy synagogue of Naro for her salvation.

The *menorot* seem to serve as markers of ethnic identity on a carpet mosaic that is otherwise completely secular. A niche stood on the eastern (Jerusalem) wall of the "holy synagogue." Goodenough suggests that this apse served to hold the holy books during the synagogue service.⁷⁰ If this is the case, the cult object of this "holy synagogue" was the Torah scroll that was housed in a Jerusalem-aligned apse.⁷¹ This scenario is commonplace in Palestine. It also appears commonly in the synagogues of the Greco-Roman Diaspora, where the Torah shrine aligned toward Jerusalem often is the essential sacred element of the synagogue interior.

The synagogue of Dura Europos was constructed within a converted private house, as were the church and the mithraeum down the street.⁷² The building was first used as a synagogue sometime before 244–245 C.E. In this year, dedicatory inscriptions suggest, the synagogue was renovated and enlarged (*itbanei, benei*).⁷³ In the atrium of the synagogue complex there was a laver for ablutions before entering the synagogue. This behavior was apparently taken over from the general context to this synagogue, though a relation between this ablution and that which was practiced in the Temple of Jerusalem is possible. Like the nearby church baptistery and the mithraeum, a focal point dominated by a niche was constructed on one wall of the synagogue. A Torah shrine stood at the center of the Jerusalem wall in both the first and the second phases of the synagogue.⁷⁴ In the second phase benches were constructed around the walls of the hall, focusing attention upon the center of the room where the Scriptures were probably read.⁷⁵

During both phases of the building, mural painting was centered above the Torah shrine. The upper facade of aedicula was apparently decorated during the first phase and this painting was preserved in the second.⁷⁶ This keystone of the synagogue interior was decorated with images related to the Temple cult. At its center, the Temple facade, to its left the *menorah*, *lulav* and *ethrog*, and to its right the Binding of Isaac, which biblical tradition suggests occurred on the Temple Mount.⁷⁷ The entrance portal of the Temple is crowned by a large conch shell. This shell directly parallels the upper register of the Torah niche, which is formed like a conch. As we have noted, this was a form that was specifically used to frame religious images during Greco-Roman antiquity. It appears often within the religious buildings of Dura Europos.⁷⁸ A dedicatory "graffito" on the left side of the aedicula's facade and below the *menorah* helps to establish the visual rela-

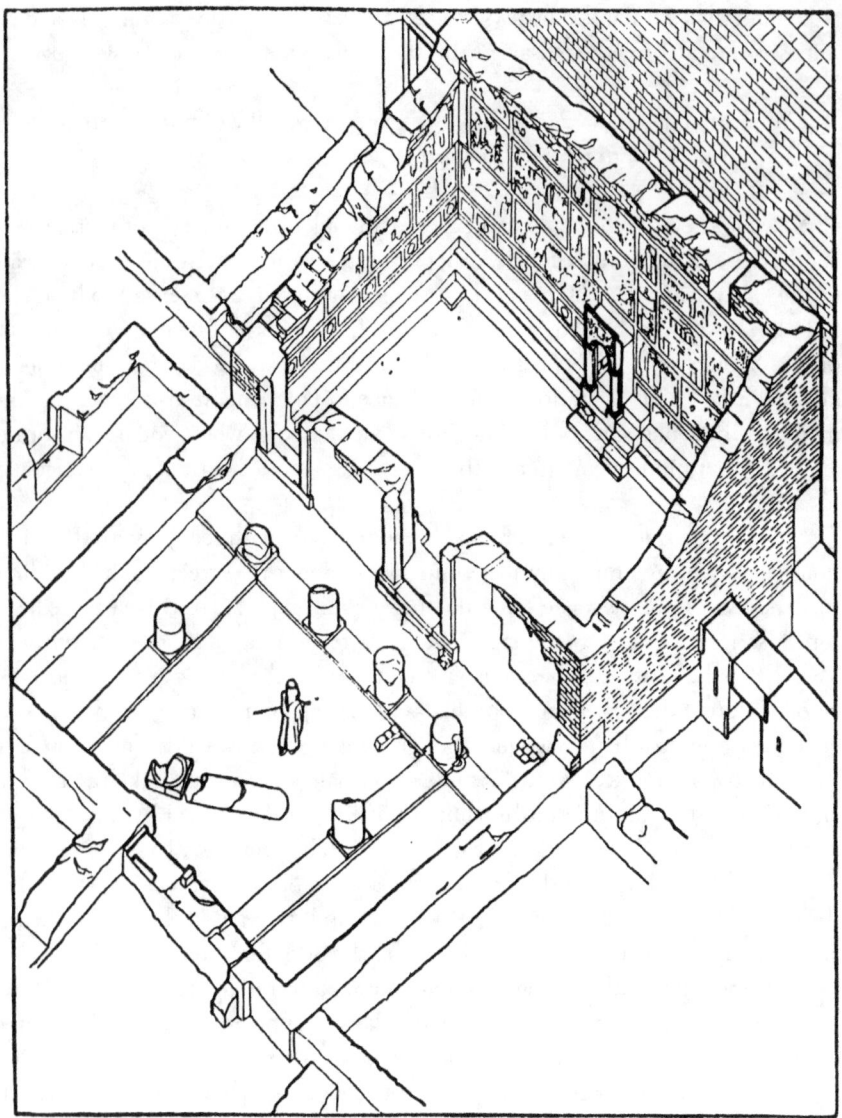

Isometric drawing of the Dura Europos Synagogue.

tionship between the Temple tympanum and the conch of the niche. The Aramaic inscription reads:

> (I . . .) donated (or, made) the beit arona.
> Joseph son of Abba. . . .[79]

The Dura Europos Synagogue, drawing of the interior by Nahman Avigad.

The aedicula is called the *beit arona* in this inscription. As at Naveh in the Jebel Druze, it is, literally, the "house of the ark."[80] As there, it is unclear whether this phrase suggests that a movable ark (*arona*) was stored in the *beit arona*,[81] or whether the shrine itself is the ark. In any event, a word that often hearkens back to the ark of the Jerusalem Temple is here used to describe a Torah synagogue shrine that is decorated with the image of the Temple and shares an iconographic

Moses holding the scroll of the Torah from the Dura Europos Synagogue.

characteristic with it. The literary and visual message of the Torah niche is that the synagogue Torah shrine and the Temple of Jerusalem bear an intimate relationship. This relationship is established by the fact that the shrine stands on the wall that is aligned with Jerusalem.

During the second stage of mural painting, the walls of the synagogue hall were covered with wall paintings. These wall paintings project mostly narratives that appear in the text of the Scriptures through the lens of late antique Jewish tradition and onto the walls of the synagogue. A central feature above and to the right of the Torah shrine is an iconic image of Moses holding an open Torah scroll. While most of the individual scenes in the paintings within this complex iconographic program do not speak explicitly to the issue of synagogue sanctity, together present a statement of the significance of Scripture to this community.[82]

Particularly important for our study is the great concern shown for the Ark of the Covenant in the wall paintings.[83] In four images the ark is portrayed as a chest, which Carl H. Kraeling suggests is in "the form of ancient Scroll Chests themselves ... is related on the one hand to the aediculae constructed to house them, and on the other to the Ark of the Covenant as portrayed at Dura."[84] He also posits that the aedicula was enclosed by a curtain.[85] If he is correct, the shrine must have looked much like the central portal of the Tabernacle in the scene which Kraeling calls "The Consecration of the Tabernacle and its Priests."[86] Following Kraeling, Joseph Gutmann[87] is correct that "in the second band of the Dura paintings, the largest of the three figurative bands, the substitution of the biblical ark for the Torah ark-chest (the container of God's entire revelation to Israel) is done purposely. The Torah shrine and scrolls cabinet look like Temple and the Ark of the Covenant, and the Temple and the Ark look like them."[88] This parallels the use of the term *arona* in reference to the synagogue ark in the aedicula dedicatory inscription.

The sanctity of the Dura synagogue is expressed most clearly, then, through the representation of stories derived from the Holy Books onto its walls, through the centrality of the Holy Books and their shrine, through the physical alignment of the community toward the Jerusalem Temple, which appears often in the paintings, and through the large number of ark-related scenes in the iconographic program. Other sources of sanctity are hinted at as well. Two plaques showing magical eyes decorated the synagogue's ceiling. Goodenough aptly describes the iconography of one of these eye tiles:[89]

> [The eye is] being attacked by snakes and three daggers, above which du Mesnil was certain that he could make out the letters IAO. A beetle or scorpion advances to attack the eye from below, while lines down from the eye apparently indicate two streams of tears.

Goodenough argues that the eye "labeled Iao, it certainly is not itself the 'evil eye,' but a good eye, suffering and hence potent against the evil eye." He suggests that such representations are part of general Greco-Roman magical tradition.[90] Perhaps the Dura synagogue was a place attributed with magical power. This fits well with Chrysostom's fourth-century claim that some Christians considered synagogues to be places of magic and with amulets discovered in Palestinian synagogues of a somewhat later period.[91]

Of similar interest are remains of human "finger" bones that were deposited in an extension of the hinge socket under the door sill of the synagogue's main door.[92] Kraeling reports that "analogous remains" were discovered in the hinge

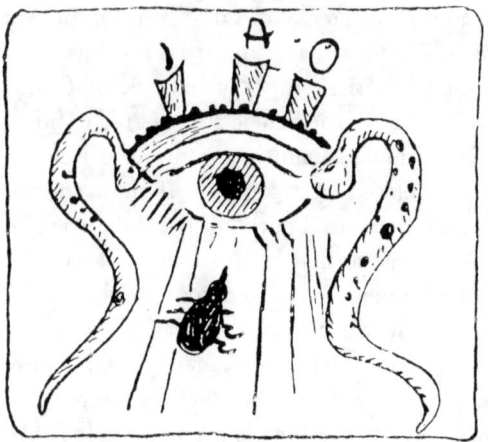

Ceiling tile with the image of the evil eye from the Dura Europos Synagogue.

socket of the right doorway. Their placement was thus no accident. He notes that similar foundation deposits were discovered in polytheistic structures at Dura.[93] The discovery of the buried finger bones is particularly striking in light of biblical purity prohibitions against contact with the dead,[94] particularly by "priests" like Samuel the synagogue leader,[95] and the seemingly close similarity between the synagogue's decorative program and Rabbinic sources.

Evidence that the synagogue was treated as a kind of Jewish temple is expressed in one of the more than thirteen Middle Iranian graffiti that were scratched into the paintings before the synagogue's destruction around 256 C.E.[96] One rather expansive text was scratched into the right leg of Hamman in the Mordecai and Esther panel. This graffito commemorates a visit to the synagogue by seemingly non-Jewish Persians in the company of the synagogue "scribe." In it the synagogue is called by the visitors the "edifice (*ptlstky*) of the God of Gods of the Jews. . . ."[97] The terminology used in this graffito suggests that the visitors, whose names are Persian, were not Jews.[98] An insider would most likely not have had reason to identify the "God of Gods" as the Jewish God. The visitors described the synagogue in distinctly Persian categories, seeing it as a local Jewish temple.

While the Judaism shared by the Dura community with the Palestinian Sages was indeed profound, their manner of marking the synagogue as a temple among the Dura temples was surely at variance with that of the Rabbinic Sages in Palestine and in Sassanian Babylonia. A parallel example of bones within a synagogue context seems to have existed in the fourth-century "Synagogue of the Maccabean Martyrs" in Antioch.[99] Though sources for the Antiochene synagogue are difficult, it appears that the relics of these martyrs were present within the synagogue and afforded it a special status at a time when the "cult of the saints" was central to Christian religious expression.[100]

Like the Jews of Dura and Stobi, the Jews of Priene met for communal life in a converted house.[101] According to the excavators, it was refurbished for this purpose during the fourth or fifth century.[102] The focal point of the meeting room was the Torah shrine, which stood on the eastern wall of the synagogue. According to A. Thomas Kraabel, the remains of a Torah niche 1.5 meters wide by 1.5 meters deep set "deep in the east wall, the side closest to Jerusalem" could still be seen in 1979.[103] On the floor of the synagogue was discovered opposite the Torah shrine a framed, rectangular relief that shows a *menorah*, a lulav to its left, and an unidentifiable object to the right. This composition is flanked by birds.[104] The *menorah* appears two more times at Priene; carved on a stele[105] and on a square piece of marble that was retrieved "from a church in the neighborhood."[106] This relief bears the image of a *menorah*, its branches surmounted by a cross-bar, flanked by an *ethrog* to the left, and a *shofar* and a palm frond to its right. Between the *menorah*'s branches and its legs, its stem is flanked by two spirals which Sukenik identified as the ends of biblical scrolls.[107] If he is correct, which Leonard V. Rutgers and I recently argued he was, this image forges a powerful relationship between the Temple *menorah* and the synagogue scrolls.[108] To the right of the Torah shrine was discovered an installation for ablutions. This location, assuming that it is original, suggests that ablution was an integral part of the synagogue service, not a purification rite performed before entry into the synagogue. Though distant in date and place from Dura, the Jews of Priene used similar strategies to differentiate their synagogue from the buildings of other religious associations in this city. These included the construction of a large Torah shrine with images of the *menorah* on the eastern, Jerusalem wall. The sanctity of the Torah was central within this synagogue, and the image of the *menorah* was drawn from the Temple context. The close conceptual relationship between Torah and Temple is set out in shorthand in the Priene *menorah* tablet with its images of two scriptural scrolls. The location of the ritual ablutions is unique to this synagogue, perhaps suggesting that this practice was extremely important to the community that gathered in the Priene synagogue.

During the second half of the third century a monumental building in the gymnasium complex at Sardis had been handed over to the Jewish community to serve as a synagogue.[109] This structure is the largest synagogue to be preserved from antiquity.[110] The building was constructed as part of the gymnasium on an east-west axis, an apse with seating capacity for seventy at its western end. The present interior plan of the building dates to the fourth century.[111] Jewish renova-

Menorah plaque from the Priene Synagogue.

tors installed two aediculae on the eastern end of the building between the three entrances at this time, realigning the focal point of the building from the west toward the east.[112] They also covered the seats of the apse with marble. This arrangement is reminiscent of the fourth-century building at Ostia, which was also realigned toward a Torah shrine on its eastern side during the fourth-century. Like a small number of Palestinian synagogues and like the synagogue at Ostia, the Torah shrines at Sardis were placed next to the entrances of the hall on the Jerusalem wall at this time.[113] These aediculae are set upon high pedestals. An inscription found within the hall refers to the *nomophylakion*, "the place that protects the Law (or, 'Torah')."[114] A second inscription demands pious religious behavior toward the Scriptures: "Find, open, read, observe."[115] Robert suggests that this inscription, also on marble, "must have been let onto the base on which

The Sardis Synagogue.

The Sardis Synagogue, model by Andrew Seager.

stood the cupboard or shrine of the Torah."[116] Kraabel notes that *phylaxon*, "observe" refers to "My commandments" in common Septuagint usage.[117] All the Hebrew inscriptions found were discovered "next to the southern shrine" as was a plaque bearing a *menorah* and a *shofar*. The original arrangement of scrolls within the Torah shrine at Sardis is represented in a fragmentary relief showing a Torah shrine with three scrolls lying horizontally within it.[118] This is the same arrangement illustrated in numerous exemplars from Rome at about the same time. It is significant that the Torah shrine was not merely a cabinet for Holy Books, but, as in Rome and in Palestine, it served as a visual symbol.

A lightweight wooden platform "on marble colonettes" stood at the center of the hall. A mosaic inscription "set among the stone slabs"[119] near the platform mentions "a priest (*heuron*) and *sophodidaskalos*," a "teacher of wisdom" or "wise teacher."[120] Perhaps the proximity of this inscription to the platform is significant, the platform being where "teaching" took place.[121] Perhaps this is the type of priestly synagogue official intended in Constantine's permission for "priests" who serve in synagogues not to pay corporal liturgies. A fragment of a large marble *menorah*, the branches of which once spanned over one meter,[122] a "small fragment of a bronze *menorah*,"[123] and an inscription recording the donation of a *heptamyxion*, a "seven-branched lamp," have been discovered.[124] The Sardis synagogue, like Dura and Priene, was a place dedicated to Torah. From the fourth century on the sacred books were kept within aediculae, called "the place that protects the law," which themselves were aligned toward the east. Three dimensional *menorot* were part of the synagogue's furnishings, and representation of the *menorah* adorned the synagogue. The honorific of the "priest and teacher of wisdom" bring to bear the elements that might have made this synagogue holy: the presence and reading of the scrolls, the official status of its "priest and teacher," and the use of Temple imagery.

Much archaeological evidence of Jewish culture in the vicinity of Rome has been uncovered in recent centuries.[125] The only extant synagogue remains, however, were uncovered in 1961 at Ostia, the ancient port of Rome.[126] The synagogue building was first constructed toward the end of the first century of the Common Era, though it is doubtful that it served as a synagogue at this stage.[127] The building was enlarged and used as a synagogue the second and third, and was enlarged further and partly rebuilt at the beginning of the fourth. The triple entrances in the facade of the second-third century basilica are aligned toward the east-southeast, perhaps in the direction of Jerusalem. A stepped podium stood on the wall opposite the main entrance. Firm evidence for the existence of a Torah shrine in this building occurs in a Latin and Greek inscription that was used to repair the floor of the fourth century building:[128]

Torah shrine of the Ostia Synagogue.

> For the well-being of the emperor!
> Mindus Faustus established and built
> (it) and set up the ark (*keiboton*)
> of the Holy Torah (*nomo hagio*). . . .

Relevant to our discussion is the object of benefaction, "the ark for the holy Torah." We have seen that *hagios nomos* is used as early as the first century to describe the Torah. As Kraabel notes, *kibotos*, "ark," is "a word with heavy meanings in Jewish Greek, where it is used for the ark of Noah[129] and the Ark of the Covenant as well as the Torah shrine."[130]

During the fourth century the southernmost entrance portal on the eastern wall of the synagogue was sealed, and replaced with a Torah shrine. The Torah shrine was constructed as a large, free-standing aedicula.[131] It was built of *opus vittatum*—alternating courses of bricks and small tufa blocks—which was the standard building technique of fourth-century Ostia. The first phase of the shrine consisted of a large apse (3.62 m. wide), flanked by two small columns of marble with composite capitals (about 3.90 m. tall). Two architraves (measuring 1.82 x 0.31 m.) extended from the front of the apse, and rested on the capitols of the small columns. They end in identical corbels which were carved with the *menorah*, flanked by a *shofar* on the right and by a palm frond and an *ethrog* on the left. The *menorah* is ornamented with a carved designs imitating jewels. Traces of pigment that have been interpreted as glue for gilding were noted by the excavator. The outer sides of the architraves are carved with simple cornices, the inner sides were not properly finished; each bears a deep notch (about .18 m. deep and .26 m. wide), designed to carry a traverse member that probably supported a pediment. A low wall, approximately .75 m. from the back of the apse, ran across the aedicula and may have supported a cabinet for storing sacred scrolls. Originally, the shrine

Reconstruction drawing of the Ostia Synagogue Torah shrine.

was approached by a small podium, which was expanded at a later date. The later podium stood approximately .92 m. above the floor of the hall, and extended approximately 2.5 m. from front to back. It was built across the entire width of the aedicula and in front of the column bases. A flight of four steps (1.49 m. wide) was constructed on the face of the podium, at the center. The stairs are flanked by four

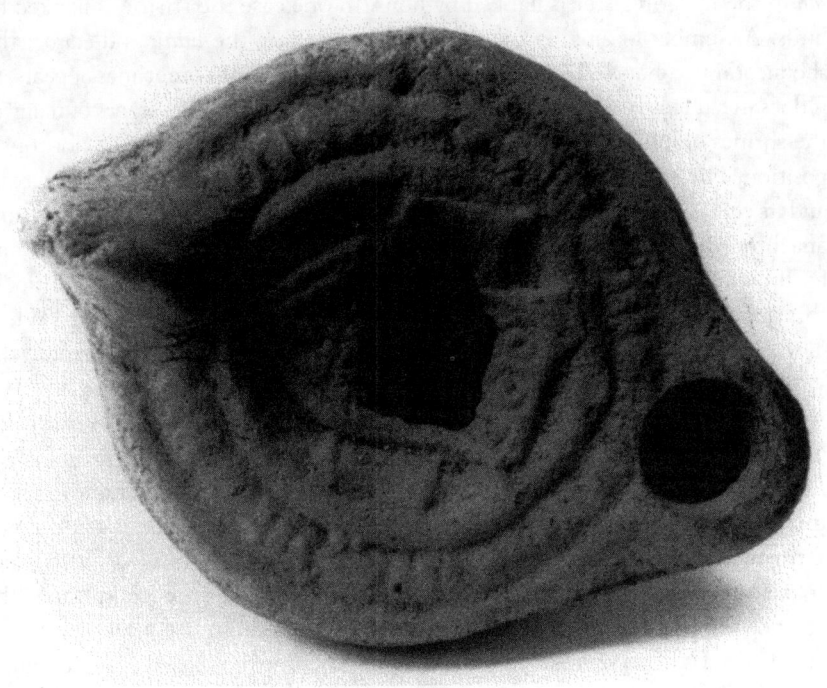

Oil Lamp with an image of a Torah shrine, discovered in Ostia.

small decorative niches, two on each side. These were faced with polychrome marble.

The *menorot* on the corbels specify the ethnicity of this community, and inject clear Temple imagery into the Torah shrine. The shrine was made much more impressive with the construction of the podium during the second stage. One can only wonder what types of objects were kept in the small niches on the base of the podium. The form of the renovated Torah shrine must have been much like the shrines represented in images that appear on oil lamps found in Ostia, one in the synagogue,[132] and in roughly contemporaneous images from the Roman catacombs.[133] As at Sardis, Gush Ḥalav, Meroth, and perhaps at Chorazin, the Torah shrine at Ostia was against the front wall of the fourth-century Ostia synagogue, and beside the main entrance.

In gold glass compositions the Torah shrine flanked by *menorot* often appears, as do images of one or two *menorot* in the lower register of some gold glasses. The *menorot* in turn are flanked by other ritual objects. In two cases the shrine is flanked not by *menorot*, but by lions, and in one exemplar a single *menorah* in the lower register is flanked by lions. In one case the shrine is flanked by birds. A number of smaller objects appear, including the *lulav* and *ethrog*, the shofar, and two-handled amphorae. The Torah scroll alone sometimes appears, as it does in catacomb wall paintings and inscriptions.[134] The open doors of many of the shrines emphasize the scrolls, which, as in Sardis, are stored in a horizontal position. The iconography of the scroll reflects a unique feature of the synagogue and its cult object. We have noted previously that the scroll form was by this time anachronistic, having been supplanted by the codex used for secular purposes and for liturgical uses in the church.[135] As in Palestine and in Chrysostom's Antioch, this anachronism seems to have been translated into greater holiness. While Christians used the codex form to signify their holy books, Jews emphasized the scroll form.[136]

The major symbolic elements illustrated in gold glass compositions were most probably elements of synagogue design, particularly the shrine (as at Ostia), the *menorot*, the lions and birds. A small fragment of a lion's mane discovered on the floor of the synagogue opposite the Torah shrine may suggest that the Ostia shrine was decorated with lions.[137] As we have seen, *menorot* and lions were synagogue furnishings both in Palestine and in Asia Minor. Open curtains frame the composition at the Villa Torlonia catacomb, as they do in the upper register of one gold glass. This suggests that the shrine area might be closed off by curtains, as in the Beth Alpha mosaic.[138]

One apparently Jewish gold glass, discovered "beneath the ruins of a cubiculum in the (Christian) cemetery of Sts. Peter and Marcellinus in 1882"[139] shows the image of a shrine, apparently flanked by free-standing columns. A lit *menorah* stands before the shrine, flanked by smaller appurtenances. The shrine stands within a closed compound and surrounded by smaller buildings and palm trees. The inscription around the picture of the shrine and the *menorah* "house of peace (*oikos ire[ne]s*). Accept a blessing (?) . . . . with all yours."[140] Scholars have identified this "house of peace" as Solomon's Temple, though it seems to me that it makes small difference whether this is Solomon's Temple, the Second Temple, or the desert Tabernacle. Goodenough[141] suggests that the inscription identifies the shrine as a tomb, while Hugo Gressmann,[142] followed by Sukenik,[143] identified it as a Torah shrine. Gressmann understood, however, the multivalent nature of this image: "I am inclined to believe that the heavenly temple is really meant here, or more exactly the heavenly Torah shrine in the form of the heavenly

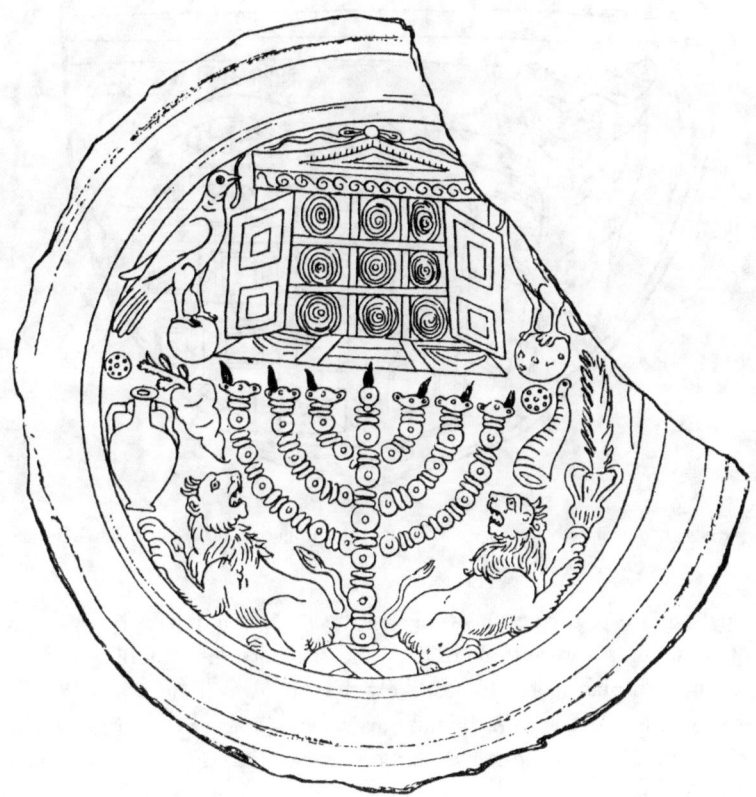

Gold glass with an image of a Torah shrine from the Jewish catacombs of Rome.

temple."[144] This ambiguity, as St. Clair notes, "reflects the desire of later Judaism to model its structures on ancient sacred models, particularly the Temple, as well as the tendency of the artist to represent such models in the familiar form of contemporary temple architecture."[145] In this gold glass illustration the dialectical relationship between the Torah shrine and Temple iconography becomes evident. Just as the Torah shrine was modeled upon the Temple of Jerusalem, the Temple of Jerusalem came to be seen in terms of the synagogal Torah shrine.[146] Extant Jewish gold glasses are the bases of drinking cups that were apparently used by their owners while they were still among the living, and suspended as grave markers after death. It is unknown how these cups were used by their owners, though some ceremonial context is possible. That this imagery was used to decorate lamps and glasses, the glasses having clearly been the possessions of

Gold glass fragment with an image of a Torah shrine from the Jewish catacombs of Rome.

individuals, points to the persuasiveness of this iconography. It is unclear why the sides of these glasses were broken away and the bottoms attached to the catacomb walls with plaster. It is quite likely that this was done as a relatively inexpensive way to place within the funerary setting imagery that otherwise might have been carved on stone grave markers or painted in costly wall paintings. From the synagogue, to the home, to the grave there were Jews in Rome who surrounded themselves in the imagery of the Torah shrine, bringing the holiness of the Torah scrolls and of the Temple itself into their lives (and into their afterlives).[147]

Summary

Evidence for synagogue sanctity in the diasporas during late antiquity is spotty. Babylonia is known only from literary sources, principally the Babylonian Talmud; while the Roman Diaspora is known from archaeological and non-Jewish literary sources. The sanctity of the sacred scrolls and the application of Temple motifs to the synagogue context was a component of synagogue sanctity throughout the Diaspora during late antiquity, as it was in the Land of Israel itself. This is reflected in literary as well as archaeological sources, in the Babylonian Talmud and in the writings of John Chrysostom. To be sure, communities must have had their own distinctive ways of expressing synagogue holiness, the magic ascribed to Antioch synagogues and the synagogue at the tomb of the Maccabean martyrs being prime examples. In Babylonia the synagogues of *Shaf ve-Yatev* and *Hutsal* served as objects of local patriotism, and thus were attributed with greater holiness than other Babylonian synagogues. These were the centers of Babylonian Jewry, places where sanctity had been firmly localized. The presence of an "ark" and free standing *menorot* within many extant Diaspora synagogues directly parallels the situation in Palestine, as does the use of the *menorah* and the Torah shrine in symbolic contexts. Leonard Rutgers[148] correctly suggests that "the fact that the same, confined repertoire of Jewish motifs recurs at most Jewish sites all over the Mediterranean, suggests that at least some coherent system of imagery existed in the symbolism of the depicted objects and that many Jews identified with this pictorial language." The common iconography of synagogues ranging from the Roman to the Sassanian empires eloquently expresses the "common Judaism" shared by Jews throughout this great expanse and the amazingly uniform way in which synagogue sanctity was expressed.

Conclusion

In this study we have traced the process by which late antique synagogues came to be considered "holy places." Beginning with the earliest synagogues during the Second Temple period, the cult object of the synagogue was the "Sacred Scripture" that was studied and probably stored there. The development of the synagogue was related to the increasing mobility of religion in Greco-Roman period away from temples and in the direction of smaller religious communities. While others focused upon the holy person, Jews set their attention upon their own cult objects, the scroll of the "Sacred Scriptures."

We have argued that the synagogue in the Land of Israel became the primary institutional locus for the Rabbinic revitalization of Judaism after the destruction of the Jerusalem Temple. Throughout its development Rabbinic sources show a tension between the mobility of the synagogue and the desire to root the synagogue in a more permanent manner. The conception that synagogues were "holy" was the ideological underpinning for this process, providing the essential rubric for the conceptual development of this institution throughout the Greco-Roman world. For the Rabbinic Sages the synagogue became the sacred institution of *zeman ha-zeh*, the time between the Temple's destruction and its ultimate messianic reconstruction. The synagogue was so successful that it itself was projected into sacred time. The notion of synagogue sanctity was embraced by Jews of various social groupings in late antique Palestine, as well as communities throughout the Greco-Roman and Babylonian diasporas. It is striking evidence of the "common Judaism" shared by Jewish communities the world over.

This is not to say that various communities did not have their own specific ways of expressing synagogue sanctity during late antiquity. We have discussed, for example, the "extra-holy" synagogues of Babylonia, the human bones deposited in the foundations of the Dura-Europos synagogue, and the exclusion of menstruating women from some synagogues in Palestine. Throughout the inhabited world (*oikomene*), however, two factors predominated in the sanctification of synagogues: the sanctity of the biblical scrolls that were publicly read (and often stored) in synagogues and the application of imagery derived from the Jerusalem Temple.

While hints of these factors exist in sources of the latter Second Temple period, they were first developed in a systematic way by the Tannaitic Sages. From Tannaitic literature onward the synagogue environment was differentiated from other settings as a realm of Torah. The reading of Scripture in the "holy tongue," the sounds of bells dangling from richly colored textiles in which the "holy writings" were wrapped, and the provisioning of other fine furnishings surely differentiated the Tannaitic period synagogue. One Tannaitic tradition suggests that the community aligned itself toward the chest, which was the focal point of the synagogue interior. This alignment is expressed with ever greater profundity in Amoraic, post-Amoraic, and archaeological sources from Palestine, where the Torah shrine and its compound were made increasingly larger and more ornate. The sanctity of the synagogue scrolls was acknowledged by Christians as well. John Chrysostom polemicized against Christian veneration of the synagogue scrolls in fourth-century Antioch. Jewish literary sources from Babylonia and archaeological sources from the Greco-Roman Diaspora reflect a situation similar to that which appears in Palestinian literature.

We have called the application of forms derived from the Jerusalem Temple to synagogues *imitatio templi*. This notion seems to appear in nascent form in a source from Qumran, though it is otherwise unknown in sources from the Second Temple period. *Imitatio templi* appears in Tannaitic sources in both subtle and less subtle ways. The notion of "ascent in holiness" with the Torah scroll at the pinnacle, for example, is apparently derived from the Temple context. Many of the rules of proper synagogue decorum described in Tannaitic sources are presented elsewhere as having been in effect in the Temple. Similarly, the great Alexandrian synagogue is described as having looked and functioned something like the Jerusalem Temple. Seven-branched *menorot* may have illuminated second-century Palestinian synagogues. According to one text synagogues were to be built at the high point of the town, doors open to the east like those of the Temple. The interior was to be aligned through the Torah cabinet toward Jerusalem. While communal prayer modeled upon the Temple service is evidenced in Second Temple period contexts, it seems to have been restricted to fringe groups like the Qumran community and the Masada rebels. After 70, however, such prayer was developed by the Tannaim and came to be localized in synagogues. On the model of the Temple, synagogues became places where through liturgy Jews could encounter the Divine.

In Amoraic and post-Amoraic literature synagogues were increasingly conceptualized in terms of the Temple. Synagogues and study houses are called "small temples" in one representative tradition. The Torah shrine was transformed into an "ark," a curtain named for the Temple veil suspended before it. In post-Amoraic Palestinian literature additional Temple forms and notions were applied to synagogues, including the burning of incense and the taboo against menstruating women entering sacred domain. Archaeological evidence from both Palestine and the Greco-Roman Diaspora parallel Palestinian literary sources. The large majority of the synagogues that have been excavated had Torah shrines that were aligned toward Jerusalem, and many were illuminated with seven-branched *menorot*.

Despite these developments, the application of Temple forms to synagogues never constituted more than a conceptual veneer. In an age when temple culture was the dominant form of religion, the Tannaim applied Temple language and concepts to synagogues. They were careful, however, that synagogues not become temples in their own right. Such safeguards do not appear in Amoraic or post-Amoraic literature. This may be attributable to a perception that temple culture was in decline, to the success of the Rabbinic movement, and to the increasingly distant and mythic Temple. By the close of Tannaitic literature the form of the synagogue was essentially set, and there was little concern that synagogues might become replacements for the Temple. As in Tannaitic literature, the application of Temple concepts and forms to synagogues legitimized contemporary practice. Temple categories provided the terminology through which holiness was expressed. The long-standing scholarly hypothesis that saw the synagogue as a "replacement" for the Temple has been shown to overly stress the importance of Temple imagery in the ideological formation of this institution. The transformation of synagogues into places where communities would assemble to encounter the Divine was often articulated in terms derived from the Temple. The sanctity of this institution was dependent in the most profound sense, however, upon the community and its sacred scrolls.

With this we have concluded our study of the sanctity of the synagogue in the Greco-Roman world: how it became a holy place and the factors that led to this development. Over the thirteen hundred or so years since the close of antiquity the synagogue and notions of synagogue sanctity have matured in ever new and always fascinating ways. Subsequent development of this institution has its roots in the rich soil of ancient Judaism and takes its nourishment from the sources that we have assembled and analyzed here. The Rabbinic sources that we have discussed were central to the development of the synagogue throughout the millennia. It is my hope that this discussion will prove useful to contemporary communities of every allegiance as they reenergize their sacred spaces and resanctify their sanctuaries. Whether constructed in medieval Prague, eighteenth-century Baghdad, or twentieth-century Baltimore, medieval and modern synagogues are in truth the spiritual descendants of the late antique synagogue. They are the progeny of those long lost meeting houses that were first called *hadain atra qadisha*, "this holy place."

Postscript

Reflections after Twenty Years

THIS HOLY PLACE WAS a step in a journey that began in my teen years and has continued ever since.[1] It reflects learning that commenced even before I entered the university and that continued as I—then a nice third-generation American Jewish boy from a San Diego suburb—trekked through the history of religions, art history, and Jewish history, stopping off, by and by, at the University of California, Santa Barbara, the University of Southern California, UCLA, various *yeshivot*, and (more than once) the Hebrew University of Jerusalem. Like many dissertation books, it is a palimpsest, reflecting the breadth of my academic experiences to that point. It also contains within it themes, issues, and subjects that I have continued to think about since. This trek reflects both my abiding curiosity as a historian and my personal search for meaning in the texts, artifacts, and approaches that I have encountered along the way. It is fair to say that *This Holy Place* has been with me from project to project, and from book to book.

Thinking about this research during the years that followed the publication of *This Holy Place*, I took the unusual (but not unheard of) step of

---

1. Many thanks to Joseph Angel, Jonathan Dauber, Vukan Marinković, and Ronnie Perelis for their insightful comments on this essay.

responding to its weaknesses in my second book, *Art and Judaism in the Greco-Roman World: Toward a New Jewish Archaeology* (Cambridge University Press, 2005; rev. ed., 2010). There I set out—in part—to expand upon many of the methodological issues of *This Holy Place* that I felt had been unresolved. My comments concluded the final section, "Reading Holistically: Art and the Liturgy of Late Antique Synagogues":

> Completing *This Holy Place*, I was left with the overwhelming sense that something was missing—that there was more to say, yet I did not know how to say it. This becomes painfully clear in my discussion of zodiac mosaics, where I frankly admitted that "I can think of no reason why this image in itself is holy..."[2] A decade after I penned these words, I look back upon them with the horror of a (more) mature scholar reading the work of a doctoral student. In defining synagogue sanctity, my approach was far too tied to the ways that late antique Jews might have verbalized this notion (that is, to "philology") and not focused enough upon the broader phenomenon. The zodiac and all the other imagery within synagogues did indeed form a single matrix, expressed in the notion of "holy place." Together with the Torah shrine, Temple imagery, inscriptions that often only Jews could read that praise donors through liturgically based formulae (and at Reḥov, instructed Jews how to live a sacred life), and the blatantly secular motifs decorating virtually all synagogue remains, the zodiac was (or at least, became) a projection of conceptions that are central to the "holy people" and its "holy Torah" (particularly in a "Holy Land" increasingly populated and controlled by Bible-reading colonialists). The synagogue was the place where this content was expressed and acted out, where the value concept (to borrow a term from Max Kadushin[3]) of *qedushah*, holiness, a central organizing principle of Jewish practice and belief, was given liturgical life. Every element of this "set" worked with every other to facilitate the notion of a synagogue as a "holy place"—an alternate and distinctly Jewish space. This is a sloppy definition, one for which earlier scholarship on the synagogue—and my own training—were ill prepared. It is, however, a most human

---

2. Fine, *This Holy Place*, 124.

3. Kadushin, *The Rabbinic Mind* (New York: Jewish Theological Seminary of America, 1952), 167–93, and Kadushin, *Worship and Ethics* (Evanston: Northwestern University Press, 1963), 216–34.

definition. Constructed in three and not two dimensions, my current approach does not assume a consecutive and authoritative narrative but a flowing notion of sanctity that flexed across categories and was never static—even as it coagulated in different ways within the bounds of the generally shared common Judaism as it developed through the very long period covered in this study. Kadushin's fluid notion of the value concept well describes the many themes and impulses that led to the construction, decoration, and maintenance of distinctly Jewish "holy places" throughout the Roman and Sasanian Empires.[4]

It has been more than a decade since I wrote this critique of my own work and nearly twenty years since *This Holy Place* went to press. I will refrain here from adding yet another level of reflection and mention only a few developments that affect the reception of this study.[5] The first-century Magdala synagogue, with its iconographically significant carved ashlar, may be of some significance. This stone bears the image of a large menorah, likely resting atop a square base.[6] This object—whatever its original purpose—supports my claim in *This Holy Place* that "the extant evidence [for synagogue holiness during the latter Second Temple period] stems from marginal groups within Jewish society of the time, the defenders of Masada, the Qumran sectarians, and Philo's Essene. There is no evidence to suggest that these phenomena were prevalent among wider segments of Jewish society, though that may be a factor of our sources and not representative of historical reality."[7] The menorah from Magdala suggests an interest in Temple themes within a nonsectarian context. For sheer ingenuity, the life-size first-century synagogue model at Nazareth Village and the stone-by-stone reconstruction of the late antique Umm el-Qanatir synagogue, especially the Torah shrine, deserve special mention. Each

---

4. Fine, *Art and Judaism in the Greco-Roman World*, 209–11.

5. *Art and Judaism*, xv–xxii, and *Art, History and the Historiography of Judaism in Roman Antiquity* (Boston: Brill, 2013), 1–19.

6. See my essay "The Magdala Ashlar: From Synagogue Furnishing to Media Event," in *Symposium: Constructing and Deconstructing Jewish Art*, ed. Ilia Rodov, Mirjam Rajner, and Sara Offenberg (forthcoming).

7. Fine, *This Holy Place*, 33.

conveys a taste of being "inside" an ancient synagogue environment, an experience that I have striven for throughout my career.⁸

In recent years, I had imagined that I had (finally) moved on from *This Holy Place*—until just recently when a Yeshiva University doctoral student, participating in my historiography seminar, brought me back to it again. In that course, I asked each student to choose one historian, read all of her or his oeuvre, do archival research, and explore the relationships between the published work, archival sources, and the time in which this work was carried out. With quite a bit of chutzpah, Vukan Marinković, a student of Jewish thought and not of ancient Judaism, asked to write about . . . *me*. I laughingly agreed, gave him access to my files, and was fascinated with the result. Marinković focused his analysis on *This Holy Place*. His study hit on a point that I had long ago put aside—and nearly forgotten. Marinković argued that a main argument of my book was not directed exclusively to the Jewish history/ancient Judaism/late antiquity conversation—though it was certainly most at home there and caused some ripples. Marinković adduced, correctly, that my main argument was with the basic structures of the history of religions as then practiced—a direct response to Mircea Eliade and his foundational volume, *The Sacred and the Profane: The Nature of Religion* (1959). Marinković perceptively argued that Eliade, and the history of religions broadly, was at the core of my project (and in many ways still is).

This Holy Place was indeed a kind of return to Eliade, to my *gersa de-yanquta* (as the ancient rabbis called it), to my earliest university studies. I encountered him in the fall of 1976 in a freshman introduction to religious studies course at the University of California, Santa Barbara. It was, I now know, a best books course—not of religious traditions, as I had expected, but of religious phenomenology. Readings ranged from John G. Neihardt's *Black Elk Speaks: Being the Life Story of a Holy Man of the Oglala Sioux* (1932) to Carlos Castaneda's *Teachings of Don Juan: A Yaqui Way of Knowledge* (1968); to theoretical classics like William James' *Varieties of Religious Experience* (1902) and Eliade's *Sacred and the Profane*. All of this was common fare in religious studies at UCSB, where the spirit of Eliade's "Chicago School" predominated⁹

---

8. On Nazareth Village, see Joel Kauffman, *The Nazareth Jesus Knew* (Nazareth: Nazareth Village, 2005); on Umm el-Qanatir, see Chaim Ben-David, "Um el-Kanatir: Putting Humpty Dumpty Back Together Again," *Biblical Archaeology Review* 42 (2016), 40–49.

9. For a generally affirmative presentation of these scholars by an Eliade student, see

and Joseph Campbell, with his associations with the nascent Pacifica Graduate Institute and the Esalen Institute to the north in Big Sur,[10] was in the air. A famously individualistic, experimental, and "secular" religious culture predominated. Of all the readings in that course, Eliade's volume was most significant to my development. In Eliade I found a theory of "sacred place" that seemingly explained a phenomenon that had long attracted me. His theory of *hierophany*, of divine intervention in space, creating a unique and eternal *axis mundi*, seemed to explain the religious significance of the Jerusalem Temple in broad and universal terms.

I was smitten, and the cultural environment, both within the university and beyond, reinforced my admiration. Eliade's approach fit well with a work that I had studied intensely while in high school, Erwin R. Goodenough's thirteen-volume *Jewish Symbols in the Greco-Roman Period* (1953–68), with its seemingly authoritative and, again, comparative approach. Relying upon a kind of Jungian interpretation of archaeological remains, Goodenough's magnum claimed to discover a "mystical Judaism" that was at odds with the religion of the ancient rabbis (whose literature, it turned out, he could not read without the mediation of translation and modern interpreters). Little did I know that a third "hero" of my college education, the venerable doyen of Jewish mysticism, Gershom Scholem,[11] was also part of a scholarly collegium known as the Eranos circle that met yearly in Ascona, Switzerland, a group that was convened by Carl Gustav Jung.[12] Eliade, Goodenough, and Camp-

Robert S. Ellwood, *The Politics of Myth: A Study of C. G. Jung, Mircea Eliade, and Joseph Campbell* (Albany: SUNY Press, 1999). This should be read in conjunction with Steven M. Wasserstrom, *Religion After Religion: Gershom Scholem, Mircea Eliade, and Henry Corbin at Eranos* (Princeton: Princeton University Press, 1999) and Moshe Idel, *Mircea Eliade: From Magic to Myth* (New York: P. Lang, 2014).

10. On Campbell and Esalen, see Jeffrey J. Kripal, *Esalen: America and the Religion of No Religion* (Chicago: University of Chicago Press, 2007), 188–92. See also "Joseph Campbell and Pacifica Graduate Institute," http://www.pacifica.edu/joseph-campbell-at-pacifica.

11. For my experience of Scholem while at UCSB, see my "Review of Gershom Scholem, *Magen David: Toldotav shel Semel* (*The Star of David: History of a Symbol*), ed. A. Shapira, tr. and ed. G. Hazan-Rokem (Ein Harod: Mishkan Le-Omanut, 2008), Hebrew," *Images: A Journal of Jewish Art and Visual Culture* 5 (2011) 128–30.

12. Wasserstrom, *Religion After Religion*. See now: Noam Zadoff, *From Berlin to Jerusalem and Back: Gershom Scholem between Israel and Germany* (Jerusalem: Carmel, 2015), 294–331, Hebrew.

bell were also members of this group. It was dedicated—each "mythologist" in his own way—to uncovering and foregrounding the religious experience of the individual virtuoso, religion beyond authority structures, and universal experience. Little did I know that under the eucalyptus trees and blue skies of Santa Barbara, I was an inductee to a modern mystery religion of its own making—in an environment that reinforced and was supported by the larger (unstated) tenants of this new religion.

My infatuation with this culture began its slow descent soon after I landed at Lod Airport near Tel Aviv to begin my junior year of study at the Hebrew University of Jerusalem (1977–78). These were the glory years of the Hebrew University, and I was fortunate to study with the best—folklorist Dov Noy, historian Isaiah Gafni, historical geographer Yehoshua Ben Arieh, art historian Bezalel Narkiss, city planner Israel Kimhi, and many others. Perhaps most importantly, I spent the year as an intern (and assistant to Professor Narkiss) in the Department of Judaica of the Israel Museum, my charge from curator Chaya Benjamin being to "touch and get to know every object in the collection." I studied artifacts and texts, art, archaeology, Talmud and Midrash, learning to focus on the small before asking the kinds of big questions that had dominated my earlier education. Each of these scholars influenced me profoundly, slowly convincing me that great history is in the details and that what we call today "micro-history" must proceed—and never follow after—macro-theories.

My MA studies in art history (at USC, especially my engagement with Pratapaditya Pal) and much of my doctoral program (under the mentorship of Amos Funkenstein at UCLA, then in Jerusalem with Lee Levine and Lawrence Schiffman) were spent working out my early fascination with the "big ideas" of the history of religions and my love of philology (particularly of rabbinic literature), close reading, artifacts—and most of all, the real people whom I had taken it upon myself to "find" between the manuscripts and rocks that are all that now remain of Jews in the Greco-Roman world. In my dissertation, the base text for *This Holy Place*, I returned to Eliade, this time hoping to avoid the pitfalls of overgeneralization and "phenomenology," yet hoping to maintain the sense of largeness and experience that I so appreciated in his work. As a beginning academic, I was (naively) astonished that Eliade's "phenomenology of religion" left no place for synagogues, churches, and mosques as holy places, even though late antique synagogues, the topic of my interest, were labeled explicitly as "holy places" in their inscriptions and in literary sources. How could a synagogue be holy to ancient Jews but not to the modern master of spatial sanctity? I was aware that a wholesale re-evaluation of Eliade was underway in the American academy, both within religious studies (by Jonathan Z. Smith and others) and beyond. It was time to respond, I thought, from within Jewish studies.

I engaged the then-recent scholarship of Peter Brown, with his emphasis upon the "sacred" in late antiquity, the still new anthropological turn of history later associated with Clifford Geertz and Victor Turner, and the liturgically focused art history of Thomas Matthews.[13] I hoped to explain the "sanctity" of the synagogue from the inside out, rather than imposing theory on my subjects. With Brown, I adopted a synthetic discourse, positing a "Jewish koine" that paralleled both his late antique "Christian koine" and the "common Judaism" that E. P. Sanders sees in the various Jewish expressions known from Jewish texts of the Second Temple period. I particularly appreciated Brown's often exuberant regard for his subjects, which I sought to emulate. Taking on this approach, I was responding directly to Goodenough's sectarianization—even marginalization—of the ancient rabbis, a notion promoted actively by his younger colleague, the Scholem acolyte Morton Smith, and in differing though recognizable ways by Smith's students. This approach was then widespread among American scholars of ancient Judaism. After my experience with a rather totalizing (and often anti-clerical) history of religions, I was not convinced. At the urging of my advisors, I left this issue for my next book.

I explored the thought of Erwin Goodenough, Morton Smith, and Smith's students in great detail in *Art and Judaism*, laying out for the first time the intellectual and communal roots of their project.[14] It was only as Dan Brown's *The Da Vinci Code* (2003) was reaching the apex of popularity (and my students were asking me questions based on the novel), however, that I reluctantly returned to

---

13. See my *Art, History and the Historiography of Judaism in the Greco-Roman World*, 5–16. What I did not recognize there, however, was my continuing engagement with the "Chicago School."

14. Gershom Scholem and Morton Smith, *Morton Smith and Gershom Scholem, Correspondence 1945–1982*, ed. and introduced by Guy G. Stroumsa. (Leiden: Brill, 2008). Scholem evaluated the Eranos phenomenon in a letter to Smith dated dated December 30, 1950 (pp. 50–51).

reread Eliade, his students, and his fellow travelers.[15] I was not surprised when Brown identified Campbell as a major influence, nor that George Lucas had forged a strong bond with him through his *Star Wars* trilogy (1977–83). I revisited questions of symbols as interpreted by historians of religion and lectured widely as a real live "symbologist" (a term devised by Brown to describe the professor-hero of his novel).[16] My newest book, *The Menorah: From the Bible to Modern Israel* (Harvard University Press, 2016), explores this preeminent Jewish "symbol" not through the essentializing lenses of Jung, Goodenough, Eliade, Campbell, and the like but as an actual historical phenomenon. Few scholars take the theses developed by these mid-century thinkers seriously anymore—except as examples of mid-century thinking. The legacies of Eliade, Campbell, and Jung are further tainted by their rightist—in Eliade's case, nearly fascist—associations and by predilections against Jews and Judaism (they didn't much like Christianity either!). In general, scholarship has developed less explicitly globalizing approaches—often, alas, choosing the. In the "big world," however—from *Star Wars* to *The Da Vinci Code*—Jung, Eliade, and (most of all) Campbell are alive, well, and meaningful. In a real sense, *The Menorah* forms a continuum with *This Holy Place*, being yet another response to the big and diachronic questions raised by these now troubling scholars and the implications of their approaches for contemporary culture. Once again, I begin by mulling over their questions, though I provide very different historically, philologically, and art historically grounded answers. Still, my framing of both *The Menorah* and this short essay

---

15. Regarding my reluctance, see my review of *The Hermeneutics of Sacred Architecture: Experience, Interpretation, Comparison*, by Lindsay Jones, *Religion* 34 (2004) 253–56. See "Dan Brown: By the Book," *New York Times Sunday Book Review*, June 23, 2012, 8. On Lucas and Campbell, see, for example, Joseph Campbell, *The Hero's Journey: The World of Joseph Campbell; Joseph Campbell on His Life and Work*, ed. Phil Cousineau (San Francisco: Harper & Row, 1990).

16. In a related development, see my 2007 comments on the Society for Biblical Literature's website, "Concerning the Jesus Family Tomb," *SBL Forum*, http://sbl-site.org/article.aspx?articleid=655. There I refer to the "Da Vinci codification" of our culture. More recently, see my *Art, History and the Historiography of Judaism in Roman Antiquity*, 160–80. See also the comments of Ariel Sabar, "The Unbelievable Tale of Jesus's Wife," *The Atlantic*, July/August 2016, http://www.theatlantic.com/magazine/archive/2016/07/the-unbelievable-tale-of-jesus-wife/485573/. I return to this theme in "The Magdala Ashlar: From Synagogue Furnishing to Media Event."

as a personal "trek" is largely beholden to these authors, for whom such "heroic" personal journeys are central to religious experience.

I am thrilled that *This Holy Place* is again in print, nearly twenty years since its original publication. I invite you to join me on the path that leads through it on my search of the holy, the tactile, and the deeply human in the Jewish historical experience.

Steven Fine
Yeshiva University
New York

Notes

Preface

1. On *Guernica*, see H. Chipp, *Picasso's Guernica: History, Transformations, Meanings* (Berkeley and Los Angeles: University of California Press, 1988).
2. Synagogue and Sanctity: The Late Antique Palestinian Synagogue as a "Holy Place," doctoral dissertation, Hebrew University of Jerusalem, 1993.
3. *Sacred Realm: The Emergence of the Synagogue of the Ancient World*, ed. S. Fine (New York: Oxford University Press, 1996). A related project that influenced my academic development in unexpected ways will appear as S. Fine and L. B. Fine, *Where God Dwells: A Child's History of the Synagogue* (Los Angeles: Torah Aura, forthcoming), especially chapter 3.
4. 2 Kings 8:4; y. Megillah 3:1, 73d.

Introduction

1. This poem is reproduced in *Stone Bird: Jerusalem in Modern Hebrew Poetry*, ed. H. Be'er (Tel Aviv: Shva Publishers, 1983), 66, Hebrew. It first appeared in the newspaper *Lamerhav*, January 4, 1963.
2. On the sanctity of the synagogue in modern American Judaism, see B. Litvin, *The Sanctity of the Synagogue* (Hoboken: Ktav, 1987); L. A. Hoffman, *Beyond the Text* (Bloomington: University of Indiana Press, 1989), 149–171, esp. 152–153; S. Schechter, "Lovingkindness and Truth," in *Seminary Addresses and Other Papers* (New York: Arno Press and The New York Times, 1969), 251–253.
3. On the history of the synagogue in general, see S. W. Baron, *A Social and Economic History of the Jews* (New York: Columbia University Press, 1958–1983), *passim*. On synagogue art and architecture, see *Jewish Art*, ed. C. Roth, 2nd ed. (London: Vallentine, Mitchell, 1971), 103–131, 275–285; C. H. Krinsky, *Synagogues of Europe: Architecture, History, Meaning* (New York and Cambridge, Mass.: M.I.T. Press, 1985). On the American synagogue, see S. C. Heilman, *Synagogue Life: A Study in Symbolic Interaction* (Chicago and

London: University of Chicago Press, 1976), and the articles in *The American Synagogue: A Sanctuary Transformed*, ed. J. Wertheimer (New York, 1987).

4. All of the terms used to designate the period or periods between the coming of Alexander the Great to the East and the Fatimid dynasty are problematic in one way or the other. We use "late antiquity" to refer to the period after the destruction of the Jerusalem Temple in 70 C.E., continuing through the early Islamic period. This designation corresponds with the "Period of the Mishnah and Talmud" and with the later "Greco-Roman Period."

5. In this study "sacred" and "holy" are used as synonyms. On the semantic ranges of these terms, see W. G. Oxtoby, "The Idea of the Holy," in the *Encyclopedia of Religion*, ed. M. Eliade (New York and London: Macmillan, 1987), 413–438.

6. On Tannaitic literature, the *Talmudim* and the *Midrashim* in general, see H. L. Strack and G. Stemberger, *Introduction to the Talmud and Midrash*, tr. M. Bockmuehl (Edinburgh: T. & T. Clark, 1992), 119–244, 254–393. On Targum: P. Alexander, "Jewish Aramaic Translations of Hebrew Scriptures," in *Mikra*, ed. M. J. Mulder (Assen/Maastricht: Van Gorgum and Philadelphia: Fortress Press, 1990), 217–253. On Prayer and Piyyut: I. Elbogen, *Jewish Liturgy: A Comprehensive History*, tr. R. P. Scheindlin (Philadelphia: Jewish Publication Society, 1993); E. Fleischer, *Hebrew Liturgical Poetry in the Middle Ages* (Jerusalem: Keter, 1975), 23–275. On Post-Talmudic legal (halakhic) literature from the Land of Israel: Z. Safrai, "Post-Talmudic Halakhic Literature in the Land of Israel," in *Literature of the Sages*, tr. S. Safrai (Assen/Maastricht: Van Gorgum and Philadelphia: Fortress Press, 1987). See the extensive bibliographies cited by each.

7. S. Krauss, *Synagogale Altertümer* (Berlin and Vienna: B. Harz, 1922).

8. Though their excavations took place between 1905 and 1907, the final report was not published until 1916 as *Antike synagogen in Galilaea* (Leipzig: J. C. Heinrich, 1916).

9. See, most recently, *Ancient Synagogues: Historical Analysis and Archaeological Discovery*, ed. D. Urman and P. V. M. Flesher (Leiden: E. J. Brill, 1995), and my review of this collection in *Biblical Archaeology Review* 22 (1996).

10. E. R. Goodenough, *Jewish Symbols in the Greco-Roman Period* (New York: Pantheon, 1953–1968).

11. M. Smith, "Goodenough's Jewish Symbols in Retrospect," *Journal of Biblical Literature* 86 (1967): 66. In this essay Smith discusses the reviews of Goodenough until 1967. The most important discussion of Goodenough to appear since then is R. Brilliant, "Jewish Symbols: Is That Still Good Enough?" in *Commentaries on Roman Art: Selected Studies* (London: Pindar, 1994), 233–244.

12. G. F. Moore, *Judaism in the First Centuries of the Common Era* (Cambridge, Mass.: Harvard University Press, 1927–1930).

13. See, for example, S. Krauss, *Synagogale Altertümer*.

14. See M. Smith, "Goodenough's Jewish Symbols"; R. Brilliant, "Is That Still Good Enough?" 243–244.

15. For the interpretation of visual images, Erwin Panofsky's work, though somewhat dated, is still basic. See Panofsky, *Meaning of the Visual Arts* (Garden City: Doubleday,

1955), especially 26–54. For the history of methodological approaches in the history of art, see W. E. Kleinbauer, *Modern Perspectives in Art History* (Toronto: University of Toronto Press, 1994). More recent approaches are surveyed by N. Bryson, M. A. Holly, and K. Moxey, *Visual Culture: Images and Interpretations* (Hanover: University Press of New England, 1994). On the relationship between church art, architecture, and liturgy, see T. F. Mathews, *The Early Churches of Constantinople: Architecture and Liturgy* (University Park, Penn.: Pennsylvania State University Press, 1971); S. De Blaauw, "Architecture and Liturgy in Late Antiquity and the Middle Ages: Traditions and Trends in Modern Scholarship," *Archiv für Liturgie-Wissenschaft* 33.1 (1991): 1–34; S. Sinding-Larsen, *Iconography and Ritual: A Study of Analytical Perspectives* (Oslo: Universitetsforlaget As, 1984); Gier Hellemo, *Adventus Domini: Escathological Thought in 4th-Century Apses and Catecheses* (Leiden: E. J. Brill, 1989). On the application of liturgical models to synagogue art: S. Fine, "Art and the Liturgical Context of the Sepphoris Synagogue Mosaic," in *Proceedings of the Second International Conference on Galilee*, ed. E. M. Meyers et al. (Atlanta: Scholars Press, forthcoming).

16. S. Lieberman, *Greek in Roman Palestine* (New York: Jewish Theological Seminary, 1942), 5.

17. See J. Neusner, *Development of a Legend* (Leiden: E. J. Brill, 1970); W. S. Green, "What's in a Name? The Problematic of Rabbinic Biography," in *Approaches to Ancient Judaism: Theory and Practice* (Missoula: Scholars Press, 1978); D. Goodblatt, "Towards the Rehabilitation of Talmudic History," in *History of Judaism: The Next Ten Years*, ed. B. Bokser (Chino: Scholars Press, 1980), 34–35.

18. On Rabbinic literature as a historical source, see Goodblatt, "Towards the Rehabilitation"; S. S. Miller, *Studies in the History and Traditions of Sepphoris* (Leiden: E. J. Brill, 1984), 8–12; L. I. Levine, *The Rabbinic Class of Roman Palestine* (Jerusalem: Ben Zvi Institute, New York: Jewish Theological Seminary, 1989), 16–22, and bibliography cited by each.

19. B. M. Bokser, "Rabbinic Responses to Catastrophe: From Continuity to Discontinuity," *Proceedings of the American Academy of Jewish Research* 50 (1983): 37–61; "The Wall Separating God and Israel," *Jewish Quarterly Review* 73, no. 4 (1983): 349–374; *The Origin of the Seder* (Berkeley and Los Angeles: University of California Press, 1984); "Approaching Sacred Space," *Harvard Theological Review* 78, nos. 1–3 (1985): 279–299; and "Rabbinic Continuity and Revisions in the Notion of Sacred Space: Applying Deuteronomy 23:10–15," *Proceedings of the Ninth World Congress of Jewish Studies*, Division C (1986), 7–14.

20. See most recently J. L. Rubinstein, *The History of Sukkot in the Second Temple and Rabbinic Periods* (Atlanta: Scholars Press, 1995) and his comments on the limits of this approach (pp. 6–7).

21. See Lieberman's comment cited above and D. Sperber, *Material Culture in Eretz–Israel during the Talmudic Period* (Jerusalem: Ben Zvi Institute, 1993), 7–9.

22. See L. Jacobs, "Are There Fictitious Baraitot in the Babylonian Talmud?" *Hebrew Union College Annual* 42 (1971): 185–196.

23. For example, D. Sperber, "On the Unfortunate Adventures of Rav Kahana: A Passage of Saboraic Polemic from Sasanian Persia," *Irano-Judaica* 1 (1982): 83–100.
24. See especially Neusner, *Development of a Legend*; J. Fraenkel, "Hermeneutical Problems in the Study of the Aggadic Narrative," *Tarbiz* 47 (1978): 140–358.
25. See Neusner, *Development of a Legend*; P. Schäfer, *Die Vorstellung vom heiligen Geist in der rabbinischen Literatur* (Munich: Kosel-Verlag, 1972); D. Goodblatt, *Rabbinic Instruction in Sassanian Babylonia* (Leiden: E. J. Brill, 1975); Bokser, *Origin of the Seder*; S. D. Fraade, *From Tradition to Commentary: Torah and Its Interpretation in the Midrash Sifre to Deuteronomy* (Albany: State University of New York Press, 1991).
26. E. P. Sanders, *Paul and Palestinian Judaism* (London and Philadelphia: Fortress Press, 1977), 69–70.
27. This phenomenon is discussed by P. V. M. Flesher, "Rereading the Reredos: David, Orpheus and Messianism in the Dura Europos Synagogue," in *Ancient Synagogues: Historical Analysis and Archaeological Discovery*, ed. D. Urman and P. V. M. Flesher (Leiden: E. J. Brill, 1995), 2.346–366, who in turn underestimates the messianic content of the Dura Europos synagogue wall paintings. See also Z. Weiss and E. Netzer, *Promise and Redemption: A Synagogue Mosaic from Sepphoris* (Jerusalem: Israel Museum, 1996); S. Fine, "Art and the Liturgical Context."
28. S. Mac Cormack, *Art and Ceremony in Late Antiquity* (Berkeley and Los Angeles: University of California Press, 1981), 10.
29. Krauss, *Synagogale Altertümer*, 17–18, 66–102, 413–433; M. Hengel, "Die Synagogeninschrift von Stobi," *Zeitschrift für die neutestamentliche Wissenschaft* 57 (1966): 173–174; A. T. Kraabel, "The Diaspora Synagogue: Archaeological and Epigraphic Evidence since Sukenik," *Aufstieg und Niedergang der Römische Welt* (Berlin and New York: Walther de Gruyter, 1979), 502; K. Schubert, "The Holiness of the Synagogue and Its Figurative Decoration," in *Jewish Historiography and Iconography in Early and Medieval Christianity*, eds. H. Schreckenberg and K. Schubert (Assen/Maastricht: Van Gorgum and Minneapolis: Fortress Press, 1992), 162. See also H. W. Turner, *From Temple to Meeting Place: The Phenomenology and Theology of Places of Worship* (The Hague: Mouton, 1972).
30. Kraabel, "The Diaspora Synagogue," 502.
31. S. J. D. Cohen, "The Temple and the Synagogue," in *The Temple in Antiquity*, ed. T. G. Madsen (Provo: Brigham Young University Press, 1984), 151–174. See also Cohen, "Pagan and Christian Evidence on the Ancient Synagogue," in *The Synagogue in Late Antiquity*, ed. L. I. Levine (Philadelphia: American Schools for Oriental Research, 1987), 163–164.
32. S. J. D. Cohen, "The Temple and the Synagogue," 168–169.
33. J. Lightstone, *The Commerce of the Sacred: Mediation of the Divine among Jews in the Greco-Roman Diaspora* (Chico: Scholars Press, 1984), 119.
34. See L. I. Levine, "From Community Center to Small Temple: The Furnishings and Interior Design of Ancient Synagogues," *Cathedra* 60 (1991): 79–84; "The Nature and Origin of the Palestinian Synagogue Reconsidered," *Journal of Biblical Literature* 115, no. 3 (1966): 445–447; see Z. Safrai, "From Synagogue to Little Temple," *Proceedings of the Tenth*

World Congress in Jewish Studies, Division B (Jerusalem, 1990) and recently "From House of Assembly to Miniature Temple," *Israel People and Land* 6–7 (1991–1993); M. Goodman, "Sacred Space in Diaspora Judaism," in *Studies on the Jewish Diaspora in the Hellenistic and Roman Periods* (=*Te'uda 12*) ed. B. Isaac and A. Oppenheimer (Tel Aviv: Tel Aviv University Press, 1996). Their use of sources and independent conclusions often parallel my own. I thank Professor Goodman for making his essay available to me prior to its publication. J. M. Branham has written extensively on the sanctity of the ancient synagogue, bringing to bear methods developed by scholars of literature. Branham focuses on the synagogue as a "competitor" with the Temple for sanctity. Her approach, which does not sufficiently take into account the philological backgrounds of the texts discussed, is a variant of the replacement hypothesis. See Branham, "Sacred Space under Erasure in Ancient Synagogues and Churches," *Art Bulletin* 74 (1992); "Vicarious Sacrality: Temple Space in Ancient Synagogues," in *Ancient Synagogues: Historical Analysis and Archaeological Discovery,* ed. D. Urman and P. V. M. Flesher (Leiden: E. J. Brill, 1995) and my review of her thesis in "'Chancel' Screens in Late Antique Palestinian Synagogues: A Genizah Source," in *Religious and Ethnic Communities in Late Roman Palestine,* ed. H. Lapin (College Park, Md.: University of Maryland, forthcoming).

35. L. I. Levine, "The Nature and Origin of the Palestinian Synagogue Reconsidered," 447. On the early Christian *hieros topos,* see P. C. Finney, "Hieros Topos and christlicher Sakralbau un vorkonstantinischer Ueberliegerung," *Boreas* 7 (1984). H. L. Kessler, "Through the Veil: The Holy Image in Judaism and Christianity," in *Studies in Pictorial Narrative* (London: Pindar, 1994), contrasts Jewish and Christian approaches. See below, p. 206, n. 248. On the development of Christian "holy places" and "holy land," see E. D. Hunt, *Holy Land Pilgrimage in the Later Roman Empire a.d. 312–460* (Oxford: Oxford University Press, 1982); P. W. L. Walker, *Holy City, Holy Places?* (Oxford: Oxford University Press, 1991); R. Wilken, *The Land Called Holy: Palestine in Christian History and Thought* (New Haven: Yale University Press, 1993); R. A. Markus, "How on Earth Could Places Become Holy? Origins of the Christian Idea of Holy Places," *Journal of Early Christian Studies* 2, no. 3 (1994), 257–271.

36. E. P. Sanders, *Judaism: Practice and Belief 63 BCE–66 CE* (London and Philadelphia: Trinity International, 1992), ix. See the very different reviews of Sanders' approach by M. Hengel and R. Deines, "E. P. Sanders' 'Common Judaism', Jesus, and the Pharisees," *Journal of Theological Studies,* New Series, 46 (1995): 1–70 and of J. Neusner, *Ancient Judaism and Modern Category Formation* (New York: University Press of America, 1986), 111–119; B. Chiton and J. Neusner, *Judaism in the New Testament: Practices and Beliefs* (London and New York: Routledge, 1995).

37. E. P. Sanders, *Judaism: Practice and Belief,* esp. 47–51; *Paul and Palestinian Judaism,* esp. 419–428. A similar approach is suggested by L. Schiffman, *From Text to Tradition: A History of the Second Temple and Rabbinic Judaism* (Hoboken: Ktav, 1991), 4–5, and J. Burtchaell, *From Synagogue to Church: Public Services and Offices in the Earliest Christian Communities* (Cambridge: Cambridge University Press, 1992), xiii–xv.

38. P. Brown, *Society and the Holy in Late Antiquity* (Berkeley and Los Angeles: University of California Press, 1989), 166–195, esp. 173, 181.

39. Approaches to "sacred space" in the "history of religions" are surveyed and evaluated by R. Friedland and R. Hecht, "The Politics of Sacred Space: Jerusalem's Temple Mount/al-haram al sharif," in *Sacred and Profane Spaces: Essays in the Geographics of Judaism, Christianity, and Islam*, ed. J. Scott and P. Simpson-Housely (New York: Greenwood Press, 1991). On Eliade's approach, see M. Eliade, *The Sacred and the Profane: The Nature of Religion* (New York: Harper and Row, 1961); K. Rudolph, "Mircea Eliade and the 'History' of Religions," tr. G. D. Alles, *Religion* 19 (1989); L. Hoffman, *Covenant of Blood: Circumcision and Gender in Rabbinic Judaism* (Chicago and London: University of Chicago Press, 1996), 156–157. J. Branham extensively engages Eliade's approach as it impacts on ancient synagogue studies. She is absolutely correct that "The late-antique synagogue does not share in the definition of sacred space that Eliade associates with the Jerusalem Temple" ("Vicarious Sacrality: Temple Space in Ancient Synagogues," 330).

40. J. Z. Smith, *Map Is Not Territory: Studies in the History of Religions* (Leiden: E. J. Brill, 1978), 291–293.

41. Ibid., 187.

42. P. Brown, *The World of Late Antiquity* (London: Thames and London, 1971), 96–103; *Society and the Holy*, 5–8, 163–165.

43. P. Brown, "Art and Society in Late Antiquity," in *The Age of Spirituality: A Symposium*, ed. K. Weitzmann (New York, 1980); *The Cult of Saints* (Chicago and London: University of Chicago Press, 1981); and *Society and the Holy*, 6–7.

44. P. Brown, *Cult of Saints*; *Society and the Holy*, 6–7.

45. See M. Barasch, *Icon: Studies in the History of an Idea* (New York: New York University Press, 1992); P. Brown and S. Mac Cormack, "Artifices of Eternity," in *Society and the Holy in Late Antiquity*, ed. P. Brown (Berkeley and Los Angeles: University of California Press, 1989).

46. P. Brown, "Art and Society in Late Antiquity," 25.

47. Sanctity in biblical literature has recently been discussed by P. Jenson, *Graded Holiness: A Key to the Priestly Conception of the World* (Sheffield: Sheffield University Press, 1992) and by D. Wright, "Holiness, Old Testament," *Anchor Bible Dictionary*, ed. D. N. Freedman (New York: Doubleday, 1992), though a comprehensive study of the implications of q-d-sh has yet to be written. Sanctity in the Apocryphal and Pseudepigraphic literature surveyed by A. Fridrichsen also seems to parallel biblical models (*Hagios-Qados: Ein Beitrag zu den Voruntersuchungen zur Christlichen Begriffsgeschichte, Skrifter utgit av Videnskapsselskapet i Kristiania* [Kristiania: J. Dywad, 1916], 53–64). For partial sources in Qumran literature and most sources in Tannaitic literature, see Academy of the Hebrew Language, *The Historical Dictionary of the Hebrew Language: Materials for the Dictionary, Series I, 200 B.C.E.–300 C.E.* (Jerusalem: Academy of the Hebrew Language, 1988): 15933–16033. On biblical, Rabbinic, and later literature, see E. Ben Yehuda, *A Complete Dictionary of Ancient and Modern Hebrew* (New York: Thomas Yoseloff, 1959), 12: 5775–5801.

48. A. Marmorstein, *The Doctrine of Merits in Old Rabbinic Literature and the Old Rabbinic Doctrine of God* (New York: Ktav, 1968), 208–217. M. Kadushin, *The Rabbinic Mind* (New York: Jewish Theological Seminary, 1952), 167–193, and *Worship and Ethics* (Chicago

and London: University of Chicago Press, 1964), 216–234. On Kadushin's methodology, see J. Goldin, "The Thinking of the Rabbis," *Judaism* 5, no. 1 (1956); A. Holtz, *Rabbinic Thought: An Introduction to the Works of M. Kadushin* (Tel Aviv: Sifriyat Poalim, 1978); and the essays assembled by P. Ochs, *Understanding the Rabbinic Mind: Essays in the Hermeneutics of Max Kadushin* (Atlanta: Scholars Press, 1990). See now J. Dan, *On Sanctity: Religion, Ethics, and Mysticism in Judaism and Other Religions* (Jerusalem: Magnes, 1997).

49. L. Hoffman, *Covenant of Blood*, 156–163.

50. M. Douglas, *Purity and Danger: An Analysis of the Concepts of Pollution and Taboo* (London: London and Boston: Ark Paperbacks, 1984), 49.

51. L. Hoffman, *Covenant of Blood*, 158.

52. Ibid.

53. Wright, "Holiness, Old Testament," 239–243.

54. Ibid., 243.

55. Ibid., 243–244; Jenson, *Graded Holiness*, 182–209; J. Milgrom, *Studies in Levitical Terminology* (Berkeley: University of California Press, 1970), 80–81, n. 297.

56. See Wright, "Holiness, Old Testament," 238–239.

57. Ibid., 239.

58. Ibid., 238–239; Jenson, *Graded Holiness*, 50.

59. Wright, "Holiness, Old Testament," 237–238.

60. On the interrelatedness of each of the four categories mentioned in Lev. 10:10, see Wright, "Holiness," 246–247 and the sources cited there. See also J. Klawans, "Gentile Impurity in Ancient Judaism," *AJS Review*, 20.2 (1995): 288–292. For their interrelationship in Rabbinic thought, see Jacob Neusner, *The Idea of Purity in Ancient Judaism* (Leiden: E. J. Brill, 1973), 72–107, esp. 78–80 and Marmorstein, *Doctrine of Merits*, 210.

61. See L. Hoffman, *Covenant of Blood*, 157; Neusner, *Idea of Purity*, 124.

62. Cf. L. Hoffman, *Covenant of Blood*, 160.

63. For the denotations of the root Hal. in biblical literature, see W. Dommeshausen, "ḥll," *Theological Dictionary of the Old Testament* (Grand Rapids: Zondervan, 1980). See *American Heritage Dictionary of the English Language* [1991]: 988. I also avoid "profane" in order to differentiate the Rabbinic concept from the specific loadings associated with this term by Durkheim (*The Elementary Forms of Religious Life*, tr. J. S. Swain [New York: Free Press, 1965], 52–57) and his followers.

64. See also Ez. 22:26, 44:23.

65. See Klawans, "Notions of Gentile Impurity in Ancient Judaism," esp. 292.

66. See R. Rabbinowicz, *Dikduqei Sofrim* (New York: M. P. Press, 1976), ad loc. Cf. *b. Hul.* 26b. Elbogen, *Jewish Liturgy*, 41–42.

67. *m. Hul.* 1:7.

68. As, for example, *m. Meg.* 4:2. See J. N. Epstein, *Introduction to the Text of the Mishnah* (Jerusalem: Magnes Press, 1948), 634, n. 2.

69. Eg. *m. Rosh. Hash.* 2:7 for the "sanctification" of the new moon. For the "sanctification" of a woman in marriage, *see m. Qid.* 2:1, and especially the name of the tractate itself.

70. See, for example, the examples delineated in m. Meg. 1:5–11.

71. B. Levine, "Biblical Temple," *Encyclopedia of Religion*, ed. M. Eliade (New York: Macmillan, 1987), 2.213.

72. Bokser, "Approaching Sacred Space," 289–290; R. Sarason, "The Significance of the Land of Israel in the Mishnah," in *The Land of Israel: Jewish Perspectives*, ed. L. A. Hoffman (Notre Dame, Ind.: University of Notre Dame Press, 1986); J. Z. Smith, *Map Is Not Territory*, 112–115.

73. m. Kelim 1:9.

74. See M. H. Ben Shammai, "The Sanctity of the Land," *Encyclopaedia Biblica* (Jerusalem: Bialik Institute, 1955).

75. m. Kelim 1:6.

76. See C. Albeck's 1979 edition of the Mishnah, ad loc.

77. On the Temple in Rabbinic sources, see J. R. Brown, *Temple and Sacrifice in Rabbinic Judaism* (Evanston, Ill.: Seabury-Western Theological Seminary, 1963). See also m. Avot 1:2 and B. T. Viviano, *Study as Worship: Aboth and the New Testament* (Leiden: E. J. Brill, 1978), 7–8.

78. Ibid., 7–8.

79. See Albeck's comment, 6: 313; E. P. Sanders, *Judaism: Practice and Belief*, 59.

80. G. Alon, *The Jews in Their Land in the Talmudic Age*, tr. G. Levi (Cambridge, Mass: Harvard University Press, 1989), 50–55.

81. This shift is discussed most concisely by M. Fishbane, "From Scribalism to Rabbinism: Perspectives on the Emergence of Classical Judaism," in *The Scribe in Israel and the Ancient Near East*, ed. J. G. Gambie and L. G. Perdue (Winona Lake, Ind.: Eisenbrauns, 1990), esp. 440–445.

82. See R. Beckwith, "Formation of the Hebrew Bible," in *Mikra*, ed. M. J. Mulder (Assen/Maastricht: Van Gorgum and Philadelphia: Fortress Press, 1990), 39–40; R. Kasher, "The Interpretation of Scripture in Rabbinic Judaism," in *Mikra*, ed. M. J. Mulder (Assen/Maastricht: Van Gorgum and Philadelphia: Fortress Press, 1990), 548.

83. On the Hebrew *Vorlage* of 1 Maccabees, see S. Zeitlin, "Introduction," *The First Book of Maccabees*, tr. S. Tedesche (New York: Harper, 1950), 33–34.

84. War 2:229, Ant. 20:115:. See also Ant. 16:164. Cf. M. Haran, "Torah and Bible Scrolls in the First Centuries of the Christian Era," *Shnaton: An Annual for Biblical and Ancient Near Eastern Studies* 19 (1986): 93.

85. Line 177.

86. Line 317.

87. M. Goodman, "Sacred Scripture and 'Defiling the Hands'," *Journal of Theological Studies* 41 (1990): 99–107, and "Sacred Space," 3–4.

88. Haran discusses development of these traditions during the Second Temple and early Rabbinic periods. See Haran "Bible Scrolls in Eastern and Western Jewish Communities from Qumran to the High Middle Ages," *Hebrew Union College Annual* 56 (1985); and "Torah and Bible Scrolls."

89. Particular care was taken in cave four. On the parchment, see Haran, "Bible Scrolls." On the writing of the scrolls, see E. Tov, *Textual Criticism of the Hebrew Bible*

(Minneapolis: Fortress Press and Assen/Maastricht: Van Gorgum, 1992), 107–111, 201–233. On the storage of the scrolls, see D. Barthélemy and J. T. Milik, *Discoveries in the Judean Desert: Qumran Cave I* (Oxford: Oxford University Press, 1956), 8–9, 18–38, 2.4–7; *Assumption of Moses* 1:16–17; *b*. Meg. 26b.

90. Tov, *Textual Criticism*, 203.

91. On similarities between parchment found at Qumran and that which is described in Rabbinic sources, see Haran, "Bible Scrolls," 37–40.

92. Haran, "Torah and Bible Scrolls," 95, n. 7; Beckwith, "Formation of the Hebrew Bible," 51–61. See also N. Wieder, "'Sanctuary' as a Metaphor for Scripture," *Journal of Jewish Studies* 7, nos. 3–4 (1957).

93. See, for example, J. A. Sanders, *Torah and Canon* (Philadelphia: Fortress Press, 1972), 95.

94. S. Leiman, *The Canonization of Hebrew Scripture: The Talmudic and Midrashic Evidence* (Hamden, Conn.: Connecticut Academy of Arts and Sciences by Archon Books, 1976), 111–118, 125–135.

95. Sources are assembled and analyzed by Leiman, *Canonization of Hebrew Scripture*, 104–118.

96. G. Alon, "The Bounds of the Laws of Levitical Cleanliness," in *Jews, Judaism and the Classical World*, tr. I. Abrahams (Jerusalem: Magnes Press, 1977), 191–199.

97. m. Yad. 4:6. Cf. m. Ed. 5:3; t. Yad. 2:19. Hand defilement has been discussed by numerous modern scholars. See Albeck's commentary, ad. loc., 6: 608–609; Leiman, *Canonization of Hebrew Scripture*, provides a comprehensive discussion of research and bibliography previous to his own. Add to these M. Goodman, "Sacred Scripture"; S. Friedman, "The Holy Scripture Defile the Hands—The Transformation of a Biblical Concept in Rabbinic Theology," in *Minhah le-Nahum: Biblical and Other Studies Presented to Nahum M. Sarna in Honour of his 70th Birthday*, ed. M. Brettler and M. Fishbane (Sheffield: Sheffield University Press, 1993). Leiman (pp. 102–105) suggests on the basis of m. Yad. 4:6 (and parallels) that "a decree promulgated no later than the end of the first half of the first century C.E., and perhaps much earlier, ordained that the sacred books defile the hands" (p. 119).

98. m. Yad. 3:5. Cf. t. Yad. 2:14.

99. y. Shab. 15:1, 15b. See also b. Meg. 7a. See M. Goodman, "Sacred Scripture," 100–101.

100. b. Shab. 14a, Meg. 32a; Rashi to b. Meg 32a; to b. Shab. 14a; B. M. Lewin, *Otzar ha-Gaonim: Thesaurus of the Gaonic Responsa and Commentaries* (Jerusalem: H. Vagshal, 1984), ad loc.; Tosafot, ad loc.; *Sof.* 3:16.

101. See y. Ber. 3:6, 6d; L. Ginzberg, *A Commentary on the Palestinian Talmud* (New York: Jewish Theological Seminary, 1941), 2:300. See Haran, "Torah and Bible Scrolls," 100.

102. y. Meg. 4:1, 74d.

103. y. Moed Qat. 3:1, 81d; b. Ber. 8b and sources collected by R. Margaliot, "The Death of R. Judah the Prince," *Sinai* 50 (1962).

104. See also b. Meg. 26a.

105. Scholars generally agree that this text is principally of Palestinian origin. See Elbogen, *Jewish Liturgy*, 272; ed. Higger of the *Tractate Sofrim*, 22–23. Cf. M. B. Lerner, "The External Tractates," in *Literature of the Sages*, ed. S. Safrai (Assen/Maastricht: Van Gorgum and Philadelphia: Fortress Press, 1987), 399. Strack and Stemberger, *Introduction to the Talmud and Midrash*, 248, note that, "This tractate . . . in its present form cannot be dated prior to the eighth century, even if earlier forms must be assumed."

106. On the development from the scroll to the codex, see S. Lieberman, *Hellenism in Jewish Palestine* (New York: Jewish Theological Seminary, 1962), 203–208; M. Beit Arié, "How Hebrew Books Are Made," in *A Sign and a Witness: 2,000 Years of Hebrew Books and Illuminated Manuscripts*, ed. L. S. Gold (New York: Oxford University Press, 1988), 35–37.

107. 4Q464, published by E. Eshel and M. Stone, "The Holy Language at the End of Days in Light of a New Fragment Found at Qumran," *Tarbiz* 62, no. 2 (1993).

108. Ibid., 177.

109. J. Fitzmyer, "The Languages of Palestine in the First Century A.D.," *Catholic Biblical Quarterly* 32, no. 1 (1970).

110. Scholars have suggested numerous specific denotations for *leshon ha-qodesh*. S. Federbush considers Hebrew to be the natural language, the language of the supernal realm (*The Hebrew Language in Israel and Among the Nations* [Jerusalem: Rav Kook Institute, 1967], 12–14. See also M. Bar Ilan, "The Blessings and Curses That Are Read before Rosh ha-Shanah," *Sinai* 55 [1992]: 29; F. Millar, "The Jews of the Greco-Roman Diaspora between Paganism and Christianity," in *The Jews Among Pagans and Christians*, ed. J. Lieu, J. North, and T. Rajak [London and New York: Routledge, 1992], 113). Schäfer suggests that it originally referred to Hebrew as the "language of the Temple" (*Die Vorstellung vom heiligen Geist*, 138–139); see J. Heinemann's 1973 review of Schäfer's study in *Kirjath Sepher* 48.

111. Fitzmyer, "Languages of Palestine"; J. Greenfield, "The Languages of Palestine, 200 B.C.E.–200 C.E.," in *Jewish Languages: Theme and Variation* (Cambridge, Mass: Association for Jewish Studies, 1978), 153.

112. See Federbush, *The Hebrew Language*, 12–14, 27–45; Greenfield, "Languages of Palestine," 153; *Sifre Deut.* 46: 104 and n. 6; 333: 383, n. 14.

113. Sources are collected by Eshel and Stone, "Holy Language," 172–173.

114. Marmorstein, *Doctrine of Merits*, 97.

115. See E. E. Urbach, *The Sages—Their Concepts and Beliefs*, tr. I. Abrahams (Jerusalem, Magnes Press, 1975), 78.

116. Marmorstein, *Doctrine of Merits*, 92–93, 97, 129–147; S. Esh, *Der Heilige (Er Sei Gepriesen): Zur Geschichte einer Nachbiblisch-Hebraeischen Gottesbezeichnung* (Leiden: E. J. Brill, 1957).

117. Eg. *Lev. Rab.* 24.9; y. *Ber.* 13a (and parallels). See Marmorstein, *Doctrine of Merits*, 216. The complex concept of *ruaḥ ha-qodesh*, "holy spirit," has been studied most recently by Schäfer, *Die Vorstellung vom heiligen Geist*, who holds that *ruaḥ ha-qodesh* refers to the "spirit of the Temple." See J. Heinemann's review of this book (n. 110, above), where Heinemann correctly argues for a less limited interpretation.

118. Ibid.

119. The most recent discussion is by A. Green, *Keter: The Crown of Glory in Early Jewish Mysticism* (Princeton: Princeton University Press, 1997), 12–19 and the bibliography there. This is discussed briefly on p. 53 below.

120. *The Liturgical Poetry of Rabbi Yannai*, ed. Rabinovitz (Jerusalem: Bialik Institute, 1985–1987), 1.45. The *qedushah* is of great significance within Hekhalot literature as well. This literature is closely aligned with liturgical context. See M. Swartz, *Mystical Prayer in Ancient Judaism: An Analysis of Ma'aseh Merkavah* (Tubingen: J. C. B. Mohr, 1992); I. Gruenwald, "The Song of Angels, the *Qedushah*, and the Composition Hekhalot Literature," in *Jerusalem in the Second Temple Period: Abraham Schalit Memorial Volume*, ed. A. Oppenheimer, J. Rappaport, and M. Stern (Jerusalem: Ben Zvi Institute, 1980); A. Green, *Keter*, 16–17.

121. While a fine edition of Yannai's poems was prepared by Z. M. Rabbinowitz and numerous scholarly articles have been written on the works of Yannai, no monograph that focuses on Yannai's religious outlook has yet been undertaken. See the comments in ibid., 1.59–68.

122. Ibid., 1.11–12.

123. Ibid., 1.105–106.

124. Ibid., 1.170–171.

125. See m. Yoma 1:1–7, where the centrality of the priesthood to proper ritual is asserted. The heroes of this text are the Sages, the priest being a disgrace to his exalted office. C. Licht (*Ten Legends of the Sages: The Image of the Sage in Rabbinic Literature* [Hobocken: Ktav, 1991], 91–100, 103–119) discusses Rabbinic attitudes toward the latter Second Temple period priesthood. Licht's *Tradition and Innovation: Studies in Rabbinic Literature* (Givat-Haviva: Givat-Haviva Press, 1989), 23–32, also discusses the priority of the Sage over the prophet in Rabbinic literature.

126. Bokser, "Approaching Sacred Space," 287–299.

127. For example, m. Hor. 3:10.

128. On the application of Temple purity laws within the Rabbinic community, see Alon, "Bounds of the Laws." For Qumran parallels, see L. Schiffman, *Sectarian Law in the Dead Sea Scrolls* (Chico: Scholars Press, 1983), 191–210. On Qumran and the Jesus sect, see J. Baumgarten, *Studies in Qumran Law* (Leiden: E. J. Brill, 1977), 39–97; Bokser, "Approaching Sacred Space," 281–287; Schiffman, op. cit., esp. 191–210, 215–216, and "The Dead Sea Scrolls and the Early History of Jewish Liturgy," in *The Synagogue in Late Antiquity*, ed. L. I. Levine (Philadelphia: American Schools for Oriental Research, 1987), 34–35.

129. y. Maas. S. 5:5, 56b; Pesiq. Rab. Kah. 10:10, ed. Mandelbaum, 172; L. I. Levine, *The Rabbinic Class*, 71 and bibliography there.

130. J. Heinemann, *Prayer in the Talmud*, tr. R. S. Sarason (Berlin and New York: Walther de Gruyter, 1977), 52–53, 55; Elbogen, *Jewish Liturgy*, 5–6, 193.

131. Kadushin, *Rabbinic Mind*, 173.

132. Sifra, Qedoshim 9:2, Aharei 13:9; Sifre Deut. 85.

133. A. Büchler, *Types of Jewish Palestinian Piety* (London: Jews' College, 1922), 50–55. This type of separatism is called "asceticism" by S. D. Fraade, "Ascetical Aspects of

Ancient Judaism," in *Jewish Spirituality from the Bible through the Middle Ages* (New York: Crossroad, 1986), 253–288.

134. *Sifra, Qedoshim*, 1:1, *Shemini* 12:4; *Lev. Rab.* 24:4; *Mekhilta of Rabbi Ishmael, Ba-Hodesh* 2, ed. Horowitz-Rabin: 209; ed. Lauterbach 2: 206. Fraade, "Ascetical Aspects," discusses the concept of *perishut* in Rabbinic sources. See also Marmorstein, *Doctrine of Merits*, 208–213; D. Biale, *Eros and the Jews: From Biblical Israel to Contemporary America* (New York: Basic Books, 1992), 36.

135. Compare, however, the Tannaitic tradition cited in m. *Sota* 9:15 (=y. *Shab.* 1:5, 3c; b. *Abod. Zar.* 20b) and the comments of J. N. Epstein, *Introduction*, 976–977; Fraade, "Ascetical Aspects," 270–271; Büchler, *Types of Jewish Palestinian Piety*, 52–53.

136. b. *Ber.* 9b. See S. Safrai, "The Holy Community of Jerusalem," in *Eretz Israel and Its Sages during the Period of the Midrash and the Talmud* (Israel: Hakibbutz Hameuchad, 1983), n. 1; b. *Rosh. Hash.* 19b; *Yoma* 69a; *Besa* 27a; *Tamid* 27b. See C. Rabin, *Qumran Studies* (London: Oxford University Press, 1957) 37–43.

137. See Rabin, *Qumran Studies*, 38; S. Safrai, "Holy Community of Jerusalem," 54.

138. See Rabin, *Qumran Studies*, 41–42; S. Safrai, "Holy Community of Jerusalem," 54–55.

139. Sources are cited by Rabin, *Qumran Studies*, 37–38. See S. Safrai, "Holy Community of Jerusalem," 53.

140. Büchler, *Types of Jewish Palestinian Piety*, 43–44 was the first to notice this fact.

141. = *Gen. Rab.* 100:7 and parallels cited in the Theodor-Albeck edition: 1291; see also b. *Sanh.* 23a. Ginzberg, *Commentary on the Palestinian Talmud*, 1: 385; Marmorstein, *Doctrine of Merits*, 213.

142. y. *Meg.* 1:11, 72b; y. *Sanh.* 10:5, 29c; y. *Abod. Zar.* 3:1, 42c; b. *Pesah.* 104a, b. *Abod. Zar.* 50a. On "Nahum of the Holy of Holies," see *Eccl. Rab.* 9:10; Marmorstein, *Doctrine of Merits*, 215–216; L. I. Levine, *The Rabbinic Class*, 85–86. On Rabbi Judah the Prince, see b. *Shab.* 118b. In the Babylonian Talmud other early Amoraim are referred to as holy. Rabbi Hanina and Rabbi Hoshaya are called "Our Holy Masters of the Land of Israel" in b. *Pesah.* 113b and in b. *Pesah.* 104a (=*Abod. Zar.* 50a) Nahum of the Holy of Holies is called "the son of *qedoshim*."

143. See Fraade, "Ascetical Aspects," 261: Büchler, *Types of Jewish Palestinian Piety*, 50, and n. 3; Marmorstein, *Doctrine of Merits*, 213.

144. See Büchler, *Types of Jewish Palestinian Piety*, n. 2.

145. y. *Sanh.* 10:2, 29b; *Lev. Rab.* 24:6; b. *Ber.* 10b. See L. Ginzberg, *Legends of the Jews* (Philadelphia: Jewish Publication Society, 1954), 4: 242–244; 6: 346, n. 12. Abraham is described as having a "holy body" in *Gen. Rab.* 45:3. On "holy men" during late antiquity: P. Brown, *Cult of Saints; Society and the Holy*, 103–166; R. Kirschner, "The Vocation of Holiness in Late Antiquity," *Vigiliae Christianae* 37 (1984). On "holy men" in Rabbinic sources: W. S. Green, "Palestinian Holy Men: Charismatic Leadership and Rabbinic Tradition," in *Aufstieg und Niedergang der Römische Welt* (Berlin and New York: Walther de Gruyter, 1979); Kirschner, "Vocation of Holiness," 114–119.

A Hebrew funerary inscription from Beth She'arim, memorializes "the holy ones, the sons (of . . .)" (Catacomb 20, no. 17; N. Avigad, *Beth She'arim*," 3 [New Brunswick: Rutgers

University Press, 1976], 244–245: *Ha-qedoshim banav sh[el]* . . .). The meaning of this title is unclear. There is apparently something special about these "holy ones," since other internees at Beth She'arim are not so designated (ibid., 244–245). A Greek inscription from the same catacomb may also reflect this phenomenon (M. Schwabe and B. Lifshitz, *Beth She'arim*, 2 [New Brunswick, N.J.: Rutgers University Press, 1974], no. 193: 179–180). See N. Avigad, "Excavations at Beth She'arim: Preliminary Report," *Israel Exploration Journal* 7, no. 4 (1957): 246, G. W. Bowersock, *Hellenism in Late Antiquity* (Ann Arbor: University of Michigan Press, 1990), 16. Compare, however, Schwabe and Lifshitz, ad loc.). E. E. Urbach suggests that the connotation of *ha-qedoshim* here is the same as in Rabbinic sources ("The Rabbinical Laws of Idolatry in the Second and Third Centuries in Light of Archaeological and Historical Facts," *Israel Exploration Journal* 9, nos. 3–4 [1959]: 152–153; 1979: 78–79).

146. y. *Yeb.* 2:4, 3d; *Lev. Rab.* 24:6. Cf. b. *Yeb.* 20a, ed. Liss.

147. On ascetic tensions in Rabbinic literature, see Fraade, "Ascetical Aspects," 269–277, esp. n. 883; Biale, *Eros and the Jews*, 33–59.

148. See above, note 144.

149. Ibid.

150. *Midrash Tehillim* 16:2. Cf. P. Brown, *Cult of Saints*, 3; Marmorstein, *Doctrine of Merits*, 216.

151. Z. Safrai, *The Economy of Roman Palestine* (London and New York: Routledge, 1994) and bibliography cited there.

152. Z. Safrai, "Sacred Tombs and Holy Sites in the Jewish Tradition," in *Zev Vilnay's Jubilee Volume* ed. E. Schiller (Jerusalem: Ariel, 1984), 304–307.

153. Jer. 1:5; L. Hoffman, *Covenant of Blood*, 112.

154. See G. Stroumsa, "Religious Contacts in Byzantine Palestine," *Numen* 36, no. 1 (1989).

155. On Christian sources, see Y. Meimaris, *Sacred Names, Saints, Martyrs, and Church Officials in the Greek Inscriptions and Papyri Pertaining to the Christian Church of Palestine* (Athens: Kentron Hellenikeskai Romaikes Archaiotetos Ethnik Hydryma Ereunon, Paris: Diffusion de Boccard, 1986), 17; J. Wilkinson, *Egeria's Travels to the Holy Land* (Jerusalem: Ariel and London: Aris and Phillips, 1981), 15 and p. 98 below.

156. y. *Ned.* 6:13, 40a; y. *Sanh.* 1.19a. See Marmorstein, *Doctrine of Merits*, 216.

157. S. Safrai, "Synagogues South of Mt. Judah," *Immanuel* 3 (1974): 49.

158. "The holiness of my master Rabbi Issi, the honored priest . . ." (J. Naveh, *On Stone and Mosaic: The Aramaic and Hebrew Inscriptions from Ancient Synagogues* [Israel: Maariv, 1978], 115–116).

159. *Qaddish*: G. Foerster, "Synagogue Inscriptions and Their Relation to Liturgical Versions." *Cathedra* 17 (1981): 23–26; *Mi-sheberakh: Seder Avodat Israel*, ed. Z. Baer: 230; A. Yaari, "The *Mi' Sheberakh* Prayers: History and Texts," *Kirjath Sepher* 33, nos. 1–2 (1957–1958): 118–120. Susiya: Naveh, *On Stone and Mosaic*, 123; Jericho, ibid., 104. See also Beth Shean B, ibid., 77–78.

160. See J. Le Goff, *History and Memory* (New York: Columbia University Press, 1992), 11–13.

161. See especially S. Lieberman, "Some Aspects of the Afterlife in Early Rabbinic Literature," in *Harry Austryn Wolfson Jubilee Volume* (Jerusalem: American Academy for Jewish Research, 1965), 2: 495–532.

162. See L. Hoffman, *Beyond the Text*, 82–86, 116–144; B. Z. Wacholder, *Messianism and Mishnah: Time and Place in the Early Halakhah* (Cincinnati: Hebrew Union College Press, 1978), esp. 8-9.

163. *Zeman ha-zeh* appears in m. *Maas. Sh.* 5:7, Albeck, ad loc.; *Maas. Sh.* 1:15, 3:13–14, t. *Sanh.* 3:6; *Zebaḥ.* 13:1; t. *Bek.* 3:2, 7:15; t. *Arak.* 2:7, b. *Yebam.* 47a–b; b. *Git.* 36a.

164. y. *Ter.* 16a, 40b "The time of the Temple" is referred to as "The time (*zeman*) when the Temple exists" in y. *Ned.* 30a.

165. Eg. b. *Ber.* 62b, *Pesaḥ.* 44a, 72b; *Taan.* 14b; *Meg.* 2a.

166. M. Friedman, *Jewish Marriage in Palestine* (Tel Aviv: Tel Aviv University and New York: Jewish Theological Seminary, 1980–1981), 1.104–106 and bibliography cited there. During the Geonic period dating according to the Seleucid era was common in Babylonia and in Genizah documents from Egypt, though not in Palestine (p. 106). Dating from the destruction of the Temple, together with dating from the creation, was practiced by communities that followed the Byzantine-Jewish rite (such as Corfu and Avolna) into the modern period. See S. Sabar, *Ketubbah: Jewish Marriage Contracts of the Hebrew Union College Skirball Museum and Klau Library* (Philadelphia: Jewish Publication Society, 1990), 11, 236, 258–261.

167. On this, see N. Glatzer, "The Attitude toward Rome in Third-Century Judaism," in *Essays in Jewish Thought* (Alabama: University of Alabama Press, 1978).

168. See *Pesiq. Rab. Kah.*, 26:2 ed. Mandelbaum: 386; *Eccl. Rab.* 2:8. On synagogues in the future, see below, pp. 65–66, 110–111.

169. Y. Yerushalmi, *Zakhor: Jewish History and Jewish Memory* (Seattle: University of Washington Press, 1982), 24.

1. "Sacred Places That They Call Synagogues"

1. J. Gutmann summarizes theories of synagogue origins in "The Origin of the Synagogue," *Archaeologischer Anzeiger* 87 (1972). See also L. Grabbe, "Synagogues in Pre-70 Palestine: A Reassessment;" J. G. Griffiths, "Egypt and the Rise of the Synagogue," in *Ancient Synagogues: Historical Analysis and Archaeological Discovery*, ed. D. Urman and P. V. M. Flesher (Leiden: E. J. Brill, 1995); L. I. Levine, "Nature and Origin," 425–445.

2. E. Rivkin, "Prolegomenon," in *Judaism and Christianity*, ed. W. O. E. Oesterley (New York: Ktav, 1969), xxvi–xxvii; Gutmann, "Origin of the Synagogue," 39–40.

3. *Apion*, 2:175; Acts 15:21. See also y. *Meg.* 4:1, 75a.

4. Z. Smith, *Map Is Not Territory*, 187.

5. M. White, *Building God's House in the Roman World* (Baltimore and London: Johns Hopkins University Press, 1990), 26–40.

6. J. Z. Smith, *Map Is Not Territory*, 104–128, esp. 128.

7. Rivkin, "Prolegomenon," xxvi–xxvii; Gutmann, "Origin of the Synagogue," 39–40; Grabbe, "Synagogues in Pre–70 Palestine," esp. 24–25.

8. In one case *eucheion*, which also means "prayer place" is used. See V. A. Tcherikover, A. Fuks, and M. Stern, *Corpus Papyrorium Judaicarum* (Cambridge, Mass: Harvard University Press, 1957–1964), 2.220–224. M. Hengel, "Proseusche und Synagoge: Jüdische Gemeinde, Gotteshaus und Gottesdienst in der Diaspora und in Palaestina," *Tradition und Glaube, Das fruehe Christentum in seiner Umwelt, Festgabe für Karl Georg Kuhn zum 65 Geburtstag*, ed. G. Jeremias et al. (Göttingen: Vanderhoeck and Ruprecht, 1971), 157–183; W. Horbury and D. Noy, *Jewish Inscriptions of Graeco-Roman Egypt* (Cambridge: Cambridge University Press, 1992), 276. See also David Noy, "A Jewish Place of Prayer in Roman Egypt," *Journal of Theological Studies*, n.s. 43, no. 1 (1992): 119–120.

9. The supposed synagogue on Delos is not included in this discussion because of the inconclusive nature of the evidence. See White, *Building God's House*, 64–67 and my "Relations between Egypt and Palestine during the Greco-Roman Period: The Evidence of the Synagogue," in *Proceedings of the Conference on Israel-Diaspora Relations during the Greco-Roman Period*, ed. A. Baumgarten, I. Gafni, L. Schiffman (Jerusalem, forthcoming).

10. Sources are discussed at length by P.-E. Dion, "Synagogoues et Temples dans l'Egypte Hellenistiques," *Science et Espirit* 29 (1977); Griffiths, "Egypt and the Rise of the Synagogue."

11. Ibid., 9–10, 15.

12. Dion, "Synagogoues et Temples," 48–55; H. Liddell and R. Scott, *A Greek-English Lexicon*, 9th ed. (Oxford: Oxford University Press, 1940), 820–823, esp. 822.

13. Apparently referring to the land belonging to the synagogue as holy. Tcherikover, Fuks, and Stern, *Corpus Papyrorium*, 1.248–249 and the commentary, ad loc. Lit.: "A *proseuche* of the Jews" (*proseuchas Ioudaion*) represented by Pertollios, and a consecrated garden cultivated (*hieras para[deisou] g[amisu]*) by a tenant." A. Kasher, *The Jews in Hellenistic and Roman Egypt* (Tubingen: J. C. B. Mohr, 1985), 138–139; and "Synagogues as 'Houses of Prayer' and 'Holy Places' in the Jewish Communities of Hellenistic and Roman Egypt," in *Ancient Synagogues: Historical Analysis and Archaeological Discovery*, ed. D. Urman and P. V. M. Flesher (Leiden: E. J. Brill, 1995), 216.

14. Horbury and Noy, *Jewish Inscriptions of Graeco-Roman Egypt*, 13–15: . . .*t]on hieron peribolon (?) kai ton pros[euchan kai ta sug]kuronta*. D. M. Lewis ("The Jewish Inscriptions in Egypt," in *Corpus Papyrorium* [1964], no. 1433) notes that "*ta sugkuronta* of the subsidiary buildings of a temple or shrine is not uncommon in Ptolemaic Egypt." See also Horbury and Noy, op. cit., 14, 42–43 and Dion, "Synagogoues et Temples," 60–61; A. Kasher, "Synagogues as 'Houses of Prayer'," 216.

15. Horbury and Noy, *Jewish Inscriptions of Graeco-Roman Egypt*, 40–42 and bibliography cited there. A. Kasher, "Synagogues as 'Houses of Prayer'," 216.

16. Dion, "Synagogoues et Temples," 61–65; Griffiths, "Egypt and the Rise of the Synagogue," 11–12.

17. Dion, "Synagogoues et Temples," 55–57; A. Kasher, "Synagogues as 'Houses of Prayer'," 218–219; Horbury and Noy, *Jewish Inscriptions of Graeco-Roman Egypt*, 19–21, 35–37, 40–43, 45–50, 201–203.

18. Ibid., 212–216 and bibliography cited there. A. Kasher, *Jews in Hellenistic and Roman Egypt*, 11; 1987: 128–129, and "Synagogues as 'Houses of Prayer',", 215, 218; Griffiths, "Egypt and the Rise of the Synagogue," 12. On rights of asylum in Egypt, see M. Rostovtzeff, *Social and Economic History of the Hellenistic World* (Oxford: Oxford University Press, 1941), 2.899–903.

19. L. I. Levine, "The Second Temple Synagogue: The Formative Years," in *The Synagogue in Late Antiquity*, ed. L. I. Levine (Philadelphia: American Schools for Oriental Research, 1987), 23. See Dion, "Synagogoues et Temples," 65–74.

20. Cf. A. Kasher, "Synagogues as 'Houses of Prayer',", who relates the sanctity of Egyptian synagogues to that of the Jerusalem Temple.

21. V. Tcherikover, *Hellenistic Civilization and the Jews* (Philadelphia: Jewish Publication Society, 1959), 315.

22. *Flaccus*, line 46. H. A. McKay, *Sabbath and Synagogue: The Question of Sabbath Worship in Ancient Judaism* (Leiden: E. J. Brill, 1994), 61–77, discusses in detail sources in Philo.

23. Line 48. Translation follows F. H. Colson.

24. Line 49. See also *Embassy to Gaius*, line 137.

25. Line 133, tr. F. H. Colson.

26. See S. Fine and M. Della Pergola, "The Ostia Synagogue and Its Torah Shrine," in *The Jews of Ancient Rome*, ed. J. G. Westenholz (Jerusalem: Bible Lands Museum, 1994), 50–52.

27. See n. 14 above. The same term is used by Josephus to describe the Temple Mount in Jerusalem in *War*, 4:400.

28. *On Dreams*, 2, line 127.

29. *The Life of Moses*, 2, line 216. Translation follows Goodenough, *Jewish Symbols*, 2. 88. See also *Embassy to Gaius*, line 132.

30. *Antiquities* 14:260: *tas patrious euxas kai thusias to theo*. See E. Bickerman, "The Altars of the Gentiles: A Note on the Jewish 'Ius Sacrum'," in *Studies in Jewish and Christian History*, part 1 (Leiden: E. J. Brill, 1980); M. Stone, *Scripture, Sects and Visions: A Profile of Judaism from Ezra to the Jewish Revolts* (Philadelphia: Fortress Press, 1980), 80–81; L. I. Levine, "The Second Temple Synagogue," 14–15; M. Goodman, "Sacred Space," 4–5.

31. Levine, "The Second Temple Synagogue," 14.

32. *War* 4:408, 7:144; and perhaps *Apion*, 1:209. See also 3 Mac. 2:28 and S. J. D. Cohen, "Pagan and Christian Evidence," 161–162.

33. *War* 7:44–45. See S. Zeitlin, "Tefillah, the Shemoneh Esreh: An Historical Study of the Canonization of the Hebrew Liturgy, "*Jewish Quarterly Review* 54 (1963–1964): 236; McKay, *Sabbath and Synagogue*, 81–82.

34. See especially *Embassy to Gaius*, 133.

35. Tacitus too describes how Jews did not have images in their "temples" (*templis*) in their cities (*Histories*, 5:4:4). As M. Goodman ("Sacred Space," 10) notes, this author "may have intended to refer to synagogues by the plural *templa*."

36. Synagogues during the Second Temple period are discussed by L. I. Levine, "The Second Temple Synagogue."

37. The removal of the Torah from a Caesarea synagogue in the wake of a Greek provocation in 66 C.E. is described by Josephus (*War* 2:289–292). See M. Goodman, "Sacred Scripture," 103–104; "Sacred Space," 3–4.

38. Literary and archaeological sources are discussed by L. I. Levine, "The Second Temple Synagogue."

39. Translation follows L. I. Levine, "The Second Temple Synagogue," 17. On this inscription, see L. Roth-Gerson, *Greek Inscriptions in the Synagogues in Eretz-Israel* (Jerusalem: Ben Zvi Institute, 1987), 76–86 and bibliography cited there. H. C. Kee and H. McKay date this inscription some centuries later. See Kee, "The Transformation of the Synagogue after 70 C.E.: Its Import for Early Christianity," *New Testament Studies* 36 (1990); "The Changing Meaning of Synagogue: A Response to Richard Oster," *New Testament Studies* 40 (1994); "Defining the First-Century CE Synagogue: Problems and Progress," *New Testament Studies* 41 (1995); McKay, *Sabbath and Synagogue*, 242–245. There is no basis for this interpretation, as is correctly argued by E. P. Sanders, *Jewish Law from Jesus to the Mishnah* (London and Philadelphia: Trinity International, 1990), 341–343; R. E. Oster, "Supposed Anachronism in Luke-Acts' Use of *Sunagoge*: A Rejoinder to H.C. Kee," *New Testament Studies* (1993); R. Riesner, "Synagogues in Jerusalem," in *The Book of Acts in Its Palestinian Setting*, ed. R. Bauckham (Grand Rapids: Eerdmans and Carlisle: Paternoster Press, 1995); P. van der Horst, "Was the Ancient Synagogue a Place of Sabbath Worship?" in *Jews, Christians and Polytheists in the Ancient Synagogue: Cultural Interaction During the Greco-Roman Period*, ed. S. Fine (London and New York: Routledge, forthcoming).

40. See L. I. Levine, "Judaism from the Destruction of Jerusalem to the End of the Second Revolt," in *Rabbinic Judaism and Christianity: A Parallel History of Their Origins and Early Development*, ed. H. Shanks (Washington, D.C.: Biblical Archaeology Society, 1992), 129, n. 7.

41. See the final report of this excavation: E. Netzer, *Masada III, The Yigael Yadin Excavations 1963–1965, Final reports, The Buildings: Stratigraphy and Architecture* (Jerusalem: Israel Exploration Society, 1991), 402–413. See also Y. Yadin, "The Synagogue at Masada," 20–21; G. Foerster, "The Synagogues at Masada and Herodium," both in *Ancient Synagogues Revealed*, ed. L. I. Levine (Jerusalem: Israel Exploration Society, 1981).

42. M. J. S. Chiat and P. V. M. Flesher have argued that the Masada synagogue was not a synagogue at all. Neither, however, provides a definition of what a synagogue is, so it is unclear what either would consider to be one. (See Chiat, "First-Century Synagogue Architecture: Methodological Problems," in *Ancient Synagogues: The State of the Research*, ed. J. Gutmann [Chino: Scholars Press, 1981], 52–53, and Flesher, "Palestinian Synagogues before 70 C.E.: A Review of the Evidence" in *Ancient Synagogues: Historical Analysis and Archaeological Discovery*, ed. D. Urman and P. V. M. Flesher [Leiden: E. J. Brill, 1995], esp. 1:35–37.)

43. See E. Fleischer, "On the Beginnings of Obligatory Jewish Prayer," *Tarbiz* 59, nos. 3–4 (1989–1990): 407.

44. Designated "room 1043" by the excavator.

45. Yadin, "The Synagogue at Masada," 21–22; Netzer, *Masada III*, 410. Various objects were assembled and burned in the cell, presumably during the conflagration of 74 C.E.

See ibid., 422; Y. Yadin, "The Excavation of Masada 1963/64 Preliminary Report," *Israel Exploration Journal* 15 (1965): 78.

46. See Yadin ("The Excavation of Masada," 78; "Synagogue at Masada," 20, n. 1), who suggests a parallel between this building and the Ecclesiasterium at Priene. See also Foerster, "Synagogues at Masada and Herodium," 26–28; A. Ovadiah and T. Michaeli, "Observations of the Origin of the Architectural Plan of Ancient Synagogues," *Journal of Jewish Studies* 38, no. 2 (1987): 238; Z. Ma'oz, "The Synagogue in the Second Temple Period—Architectural and Social Interpretation," *Eretz-Israel* 23 (1992). Compare Z. Safrai, "Dukhan, Aron and Teva: How Was the Ancient Synagogue Furnished?" in *Synagogues in Israel*, ed. R. Hachlili (London: BAR International, 1989), 71.

47. Cf. Yadin, "The Synagogue at Masada," 20.

48. Cf. t. Meg. 3:21.

49. Netzer, *Masada III*, 410–412.

50. *Every Good Man is Free*, lines 81–82, tr. F. H. Colton. See M. Goodman, "Sacred Space," 4.

51. L. I. Levine, "The Second Temple Synagogue," 9.

52. L. I. Levine, "The Second Temple Synagogue," 11–12, and Riesner, "Synagogues in Jerusalem," survey archaeological evidence for synagogues during this period.

53. See L. I. Levine, "The Second Temple Synagogue,"; Fleischer, "On the Beginnings of Obligatory Jewish Prayer."

54. See van der Horst, "Was the Ancient Synagogue a Place of Sabbath Worship?"

55. *Life* 54, 276–282; compare Fleischer, "On the Beginnings of Obligatory Jewish Prayer," 408–410.

56. C. Newsom, *Songs of the Sabbath Sacrifice: A Critical Edition* (Atlanta: Scholars Press, 1985), 18–20, 72.

57. A number of scrolls were uncovered in the nearby "Casement of the Scrolls" (Casement 1039) which were "assembled there" and "sifted through repeatedly" near the end of the Masada campaign (Netzer, *Masada III*, 422). Netzer conjectures that they were collected together with other valuables either by the defenders immediately before the fall of Masada or by Roman soldiers or other looters after the battle. Significantly, most of the Hebrew and Aramaic parchments discovered on Masada stem from the synagogue or within 20 or so meters of the synagogue. See Netzer, op. cit., 415, plan 36. S. Talmon notes the significance of this proximity to the synagogue in discussing a fragment that he considers to be Samaritan that was discovered in the "Casement of the Scrolls" ("Fragments of Scrolls from Masada," *Eretz-Israel* 20 [1989]: 284, and historical comments there). See, however, H. Eshel, "The Prayer of Joseph, a Papyrus from Masada and the Samaritan Temple on ARGARIZIN," *Zion* 56, no. 2 (1991): 134–136, who considers this fragment to be a Jewish prayer text. Fragments of a parchment scroll were also found in room 1045, adjacent to the synagogue (Netzer, op. cit., 396). The texts from the "Casement of the Scrolls" are discussed by Yadin, "Excavation of Masada," 80–81, 103–109. On the "Songs of the Sabbath Sacrifice," see Yadin, op. cit., 80–81, 105–108; C. Newsom and Y. Yadin,

"The Masada Fragment of the Qumran Songs of the Sabbath," *Israel Exploration Journal* 34 (1984); Newsom, *Songs of the Sabbath Sacrifice*, 5–21, 59–72; Talmon, op. cit.

58. 11:21–22; 4Q271 (photo CAM 43280). This text was recently discussed by A. Steubel, "The House of Prostration, CD XI, 21–XII, 1—Duplicates of the Temple (1)," *Revue de Qumran* 16, no. 1 (1993).

59. See C. Rabin, *The Zadokite Documents* (Oxford: Oxford University Press, 1958), 59, line 22, n. 1; L. Ginzberg, *An Unknown Jewish Sect* (New York: Jewish Theological Seminary, 1976), 374; Bokser, "Approaching Sacred Space," 284.

60. Schiffman, "Dead Sea Scrolls and Early History," 35. Cf. L. I. Levine, "The Second Temple Synagogue," 13.

61. On purity at Qumran, see Schiffman, "Dead Sea Scrolls and Early History," 44.

62. On prayer at Qumran, see ibid.; S. Talmon, *The World of Qumran from Within* (Jerusalem: Magnes Press, 1989), 200–243; Fleischer, "On the Beginnings of Obligatory Jewish Prayer," 414–415. On prayer in other Second Temple period literatures, see L. I. Levine, "The Second Temple Synagogue," 19–23; Fleischer, op. cit.

2. "They Are Sacred Even When Destroyed"

1. See Bokser, "Rabbinic Responses to Catastrophe," "The Wall Separating God and Israel," *Origin of the Seder*, "Approaching Sacred Space," and "Rabbinic Continuity." See now Rubinstein, *The History of Sukkot*.

2. See Bokser, *Origin of the Seder*.

3. m. Meg. 3:4–6, 4:3–4; t. Meg. 2:18. Traditions in y. Meg. 4:1, 75a date the institution of public Torah reading to Moses and to Ezra. See Elbogen, *Jewish Liturgy*, 130, nn. 3–6.

4. These new functions include:
   a. Recitation of Aramaic translations of the Torah reading (m. Meg. 4:6,10).
   b. Torah blessings (t. Kipp. 3:18).
   c. Communal prayer (m. Ber. 7:3).
   d. *Shofar* blowing on Rosh Hashanah (m. Rosh. Hash. 3:7).
   e. Additional use of *Lulavim* on the feast of Sukkot (m. Sukk. 3:13. Cf. t. Sukk. 2:10 and A. Oppenheimer, "Benevolent Societies in Jerusalem," in *Jerusalem in the Second Temple Period: Abraham Schalit Memorial Volume*, ed. A. Oppenheimer [Jerusalem: Ben Zvi Institute, 1980], 180).
   f. *Megillah* reading on Purim (ibid. Possibly even by women. See m. Meg. 2:4).
   g. Recitation of the *Hallel* psalms (t. Pesah. 10:8).
   h. Eulogies (t. Meg. 2:18, Cf. Sof. 18:12).
   i. Public oaths (m. Sheb. 4:10).
   j. Local charity collection (t. Shab. 16:22; t. Ter. 1:10; t. B. Bat. 8:4; Matt. 6:2).
   k. Communal meals (m. Zav. 3:2; Bek. 5:5).

On the functions of synagogues in late antique sources, see Z. Safrai, "The Communal Functions of the Synagogue in the Land of Israel in the Rabbinic Period," in *Ancient Syna-*

gogues: Historical Analysis and Archaeological Discovery, ed. D. Urman and P. V. M. Flesher (Leiden: E. J. Brill, 1995), 1:181–204. Z. Zahavy, *Studies in Jewish Prayer* (Lanham: University Press of America, 1991), 55–79, discusses each appearance of "synagogue" in the Mishnah and Tosefta. Synagogue functions before 70 are detailed by L. I. Levine, "The Second Temple Synagogue," 14.

5. See L. I. Levine, "The Second Temple Synagogue" and Fleischer, "On the Beginnings of Obligatory Jewish Prayer."

6. See Rashi to *b. Meg.* 28b.

7. See *y. Ber.* 2:7, 5a–b; *b. Meg.* 28b; *b. Moed Qat.* 25b; J. Fraenkel, *The Ways of Aggadah and Midrash* (Israel: Yad la-Talmud, 1991), 41–42.

8. Greenfield, "Languages of Palestine," 153; C. Rabin, "The Linguistic Investigation of the Language of Jewish Prayer," in *Studies in Aggadah, Targum, and Jewish Liturgy in Memory of Joseph Heinemann*, ed. J. J. Petuchowski and E. Fleischer (Jerusalem: Magnes Press, 1981), 163, 167–168.

9. Ibid.

10. *m. Meg.* 1:8.

11. This may have been the case even of members of the Tannaitic circle. See *b. Meg.* 18a; Rashi, ad loc.

12. See Fitzmyer, "Languages of Palestine," 514–515, 528–531.

13. Discussed below, p. 46.

14. *t. Meg.* 2:14,16.

15. *t. Meg.* 2:14. In Tannaitic literature *menorah* is used to refer both to a seven-branched candelabrum and to an ordinary house lamp. It is unclear which is referred to here. For sources on the *menorah* in Rabbinic literature, see J. Brand, *Ceramics in Talmudic Literature* (Jerusalem, 1953), 296–314; L. I. Levine, "From Community Center to Small Temple: The Furnishings and Interior Design of Ancient Synagogues," *Cathedra* 60 (1991) 77–78; Sperber, *Material Culture in Eretz-Israel*, 97–101. On lamps in Rabbinic literature, see U. Zevulun, *Form and Function in the Talmudic Period* (Tel Aviv, 1979), 74–85, 39*–43*.

16. *t. Meg.* 2:13, *t. Meg.* 2:16.

17. *m. Kelim* 16:7. See *The Gaonic Commentary On The Order Tohorot Attributed to Rav Hay Gaon*, ed. J. N. Epstein (Tel Aviv: Dvir and Jerusalem: Magnes Press, 1982), 47–48; Maimonides, Commentary to *m. Kelim* 16:7; Albeck, ad loc. R. Hachlili, *Ancient Jewish Art and Archaeology in the Land of Israel* (Leiden: E. J. Brill, 1988), 95.

18. *m. Kelim* 16:7. See Albeck's comment, ad loc. In fact, the Greek loan word *geluskama* can denote both an ossuary and a secular chest or a chest for books. M. Jastrow, *Dictionary of the Targumim, the Talmud Babli, and Yerushalmi, and the Midrashic Literature* (New York: Traditional Press, 1982), 247; E. M. Meyers, *Jewish Ossuaries: Reburial and Rebirth. Secondary Burials in Their Near Eastern Setting* (Rome: Biblical Institute, 1971), 52–55.

19. *m. Kelim* 16:7.

20. *m. Kelim* 28:4.

21. *t. Kelim, B. Mes.* 1:13 and parallels.

22. This text is discussed on pp. 43–45.

23. On the town in Tannaitic and later Rabbinic literature, see S. Safrai, "The Jewish City in Eretz Israel during the Period of the Mishna and the Talmud," *Town and Country: Lectures Delivered at the Twelfth Convention of the Historical Society of Israel*, December 1966 (Jerusalem, 1967); Z. Safrai, *The Economy of Roman Palestine* (London and New York: Routledge, 1994), 39–64, 75–77.

24. Communal possessions are listed in m. Ned. 5:5 as: "the (town) square, the bath house, the synagogue, the (scrolls) chest, and the (holy) books."

25. The identification of *sefarim* is unclear. t. Meg. 3:20, suggest an ascending hierarchy consisting of the Prophets, individual books of the Pentateuch, and the Pentateuch scroll. All three were similar in form, "written in Assyrian (square Hebrew) script on parchment with ink" (m. Meg. 2:2, 1:8; Yad. 4:5). See N. Sarna, "Bible," *Encyclopedia Judaica* (1970), 4:816–817; Haran, "Torah and Bible Scrolls," esp. 97–99.

26. Compare Haran, "Torah and Bible Scrolls."

27. According to the Kaufmann and Parma A (De Rossi 138) manuscripts; the printed editions and manuscripts of the Palestinian and Babylonian Talmudim. Compare the Cambridge manuscript of the Mishnah, which reads "Rabbi Judah."

28. m. Sheqal. 6:4, according to the Kaufmann manuscript.

29. According to the form-critical model developed by Jacob Neusner (*A History of Mishnaic Law of Appointed Times*, Part 5 [Leiden: E. J. Brill, 1983], 233–234), the anonymous sections of m. Meg. 3:1 should be dated to Usha. S. J. D. Cohen ("Jacob Neusner, Mishnah and Counter-Rabbinics," *Conservative Judaism* 37 [1983]: 53), notes, however, that "just as later tannaim who build upon the opinions of their predecessors thereby verify the ascriptions of those opinions to their predecessors, so too later tannaim who build upon, or refer to, the opinions of anonymous texts, thereby verify that the opinions expressed in those texts precede their own generation." If the anonymous section of m. Meg. 3:1 received its literary form at the late date suggested by Neusner, the content certainly predates Rabbi Meir. Additional responses to Neusner's methodology include S. D. Fraade, "Interpreting Midrash 1: Midrash and the History of Judaism," *Prooftexts* 7, no. 2 (1987): 179–194; E. P. Sanders, *Jewish Law from Jesus to the Mishnah*, 308–331.

30. t. Meg. 3:20.

31. On the storage of Roman books, see J. Clark, *The Care of Books* (Cambridge: Cambridge University Press, 1902), 36. This is the arrangement in images of Torah shrines from the Roman catacombs and on one from Sardis. Sources are collected by E. Budde, *Armarium und Kibotos* (Würzburg: Conrad Triltsch, 1939), pl. 30, 32–34, 36–37; Fine and Della Pergola, "Ostia Synagogue," 55–57. See figures pp. 152, 153, 155, 156.

32. *Thekē* in Greek. See W. Bacher, "Synagogue," *A Dictionary of the Bible*, ed. J. Hastings (New York, 1903), 369; A. Kohut, *Aruch Completum* (New York: Pardes, 1955), 8: 262–263; S. Krauss, *Griechische und lateinische Lehnwörter im Talmud, Midrasch und Targum* (Berlin: S. Calvary and Co., 1898–1899), 588; Budde, *Armarium und Kibotos*, 5. See Naveh, *On Stone and Mosaic*, 144.

33. t. Yad. 2:12, see S. Lieberman, *Tosefta Kifshuto* (New York: Jewish Theological Seminary, 1955–1988), 4: 156.

34. From the Greek, *analogion*. See Albeck, ad loc.; other opinions are collected by L. I. Levine, "From Community Center to Small Temple," 56–57. See also Brand, *Ceramics*, 42–44; *Glass Vessels in Talmudic Literature* (Jerusalem: Rav Kook Institute, 1978), 216–217; G. W. H. Lampe, *A Patristic Greek Dictionary* (Oxford: Oxford University Press, 1961), 111, and Daniel Sperber, *Greek and Latin Legal Terms in Rabbinic Literature* (Ramat Gan: Bar Ilan University Press, 1984), 37, n. 1. Archdeacon Seraphim, formerly of the Monastery of the Cross in Jerusalem, has brought it to my attention that the pedestal upon which the Scriptures are read in contemporary Greek Orthodox churches is called an *analogeion*.

35. See also *b. Meg.* 26a.

36. See *y. Bik.* 3:7, 65d; *b. Meg.* 27a.

37. *m. Meg.* 3:1, lines 20–21.

38. This reading is based upon the Erfurt manuscript. Cf. Lieberman, *Tosefta Kifshuto*, 5: 1162. The same principle is anonymously applied in *t. Meg.* 2:14 to synagogue appurtenances. See Lieberman, *Tosefta Kifshuto*, 5: 1154–1155. The traditions of Rabbi Eleazar son of Zadok are analyzed by Oppenheimer, "Benevolent Societies in Jerusalem," esp. 182–183.

39. Rashi to *b. Meg.* 27b remarks that Rabbi Meir requires this stipulation: "even from community to community Rabbi Meir forbade complete sale, for it is disgraceful."

40. This is consistent with the position attributed to him in *t. Meg.* 2:12, where he argues that if the "town leaders" agree they may sell an holy object from any step of *m. Meg.* 3:1's pyramid and do with the funds as they please.

41. *t. Sanh.* 4:4, 4:8; *m. Abod. Zar.* 3:4; *t. Ber.* 2:20; *Sifre Deut.*: 258. See Y. Hirschfeld, *Dwelling Houses in Roman and Byzantine Palestine* (Jerusalem: Ben Zvi Institute, 1987), 180–181.

42. Ibid.

43. This principle is applied anonymously by *t. Meg.* 2:14 to synagogue lamps. Once the names of the donors are worn off the lamp, it may be used for any purpose.

44. The term "*Imitatio Templi*" was suggested to me by Ziony Zevit.

45. J. N. Epstein, *Introduction to Tannaitic Literature*, ed. E. Z. Melamed (Jerusalem: Magnes Press, 1957), 656–658; E. Z. Melamed, *Halachic Midrashim of the* Tannaim *in Babylonian Talmud* (Jerusalem: Magnes Press, 1973), 192; E. P. Sanders, *Paul and Palestinian Judaism*, 67–69; Strack and Stemberger, *Introduction to the Talmud and Midrash*, 286–287.

46. *Sifra, Beḥukotai* 6; Cf. D. Z. Hoffmann, *Das Buch Leviticus*, tr. Z. Har Shepper and A. Lieberman (Jerusalem: Rav Kook Institute, 1967), 253–254; parallels cited by Lieberman, *Tosefta Kifshuto*, 5: 1204–206; Bokser, "Approaching Sacred Space," 290–292; Zahavy, *Studies in Jewish Prayer*, 18–19.

47. "Your temples" is set in a parallel construction with "Your cities." Cf. Hoffmann, *Das Buch Leviticus*, 253.

48. E. Kautzsch, *Gesenius' Hebrew Grammar*, tr. A. E. Cowley (Oxford: Oxford University Press, 1910), 264–265, 399–400.

49. See B. Epstein, *Torah Temimah* (Vilna: Romm, 1902), 3: 566–567, note 42.

50. See Bokser, *Origin of the Seder*, 41.

51. Ibid.

52. L. Gordon, "Becoming a Rabbi in First-Century Palestine," *Proceedings of the Eastern Great Lakes Biblical Society* 7 (1987), analyzes Tannaitic references to the study house.

53. The formula "synagogues and study houses" appears in m. *Ter.* 11:10 and m. *Pesah.* 4:4 in regard to the procurement of oil to light these institutions.

54. L. I. Levine, *The Rabbinic Class*, 28–29.

55. *Qapanderia.* See Krauss, *Griechische und lateinische Lehnwörter*, 374.

56. m. *Ber.* 9:5, *Sifre Deut.* 258.

57. See Maimonides and Albeck, ad loc.; Cf. t. *Sukk* 4:1.

58. See Bokser, "Approaching Sacred Space," 290; T. Zahavy, *The Mishnaic Law of Blessings and Prayers* (Atlanta: Scholars Press, 1987), 125.

59. Bokser, "Approaching Sacred Space," notes that the regulation of proper synagogue decorum legislated by t. *Meg.* 2:19 transfers biblical and Tannaitic modes of regulating behaviors in the Temple to the synagogue context. Following Eliade, Bokser calls the preparations taken before entering the Temple and behavior that must be maintained while there, "gestures of approach." He suggests that "this text is surely taking up the principle of m. *Ber.* 9:5."

60. b. *Meg.* 28a.

61. Following the Erfurt manuscript.

62. A section from a biblical scroll; Lieberman, *Tosefta Kifshuto*, 4: 892.

63. See Alon, *Jews in Their Land*, 170; A. Kasher, *Jews in Hellenistic and Roman Egypt*, 350, n. 28; J. Schwartz, *Jewish Settlement in Judaea* (Jerusalem: Magnes Press, 1986), 73; M. Ayali, *Workers and Craftsmen: Their Labor and Their Status in Rabbinic Literature* (Israel: Yad la-Talmud, 1987), 118.

64. t. *Sukk* 4:6; y. *Sukk* 5:1, 55a–b; Lieberman, *Tosefta Kifshuto*, 4: 889–892. A. Kasher, *Jews in Hellenistic and Roman Egypt*, 350–351, compares the versions and scholarly discussion of this tradition.

65. E. Levi, *Foundations of the Liturgy* (Tel Aviv: Avraham Ziony, 1963), 81. Cf. Elbogen, *Jewish Liturgy*, 355. See also 130–131.

66. m. *Sota* 7:8, t. *Sota* 7:13–14. Levi, *Foundations of the Liturgy*, 81. On *Haqhel*, see L. I. Rabinowitz, "Hakhel," *Encyclopedia Judaica* 7 (1970).

67. m. *Sota* 7:8.

68. m. *Yoma* 1:7; t. *Sukk* 4:8, 11–12; t. *Taan.* 1:13.

69. t. *Taan.* 1:13, *Meg.* 3:21; *Bik.* 2:8. On the duties of this functionary, see J. Zuri, *The Rule of the Patriarchate and the Council* (Paris, 1931), 1: 243–244. Cf. Zahavy, *Studies in Jewish Prayer*, 63–64.

70. See S. Lieberman, "Ḥazanut Yannai," *Sinai* 4 (1939): 222. Similarly, Tannaitic literature applies the title "Head of the Community" (*rosh ha-knesset*) both to a Temple functionary (m. *Yoma* 7:1; m. *Sota* 7:7–8), and to the "Head of the Community of Kziv" (t. *Ter.* 2:13; A. Neubauer, *La Géographie du Talmud* (Paris: M. Levy, 1868), 233; P. Neaman, *Encyclopedia of Talmudic Geography* (Tel Aviv: Joshua Chachik Publishing House, 1971), 2.15–19. *Rosh ha-Knesset* is the Hebrew equivalent of the Greek *archisynagogos* known from the later Second Temple Period and from later sources from Palestine and the Greco-Roman Diaspora. T. Rajak, "The Jewish Community and Its Boundaries," in *The*

Jews Among Pagans and Christians, ed. J. Lieu, J. North, and T. Rajak (London and New York: Routledge, 1992), 23–24, suggests that this term "would seem to have originated in Hebrew." See Roth-Gerson, *Greek Inscriptions,* 79 and the sources cited there; S. Hoenig, "The Ancient City Square: The Forerunner of the Synagogue," in *Aufstieg und Niedergang der Römische Welt* (Berlin and New York: Walther de Gruyter, 1979), 452–454; Burtchaell, *From Synagogue to Church,* 240–244.

71. y. *Taan.* 3:11, 66d, Josephus, *War,* 5:190, *Ant.* 15:396, 411–416. On basilicas in Rabbinic literature, see H. Gordon, "The Basilica and the Stoa in Early Rabbinical Literature," *Art Bulletin* 13 (1931).

72. b. *Ber.* 33b, b. *Pesah.* 13b.

73. Within the Tosefta this tradition follows a discussion of the Temple synagogue.

74. See Rabbinowicz, *Dikduqei Sofrim:* ad loc., note *samekh.* Cf. Rashi, Tosafot, ad loc.; compare the Palestinian Talmud version, which lists 70 elders. Sources collected by Lieberman, *Tosefta Kifshuto,* 4: 891; D. B. Ratner, *Ahavat Zion ve-Yerushalem* (Vilna: Romm, 1916), ad loc. Cf. A. Kasher, *Jews in Hellenistic and Roman Egypt,* 350, n. 24, 351.

75. The Palestinian Talmud version adds that they were "covered with fine stones and pearls."

76. See M. Goodman, "Sacred Space," 4.

77. *Embassy to Gaius,* line 133.

78. *War,* 7:44–45.

79. Lieberman, *Tosefta Kifshuto,* 4: 891; L. I. Levine, "From Community Center to Small Temple," 52.

80. On Alexandrian contact with Palestinian Rabbinic Sages, see A. Kasher, *Jews in Hellenistic and Roman Egypt,* 349. Historical sources are discussed by Lieberman, *Tosefta Kifshuto,* 4: 489. See also Alon, *Jews in Their Land,* 170–171, 397–405.

81. On attitudes toward history in Rabbinic literature, see N. Glatzer, *Untersuchungen zur Geschichtslehre der Tannaiten* (Berlin: Schocken, 1933); Yerushalmi, *Zakhor,* 16–26; L. I. Levine, "The Second Temple Synagogue," and *The Rabbinic Class,* 16–17. The closest literary parallels to our text are aggadic discussions of the Herodian Temple and its service. See J. Fraenkel, *Studies in the Spiritual World of the Homiletical Story* (Israel: Kibbutz Hameuchad, 1981), 119–137. On the literary quality of Rabbinic "historiography," see J. Fraenkel, "Hermeneutical Problems"; E. Slomovic, "Patterns of Midrashic Impact on the Rabbinic Midrashic Tale," *Journal for the Study of Judaism* 19, no. 1 (1988); D. Boyarin, "The Eye in the Torah: Ocular Desire in Midrashic Hermeneutic," *Critical Inquiry* 16, no. 3 (1990). See also R. Krautheimer, "The Constantinian Basilica," *Dumbarton Oaks Papers* 21 (1967): 124, n. 22.

82. In m. *Sukk* 3:1 the rejoicing of the water drawing ceremony in the Temple is described using similar language. In a *baraita* in b. *Sukk* 51a this terminology is applied to the Temple and to the city of Jerusalem.

83. See L. Hoffman, *Beyond the Text,* 194, n. 38. All of the trades mentioned in our tradition are known to have been practiced by Jews in Palestine. See Ayali, *Workers and Craftsmen:* goldsmiths: 114; silversmiths: 84; common weavers: 10–11, Tarsian weavers:

118; blacksmiths: 19. On Jewish participation in trades in the Roman Diaspora, see W. Meeks, *The First Urban Christians: The Social World of the Apostle Paul* (New Haven: Yale University Press, 1983), 39; A. Kasher, *Jews in Hellenistic and Roman Egypt*, 352–353. No indisputably Tannaitic source mentions contemporary synagogues belonging to specific groups of tradesmen, such synagogues do appear in Amoraic sources. Note the "Synagogue of the Tarsian (weavers)" in y. *Sheqal.* 2:7, 47a and Alon, *Jews in Their Land*, 170. I discussed this text in greater detail in "Relations between Egypt and Palestine during the Greco-Roman Period: The Evidence of the Synagogue."

84. Following J. Wilkinson, "Orientation, Jewish and Christian," *Palestine Exploration Quarterly* 116, no. 1 (1984) and A. Seager, "The Recent Historiography of Ancient Synagogue Architecture," in *Ancient Synagogues in Israel*, ed. R. Hachlili (London: BAR International, 1989), 88, we use "alignment" rather than "orientation."

85. On the equation of wisdom with Torah, see H. Strack and P. Billerbeck, *Kommentar Zum Neuen Testament*, 2: 353–355.

86. See S. J. D. Cohen, "Pagan and Christian Evidence," 162–163, regarding eastward orientation as perceived by pagan authors.

87. Vitruvius, 1.7.1. Cf. Targum to Prov. 1:21.

88. The identification of the *qodesh* has exercised many scholars. B. Epstein, *Torah Temimah*, to Lev. 8:4; Nissim son of Reuven Gerondi to Alfasi, *Meg.* 14a; Elbogen, *Jewish Liturgy*, 359; J. Hoffman, "The Ancient Torah Service in Light of the Realia of the Talmudic Era," *Conservative Judaism* 42, no. 2 (1989–90): 45. Compare y. *Bik.* 3:3, 65c.

89. Lieberman, *Tosefta Kifshuto*, 5: 1205, relates the use of *qodesh* in t. *Meg.* 3:21 to its appearance here. See also Alon, *Jews in Their Land*, 180, n. 14.

90. t. *Ber.* 3:15–16.

91. t. *Meg.* 2:14.

92. Lieberman, *Tosefta Kifshuto*, 5: 1154–1155.

93. Brand, *Ceramics*, 211.

94. L. I. Levine, "From Community Center to Small Temple," 77–78.

95. m. *Yoma* 3:10; t. *Kipp.* 2:3, and parallels. Lieberman, *Tosefta Kifshuto*, 4: 760. See L. Schiffman, "The Conversion of the Royal House of Adiabene in Josephus and in Rabbinic Sources," in *Josephus, Judaism, and Christianity*, ed. L. H. Feldman and G. Hata (Detroit: Wayne State University Press, 1987), 299.

96. y. *Yoma* 3:8, 41a. See Lieberman, *Tosefta Kifshuto*, 4: 760; Brand, *Ceramics*, 296–315, 346; M. Sokoloff; "Epigraphical Notes on the Palestinian Talmud," *Bar Ilan* 18–19 (1980): 219; *Dictionary of Jewish Palestinian Aramaic* (Ramat Gan: Bar Ilan University Press, 1990), 319.

97. Ed. Margaliot, 440–441.

98. L. Blau, "Early Christian Archaeology from a Jewish Point of View," *Hebrew Union College Annual* 3 (1926): 185, considers this text to be of Tannaitic origin based upon D. Z. Hoffmann's reconstruction of the *Mekhilta of Rabbi Shimon bar Yohai* (1905: 114–115). This tradition does not appear, however, in the partial edition of the *Mekhilta of Rabbi Shimon bar Yohai* based upon Cairo Genizah fragments that was published by Epstein and

Melammed. See G. Blidstein, "The Tannaim and Plastic Art: Problems and Prospects," *Perspectives in Jewish Learning* 5 (1973): 20.

99. Following the Vilna edition. See Rabbinowicz, *Dikduqei Sofrim:* ad loc., Abod. Zar. 43a, Menah. 28b.

100. Krauss, *Griechische und lateinische Lehnwörter*, 44–45.

101. See S. Fine, "On the Development of a Visual Symbol: The Date Palm in Roman Palestine and the Jews," *Journal for the Study of the Pseudepigrapha* 4 (1989): 112–113.

102. L.Y. Rahmani, A *Catalogue of Jewish Ossuaries in the Collection of the State of Israel* (Jerusalem: Israel Antiquities Authority, 1994), 51–52.

103. Ibid., no. 815.

104. Ibid., no. 829.

105. V. Sussman, *Ornamental Jewish Oil-Lamps: From the Destruction of the Second Temple Period through the Bar Kokhba Revolt* (Jerusalem: Israel Exploration Society, 1982), 20; nos. 1–6.

106. Ibid., no. 6.

107. Brand, *Glass Vessels*, 209. On examples of this phenomenon during the Byzantine period, see Branham, "Sacred Space under Erasure," 389–391.

108. Blau, "Early Christian Archaeology," 184–185.

109. See the Mishnah commentaries of Maimonides and Samson son of Abraham of Sens, ad loc.

110. Ex. 25:31–40; 37:17–24.

111. Targum Neofiti, Targum Pseudo-Jonathan, ad loc.; Maimonides, Mishnah Commentary, ad loc., relates "base" in our mishnah to Onkelos' translation of *kano* in Ex. 30:28, *basisei*.

112. Schiffman, "Dead Sea Scrolls and Early History," 34–35.

113. See ibid.

114. See above and Fleischer, "On the Beginnings of Obligatory Jewish Prayer," 420, n. 52.

115. t. *Yoma* 7:1, t. *Sota* 7:7.

116. t. *Kipp*. 4:18.

117. Lieberman, *Tosefta Kifshuto*, 4: 865–866; Oppenheimer, "Benevolent Societies in Jerusalem," 180–182; Y. Elman, "Babylonian Baraitot in the Tosefta and the 'Dialectology' of Middle Hebrew," *AJS Review* 16 (1991): 9, 22–24. On the *lulav*, see m. *Rosh. Hash.* 4:1–4; m. *Sukk*. 3:12, m. *Menah*. 10:5.

118. See Fleischer, "On the Beginnings of Obligatory Jewish Prayer," 419–423.

119. m. *Sukk*. 3:12. Based upon the critical edition by H. Fox (1979), 115; m. *Rosh. Hash.* 4:1–4, *Menah*. 10:5.

120. See Oppenheimer, "Benevolent Societies in Jerusalem," 181; Rubinstein, *The History of Sukkot*, 182–187.

121. See also M. Goodman, *State and Society in Roman Galilee*, 132–212 C.E. (Totowa, N.J.: Rowman and Allanheld, 1983), 127, and M. Jaffee, "The *Taqqanah* in Tannaitic Literature: Jurisprudence and the Construction of Rabbinic Memory," *Journal of Jewish Studies* 41, no. 2 (1990): 210, n. 21.

122. See *b. Rosh. Hash.* 30a.

123. *m. Sukk.* 3:14. The date of this anonymous tradition cannot be precisely ascertained, though it certainly predates Rabbi Jose, who, in *Sukk.* 3:14, takes it as a starting point for his legal position. The anonymous tradition in 3:13 must date, therefore, before the Usha generation (circa 150 C.E.). On the *takkanah* in Tannaitic literature, including our traditions, see Jaffee, "The *Taqqanah* in Tannaitic Literature," esp. 208–210, and bibliography cited there.

124. *m. Rosh. Hash.* 3:7. See S. Safrai, "The Temple and the Synagogue," in *Synagogues in Antiquity*, ed. A. Kasher, A. Oppenheimer, and U. Rappaport (Jerusalem: Ben Zvi Institute, 1987), 37–40; Zahavy, *Studies in Jewish Prayer*, 57.

125. *t. Meg.* 10:8. See S. Safrai, "Temple and Synagogue," 43–45.

126. *m. Meg.* 4:3,6,7. See S. Safrai, "Temple and Synagogue," 33–37, who suggests that the priestly blessing was carried out in Jerusalem synagogues before 70.

127. *t. Ber.* 3:1, 3; *t. Sukk* 4:4.

128. *t. Kipp.* 4:18.

129. The reading of the Esther scroll on Purim is also mentioned, apparently on the model of Torah reading. See *m. Rosh. Hash.* 3:7; Zahavy, *Studies in Jewish Prayer*, 57.

130. See L. I. Levine, "The Second Temple Synagogue"; Fleischer, "On the Beginnings of Obligatory Jewish Prayer," 426–441.

131. *t. Ber.* 2:4; Lieberman, *Tosefta Kifshuto*, 1:15; *m. Ber.* 7:3.

132. Rabin, "Linguistic Investigation," 163.

133. *t. Ber.* 3:6.

134. Newsom, *Songs of the Sabbath Sacrifice*, 20. G. Alon, "The Halakhah in the Teachings of the Twelve Apostles (*Didache*)," *Studies in Jewish History* 1 (1978): 284–285 cites evidence for this development before 70 C.E. See Heinemann, *Prayer in the Talmud*, 15.

135. *t. Ber.* 3:1,3. See Levi, *Foundations of the Liturgy*, 149. On the *mussaf* prayer, see *m. Ber.* 4:1, *t. Ber.* 3:3; *t. Sukk.* 4:4; Elbogen, *Jewish Liturgy*, 97–98.

136. For other measures of time, see *m. Ber.* 3:1, *t. Ber.* 1:1.

137. *m. Ber.* 4:1.

138. J. Heinemann and J. J. Petuchowski, *Literature of the Synagogue* (New York: Behrman House, 1975), 2; Heinemann, *Prayer in the Talmud*, 14–15; *Sifre Deut.* 41 and parallels collected by Finkelstein, ad. loc.; Elbogen, *Jewish Liturgy*, 5.

139. *Sifre Deut.* 41.

140. Elbogen, *Jewish Liturgy*, 199–205.

141. *m. Tamid* 7:4.

142. R. Goldenberg, "The Broken Axis: Rabbinic Judaism and the Fall of Jerusalem," *Journal of the American Academy of Religion* 45.3 (1977): 872.

143. Bokser, "The Wall Separating God and Israel," 368, and parallels cited in n. 52.

144. On the development of the *Amidah*, see Elbogen, *Jewish Liturgy*, esp. 24–54; Heinemann, *Prayer in the Talmud*, 13–24, 33–36, 50; R. Kimelman, "The Daily Amidah and the Rhetoric of Redemption," *Jewish Quarterly Review* 79, nos. 2–3 (1988–1989). Rabbinic sources are collected by Levi, *Foundations of the Liturgy*, 147–155. Cf. E. Fleischer,

Eretz-Israel Prayers and Rituals as Portrayed in the Geniza Documents (Jerusalem: Magnes Press, 1988), 14–15.

145. Heinemann, *Prayer in the Talmud*, 34. On the "rhetoric of redemption" in the *Tefillah*, see Kimelman, "The Daily Amidah," esp. 175–178.

146. See Lieberman, *Tosefta Kifshuto*, 1: 53–55. The benediction for the rebuilding of Jerusalem is discussed by Heinemann, *Prayer in the Talmud*, 50–58 and his *Studies in Jewish Liturgy*, ed. A. Shinan (Jerusalem: Magnes Press, 1981), 3–11.

147. See Ginzberg, *Commentary on the Palestinian Talmud*, 268.

148. Heinemann, *Prayer in the Talmud*, 24.

149. Scholars are divided on the early history of these texts. See ibid., 24, 230–233.

150. *Apostolic Constitutions* 4 and esp. 12:84–85. The *Apostolic Constitutions* are discussed by D. Fiensey, *Prayers Alleged To Be Jewish: An Examination of the Constitutiones Apostolorum* (Atlanta: Scholars Press, 1985). In *b. Ber.* 33a the *qedushot* and *havdalot* are attributed to the "Men of the Great Assembly."

151. See manuscript traditions cited by Lieberman, ad loc.

152. Heinemann, *Prayer in the Talmud*, 24–25.

153. Hoffman, *The Canonization of the Synagogue Service* (Notre Dame, Ind.: University of Notre Dame Press, 1979), 61–62.

154. On the dating of the Mekhiltas, see Fraade, *From Tradition to Commentary*, 192, n. 9, who writes as follows: "I assume that the two Mekiltas (conventionally associated with the "schools" of Rabbi Ishmael and of Rabbi Simeon bar Yohai) not withstanding their differences from one another and from *Sifre* Deuteronomy originate from much the same sociohistorical context of third century Palestine." Compare B. Z. Wacholder, "The Date of the Mekilta De-Rabbi Ishmael," *Hebrew Union College Annual* 39 (1968); H. Fox, "'As If with a Finger'— The Text History of an Expression Avoiding Anthropomorphism," *Tarbiz* 49 (1980): 288 n. 34; M. Kahane, "Pages of the Deuteronomy *Mekhilta* on Ha'azinu and Weziot Ha-Berakha," *Tarbiz* 57 (1988).

155. Ex. 20:21, *Ba-Hodesh* 2, ed. Horovitz-Rabin: 243; ed. Lauterbach 2:287 and parallels cited by Horovitz-Rabin. See Z. Safrai, "Communal Functions," 185, n. 17.

156. The parallel to this tradition in *Sifre Num.* 39, ed. Horowitz, prohibits the pronunciation of the Tetragrammaton in the priestly blessing outside the Temple.

157. *Sifre Num.* 39, ed. Horowitz and parallels cited there.

158. Ibid.

159. *y. Ber.* 4:4, 8b, 8d–9a; *Pesiq. Rab. Kah.* 5:8, ed. Mandelbaum: 91; *b. Ber.* 6a.

160. See M. Goodman, "Sacred Space," 12–13.

161. On Qumran and the Jesus sect, B. Gartner, *The Temple and the Community in Qumran and the New Testament* (Cambridge: Cambridge University Press, 1965). See also Baumgarten, *Studies in Qumran Law*, 39–97; Bokser, "Approaching Sacred Space," 281–287.

162. Smith, *Map Is Not Territory*, 172–189.

163. See R. Goldenberg, "The Synagogue as Sacred Space," *Conservative Judaism* 38, no. 2 (1985–1986): 19.

164. According to the Vienna manuscript. See Lieberman, *Tosefta Kifshuto*, 5: 1153–1154.

165. See ibid., 5:1157–58 for parallels.

166. Ibid., 5:1158.

167. Ibid.

168. *Ba-Ḥodesh* 10, ed. Horowitz-Rabin, 241; ed. Lauterbach 2:283. See Melamed, *Halachic Midrashim*, 123.

169. *Commentary on the Pentateuch*, Ex. 20:20. Cf. Blidstein, "The Tannaim and Plastic Art," 19–20.

170. Ed. Horowitz-Rabin 241; ed. Lauterbach 2:283.

171. Ibid.

172. On the role of the editor in Tannaitic *midrashim*, see Fraade, "Sifre Deuteronomy 26 (ad Deuteronomy 3:23): How Conscious the Composition?" *Hebrew Union College Annual* 54:245–301; Sifre Deuteronomy 26."

173. B. Epstein, *Torah Temimah*, 2:218, note 109.

174. *Sifra* to Leviticus 26:31, *Beḥukotai* 6, ed. Weiss, 112b.

175. Cf. Blidstein. "The Tannaim and Plastic Art," 20.

176. See: *b. Yoma* 69a; *Megillat Ta'anit* and the Scolion, ed. Lichtenstein, 339–340; ed. Luria, 164–170. Tcherikover, *Hellenistic Civilization and the Jews*, 46–47; L. Feldman, *Josephus and Modern Scholarship (1937–1980)* (Berlin and New York: Walther de Gruyter, 1984), 537–541. On recent archaeological excavations, see I. Magen, "Mount Gerizim—A Temple City," *Qadmoniot* 23, nos. 3–4 (1990).

177. m. Menaḥ. 13:10; y. Yoma 6:3, 43c–d; b. Menaḥ. 109a–110a; b. Meg. 10a. See also E. P. Sanders, *Judaism: Practice and Belief*, 21–22.

178. Even so, the Sages do not seem to have been very concerned that Jews would turn to blatant idolatry. See M. Goodman, *State and Society*, 40–53; Lieberman, *Hellenism in Jewish Palestine*, 115–138. Evidence for Diaspora Jews who participated in pagan cult practices is collected by L. Feldman, "Proselytes and 'Sympathizers' in Light of the New Inscriptions from Aphordisias," *Revue des Etudes juives* 147, nos. 3–4 (1989): 303–304.

179. B. Epstein, *Torah Temimah*, 2: 218, note 109; Blau, "Early Christian Archaeology," 185.

180. 440–441.

181. See Elbogen, *Jewish Liturgy*, 62–64.

182. M. Meg. 4:7. In *b. Rosh. Hash.* 31b this behavior is identified as an enactment of Rabban Yohanan son of Zakkai.

183. G. Blidstein, "Prostration and Mosaics in Talmudic Law," *Bulletin of the Institute of Jewish Studies* 2 (1974): 23, suggests that "Thus, it is not unlikely that the degree to which temple practices and structures were to be imitated in the post-destruction synagogue was a matter of some debate."

184. y. Ber. 3:1, 6a. See b. Sotah 38b.

185. The meaning of this term is somewhat obscure. See the relevant bibliography cited by Z. Weiss, "The Location of the Sheliah Tsibbur during Prayer," *Cathedra* 55

(1990). See also J. Hoffman, "Ancient Torah Service," 42–44; Elman, "Babylonian Baraitot," 23.

186. Following ms. Kaufmann. This text and parallel traditions are discussed in detail by Miller, *History and Traditions of Sepphoris*, 103–115. See also Blidstein, "Prostration and Mosaics," 22 and n. 3.

187. See Miller, *History and Traditions of Sepphoris*, 104.

188. *t. Taan.* 1:13, Lieberman, *Tosefta Kifshuto*, 5: 1075.

189. On Sikhnin, see Miller, *History and Traditions of Sepphoris*, 104, n. 235.

190. Blidstein, "Prostration and Mosaics," 23.

191. *Sifra, Behar* 9:5: 110b; y. *Abod. Zar.* 4:1; 43d; b. *Meg.* 22b.

192. Blidstein, "Prostration and Mosaics," 22.

193. See above, n. 168.

3. "The Sanctity of the Synagogue"

1. See S. Reif, "The Early History of Jewish Worship," in *The Making of Jewish and Christian Worship*, ed. P. F. Bradshaw and L. A. Hoffman (Notre Dame, Ind.: University of Notre Dame Press, 1991), 124–130; Peter Schäfer, "Jewish Magic Literature in Late Antiquity and in the Early Middle Ages," *Journal of Jewish Studies* 41 (1990): 7.

2. Targum Jonathan to Ez. 11:16.

3. See Introduction, p. 8.

4. See Ratner, *Ahavat Zion ve-Yerushalem*, 117. On the Divine epithet Maqom, Urbach, *The Sages*, 66–79.

5. See *b. Meg.* 6b.

6. See *b. Ber.* 8a.

7. The Venice edition errantly reads "Rabbi Abbahu in the name of Rabbi Abbahu." Ratner, *Ahavat Zion ve-Yerushalem*, 1:121, citing *Yalqut Shimoni* to Isa. 55:6

8. So *Yalqut Shimoni* to Isa. 55:6.

9. Cf. *b. Ber.* 6a and A. L. Yellin, *Yafeh Anayim* (Vilna: Romm, 1884), ad loc.

10. C. Albeck, *Introduction to the Talmud, Babli and Yerushalmi* (Tel Aviv: Dvir: 1969), 228–229.

11. Cf. D. Urman, "The House of Assembly and the House of Study: Are They One and the Same?" in *Ancient Synagogues: Historical Analysis and Archaeological Discovery*, ed. D. Urman and P. V. M. Flesher (Leiden: E. J. Brill, 1995), 1:240. On synagogues in Tiberias, see Z. Weiss, "Ancient Synagogues in Tiberias and in Hamat," *Idan* 11 (1988).

12. Pp. 53–55.

13. 1 Sam. 1:10.

14. *Pesiq. Rab. Kah.* 5:8, ed. Mandelbaum, 90–91.

15. *Pesiq. Rab. Kah.* 28:8, ed. Mandelbaum, 431–432.

16. *Pesiq. Rab. Kah.* 28:8, ed. Mandelbaum, 432.

17. See parallels cited by Mandelbaum, ad loc.

18. On the principle of "measure for measure" in Rabbinic thought, see Urbach, *The Sages*, 436–444.
19. See also y. *Sheb.* 4:10, 35c.
20. = *Midrash Tehillim* 84:3. Cf. Targum Psalms to Ps. 84:8, Rashi, ad loc.
21. The heavenly study house to which the righteous may look forward is described in detail in a version of *Pereq Meshiah*, discussed below, pp. 110–111.
22. Compare S. J. D. Cohen, "The Temple and the Synagogue," 170 and note 50.
23. See Rabbinowicz, *Dikduqei Sofrim*: ad loc.
24. The verse is translated to accord with the homily. Cf. *Tanhuma Jethro* 1:1:241 and Rashi to Eccl. 8:10.
25. R. Gordis, *Koheleth: The Man and His World* (New York: Block, 1955), 284–286, and M. Fox, *Qohelet and His Contradictions* (Sheffield: Sheffield University Press, 1989), 250, discuss the text history and interpretation of this verse. See the new Jewish Publication Society translation (1985: 1450 and note k k).
26. This connection was first noted by S. Klein, "Inscriptions from Ancient Synagogues in the Land of Israel," *Bulletin for the Institute for Jewish Studies* 2 (1925): 29.
27. M. Hirshman, *Midrash Qohelet Rabbah (Ch. 1–4)*, doctoral dissertation, Jewish Theological Seminary of America, 1983, 25, 106–107; "The Greek Fathers and the Aggada on Ecclesiastes: Formats of Exegesis in Late Antiquity," *Hebrew Union College Annual* 59 (1988): 37.
28. Ratner, *Ahavat Zion ve-Yerushalem*, 9: 60–61.
29. See b. *Meg.* 26b–27a. and D. Halivni, *Sources and Traditions* (New York: Jewish Theological Seminary, 1975), 508–509; Urman, "House of Assembly and the House of Study," 243.
30. See L. I. Levine, "The Sages and the Synagogue in Late Antiquity: The Evidence of the Galilee," in *The Galilee in Late Antiquity*, ed. L. I. Levine (New York: Jewish Theological Seminary, 1992), 205.
31. On this text see my "Review of R. Hachlili, *Ancient Jewish Art and Archaeology in the Land of Israel*, Leiden, 1988," *Journal for the Study of the Pseudepigrapha* 13 (1995): 101–104.
32. *Pnei Moshe* to y. *Meg.* 3:1, ed. Vilna: 23a.
33. Other sources that assert the priority of the study house over the synagogue include: b. *Ber.* 54a (ed. Vilna. Cf. Rabbinowicz, *Dikduqei Sofrim*: ad loc., nn. *ayin, peh*), *Midrash Tehillim* (84:3 and Buber's note: 186, n. 12). Compare the Palestinian Talmud version of this tradition (*Sheb.* 4:10, 35c), which M. Margaliot (*Pnei Moshe* [Vilna: 1922, ad loc.]), interprets in terms of the Bavli versions. See also Gen. Rab. 63:6, and the ms. traditions and parallels cited by Theodor and Albeck, *ad loc.*, 684.
34. See L. I. Levine, *The Rabbinic Class*, 28–29. On Rabbinic attitudes toward the synagogue and the study house, see L. I. Levine, "Sages and the Synagogue."
35. y. *Meg.* 3:4, 74a.
36. Rabbi Yoḥanan allows minor loosening of forbidden synagogue behaviors within public study houses, and possibly within public synagogues. The object of Samuel's

leniency is unclear. Cf. b. Meg. 29a, Rabbinowicz, Dikduqei Sofrim: ad loc.; M. Margoliot, Pnei Moshe, to y. Meg. 3:4.

37. Ibid.

38. See D. Fraenkel, Qorban ha-Edah (1922), ad loc.

39. y. Meg. 3:1, 73d.

40. m. Kelim 16:7; t. Yad. 2:12.

41. See Krauss' discussion of synagogue appurtenances (Synagogale Altertümer, 379–392).

42. L. I. Levine ("From Community Center to Small Temple," 54–56) collects the various interpretations of the synagogue appurtenances mentioned in this pericope. See M. Sokoloff, "The Hebrew of Genesis Rabba, Manuscript Vatican 30," in Anthology of Articles in Rabbinic Hebrew, ed. M. Bar-Asher (Jerusalem, 1990), 1.493, 435; Krauss, Griechische und lateinische Lehnwörter, 545. Jastrow, Dictionary, 1375, translates "teacher's litter." L. Y. Rahmani, "Stone Synagogue Chairs: Their Identification, Use, and Significance," Israel Exploration Journal 40, nos. 2–3 (1990): 197, 198–199, suggests that this is the equivalent of the Greek/Aramaic qatedra.

43. Sokoloff, Dictionary of Jewish Palestinian Aramaic, 256. On the usage of this curtain, see y. Shab. 20:1, 17c, Esth. Rab. 2:7. See Ginzberg, Commentary on the Palestinian Talmud, 3: 302; Z. Safrai, "Dukhan, Aron and Teva," 74, 89, n. 29.

44. Sokoloff, Dictionary of Jewish Palestinian Aramaic, 96; Krauss, Griechische und lateinische Lehnwörter, 235.

45. Krauss, Griechische und lateinische Lehnwörter, 235–236, and Sokoloff, Dictionary of Jewish Palestinian Aramaic, 96, read bilan from the Greek balon. The conceptual difference is not substantial.

46. Krauss, Griechische und lateinische Lehnwörter, 150.

47. Levine suggests that levaḥin probably refers to a reading table. Cf. Elbogen, Jewish Liturgy, 359. Compare b. Meg. 32a. Rashi's comment (ad loc.) that "I do not know what they are . . ." is still quite true.

48. P. 39 above.

49. Jerome (to Matt. 23:5) notes that Jewish houses possessed shelves loaded and cases packed with books: Judaei alioquin armariae et arcae habent libros. Cited by Samuel Krauss, "The Jews in the Works of the Church Fathers," Jewish Quarterly Review, Old Series 7 (1894): 232.

50. See Ginzberg, Commentary on the Palestinian Talmud, 3: 302.

51. A. Killebrew has suggested that the "window walls" of Byzantine period houses in the Jebel Druze "may have provided space for shelves, thus serving as a kind of closet" (A. Killebrew and S. Fine, "Qatzrin—Reconstructing Village Life in Talmudic Times," Biblical Archaeology Review 27, no. 3 [1990]: 54 and n. 8). See Hirschfeld, Dwelling Houses, 61, 64, 69, 82, 83, 94, 97, 103, 104, 144. On p. 124 Hirschfeld illustrates a contemporary parallel.

52. On the identification of this place, see L. I. Levine, "From Community Center to Small Temple," n. 55.

53. Ibid.

54. Or "commissioned." See Sokoloff, *Dictionary of Jewish Palestinian Aramaic*, 289.

55. Ibid., 288.

56. y. *Moed Qat.* 3:1, 81d; b. *Ber.* 8b and sources collected by R. Margaliot, "Death of R. Judah."

57. See Jastrow, *Dictionary*, 409.

58. *Pesiq. Rab. Kah.* 1:7, ed. Mandelbaum, 12; Matt. 23:2. Archaeological finds in Israel and the Diaspora have been identified with the "chair of Moses." No chair that has been discovered is identified as such in dedicatory inscriptions. This identification must therefore be regarded as a hypothesis. See W. Bacher, "Le Siege de Moise," *Revue de Etudes Juives* 34 (1897); E. L. Sukenik, "The Throne of Moses in Ancient Synagogues," *Tarbiz* 1 (1930); C. Roth, "The 'Throne of Moses' and Its Survivals," *Palestine Exploration Quarterly* 81 (1949); I. Renov, "The Seat of Moses," *Israel Exploration Journal* 5 (1955); Rahmani, "Stone Synagogue Chairs."

59. y. *Meg.* 4:1, 74d. Cf. A. York, "The Targum in the Synagogue and School," *Journal for the Study of Judaism* 10, no. 1 (1979): 75.

60. M. Zucker, *Rav Saadya Gaon's Translation of the Torah* (New York: Jewish Theological Seminary, 1959), 170–171, n. 666.

61. y. *Bik.* 3:2, 65c.

62. No. 36, ed. Lewin (1942), 75–76; ed. Margaliot (1938), 86, 156, and manuscript variants: 86. Z. Safrai, "Post-Talmudic Halakhic Literature," 405, notes that "While the book is late (after the eighth century) it contains a summary of distinctions between Palestinian and Babylonian halakhic practice most of which are already found in talmudic literature."

63. For general comments on this text, see Fleischer, *Eretz-Israel Prayers and Rituals*, 298–299. See also S. Reif, *Judaism and Hebrew Prayer* (Cambridge: Cambridge University Press, 1993), 153. Note that "Holy" does not appear in some manuscripts. We take "Holy Ark" here to be a Babylonian or medieval expression.

64. Gush Ḥalav, Qazrin, Maon (Judea), Hammath Tiberias B, last stage. See the relevant entries in M. J. S. Chiat, *A Handbook of Synagogue Architecture* (Chino: Scholars Press, 1982); Z. Ilan, *Ancient Synagogues in Israel* (Israel: Ministry of Defense, 1991).

65. Cambridge University Library, T-S K 1.162; cited by J. Naveh, "The Aramaic and Hebrew Inscriptions from Ancient Synagogues," *Eretz-Israel* 20 (1989): 303. See Naveh on relationships between Genizah magical texts and Palestinian synagogues. On magic in synagogues, see Naveh and Shaked, *Magic Spells and Formulae: Aramaic Incantations of Late Antiquity*. (Jerusalem: Magnes Press, 1985), 35–38; Naveh, "Aramaic and Hebrew Inscriptions," 302–303. The small number of amulets discovered in Palestinian synagogues are all on metal.

66. For a general discussion of this building, see Chiat, *Handbook of Synagogue Architecture*, 243–247.

67. L. Y. Rahmani, "The Ancient Synagogue of Maon (Nirim): The Small Finds and Coins," *Louis M. Rabinowitz Fund for the Exploration of Ancient Synagogues Bulletin* 3 (1960).

68. Naveh and Shaked, *Amulets and Magic Bowls*, 16, 91–92.

69. See M. Swartz, "Scribal Magic and Its Rhetoric: Formal Patterns in Medieval Hebrew and Aramaic Incantation Texts from the Cairo Genizah," *Harvard Theological Review* 83, no. 2 (1990): 166.

70. See ibid., 165–166.

71. Naveh and Shaked, *Amulets and Magic Bowls*, no. 11.

72. Naveh and Shaked, *Amulets and Magic Bowls*, nos. 12–13. See L. Schiffman and M. Swartz, *Hebrew and Aramaic Incantation Texts from the Cairo Genizah* (Sheffield: Sheffield University Press, 1992), 46–47.

73. Naveh and Shaked, *Amulets and Magic Bowls*, no. 11: lines 1, 4; no. 12, lines 6, 16–20, 24, 27–28 (?), 40; no. 13: lines 12–22. See Swartz, "Scribal Magic and Its Rhetoric," 167–179; Schiffman and Swartz, *Hebrew and Aramaic Incantation Texts*, 33, 37–42, 57–60; J. Trachtenberg, *Jewish Magic and Superstition: A Study in Folk Magic* (Cleveland: Jewish Publication Society, 1961), 104–113.

74. Ibid., 114–115.

75. Naveh and Shaked, *Amulets and Magic Bowls*, 41, line 12; 57, line 23; Swartz, "Scribal Magic and Its Rhetoric," 178; Schiffman and Swartz, *Hebrew and Aramaic Incantation Texts*, 58.

76. Naveh, *On Stone and Mosaic*, 34, 48, 54, 57, 60, 62, 70, 86, 122.

77. Schiffman and Swartz, *Hebrew and Aramaic Incantation Texts*, 2–9.

78. Amulets in Rabbinic literature are discussed by L. Blau, *Das Altjüdische Zaberwesen* (Berlin: L. Lamm, 1914), 86–96; esp. b. *Shab.* 115a and parallels cited by Blau, 113, n. 1. See also Schiffman and Swartz, *Hebrew and Aramaic Incantation Texts*, 49; Trachtenberg, *Jewish Magic and Superstition*, 139–152. On magic in churches, see J. Engemann, "Magische Uebelabwehr in der Spätantike," *Jahrbuch für Antike und Christentum* 18 (1976): 40–48 and bibliography cited there; E. D. Maguire and H. Maguire, *Art and Holy Powers in the Early Christian House* (Urbana, Ill.: University of Illinois Press, 1989).

79. This notion is first seen in Tannaitic sources, as we have suggested in chapter 2.

80. Ed. M. Sokoloff and J. Yahalom, *Aramaic Poetry of the Byzantine Period from Eretz-Israel* (Jerusalem: Israel Academy of Sciences and Humanities, forthcoming), no. 43. Professor Joseph Yahalom kindly made this text available to me.

81. Schäfer and Shinan cite the relevant appearances of this term. See Schäfer, *Die Vorstellung vom heiligen Geist*, 137–139; A. Shinan, "*Lishon Beit Kudsha* in the Aramaic Targumim to the Pentateuch," *Beth Mikra* 3, no. 66 (1976); "The Aramaic Targum as a Mirror of Galilean Jewry," in *The Galilee in Late Antiquity*, ed. L. I. Levine (New York: Jewish Theological Seminary, 1992), 248–250; and *The Embroidered Targum: The Aggadah in Targum Pseudo-Jonathan of the Pentateuch* (Jerusalem: Magnes Press, 1992), 113–114.

82. E. Levine, "Some Characteristics of Pseudo-Jonathan Targum to Genesis," *Augustinianum* 11 (1971): 97; Schäfer, *Die Vorstellung vom heiligen Geist*, 137–139.

83. Shinan, "*Lishon Beit Kudsha* in the Aramaic Targumim," 474; "Aramaic Targum as a Mirror," 249; *Embroidered Targum*, 114.

84. Shinan, "*Lishon Beit Kudsha* in the Aramaic Targumim"; "Aramaic Targum as a Mirror," 248–250; *Embroidered Targum*, 114.

85. See E. L. Sukenik, *The Ancient Synagogue of Beth Alpha* (Jerusalem: Hebrew University, 1932), 35–47.

86. Ed. Visotzky: 6, and note 42; S. Lieberman, *Sheki'in*, 2nd ed. (Jerusalem 1970), 9; Z. Safrai, "From House of Assembly," 154.

87. S. D. Goitein, *A Mediterranean Society*, 2 (Berkeley and Los Angeles: University of California Press, 1971), 156. On Goitein's notion of "popular religion," see "Religion in Everyday Life as Reflected in the Documents of the Cairo Geniza," in *Religion in a Secular Age*, ed. S. D. Goitein (Cambridge, Mass: Harvard University Press, 1974). For Karaite parallels, see J. Mann, "Anan's Liturgy and His Half-Yearly Cycle for Reading the Law," *Journal of Jewish Lore and Philosophy* 1, nos. 1–4 (1919): 340–342.

88. On the dating of this text, see Strack and Stemberger, *Introduction to the Talmud and Midrash*, 343.

89. *Cant. Rab.* 2:5 = *Num. Rab.* 4:20, and parallels cited by Ginzberg, *Legends of the Jews*, 6: 275.

90. D. R. Dendy, *The Use of Lights in Christian Worship* (London: S.P.C.K., 1959). On Byzantine lamps, see G. Crowfoot and D. B. Harden, "Early Byzantine and Later Glass Lamps," *Journal of Egyptian Archaeology* 17 (1930); M. L. Trowbridge, *Philological Studies in Ancient Glass* (Urbana, Ill.: University of Illinois Press, 1930), 190–191; L. Bouras, "Byzantine Lighting Devices," XVI *Internationaler Byzantinstenkongress Akten* (= *Jahrbuch der Österreichischen Byzantinistik* 32, no. 3) 2, no. 3 (1982). On ritual and votive uses of oil lamps in Rabbinic thought, see Brand, *Ceramics*, 373–378.

91. The more general Modern Hebrew denotation of *ner* sometimes causes some terminological confusion. See for example, Zevulun, *Form and Function in the Talmudic Period*, 80–83. On the *ner* in Rabbinic literature, see Brand, *Ceramics*, 337–381.

92. For example, on Meroth, see Z. Ilan and E. Damati, *Meroth: The Ancient Jewish Village* (Tel Aviv: Society for the Preservation of Nature in Israel, 1987), 144; on Gush Halav, see E. M. Meyers, C. Meyers, and J. Strange, *Excavations at the Ancient Synagogue of Gush Ḥalav* (Winona Lake, Ind.: Eisenbrauns, 1990), 128–129, 158–165. The authors suggest that oil lamps were discovered in this synagogue that are "unique to Gush Halav and found nowhere outside the synagogue site." They argue that "it seems reasonable to suggest that they were manufactured solely for use within this building." At Hammath Tiberias B, level 2, M. Dothan, *Hammath Tiberias: Early Synagogues* (Jerusalem: Israel Exploration Society, 1983), 62, notes, "Almost all of the lamp fragments were found on the floor of Locus 52, which was probably the treasury of the synagogue."

93. L. A. Mayer and A. Reifenberg, "A Samaritan Lamp," *Journal of the Palestine Oriental Society* 16 (1936): 44–45; R. Pummer, "Samaritan Material Remains and Archaeology," in *The Samaritans*, ed. A. D. Crown (Tubingen: J. C. B. Mohr, 1989), 158. F. Landsberger, "Old Hanukkah Lamps," in *Beauty in Holiness*, ed. J. Gutmann (New York: Ktav, 1970), 291, n. 18, is of the opinion that "despite its small size the lamp itself is a *Ner Tamid*." On Samaritan synagogues in general, see Hüttenmeister and Reeg, *Die antiken Synagogen in Israel* (Wiesbaden: Ludwig Reichert, 1977), 2; Z. Safrai, "Samaritan Synagogues in the Roman-Byzantine Period," in *The Ancient Synagogue*, ed. Z. Safrai, 84–112; Pummer, "Samaritan Material Remains and Archaeology," 139–151.

94. Ex. 27:20 and elsewhere.

95. See Pummer, "Samaritan Material Remains and Archaeology," 142, 157–158.

96. *Ashashit:* See Jastrow, *Dictionary*, 1127–1128. *Qandila:* Greek: *kandala*, Latin: *candela*. See also Goitein, A *Mediterranean Society*, 150 notes that "In 1075 the synagogue of the Palestinians (in Fustat) was illuminated by fifty-one large and small chandeliers, called *buqandalt* i.e., *abu qandalat*), a term not found thus far elsewhere. . . ." See also S. D. Goitein, "The Synagogue Building and Its Furnishings According to the Record of the Cairo Geniza," in *Eretz Israel* 7 (1964): 170*. Trowbridge, *Philological Studies in Ancient Glass*, 190, notes that, "The first reference I find to glass lamps is in the fourth century where many large candelae are described as hanging in a church." See Bouras, "Byzantine Lighting Devices," 479; Jastrow, *Dictionary*, 1388; Sokoloff, *Dictionary of Jewish Palestinian Aramaic*, 1991: 496; *Gen. Rab.* 4:2, Theodor's comment, ad loc., and Z. W. Einhorn, *Commentary of the Maharzu* (1975), ad loc.

97. Use of the term *ner tamid* to describe lamps suspended before Torah shrines in ancient synagogues finds no warrant in Jewish literature or in Jewish archaeological remains. On the development of this term during the modern period, see Landsberger, "Old Hanukkah Lamps," 291; J. Gutmann, "How Traditional Are Our Traditions?" in *Beauty in Holiness*, ed. J. Gutmann (New York: Ktav, 1970), 417.

98. See Rashi, ad loc.

99. Munich 95, as cited by Rabbinowicz, *Dikduqei Sofrim* ad loc.

100. Ms. 110 as cited by Rabbinowicz, *Dikduqei Sofrim:* ad loc.

101. Ed. Liss, 177 and n. 59.

102. Ms. 2675.2, as cited by Rabbinowicz, *Dikduqei Sofrim:* ad loc.

103. See ed. Liss, 177.

104. L. I. Levine, "From Community Center to Small Temple," 71–72, finds evidence in *b. Erub.* 86b of the "Palestinian custom of bringing the Torah scroll to the synagogue on the Sabbath from a location that was outside the prayer hall."

105. Cf. Rashi, ad loc.; Z. Safrai, "Dukhan, Aron and Teva," 73; L. I. Levine, "From Community Center to Small Temple," 71–72. L. Ginzberg, "Beiträge zur Lexikographie des Juedische Aramäischen III," in *Essays and Studies in Memory of Linda R. Miller*, ed. I. Davidson (New York: Jewish Theological Seminary, 1938), 86–89, followed by J. Gutmann, "Programmatic Painting in the Dura Synagogue," in *The Dura Europos Synagogue*, ed. J. Gutmann (Missoula: Scholars Press, 1973), 147–148, suggests that an early *piyyut* found in *Gen. Rab.* 54:4, ed. Theodor Albeck 581–582 and parallels (ibid.) was sung when the Torah cabinet with the scroll was brought into the synagogue hall. See also G. Scholem, *Jewish Gnosticism, Merkabah Mysticism, and Talmudic Tradition* (New York: Jewish Theological Seminary, 1960); C. Kraeling, *The Synagogue. The Excavations of Dura Europos, Final Report VIII, Part I* (New Haven: Yale University Press, 1956), 105; Wieder, "'Sanctuary' as a Metaphor," 173–174.

106. See Elbogen, *Jewish Liturgy*, 158–163.

107. No. 49, ed. Lewin (1942), 99; ed. Margaliot (1938), 88, 173–174 and the ms. versions described there. See also Z. Safrai, "Dukhan, Aron and Teva," 73.

108. See no. 36, ed. Margaliot (1938), 86; ed. Lewin (1942), 75–76.
109. t. Sukk. 4:6.
110. Sof. 14:4–11.
111. Cf. Sof. 1:5.
112. Referring to Isa. 6:3.
113. Sof. 14:5.
114. Sof. 14:6.
115. Sof. 14:7
116. See Higger's note, ad loc.
117. The meaning of this section is obscure.
118. Sof. 14:9.
119. Sof. 14:10.
120. See Fleischer, *Eretz-Israel Prayers and Rituals*, 276, n. 3.
121. See Goitein, *A Mediterranean Society*, 156, above.
122. S. Lieberman, "Tractate Sofrim, ed. M. Higger," *Kirjath Sepher* 15 (1938): 59; "Ḥazanut Yannai," 9 argues that *kri'ah* is a technical term for bowing in late Rabbinic literature. Jerome notes with surprise that Jews do not kneel during prayers (Commentary to Isa. 45:2, cited by Krauss, "Jews in the Works of the Church Fathers," 236). As Lieberman himself notes, the Karaite Daniel son of Moses Al-Qumisi, polemicizes against prostration in the direction of Rabbinite Torah arks (M. Zucker, "Responses to the Karaite 'Mourners of Zion' Movement in Rabbinical Literature," in *Chanoch Albeck Jubilee Volume* (Jerusalem: Rav Kook Institute, 1963), 170–171, n. 666; Al-Qumisi, *Commentarius in Librum Duodecim Prophetarum* (1957), 5, 47; Z. Safrai, "From Synagogue to Little Temple," 26.
123. The "pure-minded ones" are mentioned in m. Git. 9:8.
124. See Sokoloff, *Dictionary of Jewish Palestinian Aramaic*, 580; L. I. Levine, "From Community Center to Small Temple," 71, n. 182.
125. Compare especially t. Meg. 3:21 and y. Bik. 3:3, 65c. and other sources collected by Z. Safrai, "Dukhan, Aron and Teva," 72.
126. Sokoloff, *Dictionary of Jewish Palestinian Aramaic*, 73. Cf. Z. Safrai, "Dukhan, Aron and Teva," 72.
127. y. Taan. 2:1, 65a.
128. In *Midrash Ecclesiastes* 1 (= *Midrash Cant.* 1) the synagogue ark is implicitly equated with the "Ark of the Covenant of God" (1 Kings 3:15). See A. Yaari, *The History of the Festival of Simhat Torah* (Jerusalem: Rav Kook Institute, 1964), 16.
129. Regarding the situation in the Babylonian Talmud, see J. Hoffman, "Ancient Torah Service," 44.
130. y. Yoma 7:1, 44b; y. Meg. 4:5, 75b; y. Sota 8:6, 22a. Sokoloff, *Dictionary of Jewish Palestinian Aramaic*, 445.
131. The transformation of the lampstand into the *menorah* is discussed above, pp. 46–49. See also y. Meg. 74a.
132. m. Yoma 3:10; t. Kipp. 2:3, and parallels. Lieberman, *Tosefta Kifshuto*, 4: 760.

133. y. *Yoma* 3:8, 41a. See Lieberman, *Tosefta Kifshuto*, 4: 760; Brand, *Ceramics*, 346; Sokoloff, *Dictionary of Jewish Palestinian Aramaic*, 483.

134. = b. *Arak.* 6b.

135. Scholars have long discussed the identity of this Antoninus. The various options are assembled by M. Stern, *Greek and Latin Authors on Jews and Judaism* (Jerusalem: Israel Academy of Arts and Sciences, 1976–1984), 2: 626–627. L. Ginzberg, "Antoninus in the Talmud," *Jewish Encyclopedia* (1901), considers these traditions to be legendary.

136. Alon, *Jews in Their Land*, 685.

137. t. *Meg.* 2:14.

138. m. *Ber.* 9:5.

139. See Rabbinowicz, *Dikduqei Sofrim*: ad loc., and the commentary of Hananel son of Hushiel in Lewin, *Otzar ha-Gaonim*, 1.72. See M. Margolioth, *Encyclopedia of Talmudic and Gaonic Literature* (Tel Aviv, 1987), 1: 171; Albeck, *Introduction to the Talmud, Babli and Yerushalmi*, 230.

140. Bokser, "Approaching Sacred Space," 290, and Zahavy, *Mishnaic Law of Blessings*, 125, consider this interpretation to be implicit in m. *Berakhot* itself.

141. y. *Bik.* 3:3, 65d = *Midrash Samuel* 7:10. On the historical context of this statement, see L. I. Levine, *The Rabbinic Class*, 173–174.

142. See E. Y. Kutscher, "Tannaitic Hebrew," in *Anthology of Articles in Rabbinic Hebrew*, ed. M. Bar-Asher (Jerusalem: Akadamon, 1972), 10–11; Sokoloff, "Hebrew of Genesis Rabba," 271–272.

143. Another exegetical application of *hekhal* to synagogues appears in y. *Sheqal.* 5:4, 49a and S. Krauss' unlikely interpretation of y. *Taan.* 3:13, 67a (*Synagogale Altertümer*, 367–368). See also B. Narkiss, "The Hekhal, Bimah, and Teivah in Sephardi Synagogue," *Jewish Art* 18 (1992): 39, 45.

144. According to most manuscript traditions. See Rabbinowicz, *Dikduqei Sofrim*: ad loc. and ms. Columbia X893–T141. The Venice edition, followed by the Vilna edition reads: Rabbi Isaac.

145. The Venice edition, followed by Vilna, continues: "which are in Babylonia." This reading is not attested, however, in the manuscript traditions. See Rabbinowicz, *Dikduqei Sofrim*, ad loc. and Ms. Columbia, ad loc.; *Yalqut Shimoni*, Psalms 659.

146. M. Greenberg, *The Anchor Bible: Ezekiel 1–20* (Garden City: Doubleday, 1983), 204; W. Zimmerli, *Ezekiel 1*, tr. R. E. Clemens (Philadelphia: Fortress Press, 1979), 262.

147. New Jewish Publication Society version (1984), 169. Cf. Greenberg, *Ezekiel 1–20*, 204.

148. Note the subtle avoidance of the terms "holy ark" and "Ark of the Covenant." See also Blidstein, "Prostration and Mosaics," 23.

149. L. Ginzberg, Genizah *Studies in Memory of Doctor Solomon Schechter* (New York: Jewish Theological Seminary, 1928–1929), 1:152–153.

150. *The Bible in Aramaic*, ed. A. Sperber (Leiden: E. J. Brill, 1962), 283.

151. Ed. M. Margaliot (1973), 131–132. Note Reif's characterization of this text (*Judaism and Hebrew Prayer*, 59).

152. Cf. Z. Safrai, "From House of Assembly," 150–151. See L. I. Levine, "From Community Center to Small Temple," 40–41. On ablution during the Second Temple period and in early Rabbinic writings, see E. P. Sanders, *Judaism: Practice and Belief*, 222–230.

153. J. Mann, "Anan's Liturgy," 344, n. 26. Al-Qumisi informs us that by analogy to the Temple, Rabbinites would not enter synagogues in a state of impurity (Zucker, *Rav Saadya Gaon's Translation of the Torah*, 171, n. 666).

154. Maon (Nirim), Maon (Judea), Meroth. See L. I. Levine, "From Community Center to Small Temple," 41. A *miqveh* is reported near the synagogue of Gamla from 67 C.E. See S. Gutman, "The Synagogue at Gamla," in *Ancient Synagogues Revealed*, ed. L. I. Levine (Jerusalem: Israel Exploration Society, 1981), 32. On immersion in the Diaspora, see E. P. Sanders, *Judaism: Practice and Belief*, 223, and note 24. See also C. Koranda, "Menora Darstellungen auf Spätantiken mosaikpavimenten," *Kairos* 30–31 (1988–1989): 219.

155. Sokoloff, *Dictionary of Jewish Palestinian Aramaic*, 124; Brand, *Ceramics*, 96–97.

156. y. *Meg.* 3:3, 74a. See Z. Safrai "Dukhan, Aron and Teva," 107. On ablution of hands before prayer, see N. Wieder, "Islamic Influences on the Hebrew Cults," *Melilah* 2 (1946): 43.

157. Chiat, *A Handbook of Synagogue Architecture*, 219–224; D. Barag, Y. Porat, and E. Netzer, "The Synagogue at En-Gedi," in *Ancient Synagogues Revealed*, ed. L. I. Levine (Jerusalem: Israel Exploration Society, 1981), 117; Z. Safrai, "Communal Functions," 184, n. 14. On other washing installations in Palestinian synagogues, see L. I. Levine, "From Community Center to Small Temple," 40, n. 26; Z. Safrai, op. cit., 184. Ablution is evidenced in the Hellenistic Diaspora during the latter part of the Second Temple period and washing installations have been uncovered in a number of late antique synagogues. Evidence is collected by L. I. Levine, op. cit., 39–41 and bibliography cited there.

158. F. van der Meer, *Early Christian Art*, tr. P. and F. Brown (Chicago and London: University of Chicago Press, 1967), 58–59; see also L. I. Levine, "From Community Center to Small Temple," 40.

159. Wieder, "Islamic Influences," 39–51. See also Goitein, *A Mediterranean Society*, 2:154, 435.

160. Though the Jewish practice may indeed have been strengthened by Moslem practice.

161. S. J. D. Cohen, "Purity and Piety: The Separation of Menstruants from the Sancta," in *Daughters of the King: Women in the Synagogue*, ed. S. Grossman and R. Haut (Philadelphia: Jewish Publication Society, 1992), 108. See Lieberman, *Sheki'in*, 22; "The Knowledge of the Halakha by the Author (or Authors) of the Heikhaloth," in *Apocalyptic and Merkavah Mysticism*, ed. I. Gruenwald (Leiden: E. J. Brill, 1980); S. Schechter, "Jewish Literature in 1890," *Jewish Quarterly Review*, Old Series 3 (1891): 338–342; M. Higger, ed., "Perek Niddah," *Alim: A Periodical for the Bibliography and History of the Jews* 3, no. 3 (1938): 60; Y. Dinari, "The Violation of the Sacred by the Niddah and the Enactment of Ezra," *Te'uda: Studies in Talmudic Literature, in Post Biblical Hebrew and in Biblical Exegesis* 3

(1983): 19. Compare, however, A. Aptowitzer, *Studies in Gaonic Literature* (Jerusalem: Rav Kook Institute, 1941), 166–168.

162. Against H. Turner, *From Temple to Meeting Place*, 282; J. R. Wegner, *Chattel of Person? The Status of Women in the Mishnah* (New York: Oxford University Press, 1988), 162. See J. Hauptman, "Review of *Chattel of Person? The Status of Women in the Mishnah*," *Religious Studies Review* 18, no. 1 (1992): 14.

163. On *niddah* and *ziva* in biblical, Second Temple period and early Rabbinic thought, see E. P. Sanders, *Judaism: Practice and Belief*, 219; S. J. D. Cohen, "Menstruants and the Sacred in Judaism and Christianity," in *Women's History and Ancient History*, ed. S. B. Pomeroy (Chapel Hill: University of North Carolina, 1991), 277.

164. See S. J. D. Cohen, "Menstruants and the Sacred," 287–290. Note especially the *Didascalia Apostolorum* (mid-third century, Syria), which criticizes roundly Christian women who, in keeping with Jewish practice, abstain from prayer, from receiving the Eucharist, and from hearing the Scriptures read during their menstrual period (ed. A. Voobus, 180: 238–239, tr. 179: 238–239).

165. See Lieberman, *Sheki'in*, 22; 1980; Schechter, "Jewish Literature," 338–342; Aptowitzer, *Studies in Gaonic Literature*, 166–168.

166. *Baraita de-Niddah*, version 1, 3:4, 30–33 and Horowitz' notes 128, 129.

167. The formula "study houses and synagogues" is unusual, reversing the usual order. See ed. Horowitz, n. 134; Dinari, "Violation of the Sacred," 18–19.

168. *Baraita de-Niddah*, version 1, 1:2, 3. See also 33, n. 133; 52, III; Schechter, "Jewish Literature," 341; M. Higger, "*Perek Niddah*," 65.

169. This point was made by S. J. D. Cohen, "Purity and Piety," 107–108. This tradition was well known in medieval Ashkenaz, where it exerted considerable influence upon the place of women in synagogue life. See Dinari, "Violation of the Sacred"; S. J. D. Cohen, "Menstruants and the Sacred."

170. L. Ginzberg, Genizah Studies, 1:77 = *Sefer Pitron Torah*: 18–19; *Midrash ha-Gadol*, Num. 8:2: 119. See Zucker, "Karaite 'Mourners of Zion Movement'," 395–398.

171. *K-me-ain ha-Miqdash*. See the *Sefer Pitron Torah*: 18–19, Urbach's comment, n. 53 and bibliography cited there. See also Z. Safrai, "From Synagogue to Little Temple," 23.

172. Ibid., 23.

173. Cf. ibid., 23–24.

174. = m. Pesah. 4:4.

175. Lieberman, *Sheki'in*, 9; Zucker, *Rav Saadya Gaon's Translation of the Torah*, 170–171, n. 666, and "Karaite 'Mourners of Zion Movement'," 395–396. Zucker suggests that these traditions reflect a Rabbinic response to Karaite polemics against synagogue lighting and to the notion that synagogues are "small temples." While this may have occasioned the formulation of these traditions, Z. Safrai, "From Synagogue to Little Temple," 27, has correctly argued that "it was not the Karaites who were responsible for this trend . . . they were simply responding to the reality of their times." See also Z. Safrai, "From House of Assembly," 153–154.

176. Lieberman, *Sheki'in*, 10; Zucker, *Rav Saadya Gaon's Translation of the Torah*, 170–171, n. 666, and bibliography cited there; Z. Safrai, "From Synagogue to Little Temple," 25.

177. See Brown, "Art and Society in Late Antiquity," 25.

178. *Against the Jews*, 6:7, ed. Migne 48:914.

179. See below, p. 121.

180. On this mosaic pavement, see below, p. 112.

181. N. Zori, "The Ancient Synagogue at Beth-Shean," *Eretz-Israel* 8 (1967): 154, 163, pl. 33.2. Zori: 163, dates this piece to the sixth or early seventh century.

182. See K. Weitzmann, *The Age of Spirituality* (Princeton: Princeton University Press, 1979), 385–386; Horbury and Noy, *Jewish Inscriptions of Graeco-Roman Egypt*, 225–226; *Sacred Realm*, ed. Fine, 155–156.

183. *Pesiq. Rab. Kah.* 24:18, ed. Mandelbaum, 377. See also *b. Taan.* 27b.

184. *yored/over lifne hatevah*. See the relevant bibliography cited by Weiss, "Location of the Sheliah Tsibbur." See also J. Hoffman, "Ancient Torah Service," 42–44; Elman, "Babylonian Baraitot," 23.

185. *y. Ber.* 4:4, 8b; Cf. *Gen. Rab.* 49:23, ed. Theodor-Albeck, 506–507 and parallels cited there.

186. See Theodor and Albeck to *Gen. Rab.* (1965), 507.

187. Jastrow, *Dictionary*, 1410. See Krauss, *Synagogale Altertümer*, 97.

188. Cited in *Hilkhot Eretz Israel*, ed. M. Margaliot, 132.

189. Additional prayers. See Buber's note: 190a–b.

190. Pp. 423–424.

191. Ginzberg, *Commentary on the Palestinian Talmud*, 433–434.

192. Some form of *Hoshana Rabba* ritual existed in synagogues during Amoraic times. See *Lev. Rab.* 37:2. Cf. Z. Safrai, "From Synagogue to Little Temple," 25, and "From House of Assembly," 152–153. See especially Ginzberg, Genizah *Studies*, 2:252–256.

193. 17:5, ed. Buber: 45 and Buber's comments there. See Z. Safrai, "Dukhan, Aron and Teva," 75–76, n. 51. Cf. 25:5.

194. Cf. Ginzberg, Genizah *Studies*, 2:252–256. A number of medieval scholars report this tradition in the name of the Palestinian Talmud, though it does not appear in extant manuscripts. *Midrash Tehillim* 17:5:45 and Buber's comments there; Ginzberg, op. cit., Z. Safrai, "Dukhan, Aron and Teva," 75–76, n. 51.

195. On this ceremony in Geonic Babylonia, Elbogen, *Jewish Liturgy*, 116; L. Hoffman, *Canonization of the Synagogue Service*, 105–106.

196. See Elbogen, *Jewish Liturgy*, 116, 175–176; Ginzberg, Genizah *Studies*, 252–259; Heinemann, *Prayer in the Talmud*, 139–150, 154–155. Following his predilection toward early dating, Heinemann believes that the *hoshanah* pattern "was not created to fulfill the demands of some local synagogue custom of circling the reading desk, which developed gradually during the Gaonic period (for, as we have seen, this pattern considerably antedated Qalir), but rather came into being to meet the needs of a fixed, ancient and festive ceremony in the Temple itself" (148).

197. *Sof.* 18:1–2; *m. Tamid* 7:4.

198. S. Assaf, "An Early Lament on the Destruction of Communities in the Land of Israel," *Texts and Studies in Jewish History* (Jerusalem: Rav Kook Institute, 1946).

199. Friedman, "Ono—New Insights from the Writings of the Cairo Genizah," in *Between Yarkon and Ayalon* (Ramat Gan: Bar Ilan University, 1983), 74.

200. E. Fleischer, cited by M. Friedman, "Ono–New Insights" 76.

201. M. Avi-Yonah, *The Jews under Roman and Byzantine Rule* (Jerusalem: Magnes Press, 1984), 251; Millar, "Jews of the Greco-Roman Diaspora," 117–120.

202. See Chiat, *A Handbook of Synagogue Architecture*, 158–161.

203. See M. Friedman, "Ono–New Insights," 74.

204. *m. Meg.* 3:1.

205. E. Fleischer, cited by M. Friedman, "Ono–New Insights," 76, notes that it is impossible to determine from the extant fragment the literary type of this *piyyut*.

206. *Yosse Ben Yosse Poems*, ed. A. Mirsky (Jerusalem: Bialik Institute, 1977), 127–178, 178–203, 222–239. See also 210–217.

207. *Liturgical Poems of Simon Bar Megas*, ed. J. Yahalom (Jerusalem: Israel Academy of Sciences and Humanities, 1984), 11.

208. *The Liturgical Poetry of Rabbi Yannai*, ed. Rabinowitz, 1:8.

209. This last notion was suggested by Michael D. Swartz in a lecture entitled "Sage, Priest, and Poet: The Tractate Yoma in the Avodah Liturgy," at the annual meeting of the Society for Biblical Literature in New Orleans on November 25, 1996.

210. Luke 1:5, 8; 4Q Mishmerot Hakohanim; B. Z. Wacholder and M. G. Abegg, *A Preliminary Edition of the Unpublished Dead Sea Scrolls* (Washington, D.C.: Biblical Archaeology Society, 1991), 60–118.

211. Sources are discussed by Hoenig, "The Ancient City Square."

212. See D. Trifon, "Did the Priestly Courses (*Mishmarot*) Transfer from Judaea to the Galilee after the Bar Kokhba Revolt?" *Tarbiz* 59, nos. 1–2 (1989–90) and bibliography cited there; L. I. Levine, *The Rabbinic Class*, 171–172 and "From Community Center to Small Temple," 83, n. 245.

213. Levine, *The Rabbinic Class*, 191.

214. Trifon, "Did the Priestly Courses (*Mishmarot*) Transfer," esp. 84 and 86, n. 58.

215. S. Klein, *Sefer ha-Yishuv*, 1 (Jerusalem: Bialik Institute, 1939), 90; Trifon, "Did the Priestly Courses (*Mishmarot*) Transfer," 78, n. 11.

216. M. Avi-Yonah, "The Caesarea Inscription of the Twenty-Four Priestly Courses," *Eretz-Israel* 7 (1964): 24–28; Naveh, *On Stone and Mosaic*, 87–88.

217. Naveh, *On Stone and Mosaic*, 89; J. Yahalom, "Synagogue Inscriptions in Palestine—A Stylistic Classification," *Immanuel* 10 (1980): 55. H. Eshel, "A Fragmentary Inscription of the Priestly Courses?" *Tarbiz* 61, no. 1 (1991): 159–161, has shown that an inscription from Kissufim is not a fragment of a *mishmarot* plaque.

218. This unpublished piece is reported by F. Vitto, "Decor mural des anciennes synagogues a la lumiere de nouvelles decouvertes," *XVI Internationaler Byzantinstenkongress Akten* (= *Jahrbuch der Österreichischen Byzantinistik* 32, no. 5).

219. H. Eshel, "A Fragmentary Inscription of the Priestly Courses?"
220. Naveh, *On Stone and Mosaic*, 93–94.
221. Ibid., 114.
222. Ibid., 115–116. Levites also appear in a number of inscriptions. Jose son of Levi the Levite is mentioned in inscriptions from Baram (pp. 19–20) and Alma in the Upper Galilee (pp. 22–23). A Levite was a donor at Hammath Gader (pp. 57–58) and Judan the Levite's donations are memorialized in two inscriptions from the Susiya synagogue (pp. 120–121, 121–122). It is interesting that both a priest and a Levite are mentioned in the Susiya synagogue.
223. = *Num. Rab.* 4:20, and parallels cited by Ginzberg, *Legends of the Jews*, 6.275.
224. *Tanḥuma*, ed. Buber, *Va-yakel*: 124 and note 32; *Tanḥuma, Va-yakel*, 1833: 336.
225. See E. E. Urbach, "The Role of the Ten Commandments in Jewish Worship," in *The Ten Commandments in History and Tradition*, ed. B. Segal and G. Levi, tr. G. Levi (Jerusalem: Magnes Press, 1990), esp. 175–181 and Fleischer, *Eretz-Israel Prayers and Rituals*, 259–274.
226. *Tanḥuma*, 1833, *Va-yakel*: 337, 339.
227. On the stoa in Rabbinic literature, see H. L. Gordon, "The Basilica and the Stoa," 366–374; Krauss, *Griechische und lateinische Lehnwörter*, 379.
228. On the redaction of Pseudo-Jonathan, see E. Levine, "Some Characteristics of Pseudo-Jonathan Targum to Genesis," 92; Y. Maori, "The Relationship of Targum Pseudo-Jonathan to Halakhic Sources," *Te'uda: Studies in Talmudic Literature, in Post Biblical Hebrew and in Biblical Exegesis* 3 (1983): 244–250; A. Shinan, "Targumic Additions in Targum Pseudo-Jonathan," *Textus* 16 (1991): 149–150.
229. See Blidstein, "Prostration and Mosaics," 39, n. 2; M. Klein, "Palestinian Targum and Synagogue Mosaics," *Immanuel* 11 (1980): 44–45; L. I. Levine, "From Community Center to Small Temple," 82.
230. See also *Sifra, Behukotai* 6; y. *Abod. Zar.* 4:1, 43d; b. *Meg.* 22b. Cf. Blidstein, "Prostration and Mosaics," 28–39; L. I. Levine, "R. Abbahu of Caesarea," in *Christianity, Judaism and Other Greco-Roman Cults*, ed. J. Neusner (Leiden: E. J. Brill, 1975): Pt. 4, 64.
231. On Palestinian mosaics in general, see E. Kitzinger, *Israel Mosaics* (New York: New American Library, 1965). Discoveries are cataloged by R. Ovadiah and A. Ovadiah, *Hellenistic, Roman, and Early Byzantine Mosaic Pavements in Israel* (Rome: "L'Erma" de Bretschneider, 1987).
232. This issue is discussed by M. Klein, "Palestinian Targum and Synagogue Mosaics," 44–45; Ovadiah and Ovadiah, *Mosaic Pavements in Israel*, 199–200.
233. See L. I. Levine, "Sages and the Synagogue," 217; M. Avi-Yonah, "Synagogue Architecture in the Late Classical Period," in *Jewish Art*, ed. C. Roth (London, 1971), 79–80.
234. S. Netter, *Commentary on Targum Jonathan* (Vienna, 1859); Lev. 26:1; Samuel Krauss, "Die Galilaeischen Synagogenruinen und die Halakha," *Monatsschrift für Geschichte und Wissenschaft des Judentums* 65 (1921): 218–219; H. L. Gordon, "The Basilica and the Stoa," 371; E. Itzchaky, *The Halacha in Targum Jerushalmi I (Pseudo-Jonathan Ben*

Uziel and Its Exegetic Methods), doctoral dissertation, Bar Ilan University, 1982, 329–330. See Targum Neofiti to Lev. 26:19,31; Targum Pseudo-Jonathan to Lev. 26:31. If Pseudo-Jonathan meant to say "synagogues" it had the resources to do so. See Ex. 18:20.

235. *Sifra Behar* 9:5; *b. Meg.* 22b and Blidstein, "Prostration and Mosaics," 20, n. 3.

236. Blidstein notes that "Although the Temple area was paved with flagstones and mosaics, whatever decoration existed was purely geometric" (ibid.). See Josephus, *War* 5:19–3; *m.* Mid. 1:6; ed. Kaufmann: 42; Krauss, *Griechische und lateinische Lehnwörter*, 2: 479–482; J. N. Epstein, *Introduction to the Text of the Mishnah*, 2:1235. All mosaics found in Jewish contexts from the Second Temple period are strictly geometric. See Hachlili, *Ancient Jewish Art*, 66–67.

237. *y. Abod. Zar.* 3:3, 42d, according to a Genizah fragment that was published by J. N. Epstein, "Additional Fragments of the Jerushalmi," *Tarbiz* 3, no. 1 (1931): 20.

238. *m. Tamid* 3:4 explicitly mentions prostration on the platform of the Temple Mount. See Josephus *War* 5:190–193; *m.* Mid. 1:6; ed. Kaufmann: 42; Krauss, *Griechische und lateinische Lehnwörter*, 2:479–482; J. N. Epstein, *Introduction to the Text of the Mishnah*, 2: 1235.

239. Avi-Yonah, *The Jews under Roman and Byzantine Rule*, 76; Lieberman, *Hellenism in Jewish Palestine*, 115–127; Y. Tsafrir, *Eretz Israel from the Destruction of the Second Temple to the Muslim Conquest, Art and Archaeology* (Jerusalem: Ben Zvi Institute, 1984), 186, 215–217, and "The Byzantine Setting and Its Influence on Ancient Synagogues," 154, n. 6; Glatzer, "Attitude toward Rome"; Bokser, "Rabbinic Responses to Catastrophe."

240. *Tanhuma,Behukotai* 3: 475; ed. Mantua, 146; *Tanhuma,*ed. S. Buber, 110.

241. Lit. "at first."

242. Cf. ed. Buber, ad. loc., n. 12. As this tradition has been transmitted, the homily is based upon the first half of the verse. See J. Mann and I. Sonne, *The Bible as Read and Preached in the Old Synagogue*, 2 (Cincinnati: Hebrew Union College Press, 1966), 146, n. 169.

243. The synagogues of Meron and H. Shema were built at the high point of the town.

244. On the movement of churches from the periphery into the traditional urban center during the Byzantine period, see D. Claude, *Die byzantinnische Stadt um 6 Jahrhundert, Byzantinisches Archiv* 13 (1969): 95–96; P. Brown, *Society and the Holy*, 189. On the Islamic period, see H. Kennedy, "From Polis to Madina: Urban Change in Late Antique and Early Islamic Syria," *Past and Present* 106 (1985): 14–15. Mann and Sonne, *Bible as Read and Preached*, 2:146, n. 169, believed that this text is reflective of a time during the Byzantine period "when Jews in Palestine were not allowed to build their synagogues in a conspicuous manner." This is in keeping with Mann's generally lachrymose approach to this period.

245. *t. Meg.* 3:23.

246. See pp. 105–112, below.

247. Ed. Kirschner.

248. Christian use of temple imagery, by contrast, was supercessionist. See Kessler, "Through the Veil." On the use of Temple imagery in late antique churches, see M. Harri-

son, *A Temple for Byzantium: The Discovery and Excavation of Anicia Juliana's Palace Church in Istanbul* (Austin: University of Texas Press, 1989), 137–144; Branham, "Sacred Space under Erasure," 380–383; K. McVey, "The Domed Church as Microcosm: Literary Roots of an Architectural Symbol," *Dumbarton Oaks Papers* 37 (1983); J. Wilkinson, "Christian Worship in Byzantine Palestine," in *Ancient Churches Revealed*, ed. Y. Tsafrir (Jerusalem, 1993). On general Christian interest in the Temple, see H. Nibley, "Christian Envy of the Temple," *Jewish Quarterly Review* 50 (1959–1960); B. Kühnel, *From the Earthly to the Heavenly Jerusalem: Representations of the Holy City in Christian Art of the First Millennium* (Rome, 1987).

4. "May Peace Be unto All Those Who Gave Charity in *This Holy Place*"

1. The most expansive published list is that of Ilan, *Ancient Synagogues in Israel*.

2. Hachlili, *Ancient Jewish Art*, 143–198; Ovadiah and Michaeli, "Observations of the Origin of the Architectural Plan of Ancient Synagogues," 235.

3. F. Vitto, "The Synagogue at Rehob," in *Ancient Synagogues Revealed*, ed. L. I. Levine (Jerusalem: Israel Exploration Society, 1981); J. Sussman, "The Inscription in the Synagogue at Rehob," ibid.; "A Halakhic Inscription from the Beth-Shean Valley," *Tarbiz* 43 (1973–74), 44 (1974–75).

4. P. 30, above.

5. t. Meg. 2:14, 16.

6. y. Meg. 3:2, 74a.

7. This material is collected by Naveh, *On Stone and Mosaic* and "Aramaic and Hebrew Inscriptions," and Roth-Gerson, *Greek Inscriptions*.

8. J. Stambaugh, *The Ancient Roman City* (Baltimore and London: Johns Hopkins University Press, 1988), 141.

9. Z. Safrai, "Financing Synagogue Construction in the Period of the Mishna and the Talmud," in *Synagogues in Antiquity*, ed. A. Kasher, A. Oppenheimer, and U. Rappaport (Jerusalem: Ben Zvi Institute, 1987); A. Kindler, "Donation and Taxes in the Society of Jewish Villages in Eretz Israel during the 3rd to 6th Centuries CE," in *Ancient Synagogues in Israel*, ed. R. Hachlili (London: BAR International, 1989).

10. M. M. Mango, *Silver from Early Byzantium* (Baltimore: Walters Art Gallery, 1986), 11.

11. C. Dauphin, "Mosaic Pavements as an Index of Prosperity and Fashion," *Levant* 12 (1980): 125.

12. *Knisha:* appears in inscriptions from Hammath Gader and Beth Guvrin (Naveh, *On Stone and Mosaic*, 60–61, 109–111). *Sunagoga:* Gerasa (Roth-Gerson, *Greek Inscriptions*, 46.); *atar:* Hammath Gader, probably in reference to the synagogue (Naveh, op. cit., 154, 156); *atra:* Naaran (ibid., 100–101); *maqom:* Baram (small synagogue) and Alma (ibid., 19–20, 22–23). It is unclear, however, whether these inscriptions refer to the synagogue upon which it is inscribed, to the village that it faced out toward, or to both. See

S. Klein, "Inscriptions from Ancient Synagogues," 29. *Atra qadisha:* Kefar Ḥananyah (Naveh, op. cit., 34–36); Hammath Tiberias B (ibid., 48–49), Beth Shean B (ibid., 77–78), Naaran (4 times, ibid., 95–96, 99–102); *hagios topos:* Ashkelon (Roth-Gerson, *Greek Inscriptions,* 25); Gaza marble fragment (ibid., 101, 103), *hagiotato topo:* Gerasa (p. 46), Gaza pavement (p. 91); *tara d'marei shumyah:* H. Ha-Ammudim (Naveh, op. cit., 40–41), interpreted following Sokoloff, "Epigraphical Notes on the Palestinian Talmud," 218, n. 2. Cf. I. Sonne, "Secondary Names for the Synagogue," *Tarbiz* 27 (1958); F. Hüttenmeister, "The Aramaic Inscription from the Synagogue at H. Ha-Ammudim," *Israel Exploration Journal* 28 (1978); Naveh, "Aramaic and Hebrew Inscriptions," 306–307.

13. See Kindler, "Donation and Taxes"; Z. Safrai, "Financing Synagogue Construction." *t. B. Mes.* 11:23 suggests that local taxation was used to finance synagogue buildings and procure sacred scrolls. (See Lieberman, *Tosefta Kifshuto,* 9: 320; *t.* B.Q. 11:3; Z. Safrai, "Financing Synagogue Construction," 78–79). Cf. White, *Building God's House,* 85. On benefaction by private pagan and Christian individuals in the villages of Roman Syria, see G. Harper, "Village Administration in the Roman Province of Syria," *Yale Classical Studies* 1 (1928): 149–150. On synagogue patronage in the land of Israel before 70 C.E., see the Theodotos inscription (Roth-Gerson, *Greek Inscriptions,* 76–86 and bibliography cited there).

14. See, for example, the two inscriptions honoring Severos at Hammath Tiberias B (Roth-Gerson, *Greek Inscriptions,* 65–68).

15. At Jericho and Susiya, Naveh, *On Stone and Mosaic,* 103–105, 123, 115.

16. "The holiness of ..." at Susiya. See ibid., 115–116.

17. P. 139 below.

18. Note, however, *a-sh-r q-d-sh* in earlier Phoenician texts. J. Gibson, *Textbook of Syrian Semitic Inscriptions,* 3: *Phoenician Inscriptions* (Oxford: Oxford University Press, 1982), 54–55; N. Slouschz, *Thesaurus of Phoenician Inscriptions* (Tel Aviv: Bialik Institute, 1942), 352.

19. Sokoloff "Epigraphical Notes," 218, n. 1.

20. M. Goodman, "Sacred Space," 13, n. 20, reached the same conclusion. He notes that *hagios topos* appears "nowhere (so far as I can discover) in pagan inscriptions. But note the use of the phrase in the story recounted by Plutarch (*Camillus* 31.3.7) about attempts made by Roman senators to mollify the people by pointing out the *choron hieron kai topon hagion* which Romulus or Numa had consecrated."

21. Meimaris, *Sacred Names,* 17. Wilkinson, *Egeria's Travels,* 15, notes this phenomenon in the fourth-century writings of Egeria: "One of the words most frequently used by Egeria is 'holy'; she applies it impartially to mountains, buildings, people, and among the holy men and women to saints of the old as well as the New Testament."

22. Meimaris, *Sacred Names,* nos. 800–801.

23. *Hagios topos:* nos. 768, 781, 802–803, and on pilgrim flasks, no. 782–799.

24. Meimaris, *Sacred Names,* nos. 802–803.

25. Ibid., no. 768. It also appears at Der-Rumsaniyeh in the Golan, no. 770.

26. Ibid., nos. 771, 772, 777, 778, 779, 780.

27. Ibid., nos. 773, 769.

28. On Transjordan, see M. Piccirillo, "Recenti Scoperte d'Archeologia Cristiana in Giordania," in *Actes du XIe Congres International d'Archeologie Chretienne* 2 (Rome, 1989); on Gaza, see Hunt, *Holy Land Pilgrimage*, 72; on Nessana, see H. D. Colt, "Introduction," *Excavations at Nessana* (London: British School of Archaeology at Jerusalem, 1962), 1.25.

29. R. Merkelbach, *Die Inschriften von Assos* (Bonn: Habelt, 1976), no. 33:70. This example is cited by M. Goodman, "Sacred Space," 13, n. 20.

30. Meimaris, *Sacred Names*, no. 769; G. E. Kirk and C. B. Welles, "Inscriptions," in *Excavations at Nessana*, ed. H. D. Colt (London: British School of Archaeology at Jerusalem, 1962), 150, no. 37. The inscription from Tabgha (Meimaris, *Sacred Names*, no. 768) is also dated to the 5th century.

31. *Hagia ekklesia*: Meimaris, *Sacred Names*, nos. 754–756, 758–766. Often in the superlative: nos. 754, 761, 762, 763, 766; *hagios euktation*: no. 757; *hagion thusiastapion*: no. 767.

32. Ibid., nos. 749, 751, 755, 756, 764.

33. See Markus, "How on Earth Could Places Become Holy" and compare L. I. Levine, "The Palestinian Synagogue Reconsidered," 447.

34. Dothan, *Hammath Tiberias*, 53, 61.

35. Sokoloff, *Dictionary of Jewish Palestinian Aramaic*, 114. Cf. Naveh, *On Stone and Mosaic*, 48.

36. Sokoloff, ibid., 170. Cf. Naveh ibid., 48–49.

37. Sokoloff, "Epigraphical Notes," 168.

38. Roth-Gerson, *Greek Inscriptions*, 69.

39. Dothan, *Hammath Tiberias*, 61–63; Roth-Gerson, *Greek Inscriptions*, 69–71.

40. Ibid., 71, my translation. See L. Roth-Gerson, "Similarities and Differences in Greek Synagogue Inscriptions of Eretz-Israel and the Diaspora," in *Synagogues in Antiquity*, ed. A. Kasher, A. Oppenheimer, and U. Rappaport (Jerusalem: Ben Zvi Institute, 1987), 133.

41. Foerster, "Synagogue Inscriptions," 14–15.

42. "Holy place" appears a number of times in the Hebrew Bible, almost always in reference to the Temple. See Lev. 6:19–20, 7:6, 10:13, 16:24, 24:9; Isa. 60:13; Ez. 42:13. On "holy place" in the Pentateuch, see D. Wright, *The Disposal of Impurity: Elimination Rites in the Bible and in Hittite and Mesopotamian Religion* (Atlanta: Scholars Press, 1987), 232–235, and "Holiness, Old Testament," 241–242. See also Ex. 3:5 and Sonne's comments ("Secondary Names for the Synagogue," 559).

43. A similar phenomenon appears in a Syriac hymn from sixth-century Edessa, where a church is called *Haykla* in place of more common terms for churches. McVey, "The Domed Church as Microcosm," 96, argues that the choice of this poetic language was "Most probably . . . deliberate, emphasizing the building as a holy place."

44. This, in fact, is Al-Qumisi's complaint against the Rabbinites (See pp. 79, 85 above). See also Goldenberg, "The Synagogue as Sacred Space," 19.

45. Following Naveh, *On Stone and Mosaic*, 99. See E. Y. Kutscher, "Jewish Palestinian Aramaic," in *An Aramaic Handbook*, ed. F. Rosenthal (Wiesbaden: Harrassowitz, 1967), 70.

46. D. Bahat, "A Synagogue at Beth-Shean," in *Ancient Synagogues Revealed*, ed. L. I. Levine (Jerusalem: Israel Exploration Society, 1981); Ovadiah and Ovadiah, *Mosaic Pavements in Israel*, 36–37.

47. Naveh, *On Stone and Mosaic*, 77–78. Cf. Dauphin, "Mosaic Pavements as an Index," 126.

48. H. J. Bornstein, "The Dispute between R. Saadia Gaon and Ben Meir," in *Nahum Sokolow Festschrift* (Warsaw: Shuldberg, 1904), 22, n. 1; M. Friedman, "The Minimum Mohar Payment as Reflected in the Geniza Documents: Marriage Gift or Endowment Pledge," *Proceedings of the American Academy of Jewish Research* 43 (1976): 33; *Jewish Marriage*, 2: 304–305; and "Ono–New Insights," 78–79, nn. 35–40; J. Mann, *The Jews in Egypt and in Palestine under the Fatamid Caliphs* (London: Oxford University Press, 1920–1922), 1.454, n. 2; Yahalom, "Synagogue Inscriptions in Palestine," 50, n. 11; Sokoloff, *Dictionary of Jewish Palestinian Aramaic*, 184. In liturgy, see *Yaqum Purqan*. See *Seder Avodat Yisrael*, ed. Baer, 229; Naveh, *On Stone and Mosaic*, 78; Elbogen, *Jewish Liturgy*, 162; Foerster, "Synagogue Inscriptions," 23–27. On *havrayya* in Rabbinic sources, see W. Bacher, "Zur Geschichte der Schulen Palaestina's im 3 und 4 Jahrhundert, Die Gnossen (*havrayya*)," *Monatsschrift für Geschichte und Wissenschaft des Judentums* 43 (1899).

49. See p. 87 above.

50. Rabbinic sources regarding this town are collected by S. Klein, *Sefer ha-Yishuv*, 2–3.

51. Assaf, "An Early Lament," 10.

52. M. Beer, "On the *Havura* in Eretz Israel in the Amoraic Period," *Zion* 47, no. 2 (1982): xiii. See also Foerster, "Synagogue Inscriptions," 27.

53. Friedman, "Ono–New Insights," 79.

54. Ovadiah and Ovadiah, *Mosaic Pavements in Israel*, 36.

55. Bahat, "A Synagogue at Beth-Shean"; Ilan, *Ancient Synagogues in Israel*, 177.

56. Bahat, "A Synagogue at Beth-Shean," 82, suggests that this niche may explain why the pattern of the southern side of the mosaic's frame is wider than the other sides.

57. No individual is mentioned in the dedicatory inscription from the synagogue in Jericho. There we read: "God knows their names," that is, the names of the benefactors (Naveh, *On Stone and Mosaic*, 77–79. See Roth-Gerson, *Greek Inscriptions*, 41–43). Ilan and Damati (*Meroth: The Ancient Jewish Village*, 72–87) suggest that a room at Meroth served as a *beit midrash*, and another room as a "study room." There is no evidence to substantiate these identifications.

58. Bahat, "A Synagogue at Beth-Shean," 85; Roth-Gerson, *Greek Inscriptions*, 41–43.

59. Ilan, *Ancient Synagogues in Israel*, 177, my translation.

60. Ibid.

61. See Urman's discussion of the literary and archaeological evidence of study houses ("House of Assembly and the House of Study") and my comments on the supposed study house on Gamla in my article on "Gamla" in the *Oxford Encyclopedia of Near Eastern Archaeology*, ed. E. M. Meyers (New York: Oxford University Press, 1996). Cf. F. Hütten-

meister, "The Synagogue and the Beth Ha-Midrash and Their Relationship," *Cathedra* 18 (1981): 42.

62. Naveh, *On Stone and Mosaic*, 34–35; Chiat, *A Handbook of Synagogue Architecture*, 55–56; Hüttenmeister and Reeg, *Die antiken Synagogen in Israel*, 1: 256–258; Ilan, *Ancient Synagogues in Israel*, 153–154.

63. Remains identified as a synagogue have been uncovered there. See Chiat, *A Handbook of Synagogue Architecture*, 55–56; Hüttenmeister and Reeg, *Die antiken Synagogen in Israel*, 1:256–258; Ilan, *Ancient Synagogues in Israel*, 153–154.

64. *Kelilah*, lit. "crown" or "garland." See Sokoloff, *Dictionary of Jewish Palestinian Aramaic*, 260. A similar usage appears in Latin. In the *Book of the Pontiffs* (*Liber Pontificalis*) we hear of *fara coronata*, "crown lamps." See discussion: 111, 113.

65. *t.* Meg. 2:14.

66. *y.* Meg. 3:1, 74a.

67. Bouras, "Byzantine Lighting Devices," 480–482.

68. Naveh, "Aramaic and Hebrew Inscriptions," 303; Cambridge University Library, Or. 1080.6.19, T-S K 1.18.

69. B. Lifshitz, *Donateurs et Fondateurs dans les Synagogues Juives* (Paris: J. Gabalda, 1967), 55; Roth-Gerson, *Greek Inscriptions*, 25–27.

70. Ibid., 101–103 and bibliography cited there.

71. Lifshitz, *Donateurs et Fondateurs*, 57, dates this piece to the sixth century. See Roth-Gerson, *Greek Inscriptions*, 103.

72. E.L. Sukenik, *The Ancient Synagogue of El-Hammeh (Hammath-by-Gadera)* (Jerusalem: R. Mass, 1935), 159. See Hüttenmeister and Reeg, *Die antiken Synagogen in Israel*, 136–137.

73. A. Ovadiah, "Excavations in the Area of the Ancient Synagogue at Gaza (Preliminary Report)," *Israel Exploration Journal* 19, no. 4 (1969): 195, and "The Synagogue at Gaza," in *Ancient Synagogues Revealed*, ed. L. I. Levine (Jerusalem, 1982), 130. See Lifshitz, *Donateurs et Fondateurs*, 58–59; Roth-Gerson, *Greek Inscriptions*, 91 and bibliography cited there.

74. Roth-Gerson, "Similarities and Differences," 133.

75. See Naveh, *On Stone and Mosaic*, 92–93.

76. See Roth-Gerson, *Greek Inscriptions*, 150.

77. See Roth-Gerson, "Similarities and Differences," and compare her conclusions, 142.

78. The translation follows Kirk and Welles, "Inscriptions," 173, n. 94. See also nos. 77, 95.

79. Though most are formulated in the third person. See the inscriptions cited by Ovadiah and Ovadiah, *Mosaic Pavements in Israel*.

80. Roth-Gerson, *Greek Inscriptions*, 47 and bibliography cited there; "Similarities and Differences," 133.

81. See Roth-Gerson, *Greek Inscriptions*, 46.

82. See Roth-Gerson, *Greek Inscriptions*, 48; Foerster, "Synagogue Inscriptions," 15–17.

83. See Naveh, *On Stone and Mosaic*, 65–66, 103, 106–108, 148.

84. E. L. Sukenik, "The Mosaic Inscriptions in the Synagogue at Apamea on the Orontes," *Hebrew Union College Annual* 28, pt. 2 (1950–1951): 545; Lifshitz, *Donateurs et Fondateurs*, 39–40.

85. See Roth-Gerson, *Greek Inscriptions*, 65, 66; Naveh, *On Stone and Mosaic*, 34, 43, 46, 48, 52, 54, 57, 60, 62, 70, 95, 99, 100, 101, 104, 107, 115–116, 122.

86. Lifshitz, *Donateurs et Fondateurs*, 74; Naveh, *On Stone and Mosaic*, 141, 146.

87. See Ovadiah and Ovadiah, *Mosaic Pavements in Israel*, 25, 88, 99.

88. See G. Foerster, "A Basilica Plan (including Apsis) as a Chronological Criterion in Synagogues," in *Synagogues in Antiquity*, ed. A. Kasher, A. Oppenheimer, and U. Rappaport (Jerusalem: Ben Zvi Institute, 1987). Architectural terminology used here generally follows R. Jacoby and R. Talgam, *Ancient Jewish Synagogues: Architectural Glossary* (Jerusalem: Center for Jewish Art of the Hebrew University, 1988). Our use of "longhouse" differs from theirs. See their illus. 9 and section 2.

89. See Kraabel, "The Diaspora Synagogue," 487; on Christian basilicas, see R. Krautheimer, *Early Christian and Byzantine Archaeology*, 3rd ed. (Baltimore: Penguin, 1979), 39–68; Meer, *Early Christian Art*, 53–69.

90. For the purpose of this discussion, "Torah shrine" is a designation for any permanent installation that was intended to contain sacred books in the main room of an ancient synagogue or study house. The visual and literary evidence do not support Hachlili's clear-cut differentiation between the Torah shrine and the Ark of the Scrolls (R. Hachlili, "The Niche and the Ark in Ancient Synagogues," *Bulletin of the American Schools for Oriental Research* 222 [1976]).

91. E. L. Sukenik, *Ancient Synagogues in Palestine and Greece* (London: Oxford University Press, 1934), 50. See L. I. Levine, "From Community Center to Small Temple," 81, n. 233. Wilkinson, "Orientation," 25–26; Seager, "Recent Historiography," 86–87; Weiss and Netzer, *Promise and Redemption*, 12–13.

92. Wilkinson, "Orientation," 18–19; Seager, "Recent Historiography," 87; Moore, *Judaism*, 1:369–374.

93. See, for example, *Shulkan Arukh*, *Orekh Ḥayyim* 150:5 and the sources cited there; M. Shapiro, *Otzar Ha-She'eloth U-Teshuvoth (Compendium Responarum)* (Jerusalem: Makhon Maharshal, 1976), 1: 124–125; J. Sarna, "The Debate over Mixed Seating in the American Synagogue," in *The American Synagogue: A Sanctuary Transformed*, ed. J. Wertheimer (New York: Cambridge University Press, 1987), 387, n. 3.

94. Most of the primary archaeological sources utilized in this discussion of Palestinian synagogues are collected and organized by Chiat, *A Handbook of Synagogue Architecture*; Hachlili, *Ancient Jewish Art*; L. I. Levine, "From Community Center to Small Temple."

95. See y. Meg. 3:1, 73d. Hachlili, *Ancient Jewish Art*, 166-187 collects the archaeological evidence.

96. A. Kloner, "The Synagogues of Horvat Rimmon," in *Ancient Synagogues in Israel*, ed. R. Hachlili (London: BAR International, 1989), 44. On the broadhouse form, see E. M. Meyers, "The Ancient Synagogue of Khirbet Shema," *Perspectives in Jewish Literature* 5 (1973): 33.

97. Note the comments of S. Gutman, Z. Yeivin, and E. Netzer, "Excavations in the Synagogue of Horvat Susiya." in *Ancient Synagogues Revealed*, ed. L. I. Levine (Jerusalem: Israel Exploration Society, 1981): 124.

98. Our discussion is based upon J. Magness, "Synagogue Typology and Earthquake Chronology at Khirbet Shema'," *Journal of Field Archaeology* 27 (1997). See the report of this excavation by E. M. Meyers, A. T. Kraabel and J. Strange, *Ancient Synagogue Excavations at Khirbet Shema', Upper Galilee, Israel, 1970–1972* (Durham: Duke University Press, 1976), 46, 49–54, 71–72 and Meyers, "The Ancient Synagogue of Khirbet Shema," 973: 32–33. See also Weiss, "Location of the Sheliah Tsibbur," 17, n. 48.

99. On regionalism in synagogue architecture, see E. M. Meyers, "Galilean Regionalism as a Factor in Historical Reconstruction," *Bulletin of the American Schools for Oriental Research* 220–221 (1976) and "The Cultural Setting of Galilee: The Case of Regionalism and Early Judaism," in *Aufstieg und Niedergang der Römische Welt* (Berlin and New York: Walther de Gruyter, 1979); M. J. S. Chiat, "Synagogues and Churches in Byzantine Beit She'an," *Jewish Art* 7 (1980).

100. Hachlili, *Ancient Jewish Art*, 146, 157. See also the synagogue at Khirbet Anis (Ilan, *Ancient Synagogues in Israel*, 302–304).

101. Schwartz, *Jewish Settlement*, 104; L. I. Levine, "From Community Center to Small Temple," 41. On this phenomenon in the Galilee, see Weiss, "Ancient Synagogues in Tiberias," 42.

102. See S. Gutman, Z. Yeivin, and E. Netzer, "Excavations in the Synagogue of Horvat Susiya," 124–125.

103. Hachlili, *Ancient Jewish Art*, 189. See Z. Yeivin, "Reconstruction of the Southern Interior Wall of the Khorazin Synagogue," *Eretz-Israel* 18 (1985): 272.

104. See G. Foerster, "Decorated Marble Chancel Screens in the Sixth Century Synagogues in Palestine and Their Relation to Christian Art and Architecture," in *Actes du XIe Congres International d'Archeologie Chretienne* (Rome: Ecole Francaise, 1989), 2. 1818–1820.

105. Z. Yeivin "Khirbet Susiya, the Bima, and Synagogue Ornamentation," in *Ancient Synagogues in Israel*, ed. R. Hachlili (London: BAR International, 1989). This piece has been reconstructed as part of the permanent exhibition at the Israel Museum, Jerusalem and is illustrated in Ilan, *Ancient Synagogues in Israel*, 312.

106. See L. A. Mayer, "Broadhouses in Jewish Religious Art," *Eretz-Israel* 5 (1958): 238.

107. Hachlili, *Ancient Jewish Art*, 161–164; "Synagogues in the Land of Israel: Art and Archaeology," in *Sacred Realm*, ed. S. Fine, 102–103.

108. Hachlili, *Ancient Jewish Art*, 156; Nabratein and Arbel have single portals, at Arbel on the eastern side. On Christian architecture in Syria, see G. Tchalenko and

E. Baccache, *Eglises de villages de la Syrie du Nord* (Paris: Librairie Orientaliste P. Guethner, 1979–80).

109. Compare Goodenough, *Jewish Symbols*, 4:113; 12:42; Y. Braslavi, "Symbols and Mythological Figures in the Early Synagogues in the Galilee," in *All the Land of Naphtali* (1967), 111–113; B. Goldman, *The Sacred Portal* (Detroit: Wayne State University Press, 1966), 69–124. Hachlili, *Ancient Jewish Art*, 156, suggests that "the triple entryway represents a recollection of the Nicanor gate which was the main entrance to the Second Temple of Jerusalem." This suggestion is not substantiated by late antique sources.

110. Cf. A. Ovadiah, "The Reciprocal Relationship between Synagogues and Churches in the Byzantine Period," in *Between and Sinai: Memorial to Amnon* (Jerusalem: Yedidim, 1977): 164–165.

111. Though not at Arbel. See L. I. Levine, "From Community Center to Small Temple," 41.

112. E. M. Meyers, J. Strange, and C. Meyers, *Excavations at Ancient Meiron, Upper Galilee, Israel, 1971–72, 1974–75, 1977* (Cambridge, Mass: Harvard University Press, 1981), 12–13.

113. Ilan and Damati, *Meroth: The Ancient Jewish Village*, 45, 49; Ilan, "The Synagogue and Study House at Meroth," in *Ancient Synagogues: Historical Analysis and Archaeological Discovery*, ed. D. Urman and P. V. M. Flesher (Leiden: E. J. Brill, 1995), 1: 258–259; Meyers, Meyers and Strange, *Excavations at the Ancient Synagogue of Gush Ḥalav*, 80–82; Hachlili, *Ancient Jewish Art*, 175.

114. S. D. Goitein, "Ambol—The Raised Platform in the Synagogue," *Eretz-Israel* 6 (1960): 162.

115. Discussed on p. 72 above. For Christian parallels, see Meer, *Early Christian Art*, 58.

116. Z. Yeivin, "Reconstruction of the Southern Interior Wall," 274–275, and "Khirbet Susiya, the Bima, and Synagogue Ornamentation," 32–33.

117. See Y. Tsafrir, "The Byzantine Setting and Its Influence on Ancient Synagogues," in *The Synagogue in Late Antiquity*, ed. L. I. Levine (Philadelphia: American Schools for Oriental Research, 1987), 152.

118. Hachlili, *Ancient Jewish Art*, 181.

119. See Tsafrir, "The Byzantine Setting," 151–152. Hachlili (*Ancient Jewish Art*, 180–182) and L. I. Levine ("From Community Center to Small Temple," 74) list appearances of the apse form.

120. Perhaps it is significant that apses generally occur in the Beth Shean valley, Hammath Gader, the Jericho region, the Gaza region and Gerasa, all areas with dense Christian populations. The exception is Hammath Tiberias B, 2a.

121. Cf. Hachlili, *Ancient Jewish Art*, 180.

122. See S. Fine, "'Chancel' Screens."

123. Hachlili, *Ancient Jewish Art*, 187–191, Foerster, "Decorated Marble Chancel Screens"; L. I. Levine, "From Community Center to Small Temple," 74–75; Branham, "Sacred Space under Erasure," esp. 379–380. Barag, Porat, and Netzer, "The Synagogue at En-Gedi," 117, report evidence for a wooden chancel screen at Ein Gedi 2.

124. On parallels between churches and synagogues, see Branham, "Sacred Space under Erasure"; Ovadiah, "Reciprocal Relationship," 1977; Tsafrir, "The Byzantine Setting"; Turner, *From Temple to Meeting Place*, 174.

125. y. Meg. 3:1 73d.

126. Branham, in "Sacred Space under Erasure," compares this division to the divisions within the Jerusalem Temple. There is no evidence, however, to support this contention. See S. Fine, "'Chancel' Screens."

127. Cambridge University Library, T-S A45.6, fol. 1v. Edited by S. Hopkins, *A Miscellany of Literary Pieces from the Cambridge Genizah Collections* (Cambridge: Cambridge University Library, 1978), 12–14.

128. See Fine, "'Chancel' Screens."

129. See Foerster, "Decorated Marble Chancel Screens."

130. Sukenik, *Ancient Synagogue of Beth Alpha*, 34, 52.

131. V. Tzaferis, "The Ancient Synagogue at Ma'oz Hayyim," *Israel Exploration Journal* 32 (1982); Hachlili, *Ancient Jewish Art*, 160; Branham, "Sacred Space under Erasure," 384–385. See Dothan, *Hammath Tiberias*, 30–32. Note, however, the opposite process at Gush Ḥalav. Meyers, Meyers, and Strange, *Excavations at the Ancient Synagogue of Gush Ḥalav*, 121; Seager, "Recent Historiography," 86 and note 17.

132. Naveh, "Aramaic and Hebrew Inscriptions," 307, and bibliography cited there.

133. See Kraeling, *The Synagogue. The Excavations of Dura Europos*, 60–61, 256–260, regarding the denotation of this phrase at Dura Europos.

134. Naveh, *On Stone and Mosaic*, 144–145. Greek: *thekē*, "Receptacle," following Krauss (*Griechische und lateinische Lehnwörter*, 588). Cf. Sokoloff, *Dictionary of Jewish Palestinian Aramaic*, 581, who translates "sheath." *Rahmana:* "The Merciful One," following Sokoloff, op. cit., 522. See also Naveh, op. cit., nos. 70–72, 106–109.

135. See W. Bacher, *Die exegetische Terminologie der jüdischen Traditionsliteratur*, tr. A. Z. Rabinowitz (Tel Aviv: Ahdut, 1923), 296–297, and note 1. See also Marmorstein, *Doctrine of Merits*, 101–102 and the synagogue inscriptions from Ein Gedi and Belvoir (Naveh, *On Stone and Mosaic*, 70–72, 107–109).

136. y. Meg. 3:1, 73d.

137. Hachlili, *Ancient Jewish Art*, 184–187, 273–274. Add to these a relief from Fahma (M. Avi-Yonah, "Remains of an Ancient Synagogue at Fahma Village," *Proceedings of the Jewish Palestine Exploration Society* 13, nos. 3–4 [1947]: 154–155; Goodenough, *Jewish Symbols*, 1: 214, 3, no. 560). Hachlili, "Niche and the Ark"; *Ancient Jewish Art*, 166–180 catalogs and categorizes various types of Torah shrines. Goodenough (op. cit., 4: 119) is correct in stating that "In the great majority of representations . . . the gable or arch of the enclosing shrine or niche seems to have been a structural part of the cabinet itself. . . ."

138. E. M. Meyers, J. Strange, and C. Meyers, "The Ark of Nabratein: A First Glance," *Biblical Archaeologist* 44, no. 4 (1981); E. M. Meyers and C. Meyers, "Finders of the Lost Ark," *Biblical Archaeology Review* 7, no. 4 (1981). M. Epstein, "The Elephant and the Law: The Medieval Jewish Minority Adapts a Christian Motif," *Art Bulletin* 76 (1994): 468, sees in these birds and lions a reference to the cherubs of the biblical Ark of the

Covenant. Unfortunately, there is no evidence to substantiate his claim. Birds atop aediculae appear with some frequency in Coptic art. See A. Gayet, *Les Monuments Coptes* (Paris: E. Leroux, 1889), fl. 24, fig. 29; pl. 86, fig. 97; Egyptian Antiquities Authority, *Coptic Museum* (Egypt, 1984), 28th plate; F. D. Friedman, *Beyond the Pharaohs: Egypt and the Copts in the 2nd–7th Centuries* A.D. (Rhode Island: Rhode Island Institute of Design, 1989), no. 176; S. Fine and L. V. Rutgers, "New Light on Judaism in Asia Minor during Late Antiquity: Two Recently Identified Inscribed Menorahs," *Jewish Studies Journal*, 3, no.1 (1996): 18–19.

139. Hachlili, *Ancient Jewish Art*, 167–187. See also Fine "'Chancel' Screens."

140. See M. Bratschkova, "Die Muschel in der antiken Kunst," *Bulletin de l'Institut Archeologique Bulgare* 12, no. 1 (1938). For Christian examples, see Wilkinson, *Egeria's Travels*, 246–252; N. Feuchtwanger, "Late Sixth Century Metal Ampoules from Jerusalem," and G. Foerster, "Christian Allegories and Symbols in the Mosaic Designs of 6th Century Eretz Israel Synagogues," both in *Jews, Samaritans and Christians in Byzantine Palestine*, ed. D. Jacoby and Y. Tsafrir (Jerusalem: Ben Zvi Institute, 1988).

141. Compare Hachlili, *Ancient Jewish Art*, 284.

142. Ibid., 273.

143. Meyers, Kraabel, and Strange, *Ancient Synagogue Excavations at Khirbet Shema'*, 52–54. The brownish coloration of the shrine in the Hammath Tiberias mosaic suggest that its model was wooden (see Dothan, *Hammath Tiberias*, 34–36).

144. Lions: Hachlili, *Ancient Jewish Art*, 322–325. See also the lions that appear on the stone *menorah* from Maon in Judea, D. Amit, "A Marble Menorah from an Ancient Synagogue at Tel Ma'on," *Proceedings of the Tenth World Congress in Jewish Studies*, Division B, 1 (1990); the reconstructed *menorah* appears in *Sacred Realm*, ed. Fine, 37. Birds: at Beth Alpha (Hachlili, op. cit., 248, 278); at Khirbet Tieba (Ilan, op. cit., 32).

145. Sources are collected by Hachlili, *Ancient Jewish Art*, 324–325. I see no need to interpret lions automatically as the "lion of Judah."

146. See Z. Gal, "Ancient Synagogues in the Eastern Lower Galilee," in *Ancient Synagogues: Historical Analysis and Archaeological Discovery*, ed. D. Urman and P. V. M. Flesher (Leiden: E. J. Brill, 1995), 1:167; Fine, ed., *Sacred Realm*, 170, fig. 2.9a.

147. Exceptions appear at Capernaum (H. Shanks, *Judaism in Stone* [New York: Harper and Row, 1979], 66), Dana (Gal, "Ancient Synagogues in the Eastern Lower Galilee," 1:167–168), Chorazin (Z. Yeivin, "Ancient Chorazin Comes Back to Life," *Biblical Archaeology Review* 12, no. 5 [1987]: 32–33, no. 7, 34, 35) and possibly Peki'in (Hachlili, *Ancient Jewish Art*, 184, pl. 32).

148. See Hachlili, *Ancient Jewish Art*, 247–249, pl. 101–105.

149. N. Slouschz, "Hamath-by-Tiberias," *Journal of the Jewish Palestine Exploration Society* 1 (1921): 32; Goodenough, *Jewish Symbols*, 1: 216, 3, fig. 562.

150. Z. Yeivin, "Reconstruction of the Southern Interior Wall," 272. Ilan, *Ancient Synagogues in Israel*, 296–297, mentions fragments of two stone *menorahs* discovered in the niches that flank the central niche at Eshtemoa, one on each side. In a letter dated 3 March 1992, Z. Yeivin, excavator of this synagogue, informs me that "The Eshtemoa *menorah* fragment was not discovered within its niche, rather nearby among the ruins. It is

our suggestion that the holy ark stood in the central niche and that in the two side niches were two *menorahs*, pieces of which were discovered also in the synagogue of Ḥorvat Susiya" (my translation).

151. Amit, "A Marble Menorah"; Ilan, *Ancient Synagogues in Israel*, 309–310.

152. Z. Yeivin, "Reconstruction of the Southern Interior Wall," 272, and "Khirbet Susiya, the Bima, and Synagogue Ornamentation," 94–95, fig. 12–13. See L. I. Levine, "From Community Center to Small Temple," 76.

153. See Hachlili, *Ancient Jewish Art*, 247, 248, 257, pl. 23, 37, 50, 54, 55, 58. See also 249–251.

154. This is clearly the purpose of the crosspiece on the stone *menorahs* from Susiya and Sardis and a cast bronze *menorah* from Ein Gedi. This lamp, 21.5 cm. wide, apparently served a decorative function in the Torah niche of the second synagogue. It shows no evidence of fixtures for burning oil and is apparently too small for this function in any case (Metropolitan Museum of Art, *Treasures of the Holy Land: Ancient Art from the Israel Museum* [New York, 1986], 246–247).

155. Ex. 25:31–40, 37:17–24. On the biblical *menorah*, see C. Meyers, *The Tabernacle Menorah: A Synthetic Study of a Symbol from the Biblical Cult* (Missoula: Scholars Press, 1976).

156. *Sifre Zutta, Ba'alotkha:* 255; b. Menah. 98b, Meg. 21b; Rashi, ad loc. See Melamed, *Halachic Midrashim*, 349.

157. This factor should not be excessively emphasized, however. Two seven-branched *menorahs* and one twelve-branched *menorah* appear in the same mosaic at Naaran (Goodenough, *Jewish Symbols*, 3, no. 643). See Branham, "Sacred Space under Erasure," 389–391.

158. This iconography occurs at a number of sites. See Hachlili, *Ancient Jewish Art*, 268–272.

159. See ibid., 269–272.

160. As in the mosaic pavement of the baptistery at Skhira in Tunisia. See M. Fendri, *Basiliques Cretiennes de la Skhira* (Paris: Presses Universitaires de France, 1961), 50–53, who recognized the similarities between the representation at Naaran and this image. A second such image appears on a Coptic stele. See Villa Hügel, *Koptische Kunst: Christentum m Nil* (Essen: Villa Hügel, 1963), 243, no. 98.

161. On Byzantine glass lamps, see Crowfoot and Harden, "Early Byzantine and Later Glass Lamps"; Trowbridge, *Philological Studies in Ancient Glass*, 190–191; Bouras, "Byzantine Lighting Devices."

162. Dendy, *The Use of Lights in Christian Worship*, 17, makes this point in regard to altar lighting in late antique churches. See Paulinius of Nola's description of lighted altars, cited by Dendy, p. 19.

163. See ibid., 17; Wilkinson, "Orientation," 20.

164. At Beth Alpha, Ma'oz Ḥayyim 3 and perhaps Ein Gedi 2.

165. Hachlili, *Ancient Jewish Art*, 192–193, catalogs the evidence. On Ein Gedi, see Barag, Porat and Netzer, "The Synagogue at En-Gedi," 117; Shanks, *Judaism in Stone*, 134–137.

166. Dothan, *Hammath Tiberias*, 31.

167. Ibid.; Lieberman, *Hellenism in Jewish Palestine*, 172.
168. Rahmani, "Ancient Synagogue of Maon."
169. Naveh and Shaked, *Amulets and Magic Bowls*, 91–92.
170. On the notion of a "symbol" in the history of religions, see J. Heisig, "Symbolism," in *Encyclopedia of Religion*, ed. M. Eliade (New York: Macmillan, 1987), 204–208; Fine, "Development of a Visual Symbol."
171. Goodenough, *Jewish Symbols*. See M. Smith, "Goodenough's Jewish Symbols"; Brilliant, "'Jewish Symbols' Is that Still Good Enough?"
172. M. Avi-Yonah, *Art in Ancient Palestine: Selected Essays*, ed. H. and Y. Tsafrir (Jerusalem, 1981): 389–392; A. Ovadiah, "The Mosaic Workshop of Gaza in Christian Antiquity," in *Ancient Synagogues: Historical Analysis and Archaeological Discovery*, ed. D. Urman and P. V. M. Flesher (Leiden: E. J. Brill, 1995), 2:367–372.
173. Maguire and Maguire, *Art and Holy Powers*, 18–22.
174. See S. Fine and B. Zuckerman, "The Menorah as Symbol of Jewish Minority Status," in *Fusion in the Hellenistic East*, ed. S. Fine (Los Angeles: University of Southern California Fisher Gallery, 1985), 26.
175. Sources are analyzed by C. Meyers, *The Tabernacle Menorah*, esp. 17–56.
176. I have argued for the significance of this criterion in my article on the date palm numismatic type. See Fine, "Development of a Visual Symbol."
177. *Mekhilta of Rabbi Ishmael, Bo*, 1 (2), ed. Horowitz-Rabin: 6.; ed. Lauterbach 1: 15–16; *Sifre Num.*, ed. Friedmann, 61; *Num. Rab.* 15:4,10; *b. Menah.* 29a and Tosafot, ad loc., s.v. *Sheloshah*; and parallels cited by Yellin, *Yafeh Anayim*, ad loc. On the textual history of these traditions, see H. Fox, "'As If with a Finger'."
178. On the *menorah* as a symbol for Judaism in Patristic sources, see Brand, *Glass Vessels*, 208.
179. One of the purposes of using the cross was apotropaic (Maguire and Maguire, *Art and Holy Powers*, 18–22). Though no literary source points to a parallel usage of the *menorah*, one wonders if this was, in fact, a consideration.
180. See Fine and Zuckerman, "The Menorah as Symbol of Jewish Minority Status," and the bibliography cited there. The notion of Jewish art as a "minority problem" was first articulated by H. Strauss, "Jewish Art as a Minority Problem," *Journal of Jewish Sociology* 2 (1960).
181. This is most clearly seen in numismatic sources. See B. Trell, "The Cult-image on Temple-Type Coins," *Numismatic Chronicle* 4 (1964); M. Price and B. Trell, *Coins and Their Cities* (London: Vecci, 1977).
182. See Fine and Zuckerman, "The Menorah as Symbol of Jewish Minority Status"; A. Ovadiah, "Mosaic Art in Ancient Synagogues of Eretz-Israel," in *Synagogues in Antiquity*, ed. A. Kasher, A. Oppenheimer, and U. Rappaport (Jerusalem: Ben Zvi Institute, 1987), 202, n. 44.
183. Millar, "Jews of the Greco-Roman Diaspora," 105–108.
184. See Feldman, "Proselytes and 'Sympathizers'," 284–285; J. Gager, "The Dialogue of Paganism with Judaism: Bar Cochba to Julian," *Hebrew Union College Annual* 44

(1973): 99–101; Y. Lewy, "Julian the Apostate and the Building of the Temple," *The Jerusalem Cathedra* 3 (1983); Millar, "Jews of the Greco-Roman Diaspora," 105–107; Nibley, "Christian Envy of the Temple."

185. On Rabbinic discussion of the Tabernacle/Temple and its cult objects, see Kirschner's comments in his edition of the *Baraita de-Melekhet ha-Mishkan* (1991), 80–83.

186. See Budde, *Armarium und Kibotos*.

187. A. Grabar, *Martyrium: Recherches sur le culte des reliques et l'art cretien antique* (Paris: College de France, 1943–1946); R. Krautheimer, "Review of Andre Grabar, *Martyrium: Recherches sur le culte des reliques et l'art antique*," *Art Bulletin* 35 (1953); Feuchtwanger, "Late Sixth Century Metal Ampoules"; Foerster, "Christian Allegories and Symbols."

188. B. Mazar, *Beth She'arim*, 1 (New Brunswick: Rutgers University Press, 1973), 111–113. See also Haran, "Torah and Bible Scrolls," 102–103.

189. S. Saller and B. Bagatti, *The Town of Nebo (Khirbet El-Mekhayyat)* (Jerusalem: Franciscan, 1949), 30–39; M. Piccirillo, *Mount Nebo* (Jerusalem: Custodia Terra Sancta, 1987), 83–87; Foerster, "Christian Allegories and Symbols," 198–200.

190. S. Gutman, Z. Yeivin, and E. Netzer, "Excavations in the Synagogue of Horvat Susiya," 125; Foerster, "Christian Allegories and Symbols," 198; Z. Yeivin, "Khirbet Susiya, the Bima, and Synagogue Ornamentation," 93.

191. Saller and Nagatti, *The Town of Nebo*, 110–111.

192. Mazar, *Beth She'arim*, 110–113.

193. Ibid., 176–177.

194. L. A. Mayer and A. Reifenberg, "Three Ancient Jewish Reliefs," *Palestine Exploration Quarterly* (1937): 136–139; Goodenough, *Jewish Symbols*, 1:174–177; 3, nos. 440–442, 445–446, L. Y. Rahmani, "Mirror-Plaques from a Fifth-Century A.D. Tomb," *Israel Exploration Journal* 14 (1964).

195. y. Ber. 5:1, 8d–9a; y. Sheb. 4:10 35c, and others. Rahmani believes that the funerary plaques bearing the image of Torah shrines flanked by *menorahs* were amulets against the evil eye (Rahmani, "Mirror Plaques"). See also Maguire and Maguire, *Art and Holy Powers*, 6–7, 218. If Rahmani is correct, then the shrine must have been considered to have special power.

196. See Goodenough, *Jewish Symbols*, 1:173; 3, no. 434; Sukenik, *Ancient Synagogue of Beth Alpha*, 23–24; Ilan, *Ancient Synagogues in Israel*, 286–287.

197. Avigad, *Beth She'arim*, 209–213.

198. See Meyers and Meyers, "Finders of the Lost Ark."

199. V. Sussman, *Ornamental Jewish Oil-Lamps*, 20–21, no. 7, suggests that the first instance dates from before the Bar Kokhba revolt. The image on this single lamp is highly schematic, however. For later lamps, see Goodenough, *Jewish Symbols*, 1:159; 3, nos. 282, 34, 336, 337. It has been held by a number of scholars that the image within the Temple doors on Bar Kokhba coins is a Torah shrine or the Ark of the Covenant. Scholarship is summarized in Y. Meshorer, *Ancient Jewish Coinage* (Dix Hills: Amphora, 1982), 2:138–140. See also Kraeling, *The Synagogue. The Excavations of Dura Europos*, 60 and E. Revel-Neher,

L'Arche d'Alliance dans Art Juif et Chrétien du Second au Dixiéme Siècles (Paris: Association des Amis des Études Archaéologiques Byzantino-Slaves et du Christianisme Oriental, 1984), 73–80. D. Barag's interpretation that this is the image of the showbread table is the most compelling so far suggested. See his "The Showbread Table and the Facade of the Temple on Coins of the Bar-Kokhba Revolt," in *Ancient Jerusalem Revealed*, ed. H. Geva (Jerusalem: Israel Exploration Society, 1994).

200. Reported by Hachlili, *Ancient Jewish Art*, 275. Professor Hachlili informs me that this piece has yet to be published.

201. As at Beth Alpha, Beth Shean A. Compare the situation at Susiya.

202. Dothan, *Hammath Tiberias*, 31–38, 69.

203. Goodenough, *Jewish Symbols*, 4: 145–166.

204. Ibid., 4:167–194.54–56.

205. Brand, *Glass Vessels*, 200–201.

206. Goodenough, *Jewish Symbols*, 4: 195–208; Lieberman, *Sheki'in*, 9–10. Braslavi, "Symbols and Mythological Figures," 118–119; Bickerman, "Altars of the Gentiles," 343, n. 65; Brand, *Glass Vessels*, 206–207; Z. Safrai, "From Synagogue to Little Temple," 25.

207. Ritual appurtenances used for other holidays simply did not fulfill this criterion. Cf. L. I. Levine, "From Community Center to Small Temple," 81, and n. 235 following Braslavi, "Symbols and Mythological Figures," 115–118.

208. See Hachlili, *Ancient Jewish Art*, 391–395 and the bibliography cited there.

209. Compare Braslavi, "Symbols and Mythological Figures," 117–118.

210. See S. Fine, "Art and the Liturgical Context."

211. The term "dome of heaven" was made popular by K. Lehmann, "The Dome of Heaven," *Art Bulletin* 27 (1945) to describe this phenomenon in late antique (including Jewish) art. This article should be read together with T. Mathews, *The Clash of the Gods: A Reinterpretation of Early Christian Art* (Princeton: Princeton University Press, 1993), 142–150 and McVey, "The Domed Church as Microcosm."

212. G. Hanfmann, "The Continuity of Classical Art: Culture, Myth and Faith," in *The Age of Spirituality: A Symposium*, ed. K. Weitzmann (New York: Metropolitan Museum of Art, 1980), 79–82.

213. Avi-Yonah, *Art in Ancient Palestine*, 396–397. See also R. Hachlili, "The Zodiac in Ancient Jewish Art: Representation and Significance," *Bulletin of the American Schools for Oriental Research* 228 (1977). Much has been written on the significance of the zodiac wheel, with the image of Helios at its center, in ancient Jewish art. Opinions regarding Helios are summarized by L. I. Levine, *The Rabbinic Class*, 178–179; Margaliot's introduction to *Sefer ha-Razim* 1966: 12–16; Naveh and Shaked, *Amulets and Magic Bowls*, 37. A chronological differentiation is necessary that takes into account the two centuries separating Hammath Tiberias from the other images. See L. I. Levine, *The Rabbinic Class*, 178. Interest in the zodiac was pervasive during late antiquity, different groups within Jewish society certainly understanding it differently. A number of scholars have dealt with the zodiac in ancient Jewish literature. See J. Charlesworth, "Jewish Astrology in the Talmud, Pseudepigrapha, the Dead Sea Scrolls, and Early Palestinian Synagogues," *Harvard Theo-*

logical Review 70, nos. 3–4 (1977); Dothan, *Hammath Tiberias*, 39–49; G. Foerster, "The Zodiac Wheel in Ancient Synagogues and Its Place in Jewish Liturgical Thought," *Eretz-Israel* 19 (1987); M. Klein, "Palestinian Targum and Synagogue Mosaics"; A. Mirsky, "Aquarius and Aries in the Ein Gedi Inscription and in Early Piyyutim," *Tarbiz* 40 (1970); M. Narkiss, "The Zodiac in Jewish Art," *Kirjath Sepher* 16 (1939–1940); Dov Noy, "Twelve Constellations and Twelve Tribes," *Mahanayim* 4 (1964); A. Ovadiah, "Mosaic Art," 190, 199; G. Sarfatti, "Introduction to the Baraita of Constellations," *Bar Ilan* 3 (1965) and "I Segni Dello Zodiaco Nell' Iconografia Ebraica," in *Scritti in Memoria di Umberto Nahon* (Jerusalem: Mosad Shelomoh Meir, Mosad Refael Kantoni, 1978); J. Yahalom, "The Zodiac Wheel in early Piyyut in Eretz-Israel," *Jerusalem Studies in Hebrew Literature* 9 (1986), and, "Piyyut as Poetry," in *The Synagogue in Late Antiquity*, ed. L. I. Levine (Philadelphia: American Schools for Oriental Research, 1987), 119–120; J. C. Greenfield and M. Sokoloff, "Astrological and Related Omen Texts in Jewish Palestinian Aramaic," *Journal of Near Eastern Studies* 48, no. 3 (1989); Schiffman and Swartz, *Hebrew and Aramaic Incantation Texts*, 56, 70, 73, 75–76.

214. Weiss and Netzer, *Promise and Redemption*, 26–29.

215. Naveh, *On Stone and Mosaic*, 106–108.

216. See Mirsky, "Aquarius and Aries"; Foerster, "Zodiac Wheel in Ancient Synagogues"; Yahalom, "Zodiac Wheel in Early Piyyut," and "Piyyut as Poetry," 119–120.

217. See Hachlili, *Ancient Jewish Art*, 167.

218. See ibid., 294–295 and pl. 26.

219. Weiss and Netzer, *Promise and Redemption*, 30–33; Ovadiah, "Mosaic Art," 187; Hachlili, *Ancient Jewish Art*, 287–295. On the binding of Isaac in Christian art, see A. M. Smith, "The Iconography of the Sacrifice of Isaac in Early Christian Art," *American Journal of Archaeology* 26 (1922); I. S. Van Woerden, "The Iconography of the Sacrifice of Isaac," *Vigiliae Christianae* 15 (1961); R. Jensen, "The Offering of Isaac in Jewish and Christian Tradition: Image and Text," *Biblical Interpretation* 11, no. 1 (1994); J. Gutmann, "The Sacrifice of Isaac: Variations on a Theme in Early Jewish and Christian Art," in *Sacred Images: Studies in Jewish Art from Antiquity to the Middle Ages* (Northampton, Variorum Reprints 1989); "Revisiting the Binding of Isaac Mosaic at Beth Alpha," *Bulletin of the Asia Institute* 6 (1992).

220. Hachlili, *Ancient Jewish Art*, 291–292, 295. C. M. Kaufmann, *Handbuch der christlichen Archaeologie* (Paderhorn: F. Schoningh, 1922), 605. See Weitzmann, *Age of Spirituality*, 469–470, no. 370; 412–413, no. 387; 429–430, no. 436; 485. Goodenough, *Jewish Symbols*, 2:109–110. K. Weitzmann and his school posit the existence of an illustrated Jewish manuscript tradition that preceded and connects the paintings of Dura Europos ultimately to medieval Jewish and Christian book illumination. See K. Weitzmann, "The Illustration of the Septuagint;" "The Question of the Influence of Jewish Pictorial Sources on Old Testament Illustration." Both articles appear in *No Graven Images: Studies in Art and the Hebrew Bible*, ed. J. Gutmann (New York: KTAV, 1971). This approach is refuted persuasively by J. Gutmann, "The Illustrated Jewish Manuscript in Antiquity: The Present State of the Question," in *No Graven Images: Studies in Art and the Hebrew Bible*, ed. J. Gut-

mann (New York, 1971). See also A. J. Wharton, "Good and Bad Images from the Synagogue of Dura Europos: Contexts, Subtexts, Intertexts," *Art History* 17, no. 1 (1994): 7–9; S. Fine, "Art and the Liturgical Context."

221. S. Schechter, *Aspects of Rabbinic Theology* (New York: Macmillan, 1909), 170. On *zekhut* and *zekhut avot*, see ibid., 170–198; Moore, *Judaism*, 1:538–546.

222. These include Rabbinic prayer, *piyyutim* and the inscription from Jericho (Naveh, *On Stone and Mosaic*, 103–105).

223. The excavator, A. Onn, reports discovery of fragments of the names "Abraham, Isaac and Jacob," though "and Jacob" cannot be discerned in the photograph or drawings that he published. See A. Onn, "The Ancient Synagogue of Kafr Misr," *'Atiqot* 26 (1994): 122, 124.

224. Naveh, *On Stone and Mosaic*, 106–109; B. Mazar, "The Inscription on the Pavement of the Synagogue of Ein Gedi," *Tarbiz* 40 (1970): 22–23, sets this invocation within the rhetoric of the entire inscription and suggests a parallel from *Cant. Rab.* 7:5.

225. This position is taken elsewhere in this mosaic, and is unique to it. The image of Virgo and each of the four seasons are also in an orens position, suggesting the appropriateness of this pose for the synagogue context.

226. Ovadiah, "Synagogue at Gaza"; P. C. Finney, "Orpheus-David: A Connection in Iconography between Greco-Roman Judaism and Early Christianity?" *Jewish Art* 5 (1978). An image at Meroth was identified by Yadin as David, though it is more properly that of a Roman soldier. Cf. Hachlili, *Ancient Jewish Art*, 297–299; Ilan, "The Synagogue and Study House at Meroth," 261–267.

227. Weiss and Netzer, *Promise and Redemption*, 18–25.

228. Tsafrir, *Eretz Israel*, 416–417. While a certain callousness might be expected in regard to visual images, the fact an expansive Rabbinic source appears in the Rehov mosaic and was laid centrally in the synagogue narthax reflects an attitude toward text that is quite alien to medieval and modern conceptions.

229. K. A. C. Creswell, *Early Muslim Architecture* (Oxford: Clarendon, 1932), 1: 269–271.

230. Samaritan iconography is in many respects the same as Jewish iconography. This subject requires further attention, particularly in light of recent discoveries a El Hirveh and Hirbet Samara. See Magen "Samaritian Synagogues." *Qadmoniot* 25 (1992).

5. "You Believe the Place Is Holy Because the Torah and Prophets Are There...."

1. This severely limits our sources, particularly in regard to issues that were beyond Rabbinic control or interest. Cf. I. Gafni, "Synagogues in Talmudic Babylonia: Traditions and Reality," in *Synagogues in Antiquity*, ed. A. Kasher, A. Oppenheimer, and U. Rappaport (Jerusalem: Ben Zvi Institute, 1987), 158.

2. I. Gafni has contrasted sources for synagogues in Amoraic Babylonia with those for synagogues in Second Temple period and Tannaitic sources from Palestine ("Synagogues

in Talmudic Babylonia"; *The Jews in Babylonia in the Talmudic Era* [Jerusalem: Zalman Shazar Institute, 1990], 109–117; and "Synagogues in Babylonia in the Talmudic Period," in *Ancient Synagogues: Historical Analysis and Archaeological Discovery*, ed. D. Urman and P. V. M. Flesher [Leiden: E. J. Brill, 1995]). Gafni's position in the 1995 version of this article is much more similar to my own.

3. J. N. Epstein, *Studies in Talmudic Literature and Semitic Languages*, ed. E. Z. Melamed, tr. Z. Epstein (Jerusalem: Magnes Press, 1983), 1: 40–41; A. Oppenheimer, *Babylonia Judaica in the Talmudic Period* (Wiesbaden: L. Reichert, 1983), 156–164, 276–293 and "Babylonian Synagogues with Historical Associations," in *Ancient Synagogues: Historical Analysis and Archaeological Discovery*, ed. D. Urman and P. V. M. Flesher (Leiden: E. J. Brill, 1995), 40–45.

4. From the Greek *pharos*, a cloth or curtain. See Krauss, *Griechische und lateinische Lehnwörter*, 2:492.

5. See Rabbinowicz, *Dikduqei Sofrim:* ad loc., note *alef*.

6. See ibid., notes *tav*, *dalet*.

7. See discussion: p. 70.

8. See Rabbinowicz, *Dikduqei Sofrim:* ad loc., note *dalet*.

9. See Kohut, *Aruch Completum*, 3:141; Jastrow, *Dictionary*, 320–321; Sokoloff, *Dictionary of Jewish Palestinian Aramaic*, 155. See also Naveh, *On Stone and Mosaic*, 36–37.

10. Cf. Gafni, "Synagogues in Talmudic Babylonia"; *The Jews of Babylonia*, 109–117; and "Synagogues in Babylonia," who assembles Babylonian sources.

11. b. Shabbat 11a.

12. See Rabbinowicz, *Dikduqei Sofrim:* ad loc., note *samekh*.

13. To the Alfasi, ad. loc.

14. Oppenheimer, *Babylonia Judaica*, 413–422, esp. 416.

15. Commentary of Ḥananel son of Ḥushiel, ad loc.

16. See L. I. Levine, *The Rabbinic Class*, 114.

17. We assume with the medieval commentators that both halves of the *baraita* refer to the synagogue context. All of the other causes of death (or troubles) collected in this pericope (32a–33b) are drawn from Jewish communal and ritual contexts that were operative during late antiquity, and are not merely exegetical.

18. See Rashi and Tosafot, ad loc., Shinan, "Aramaic Targum as a Mirror," 250.

19. Ad loc.

20. E.g. y. Meg. 3:1, 73d. Cf. Z. Safrai, "Dukhan, Aron and Teva," 72, and additional sources cited there. "Holy Ark" appears in the Talmudim only in reference to the Ark of the Covenant (J. Hoffman, "Ancient Torah Service," 44). The term "Holy Ark" in reference to the Torah shrine appears in versions of the *Differences in Religious Customs Between Babylonian and Palestinian Jewries* (no. 36, ed. Lewin [1942], 75; ed. Margaliot [1938], 86).

21. *On the Paschal Sacrifice*, lines 511, 532–533, tr. Neusner 1971, 33, 39. See S. Lieberman, *Yemenite Midrashim*, 2nd. ed. (Jerusalem: Wahrmann, 1970), 24–25; Z. Safrai, "Dukhan, Aron and Teva," 75 and notes 48–49.

22. Mann, "Anan's Liturgy," esp. 344, 350.

23. Ibid., esp. 344–346.

24. See Rashi, ad loc. Medieval discussion of this concept is summarized by Gafni, "Synagogues in Talmudic Babylonia," 155, nn. 4–6.

25. m. Meg. 3:2–3 and t. Meg. 2:18.

26. For the sake of brevity, we cite the Vilna edition. See, however, the manuscript traditions cited by Rabbinowicz, *Dikduqei Sofrim*, and also ms. Columbia X893–T141. See also Melamed, *Halachic Midrashim*, 102, note *nun*.

27. Oppenheimer ("Babylonian Synagogues," 43–44), discusses the "prominence and antiquity" attributed to Hutsal in b. Ket. 111a.

28. ed. Lewin: 73, Spanish version. See Oppenheimer, "Babylonian Synagogues," 43.

29. Ibid., 41–42.

30. Ibid.

31. On Rabbinic pilgrimage for prayer in the "Synagogue of Daniel," see b. Arub. 21a, Oppenheimer, "Babylonian Synagogues," 46–47.

32. See J. N. Epstein, *Studies in Talmudic Literature*, 40–41; Oppenheimer, "Benevolent Societies in Jerusalem," 286–287, and "Babylonian Synagogues," 40–43; I. Gafni, "Expression and Types of 'Local Patriotism' among Jews of the Sasanian Empire," in *Irano-Judaica*, 2 (1990): 66–67.

33. See Rashi, ad loc.

34. See also b. Rosh. Hash. 24b, b. Abod. Zar. 43b, b. Nid. 13a.

35. Manuscript traditions of this text are discussed on p. 81 above.

36. All manuscripts read Rava. The Venice and Vilna printed editions read: Abaye. In the parallel in Ber. 8a the printed editions and manuscripts read "Abaye." See Rabbinowicz, *Dikduqei Sofrim*: ad loc. Cf. Gafni, *Jews of Babylonia*, 111–112.

37. Venice edition, followed by Vilna. This reading is not attested, however, in the manuscript traditions.

38. See b. Ber. 8a.

39. On the struggle for hegemony between Palestine and Babylonia during late antiquity, see Gafni, "Expression and Types of 'Local Patriotism'," esp. 66; and "Synagogues in Babylonia," 230; S. Spiegel, "Regarding the Polemic of Pirkoi ben Baboi," in *Harry Austyn Wolfson Jubilee Volume* (Jerusalem: American Academy for Jewish Research, 1965), esp. 266–273.

40. The uniqueness of *Shaf ve-Yatev* is expanded upon in a famous tradition in the *Iggeret Rav Sherira Gaon* (ed. Lewin 1921: 72–73.). On the historical ramifications of this text and the Babylonian theology of exile, see Spiegel, "Regarding the Polemic of Pirkoi ben Baboi," esp. 266–273; Oppenheimer, "Babylonian Synagogues," 41–43. Additional Geonic and Medieval traditions regarding this synagogue are collected by J. N. Epstein, *Studies in Talmudic Literature*, 1:40–41.

41. *Against the Jews*, 6:7, ed. Migne 48:913; 1:3, Migne 48:847; 1.5, Migne 48:850.

42. See R. Wilken, *John Chrysostom and the Jews: Rhetoric and Reality in the Late Fourth Century* (Berkeley and Los Angeles: University of California Press, 1983), 83–94. On synagogues as places of healing, see the amulets collected by Naveh and Shaked, *Amulets and*

Magic Bowls, nos. 44, 50, 11–13 and Naveh, "Aramaic and Hebrew Inscriptions," 303. S. J. D. Cohen notes that "Many ancient texts illustrate the Jew's proficiency in magic and medicine, but the localization of magical activities in synagogues is documented nowhere but in Chrysostom's *Against the Jews*" ("Pagan and Christian Evidence," 168).

43. Wilken, *John Chrysostom and the Jews*, 80.
44. Discourses 1 and 6.
45. 6:7, ed. Migne 48:913.
46. Wilken, *John Chrysostom and the Jews*, 80–83.
47. 6:7, ed. Migne 48:914.
48. Ibid.
49. See below, p. 153.
50. 6:5, ed. Migne 48:910. Translation of this text follows ed. Harkins (1979), 164–165.
51. The titles of the "priests" and the "synagogue leaders" are preserved in their Greek forms. See A. Linder, *The Jews in Roman Imperial Legislation* (Detroit: Wayne State University Press and Jerusalem: Israel Academy of Sciences and Humanities, 1987), 137, n. 9.
52. Ibid., 72–73; 137, n. 9 and bibliography cited there.
53. See also the *Scriptores Historiae Augustae*, Alexander Severus 45:6–7, in Stern, 2: 632 and n. 7, which mentions explicitly Christian and Jewish "priests" (*sacerdotibus*). See also S. J. D. Cohen, "Pagan and Christian Evidence," 176, n. 13.
54. Linder, *The Jews in Roman Imperial Legislation*, 161–163. During the second century Tertulian (*De Jejuniis* 16) describes how the Jews abandoned their "temples" (*templis omissis*) on fast days. This term seems to have been a standard way to describe synagogues, since our author uses it without comment and without polemic.
55. Lifshitz, *Donateurs et Fondateurs*, 31, 34.
56. For the relevant bibliography regarding this inscription, see L. I. Levine, *The Rabbinic Class*, 138, n. 29. Add to this White, *Building God's House*, 71.
57. Translation generally follows L. I. Levine, *The Rabbinic Class*, 140.
58. The closest contemporaneous parallel to this term appears in the mosaic inscriptions in Hammath Tiberias B.
59. Kraabel, "The Diaspora Synagogue," 496; J. Wiseman and D. Mano-Zissi, "Excavations at Stobi, 1970," *American Journal of Archaeology* 75 (1971): 410.
60. Our translation follows Horbury and Noy, *Jewish Inscriptions of Graeco-Roman Egypt*, 25–26 and bibliography there. Cf. Lifshitz, *Donateurs et Fondateurs*, 77. See also Horbury and Noy, op. cit., 23–25, 216–218.
61. Within Palestinian synagogue contexts, see Goodenough, *Jewish Symbols*, 2: 124–134; Roth-Gerson, *Greek Inscriptions*, 19, 69, 137, 160. It appears as well in Smyrna. See Lifshitz, *Donateurs et Fondateurs*, 22 as well as funerary inscriptions. Sources are collected by Roth-Gerson, *Greek Inscriptions*, 71, n. 8.
62. Lifshitz, *Donateurs et Fondateurs*, 31.
63. Goodenough, *Jewish Symbols*, 5:82. Lifshitz, *Donateurs et Fondateurs*, 38.

64. Ibid.
65. See Goodenough, *Jewish Symbols*, 5:82.
66. See Fine and Rutgers, "New Light on Judaism in Asia Minor during Late Antiquity."
67. See Goodenough, *Jewish Symbols*, 5:82.
68. Ibid., 2:89–100.
69. Translation follows ibid., 5:91–92.
70. Ibid., 2:91.
71. Goodenough's suggestion, following Renan, that "Instruments" in two dedicatory inscriptions refers to the Scriptural scrolls is unconvincing (ibid.).
72. White, *Building God's House*, 7–8.
73. Naveh, *On Stone and Mosaic*, 127–129, 131–132.
74. White, *Building God's House*, 77. F. Landsberger, "The Sacred Direction in Synagogue and Church," *Hebrew Union College Annual* 28 (1957): 187, notes that "a striking feature of the niche is the way in which it indicates the direction of Jerusalem, thus making the wall 'holy.'"
75. See White, *Building God's House*, 131.
76. Kraeling, *The Synagogue. The Excavations of Dura Europos*, 16, 54–65.
77. 1 Chron. 3:1.
78. Kraeling, *The Synagogue. The Excavations of Dura Europos*, 22–25, 55–61; S. Downey, *Mesopotamian Religious Architecture: Alexander through the Parthians* (Princeton: Princeton University Press, 1988), 89, 97, 107–108, 110, 113–114, 116, 118, 120, 128 and bibliography cited there.
79. Naveh, *On Stone and Mosaic*, 133; C. Torrey, "The Aramaic Texts," in *The Synagogue. The Excavations of Dura Europos*, ed. C. H. Kraeling (New Haven: Yale University Press, 1956): 269.
80. See p. 112 above.
81. Kraeling, *The Synagogue. The Excavations of Dura Europos*, 60–61, 256–260.
82. I hope to provide a more detailed analysis of the Dura Europos synagogue in a forthcoming study.
83. See Gutmann, "Programmatic Painting," 147–148.
84. He continues: "for instance, in panels WB 4 and WB 2...." (Kraeling, *The Synagogue. The Excavations of Dura Europos*, 60). As well as South Band 1, and North Band 1. See also pp. 61, 98, 257.
85. Ibid., 257–259, pl. 40.2
86. Ibid., 259, suggests that with "the baldachin added, the Torah Shrine is transformed into an example of just such structures as are represented in Panel W[est] B[and] I (Wilderness Encampment and the Miraculous Well of Be'er)...." It is not at all clear, however, whether such a baldachin ever existed.
87. J. Gutmann, "Early Synagogue and Jewish Catacomb Art and Its Relation to Christian Art," in *Aufstieg und Niedergang der Römische Welt* (Berlin and New York: Walther de Gruyter, 1984), 1326.

88. See Kraeling, *The Synagogue. The Excavations of Dura Europos*, 61. M. J. Moreton, "*Eis Anatolas Blepsate:* Orientation as Liturgical Principle," *Studia Patristica* 18, no. 2 (1982): 587–588, compares the alignment of the Dura synagogue and the Dura church.

89. Goodenough, *Jewish Symbols*, 9:54.

90. Ibid., 9:54–55; Engemann, "Magische Uebelabwehr in der Spätantike."

91. Pp. 73–74 above.

92. Kraeling, *The Synagogue. The Excavations of Dura Europos*, 19. See M. Smith, Review of *The Synagogue*, by Carl H. Kraeling, with contributions by C. C. Torrey, C. B. Welles, and B. Geiger," *Journal of Biblical Literature* 76 (1957): 326–327.

93. Ibid. Interestingly, no such deposit was discovered in the Dura church.

94. Encyclopedia Hebraica and Editor, "Purity and Impurity," *Encyclopedia Judaica* (1970), 13:1405–1414, esp. 1406.

95. Torrey, "The Aramaic Texts," 263–264, 267–268.

96. See S. James, "Dura-Europos and the Chronology of Syria in the 250s AD," *Chiron* 15 (1985); D. MacDonald, "Dating the Fall of Dura-Europos," *Historia* 35 (1986). These authors independently reach similar conclusions regarding the dating of the destruction of Dura Europos and the supposed Persian occupation of the city in 253 C.E.

97. B. Geiger, "The Middle Iranian Texts," in *The Synagogue. The Excavations of Dura Europos*, ed. C. Kraeling (New Haven: Yale University Press, 1956), 306–307, no. 44.

98. Ibid., Cf. MacDonald, "Dating the Fall of Dura-Europos," 62, who suggests that the visitors "were Iranian Jews, who are known to have absorbed much of Persian culture even to the extent of adopting Iranian names, or Persians deeply interested in the Jewish religion, the Iranian equivalent of the 'God fearers' in the Roman Empire, or both."

99. W. Meeks and R. Wilken, *Jews and Christians in Antioch* (Missoula: Scholars Press, 1978), 9; J. Obermann, "The Sepulchre of the Maccabean Martyrs," *Journal of Biblical Literature* 50 (1931); E. Bickerman, "Les Maccabees de Malalas," in *Studies in Jewish and Christian History*, part 2 (Leiden: E. J. Brill, 1980); M. Schatkin, "The Maccabean Martyrs," *Vigilae Christianae* 28 (1974); S. J. D. Cohen, "Pagan and Christian Evidence," 168.

100. P. Brown, *Cult of Saints*.

101. This pattern was followed by early Christian and polytheistic communities as well. See White, *Building God's House*.

102. Goodenough, *Jewish Symbols*, 2:77. Note Kraabel's caution ("The Diaspora Synagogue," 490) that "they were surely influenced in this by their identification of it as a 'house-church'."

103. Kraabel, "The Diaspora Synagogue," 490.

104. See Kraabel's discussion, ibid., 490; Goodenough, *Jewish Symbols*, 2:77; 3, no. 882. This piece was photographed by Andrew R. Seager in 1966 and appears in Fine, ed., *Sacred Realm*, 72.

105. "Stele" is the term used by Kraabel. Sukenik (*Ancient Synagogues in Palestine and Greece*, 43), called it a "pillar." The *menorah* is incomplete. See Kraabel, "The Diaspora Synagogue," 490–491.

106. Goodenough, *Jewish Symbols*, 2:77; Sukenik, *Ancient Synagogues in Palestine and Greece*, 43.

107. Sukenik, *Ancient Synagogues in Palestine and Greece*, 34.

108. Fine and Rutgers, "New Light on Judaism in Asia Minor During Late Antiquity," 12–17.

109. Kraabel, "The Diaspora Synagogue," 485.

110. Since the final report on this excavation has not yet appeared, our conclusions must be regarded as tentative. The site was investigated by the author in July 1990.

111. Kraabel, "The Diaspora Synagogue," 485.

112. See White, *Building God's House*, n. 122.

113. Kraabel, "The Diaspora Synagogue," 487.

114. Illustrated and discussed in Fine, ed., *Sacred Realm*, 160, fig. 3.13.

115. G. Hanfmann, "The Ninth Campaign at Sardis," *Bulletin of the American Schools for Oriental Research* 187 (1967): 27–29. Illustrated in Fine, ed., *Sacred Realm*, 65.

116. Personal letter cited by Hanfmann, ibid., 27–29.

117. Ibid., 28, n. 26.

118. See Fine, ed., *Sacred Realm*, 160–161, fig. 3.15.

119. A. Seager, "The Synagogue at Sardis," in *Ancient Synagogues Revealed*, ed. L. I. Levine (Jerusalem: Israel Exploration Society, 1981), 182.

120. Hanfmann, "Ninth Campaign," 29; Kraabel, "The Diaspora Synagogue," 486; E. P. Sanders, *Judaism: Practice and Belief*, 201.

121. Kraabel, "The Diaspora Synagogue," 487.

122. Seager, "The Synagogue at Sardis," 181.

123. Ibid., 182.

124. Ibid., 182. Fine, ed., *Sacred Realm*, 161, fig. 2.19a.

125. The evidence is surveyed by H. Leon, *The Jews in Ancient Rome* (Philadelphia: Jewish Publication Society, 1960), 46–74, 195–228, 263–346; Kraabel, "The Diaspora Synagogue," 497–500; David Noy, *Jewish Inscriptions of Western Europe, 2: The City of Rome* (Cambridge: Cambridge University Press, 1995); L. V. Rutgers, *The Jews of Late Ancient Rome: An Archaeological and Historical Study on the Interaction of Jews and non-Jews in the Roman-Diaspora* (Leiden: E. J. Brill, 1995).

126. M. Floriani Squarciapino, "The Synagogue at Ostia," *Archaeology* 16, no. 3 (1963) and *La Sinagoga di Ostia* (Rome, 1964); F. Zevi, "La Sinagoga di Ostia," *Rassegna mensile di Israel* 38 (1972); Kraabel, "The Diaspora Synagogue," 497–500; Fine and Della Pergola, "Ostia Synagogue."

127. On the chronology of the building, see Fine and Della Pergola, ibid.

128. The inscription appears in Fine, ed., *Sacred Realm*, 158–159, fig. 2.18. It is discussed by Fine and Della Pergola, "Ostia Synagogue," 50–52.

129. This appears graphically in the Mopsuestia mosaic (M. Avi-Yonah, "The Mosaic of Mopsuestia—Church or Synagogue?" in *Ancient Synagogues Revealed*, ed. L. I. Levine [Jerusalem: Israel Exploration Society, 1981], 186–187).

130. Kraabel, "The Diaspora Synagogue," 499.

131. The description that follows first appeared, with minor differences, in Fine and Della Pergola, "Ostia Synagogue," 54–55. Measurements of the Torah shrine are based upon the reconstruction by Floriani Squarciapino and were taken by the author and M. Della Pergola in July 1994. They are only approximate. Cf. Floriani Squarciapino, "The Synagogue at Ostia," 196.

132. Fine, ed., *Sacred Realm*, 159, fig. 4.16.

133. Rutgers dates the Jewish catacombs of Rome to the late second through fifth century C.E. See L. V. Rutgers, "The Jewish Catacombs of Rome Reconsidered," *Proceedings of the Tenth World Congress on Jewish Studies*, Division B, 2 (1990): esp. 35; *The Jews of Late Ancient Rome*, 50–99. Visual parallels are discussed by Fine and Della Pergola, "Ostia Synagogue."

134. J.-B. Frey, *Corpus Inscriptionum Judaicarum* 1 (Rome: Pontifico instituto de archeologia critiana, 1936), 193, 225, 327, 343, 401, 460, 516, 517, 518, 522; H. W. Beyer and H. Lietzmann, *Die Jüdische Katakombe der Villa Torlonia in Rom* (Berlin: Walther de Gruyter, 1930), pl. 4, 12, 13. Fine, ed., *Sacred Realm*, 176, cat. nos. 4, 5, 6, 7, 10, 14. Cf. Haran, "Torah and Bible Scrolls," 104–106.

135. On the Hebrew Scriptures in Christian thought, see Wilken, *John Chrysostom and the Jews*, 80–83.

136. Christians: Catacomb of SS. Peter and Marcellius: G. P. Kirch, "Pitture Inedite di un Arcosolio del Cimitero dei SS. Pietro e Marcellino," *Rivisti di Archeologia Cristiana* 7 (1930): 35–36, 40, 42; C. H. Roberts and T. C. Skeat, *The Birth of the Codex* (London: Oxford University Press, 1987), 38–66 and bibliography cited there; Meer, *Early Christian Art*, 109–113; Weitzmann, *Age of Spirituality*, 527–531, 542–546, 567, 594–596.

137. Fine and Della Pergola, "Ostia Synagogue," 55.

138. See Sukenik, *Ancient Synagogues in Palestine and Greece*, 34.

139. A. St. Clair, "God's House of Peace in Paradise: The Feast of Tabernacles on a Jewish Gold Glass," *Jewish Art* 11 (1985): 6.

140. Noy, *Jewish Inscriptions of Western Europe, 2: The City of Rome*, 471–472.

141. Goodenough, *Jewish Symbols*, 2:113; St. Clair, "God's House of Peace in Paradise," and bibliography cited there.

142. H. Gressmann, "Jewish Life in Ancient Rome," in *Jewish Studies in Memory of Israel Abrahams* (New York: Jewish Institute of Religion, 1927), 180–181.

143. Sukenik, *Ancient Synagogue at Beth Alpha*, 20–21.

144. Gressmann, "Jewish Life in Ancient Rome," 181.

145. St. Clair, "God's House of Peace in Paradise," 9.

146. See also C. Roth, "Jewish Antecedents of Christian Art," *Journal of the Warburg and Courtland Institutes* 16, nos. 1–2 (1953): 26–27.

147. Rutgers, "Jewish Catacombs of Rome," 33–34, discusses the evidence for "afterworld aspirations" among Roman Jews.

148. Rutgers, "Jewish Catacombs of Rome," 34.

Bibliography

Primary Literary Sources

Hebrew Scriptures

Biblia Hebraica Stuttgartensia. 1967–1977. Ed. R. Kittel, P. Kahle, W. Rudolph, and K. Elliger. Stuttgart: Deutsche Bibelstiftung.
Tanakh: A New Translation of the Holy Scriptures. 1985. Philadelphia, New York, Jerusalem: Jewish Publication Society.

Second Temple Period Literature

The Assumption of Moses. 1897. Tr. R. H. Charles. London: Adam and Charles Black.
Baillet, Maurice, ed. 1982. *Qumran Grotte 4 III, Discoveries in the Judean Desert.* Oxford: Oxford University Press.
Barthélemy, D., and J. T. Milik, eds. 1956. *Discoveries in the Judean Desert: Qumran Cave 1.* Oxford: Oxford University Press.
Benoit, P., J. T. Milik, and R. De Vaux, eds. 1961. *Discoveries in the Judean Desert: Les Grottes de Murabbat.* Oxford: Oxford University Press.
The First Book of Maccabees. 1950. Tr. S. Tedesche, intro. and commentary by S. Zeitlin. New York: Harper. 1–66.
Josephus Flavius. 1961–1965. *The Complete Works.* Tr. H. St. J. Thackery, R. Marcus, A. Wikgren, and L. Feldman. Cambridge, Mass. and London: Harvard University Press.
Letter of Aristeas. 1951. *Aristeas to Philocrates (Letter of Aristeas).* Ed. and tr. M. Hadas. New York: Harper.
Philo of Alexandria. 1929–1962. *Philo.* Tr. F. H. Colson, G. H. Whitaker, and R. Marcus. Cambridge, Mass. and London: Harvard University Press.
Rabin, Chaim, ed. 1958. *The Zadokite Documents.* Oxford: Oxford University Press.
Wacholder, B. Z., and M. G. Abegg, eds. 1991. *A Preliminary Edition of the Unpublished Dead Sea Scrolls.* Washington, D.C.: Biblical Archaeology Society.

Rabbinic Literature, Liturgy and Targum

Assaf, Simḥa. 1946. "An Early Lament on the Destruction of Communities in the Land of Israel." In *Texts and Studies in Jewish History*. Jerusalem: Rav Kook Institute. 9–16. Hebrew.

Babylonian Talmud. 1520–1523. Venice: Bomberg. Rpt. Jerusalem.

———. 1540. Tractate Megillah, ms. X893–T141, Columbia University Library. Sana (?), Yemen.

———. 1884. Vilna: Romm.

———. 1979. *The Babylonian Talmud with Variant Readings, Tractate Sotah*. Ed. A. Liss. Jerusalem: Yad ha-Rav Hertsog. 1.

———. 1983. *The Babylonian Talmud with Variant Readings, Tractate Yebamoth*. Ed. A. Liss. Jerusalem. Yad ha-Rav Hertsog. 1.

Baraita de-Masekhet Niddah. 1889. Ed. C. M. Horowitz. In *Tosefta Atiqta*. Frankfurt. 5:1–56.

———. 1891. Ed. S. Schechter. "Jewish Literature in 1890." *Jewish Quarterly Review*, Old Series, 3:314–342.

———. 1938. Ed. M. Higger. "Perek Niddah." *Alim: A Periodical for the Bibliography and History of the Jews* 3 (3):61–69. Hebrew.

Baraita de-Melekhet ha-Mishkan. 1991. Ed. R. Kirschner. Cincinnati: Hebrew Union College Press.

The Bible in Aramaic. 1962. Ed. A. Sperber. Leiden: E. J. Brill.

Epstein, J. N. 1931. "Additional Fragments of the Jerushalmi." *Tarbiz* 3 (1): 15–26. Hebrew.

The Fathers According to Rabbi Nathan. 1967. Ed. S. Schechter. New York: Feldheim.

The Fragment-Targums of the Pentateuch. 1980. Ed. M. L. Klein. Rome: Biblical Institute.

Genesis Rabba. 1965. Ed. J. Theodor and Ch. Albeck. Jerusalem: Wahrmann.

Hopkins, Simon, ed. *A Miscellany of Literary Pieces from the Cambridge Genizah Collection*. Cambridge: Cambridge University Library.

Lamentations Rabba. 1899. Ed. S. Buber. Vilna: Romm.

Leviticus Rabba. 1993. Ed. M. Margulies. Jerusalem and New York: Jewish Theological Seminary.

Liturgical Poems of Simon Bar Megas. 1984. Ed. J. Yahalom. Jerusalem: Israel Academy of Sciences and Humanities.

The Liturgical Poetry of Rabbi Yannai. 1985–1987. Ed. Z. M. Rabinovitz. Jerusalem: Bialik Institute.

Margoliot, Mordecai, ed. 1973. *Hilkhot Eretz-Israel min ha-Geniza*. Brought to press by I. Ta-Shma. Jerusalem: Rav Kook Institute.

———. 1966. *Sefer ha-Razim*. Tel Aviv: Yediot Aharonot.

Megillat Ta'anit

———. 1931–1932. "Die Fastenrolle." Ed. H. Lichtenstein. *Hebrew Union College Annual* 8–9:257–351.

———. 1964. Ed. B. Z. Lurie. Jerusalem: Bialik Institute.

Mekhilta de-Rabbi Ishmael.
———. 1970. *Mechilta D'Rabbi Ismael.* Ed. H. S. Horovitz and I. A. Rabin. Jerusalem: Wahrmann.
———. 1976. *Mekilta de-Rabbi Ishmael.* Ed. J. Z. Lauterbach. Philadelphia: Jewish Publication Society.
Mekhilta de-Rabbi Simon b. Jochai. 1905. Ed. D. Z. Hoffmann. Frankfurt: Y. Kauffmann.
———. 1955. Ed. J. N. Epstein and E. Z. Melammed. Jerusalem: Magnes Press.
Midrash ha-Gadol to Exodus. 1967. Ed. M. Margulies. 2nd ed. Jerusalem: Rav Kook Institute.
Midrash ha-Gadol to Numbers. 1973. Ed. Z. M. Rabbinowitz. 2nd ed. Jerusalem: Rav Kook Institute.
Midrash Mishle. 1990. Ed. B. L. Visotzky. New York: Jewish Theological Seminary.
Midrash Rabba. 1975. Vilna: Romm. Rpt. Jerusalem.
Midrash Samuel. 1893. Ed. S. Buber. Cracow: Y. Fisher.
Midrash Tanhuma. 1563. Mantua. Rpt. Jerusalem: Makor, 1970–1971.
———. 1913. Ed. S. Buber. Vilna: Romm.
———. 1833. Rpt. Jerusalem, nd.
Midrash Tehillim. 1947. Ed. S. Buber. Vilna: Romm. Rpt. New York: Om.
Miqra'ot Gedolot on the Pentateuch and Five Scrolls. 1859. Vienna. Rpt. Jerusalem: Eshkol.
Mishnah.
———. 1883. *The Mishnah Upon Which the Palestinian Talmud Rests.* Ed. W. H. Lowe. Cambridge: Cambridge University Press. Rpt. Jerusalem: Makor, 1970.
———. 1929. *Codex Kaufmann A50.* Ed. G. Beer. Heidelberg. Facsimile, Jerusalem, 1968.
———. 1970. *Mishnah Codex Parma (De Rossi 138).* Facsimile. Jerusalem: Makor.
———. 1972. *The Mishnah with Variant Readings, Order Zera'im.* Ed. N. Sacks. Jerusalem.
———. 1979. Ed. C. Albeck. Jerusalem: Bialik Institute and Tel Aviv: Dvir.
———. 1979. *A Critical Edition of Mishnah Tractate Succah with an Introduction and Notes.* Ed. H. Fox. Doctoral dissertation, Hebrew University of Jerusalem. Hebrew.
———. 1991. *Tractate Middot.* Ed. A. S. Kaufmann. Jerusalem: Har Yéra'eh.
Palestinian Talmud.
———. 1523. Ed. Venice: Bomberg. Rpt. New York.
———. 1922. Vilna: Romm.
———. 1970. *Codex Vatican (Vat. Ebr. 133).* Facsimile. Jerusalem: Makor.
———. 1971. *Cod. Leiden Scal. 3.* Facsimile. Jerusalem: Makor.
———. 1979. *Tractate Shevi'it.* Ed. Y. Feliks. Jerusalem: Tsurot.
The Palestinian Targum to the Pentateuch (Neofiti 1). 1970. Facsimile. Jerusalem: Makor.
Pesiqta de Rav Kahane. 1868. Ed. S. Buber. Lyck: Mekize Nirdamim.
———. 1962. Ed. B. Mandelbaum. New York: Jewish Theological Seminary.
Pirqei de-R. Eliezer. 1862. Warsaw: Zvi Yaakov Bamberg. Rpt. Jerusalem, n.p., 1970.
Rabbinowicz, Raphael. 1976. *Dikduqei Sofrim.* New York: M. P. Press.
Seder Avodat Israel. 1937. Ed. Z. Baer. Palestine: Schocken.
Sefer Pitron Torah. 1978. Ed. E. E. Urbach. Jerusalem: Magnes Press.

Siddur Rinat Yisrael. 1976. Ed. S. Tal. Ashkenazi version. Jerusalem: Moreshet.
Sifra. 1947. Ed. I. H. Weiss. New York: Om.
Sifre on Deuteronomy. 1969. Ed. L. Finkelstein. New York: Jewish Theological Seminary.
Sifre D'Be Rab and Sifre Zutta on Numbers. 1966. Ed. H. S. Horowitz. Jerusalem.
Sokoloff, Michael, and Joseph Yahalom. Forthcoming. *Aramaic Poetry of the Byzantine Period from Eretz-Israel*. Jerusalem: Israel Academy of Sciences and Humanities.
Sperber, Alexander, ed. 1953–1973. *The Bible in Aramaic*. Leiden: E. J. Brill.
Targum des Chroniques. 1971. Ed. R. Le Deaut and J. Robert. Rome: Biblical Institute.
Targum Pseudo-Jonathan on the Pentateuch: Text and Commentary. 1984. Ed. E. G. Clarke. New York: Ktav.
Tosefta.
———. 1970. Ed. M. S. Zuckermandel. 2nd ed. Jerusalem: Wahrmann.
———. 1992. Ed. S. Lieberman. 2nd ed. New York: Jewish Theological Seminary.
Tractate Sofrim. 1937. Ed. M. Higger. New York: De-be Rabanan.
Yalqut Shimoni. 1887. Warsaw: Isaac Goldman.
Yosse Ben Yosse Poems. 1977. Ed. A. Mirsky. Jerusalem: Bialik Institute.

Gaonic and Qaraite Literatures

Daniel son of Moses Al-Qumisi. 1957. *Commentarius in Librum Duodecim Prophetarum*. Ed. I. D. Marcus. Jerusalem: Mekize Nirdamim.
Differences in Religious Customs between Babylonian and Palestinian Jewries. 1938. Ed. M. Margaliot. Jerusalem: Rav Kook Institute.
———. *Differences of Custom between Palestinian and Babylonian Jewries*. 1942. Ed. B. M. Lewin. Jerusalem: Rav Kook Institute.
The Gaonic Commentary on the Order Tohorot Attributed to Rav Hay Gaon. 1982. Ed. J. N. Epstein. Tel Aviv: Dvir and Jerusalem: Magnes Press.
Iggeret Rav Sherira Gaon. 1921. Ed. B. M. Lewin. Haifa.
———. *The Iggeres of Rav Sherira Gaon*. 1991. Tr. N. D. Rabinowich. Jerusalem: H. Vagshal. Hebrew.
Lewin, B. M. 1984. *Otzar ha-Gaonim: Thesaurus of the Gaonic Responsa and Commentaries*. Jerusalem: H. Vagshal.
She'eltot de Rab Ahai Gaon. 1963. Ed. S. K. Mirsky. Jerusalem: Rav Kook Institute.

Greek and Latin Authors

Linder, Amnon, ed. 1987. *The Jews in Roman Imperial Legislation*. Detroit: Wayne State University Press and Jerusalem: Israel Academy of Sciences and Humanities.
Plutarch. 1968. *Plutarch's Lives*. Tr. B. Perrin. Cambridge, Mass. and London: Harvard University Press. 2.
Stern, Menahem, ed. 1976–1984. *Greek and Latin Authors on Jews and Judaism*. Jerusalem: Israel Academy of Sciences and Humanities.
Vitruvius. 1970. *On Architecture*. Tr. F. Granger. Cambridge, Mass. and London: Harvard University Press.

Christian Literature

The Book of Pontiffs (Liber Pontificalis). 1989. Tr. R. Davis. Liverpool: Liverpool University Press.
Chrysostom, John. 1862. *Adversus Judaeos*. In *Patrologia Graeca*, ed. J. P. Migne. Paris: Minge. 48:839–942.
———. 1979. *Discourses against Judaising Christians*. Tr. P. W. Harkins. Washington, D.C.: Catholic University of America.
The Didascalia Apostolorum in Syriac. 1979. In *Corpus Scriptorum Christianorum Orientalium, Scriptores Syri*, ed. A. Voobus. Louvain. 179–180.
Eusebius of Caesarea. 1964. *Ecclesiastical History*. Tr. J. E. L. Oulton and H. J. Laylor. London.
Fiensey, David A. 1985. *Prayers Alleged To Be Jewish: An Examination of the Constitutiones Apostolorum*. Atlanta: Scholars Press.
New Testament. Greek-English New Testament. 1986. Ed. E. Nestle and E. Aland. Stuttgart: Deutsche Bibelstiftung.
Tertullian. 1844. *De Jejuniis*. In *Patrologia Latina*, ed. J. P. Minge. Paris: Apud Garniere Frateres. 2.

Epigraphic Corpora

Frey, Jean-Bapitiste, ed. 1936. *Corpus Inscriptionum Judaicarum*. Rome: Pontifico istituto de archeologia critiana, 1.
Horbury, William, and David Noy, eds. 1992. *Jewish Inscriptions of Graeco-Roman Egypt*. Cambridge: Cambridge University Press.
Lewis, D. M., ed. 1964. "The Jewish Inscriptions of Egypt." In *Corpus Papyrorium Judaicarum*, ed. V. A. Tcherikover, A. Fuks, and M. Stern. Jerusalem: Magnes Press and Cambridge, Mass: Harvard University Press. 3.138–166.
Lifshitz, Baruch. 1967. *Donateurs et Fondateurs dans les Synagogues Juives*. Paris: J. Gabalda.
Naveh, Joseph, ed. 1978. *On Stone and Mosaic: The Aramaic and Hebrew Inscriptions from Ancient Synagogues*. Israel: Maariv. Hebrew.
———. 1989. "The Aramaic and Hebrew Inscriptions from Ancient Synagogues." *Eretz-Israel* 20:302–310. Hebrew.
Naveh, Joseph, and Shaul Shaked. 1975. *Amulets and Magic Bowls: Aramaic Incantations from Late Antiquity*. Jerusalem and Leiden: E. J. Brill.
———. 1985. *Magic Spells and Formulae: Aramaic Incantations of Late Antiquity*. Jerusalem: Magnes Press.
Noy, David, ed. 1995. *Jewish Inscriptions of Western Europe, 2: The City of Rome*. Cambridge: Cambridge University Press.
Tcherikover, Victor A., Alexander Fuks, and Menahem Stern, eds. 1957–1964. *Corpus Papyrorium Judaicarum*. Jerusalem: Magnes Press and Cambridge, Mass: Harvard University Press.

Secondary Literature

Academy of the Hebrew Language. 1988. *The Historical Dictionary of the Hebrew Language: Materials for the Dictionary, Series I, 200 B.C.E.– 300 C.E.* Jerusalem: Academy of the Hebrew Language. Hebrew.

Albeck, Chanoch. 1969. *Introduction to the Talmud, Babli and Yerushalmi.* Jerusalem: Bialik Institute and Tel Aviv: Dvir. Hebrew.

Alexander, Phillip S. 1986. "Incantations and Books of Magic." In *The History of the Jews in the Age of Jesus Christ*, rev. and ed. G. Vermes et al. Edinburgh: T. & T. Clarke. 3.1:342–379.

———. 1990. "Jewish Aramaic Translations of Hebrew Scriptures." In *Mikra*, ed. M. J. Mulder. Assen/Maastricht: Van Gorgum and Philadelphia: Fortress Press. 217–253.

Alfasi, Isaac son of Jacob. 1884. *Sefer ha-Halakhot.* Published accompanying the Vilna: Romm edition of the Babylonian Talmud. Hebrew.

Alon, Gedalyahu. 1977. "The Bounds of the Laws of Levitical Cleanliness." In *Jews, Judaism and the Classical World*, tr. I. Abrahams. Jerusalem: Magnes Press. 190–234.

———. 1978. "The Halakhah in the Teachings of the Twelve Apostles (*Didache*)." *Studies in Jewish History* 1:274–294. Israel: Hakibbutz Hameuchad. Hebrew.

———. 1989. *The Jews in Their Land in the Talmudic Age.* Tr. G. Levi. Cambridge, Mass. and London: Harvard University Press.

American Heritage Dictionary of the English Language. 1991. Second College Edition. New York: Houghton Mifflin.

Amit, David. 1990. "A Marble Menorah from an Ancient Synagogue at Tel Ma'on." *Proceedings of the Tenth World Congress in Jewish Studies*, Division B, 1:53–60. Hebrew.

Aptowitzer, Avigdor. 1941. *Studies in Gaonic Literature.* Jerusalem: Rav Kook Institute. Hebrew.

Avigad, Nahman. 1957. "Excavations at Beth She'arim: Preliminary Report." *Israel Exploration Journal* 7 (4):239–255.

———.1976. *Beth She'arim.* 3. New Brunswick: Rutgers University Press.

Avi-Yonah, Michael. 1947. "Remains of an Ancient Synagogue at Fahma Village." *Proceedings of the Jewish Palestine Exploration Society* 13 (3–4):154–155. Hebrew.

———. 1964. "The Caesarea Inscription of the Twenty-Four Priestly Courses." *Eretz-Israel* 7:24–28. Hebrew.

———. 1971. "Synagogue Architecture in the Late Classical Period." In *Jewish Art*, ed. C. Roth. 2nd ed. London: Valentine. 65–82.

———. 1981a. *Art in Ancient Palestine: Selected Essays.* Ed. H. Katzenstein and Yoram Tsafrir. Jerusalem: Magnes Press.

———. 1981b. "The Mosaic of Mopsuestia-Church or Synagogue?" In *Ancient Synagogues Revealed*, ed. L. I. Levine. Jerusalem: Israel Exploration Society. 186–190.

———. 1984. *The Jews under Roman and Byzantine Rule.* Jerusalem: Magnes Press.

Ayali, Meir. 1987. *Workers and Craftsmen: Their Labor and Their Status in Rabbinic Literature.* Israel: Yad la-Talmud. Hebrew.

Bacher, Wilhelm. 1897. "Le Siege de Moise." *Revue de Etudes Juives* 34:299–301.

———. 1899. "Zur Geschichte der Schulen Palaestina's im 3 und 4 Jahrhundert, Die Gnossen (ḥavrayya)." *Monatsschrift für Geschichte und Wissenschaft des Judentums* 43:345–360.

———. 1903. "Synagogue." In *A Dictionary of the Bible*, ed. J. Hastings. New York. 4:636–643.

———. 1923. *Die exegetische Terminologie der jüdischen Traditionsliteratur.* Tr. A. Z. Rabinowitz. Tel Aviv: Ahdut. Hebrew.

Bachrach, Bernard S. 1985. "The Jewish Community of the Later Roman Empire as Seen in the Codex Theodosianus." In *To See Ourselves as Others See Us*, ed. J. Neusner and E. S. Frerichs. Chino: Scholars Press. 399–421.

Bahat, Dan. 1981. "A Synagogue at Beth-Shean." In *Ancient Synagogues Revealed*, ed. L. I. Levine. Jerusalem: Israel Exploration Society. 82–85.

Baker, Avrom. 1981–1982. "The Illustrations of Signs of the Zodiac for the Tal and Geshem Prayers." *Journal of Jewish Music and Liturgy* 4:11–13.

Barag, Dan. 1994. "The Showbread Table and the Facade of the Temple on Coins of the Bar-Kokhba Revolt." In *Ancient Jerusalem Revealed*, ed. H. Geva. Jerusalem: Israel Exploration Society. 272–276.

Barag, D., Y. Porat, and E. Netzer. 1981. "The Synagogue at En-Gedi." In *Ancient Synagogues Revealed*, ed. L. I. Levine. Jerusalem: Israel Exploration Society. 116–119.

Barasch, Moshe. 1992. *Icon: Studies in the History of an Idea.* New York and London: New York University Press.

Bar Ilan, Meir. 1992. "The Blessings and Curses That Are Read before Rosh ha-Shanah." *Sinai* 55:27–35.

Baron, Salo Wittmayer. 1958–1983. *A Social and Economic History of the Jews.* New York: Columbia University Press.

Baumgarten, Joseph M. 1977. *Studies in Qumran Law.* Leiden: E. J. Brill.

Beckwith, Roger T. 1990. "Formation of the Hebrew Bible." In *Mikra*, ed. M. J. Mulder. Assen/Maastricht: Van Gorgum and Philadelphia: Fortress Press. 39–86.

Be'er, Haim, ed. 1983. *Stone Bird: Jerusalem in Modern Hebrew Poetry.* Tel Aviv: Shva Publishers. Hebrew.

Beer, Moshe. 1982. "On the *Havura* in Eretz Israel in the Amoraic Period." *Zion* 47 (2):178–185. Hebrew; English summary, xiii.

Beit Arie, Malachi. 1988. "How Hebrew Books are Made." In *A Sign and a Witness: 2,000 Years of Hebrew Books and Illuminated Manuscripts*, ed. L. S. Gold. New York and Oxford: Oxford University Press. 35–46.

Ben Shammai, Meir Hillel. 1955. "The Sanctity of the Land." *Encyclopaedia Biblica.* Jerusalem: Bialik Institute. 1:741. Hebrew.

Ben Yehuda, Elieser. 1952. *A Complete Dictionary of Ancient and Modern Hebrew.* New York: Thomas Yoseloff. Hebrew.

Beyer, Hermann Wolfgang, and Hans Lietzmann. 1930. *Die Jüdische Katakombe der Villa Torlonia in Rom.* Berlin and Leipzig: Walther de Gruyter.

Biale, David. 1992. *Eros and the Jews: From Biblical Israel to Contemporary America*. New York: Basic Books.
Bickerman, Elias. 1980. "Les Maccabees de Malalas." In *Studies in Jewish and Christian History*, part 2, Leiden: E. J. Brill. 192–209.
———. 1980. "The Altars of the Gentiles: A Note on the Jewish 'Ius Sacrum'." In *Studies in Jewish and Christian History*, part 1. Leiden: E. J. Brill. 324–346.
Biebel, Franklin M. 1936. "The Mosaics of Hammam Lif." *Art Bulletin* 16 (4):541–551.
Blidstein, Gerald J. 1973. "The *Tannaim* and Plastic Art: Problems and Prospects." *Perspectives in Jewish Learning* 5:13–27.
———. 1974. "Prostration and Mosaics in Talmudic Law." *Bulletin of the Institute of Jewish Studies* 2:19–39.
Blau, Ludwig. 1902. *Studien zum althebräischen Buchwesen*. Strassburg.
———. 1914. *Das Altjüdische Zaberwesen*. Berlin: L. Lamm.
———. 1926. "Early Christian Archaeology from a Jewish Point of View." *Hebrew Union College Annual* 3:157–215.
Bokser, Baruch M. 1983a. "Rabbinic Responses to Catastrophe: From Continuity to Discontinuity." *Proceedings of the American Academy of Jewish Research* 50:37–61.
———. 1983b. "The Wall Separating God and Israel." *Jewish Quarterly Review* 73 (4):349–374.
———. 1984. *The Origin of the Seder*. Berkeley and Los Angeles: University of California Press.
———. 1985. "Approaching Sacred Space." *Harvard Theological Review* 78 (1–3): 279–299.
———. 1986. "Rabbinic Continuity and Revisions in the Notion of Sacred Space—Applying Deuteronomy 23:10–15." *Proceedings of the Ninth World Congress of Jewish Studies*, Division C. 7–14.
Bologesi, Eugenia Marta. 1985. "Relazione Preliminare di Scavo in Relazione alla Scoperta di una Sinagoga a Kafr Misr Nella Galilea Meridionale." *Revista Di Archeologia Cristiana* 61 (1–2):159–166.
Bornstein, Hayim Jehiel. 1904. "The Dispute between R. Saadia Gaon and Ben Meir." In *Nahum Sokolow Festschrift*. Warsaw: Shuldberg. 19–189. Hebrew.
Botermann, Helga. 1990. "Die Synagoge von Sardes: Eine Synagoge aus dem 4. Jahrhundert?" *Zeitschrift für die Neutestamentliche Wissenschaft* 81:103–121.
Bouras, Laskarina. 1982. "Byzantine Lighting Devices." *XVI Internationaler Byzantinstenkongress Akten* (= *Jahrbuch der Österreichischen Byzantinistik* 32.3) 2 (3):479–491.
Bowersock, G. W. 1990. *Hellenism in Late Antiquity*. Ann Arbor: University of Michigan Press.
Boyarin, Daniel. 1990. "The Eye in the Torah: Ocular Desire in Midrashic Hermeneutic." *Critical Inquiry* 16(3):532–550.
Brand, Joshua. 1953. *Ceramics in Talmudic Literature*. Jerusalem: Rav Kook Institute. Hebrew.
———. 1970. "Circuses and Theaters." *Encyclopedia Judaica*, 5:577–578.

———. 1978. *Glass Vessels in Talmudic Literature*. Jerusalem: Rav Kook Institute. Hebrew.

Branham, Joan R. 1992. "Sacred Space under Erasure in Ancient Synagogues and Churches." *Art Bulletin* 74 (3):375–394.

———. 1993. *Sacred Space in Ancient Jewish and Early Medieval Christian Architecture*. Doctoral dissertation, Emory University.

———. 1995. "Vicarious Sacrality: Temple Space in Ancient Synagogues." In *Ancient Synagogues: Historical Analysis and Archaeological Discovery*, ed. D. Urman and P. V. M. Flesher. Leiden: E. J. Brill. 2:319–346.

Braslavi, Y. 1967. "Symbols and Mythological Figures in the Early Synagogues in the Galilee." In *All the Land of Naphtali*. 106–129. Hebrew.

Bratschkova, Maria. 1938. "Die Muschel in der antiken Kunst." *Bulletin de l'Institut Archeologique Bulgare* 12 (1):1–121.

Bryson, Norman, Michael Ann Holly, and Keith Moxey. 1994. *Visual Culture: Images and Interpretations*. Hanover and London: University Press of New England.

Brilliant, Richard. 1994. "'Jewish Symbols.' Is That Still Good Enough?" *Commentaries on Roman Art: Selected Studies*. London: Pindar. 233–244.

Brooton, Bernadette J. 1982. *Women Leaders in Ancient Synagogues*. Chico: Scholars Press.

Brown, Frances, S. R. Driver, and Charles A. Briggs. 1972. *A Hebrew and English Lexicon of the Old Testament*. Oxford: Oxford University Press.

Brown, J. R. 1963. *Temple and Sacrifice in Rabbinic Judaism*. Evanston, Ill.: Seabury-Western Theological Seminary.

Brown, Peter. 1971. *The World of Late Antiquity*. London: Thames and London.

———. 1980. "Art and Society in Late Antiquity." In *The Age of Spirituality: A Symposium*, ed. K. Weitzmann. New York: Metropolitan Museum of Art. 17–28.

———. 1981. *The Cult of the Saints*. Chicago: University of Chicago Press.

———. 1989. *Society and the Holy in Late Antiquity*. Berkeley and Los Angeles: University of California Press.

Brown, Peter, and Sabine Mac Cormick. 1989. "Artifaces of Eternity." In *Society and the Holy in Late Antiquity*, ed. P. Brown. Berkeley and Los Angeles: University of California Press. 207–221.

Büchler, Adolph. 1922. *Types of Jewish Palestinian Piety*. London: Jews' College.

Budde, Erich G. 1939. *Armarium und Kibotos*. Würzburg: Konrad Triltsch.

Burtchaell, James Tunstead. 1992. *From Synagogue to Church: Public Services and Offices in the Earliest Christian Communities*. Cambridge: Cambridge University Press.

Cardman, Francine. 1982. "The Rhetoric of Holy Places: Palestine in the 4th Century." *Studia Patristica* 17a:18–25.

Charlesworth, James H. 1977. "Jewish Astrology in the Talmud, Pseudepigrapha, the Dead Sea Scrolls, and Early Palestinian Synagogues." *Harvard Theological Review* 70 (3–4):183–200.

Chiat, Marilyn Joyce Segal. 1980. "Synagogues and Churches in Byzantine Beit She'an." *Jewish Art* 7:6–24.

———. 1981. "First-Century Synagogue Architecture: Methodological Problems." In *Ancient Synagogues: The State of the Research*, ed. J. Gutmann. Chino: Scholars Press. 49–60.

———. 1982. *A Handbook of Synagogue Architecture*. Chino: Scholars Press.

Chipp, Herschel. 1988. *Picasso's Guernica: History, Transformations, Meanings*. Berkeley and Los Angeles: University of California.

Chiton, Bruce, and Jacob Neusner. 1995. *Judaism in the New Testament: Practices and Beliefs*. London and New York: Routledge.

Clark, J. W. 1902. *The Care of Books*. Cambridge: Cambridge University Press.

Claude, Dietrich. 1969. *Die byzantinische Stadt im 6 Jahrhundert*. Byzantinisches Archiv 13.

Cohen, Jeremy. 1976. "Roman Imperial Policy toward the Jews from Constantine until the End of the Palestinian Patriarchate (ca. 429)." *Byzantine Studies* (1):1–29.

Cohen, Shaye J. D. 1983. "Jacob Neusner, Mishnah and Counter-Rabbinics." *Conservative Judaism* 37 (1):48–63.

———. 1984. "The Temple and the Synagogue." In *The Temple in Antiquity*, ed. T. G. Madsen. Provo: Brigham Young University Press. 151–174.

———. 1987. "Pagan and Christian Evidence on the Ancient Synagogue." In *The Synagogue in Late Antiquity*, ed. L. I. Levine. Philadelphia: American Schools for Oriental Research. 159–183.

———. 1991. "Menstruants and the Sacred in Judaism and Christianity." In *Women's History and Ancient History*, ed. S. B. Pomeroy. Chapel Hill: University of North Carolina. 273–299.

———. 1992. "Purity and Piety: The Separation of Menstruants from the Sancta." In *Daughters of the King: Women in the Synagogue*, ed. S. Grossman and R. Haut. Philadelphia, New York, Jerusalem: Jewish Publication Society. 103–115.

Colt, H. Dunscombe. 1962. "Introduction." In *Excavations at Nessana*, ed. H. D. Colt. London: British School of Archaeology in Jerusalem. 1.1–24.

Creswell, Keppel Archibald Cameron. 1932. *Early Muslim Architecture*. Oxford: Clarendon.

Cross, Frank M. 1947. "The Tabernacle: A Study from an Archaeological and Historical Approach." *Biblical Archaeologist* 10 (3):45–68.

———. 1984. "The Priestly Tabernacle in Light of Recent Research." In *The Temple in Antiquity*, ed. T. G. Madsen. Provo: Brigham Young University Press. 90–105.

Crowfoot, Grace M., and D. B. Harden. 1931. "Early Byzantine and Later Glass Lamps." *Journal of Egyptian Archaeology* 17:196–207.

Dan, Joseph. 1997. *On Sanctity: Religion, Ethics, and Mysticism in Judaism and Other Religions*. Jerusalem: Magnes. Hebrew.

Dauphin, Claudine. 1980. "Mosaic Pavements as an Index of Prosperity and Fashion." *Levant* 12:112–134.

De Blaauw, S. 1991. "Architecture and Liturgy in Late Antiquity and the Middle Ages: Traditions and Trends in Modern Scholarship." *Archiv für Liturgie-Wissenschaft* 33 (1):1-34.

Dendy, D. R. 1959. *The Use of Lights in Christian Worship*. London: S.P.C.K.

De Sola Pool, David. 1909. *The Jewish Aramaic Prayer: The Kaddish.* Leipzig: W. Druglin.

Dinari, Yedidyah. 1983. "The Violation of the Sacred by the Niddah and the Enactment of Ezra." *Te'uda: Studies in Talmudic Literature, in Post Biblical Hebrew and in Biblical Exegesis* 3:17–37. Hebrew.

Dion, Paul-Eugene. 1977. "Synagogoues et Temples dans l'Egypte Hellenistiques." *Science et Espirit* 29:46–75.

Dommeshausen, W. "hll." *Theological Dictionary of the Old Testament.* Ed. J. Butterweck, H. Ringgren, tr. D. G. Green. Grand Rapids: Zondervan. 4:409-417.

Dothan, Moshe. 1983. *Hammath Tiberias: Early Synagogues.* Jerusalem: Israel Exploration Society.

Douglas, Mary. 1984. *Purity and Danger: An Analysis of the Concepts of Pollution and Taboo.* London and Boston: Ark Paperbacks.

Downey, Susan B. 1988. *Mesopotamean Religious Architecture: Alexander through the Parthians.* Princeton: Princeton University Press.

Durkheim, Emile. 1965. *The Elementary Forms of the Religious Life.* Tr. J. S. Swain. New York: Free Press.

Egyptian Antiquities Authority. 1984. *Coptic Museum.* Egypt.

Einhorn, Ze'ev Wolf. 1975. *Commentary of the Maharzu.* Published accompanying the Vilna: Romm edition of *Midrash Rabba.* Rpt. Jerusalem. Hebrew.

Elbogen, Ismar. 1993. *Jewish Liturgy: A Comprehensive History.* Tr. R. P. Scheindlin. Philadelphia, New York, Jerusalem: Jewish Publication Society.

Eliade, Mircea. 1958. *Patterns in Comparative Religion.* Tr. R. Sheed. London and New York: Sheed and Ward.

———. 1961. *The Sacred and the Profane: The Nature of Religion.* New York: Harper and Row.

———. 1985. *Symbolism, The Sacred and the Arts.* Ed. D. Apostolos-Cappadona. New York: Crossroad.

Elman, Yaakov. 1991. "Babylonian Baraitot in the Tosefta and the 'Dialectology' of Middle Hebrew." *AJS Review* 16:1–29.

Encyclopedia Hebraica and Editor. 1970. "Purity and Impurity." *Encyclopedia Judaica* 13:1405–1414.

Encyclopedia Judaica. 1970. "Kedushah." 7:866–872.

Engemann, Josef. 1976. "Magische Uebelabwehr in der Spätantike." *Jahrbuch für Antike und Christentum* 18:22–48.

Epstein, Barukh Ha-Levi. 1902. *Torah Temimah.* Vilna: Romm. Hebrew.

Epstein, Jacob N. 1948. *Introduction to the Text of the Mishnah.* Jerusalem: Magnes Press. Hebrew.

———. 1957. *Introduction to Tannaitic Literature.* Ed. E. Z. Melamed. Jerusalem. Hebrew.

———. 1983. *Studies in Talmudic Literature and Semitic Languages.* Ed. E. Z. Melamed, tr. Z. Epstein. Jerusalem: Magnes Press. 1. Hebrew.

Epstein, Mark Michael. 1994. "The Elephant and the Law: The Medieval Jewish Minority Adapts a Christian Motif." *Art Bulletin* 76:465–478.

Esh, Shaul. 1957. *Der Heilige (Er Sei Gepriesen): Zur Geschichte einer Nachbiblisch-Hebraeischen Gottesbezeichnung*. Leiden: E. J. Brill.

Eshel, Esther, and Michael Stone. 1993. "The Holy Language at the End of Days in Light of a New Fragment Found at Qumran." *Tarbiz* 62 (2):169–177. Hebrew.

Eshel, Hanan. 1991. "A Fragmentary Inscription of the Priestly Courses?" *Tarbiz* 61 (1):159–161. Hebrew.

———. 1991. "The Prayer of Joseph, a Papyrus from Masada and the Samaritan Temple on ARGARIZIN." *Zion* 56 (2):125–136. Hebrew.

Federbush, Shimon. 1967. *The Hebrew Language in Israel and among the Nations*. Jerusalem: Rav Kook Institute. Hebrew.

Feldman, Louis H. 1984. *Josephus and Modern Scholarship (1937–1980)*. Berlin and New York: Walther de Gruyter.

———. 1989. "Proselytes and "Sympathizers" in Light of the New Inscriptions from Aphordisias." *Revue des Etudes juives* 147 (3–4):265–305.

———. 1993. *Jew and Gentile in the Ancient World*. Princeton: Princeton University Press.

Fendri, Mohamed. 1961. *Basiliques Cretiennes de la Skhira*. Paris: Presses Universitaires de France.

Feuchtwanger, Naomi. 1988. "Late Sixth Century Metal Ampoules from Jerusalem." In *Jews, Samaritans, and Christians in Byzantine Palestine*, ed. D. Jacoby and Y. Tsafrir. Jerusalem: Ben Zvi Institute. 198–206. Hebrew.

Fine, Steven. 1989. "On the Development of a Visual Symbol: The Date Palm in Roman Palestine and the Jews." *Journal for the Study of the Pseudepigrapha* 4:105–118.

———. 1993. *Synagogue and Sanctity: The Late Antique Palestinian Synagogue as a "Holy Place."* Doctoral dissertation, Hebrew University of Jerusalem.

———. 1995. "Review of R. Hachlili, *Ancient Jewish Art and Archaeology in the Land of Israel*, Leiden, 1988." *Journal for the Study of the Pseudepigrapha*. 13:101–104.

———. 1996a. "Did the Synagogue Replace the Temple?" *Bible Review* 12 (2):18–26, 41.

———. 1996b. "Review of *Ancient Synagogues: Historical Analysis and Archaeological Discovery*, ed. D. Urman and P. V. M. Flesher. Leiden: E. J. Brill." *Biblical Archaeology Review* 22 (3):10, 69.

———. Forthcoming. "'Chancel' Screens in Late Antique Palestinian Synagogues: A Genizah Source." In *Religious and Ethnic Communities in Later Roman Palestine*, ed. H. Lapin. College Park, Md: University of Maryland.

———. Forthcoming. "Relations Between Egypt and Palestine During the Greco-Roman Period: The Evidence of the Synagogue." In *Proceedings of the Conference on Israel-Diaspora Relations during the Greco-Roman Period*, ed. A. Baumgarten, I. Gafni, and L. Schiffman. Jerusalem: Zalman Shazar Institute. Hebrew.

———. Forthcoming. "Art and the Liturgical Context of the Sepphoris Synagogue Mosaic." In *Proceedings of the Second International Conference on Galilee*, ed. E. M. Meyers. Atlanta: Scholars Press.

———, ed. 1996. *Sacred Realm: The Emergence of the Synagogue in the Ancient World*. New York: Oxford University Press and Yeshiva University Museum.

Fine, Steven, and Leah Bierman Fine. Forthcoming. *Where God Dwells: A Child's History of the Synagogue*. Los Angeles: Torah Aura.
Fine, Steven, and Miriam Della Pergola. 1994. "The Ostia Synagogue and Its Torah Shrine." In *The Jews of Ancient Rome*, ed. J. Goodnick Wesenholz. Jerusalem: Bible Lands Museum. 42–57.
Fine, Steven, and Leonard Victor Rutgers. 1996. "New Light on Judaism in Asia Minor during Late Antiquity: Two Recently Identified Inscribed Menorahs." *Jewish Studies Quarterly* 3 (1):1-23.
Fine, Steven, and Bruce Zuckerman. 1985. "The Menorah as Symbol of Jewish Minority Status." In *Fusion in the Hellenistic East*, ed. S. Fine. Los Angeles: University of Southern California Fisher Gallery. 23–30.
Finney, Paul Corby. 1978. "Orpheus-David: A Connection in Iconography between Greco-Roman Judaism and Early Christianity?" *Jewish Art* 5:6–15.
———. 1984. "Hieros Topos und christlicher Sakralbau in vorkonstantinischer Ueberliegerung." *Boreas* 7:193–225.
Fishbane, Michael. 1990. "From Scribalism to Rabbinism: Perspectives on the Emergence of Classical Judaism." In *The Scribe in Israel and the Ancient Near East*, ed. J. G. Gambie and L. G. Perdue. Winona Lake, Ind.: Eisenbrauns. 439–456.
Fitzmyer, Joseph A. 1970. "The Languages of Palestine in the First Century A.D." *Catholic Biblical Quarterly* 32:501–531.
Fleischer, Ezra. 1975. *Hebrew Liturgical Poetry in the Middle Ages*. Jerusalem: Keter. Hebrew.
———. 1988. *Eretz-Israel Prayers and Rituals as Portrayed in the Geniza Documents*. Jerusalem: Magnes Press. Hebrew.
———. 1989–1990. "On the Beginnings of Obligatory Jewish Prayer." *Tarbiz* 59 (3–4): 397–441. Hebrew.
Flesher, Paul Virgil McCracken. 1995a. "Palestinian Synagogues before 70 C.E.: A Review of the Evidence." In *Ancient Synagogues: Historical Analysis and Archaeological Discovery*, ed. D. Urman and P. V. M. Flesher. Leiden: E. J. Brill. 1:27–39.
———. 1995b. "Rereading the Reredos: David, Orpheus and Messianism in the Dura Europos Synagogue." In *Ancient Synagogues: Historical Analysis and Archaeological Discovery*, ed. D. Urman and P. V. M. Flesher. Leiden: E. J. Brill. 2:346–366.
Floriani Squarciapino, Maria. 1963. "The Synagogue at Ostia." *Archaeology* 16 (3):194–203.
———. 1964. *La Sinagoga di Ostia*. Rome.
Foerster, Gideon. 1981a. "The Synagogues at Masada and Herodium." In *Ancient Synagogues Revealed*, ed. L. I. Levine. Jerusalem: Israel Exploration Society. 24–29.
———. 1981b. "Synagogue Inscriptions and Their Relation to Liturgical Versions." *Cathedra* 17:12–40. Hebrew.
———. 1985. "The Zodiac Wheel in Ancient Synagogues and Its Iconographic Sources." *Eretz-Israel* 18:380–391. Hebrew.
———. 1987a. "A Basilica Plan (including Apsis) as a Chronological Criterion in Synagogues." In *Synagogues in Antiquity*, ed. A. Kasher, A. Oppenheimer, and U. Rappaport. Jerusalem: Ben Zvi Institute. 173–179. Hebrew.

———. 1987b. "The Zodiac Wheel in Ancient Synagogues and Its Place in Jewish Liturgical Thought." *Eretz-Israel* 19:224–234. Hebrew.

———. 1988. "Christian Allegories and Symbols in the Mosaic Designs of 6th Century Eretz Israel Synagogues." In *Jews, Samaritans, and Christians in Byzantine Palestine*, ed. D. Jacoby and Y. Tsafrir. Jerusalem: Ben Zvi Institute. 198–206. Hebrew.

———. 1989. "Decorated Marble Chancel Screens in Sixth Century Synagogues in Palestine and Their Relation to Christian Art and Architecture." *Actes du XIe Congres International d'Archeologie Chretienne*. Rome: Ecole Francaise. 2:1809–1820.

Fox, Harry. 1980. "'As if with a Finger'—The Text History of an Expression Avoiding Anthropomorphism." *Tarbiz* 49:278–291. Hebrew.

Fox, Michael V. 1989. *Qohelet and His Contradictions*. Sheffield: Sheffield University Press.

Fraade, Steven D. 1986. "Ascetical Aspects of Ancient Judaism." In *Jewish Spirituality from the Bible through the Middle Ages*. New York: Crossroad. 253–288.

———. 1987. "Interpreting Midrash 1: Midrash and the History of Judaism." *Prooftexts* 7 (2):179–194.

———. 1988. "Sifre Deuteronomy 26 (ad Deuteronomy 3:23): How Conscious the Composition?" *Hebrew Union College Annual* 54:245–301.

———. 1990. "The Early Rabbinic Sage." In *The Scribe in Israel and the Ancient Near East*, ed. J. G. Gambie and L. G. Perdue. Winona Lake, Ind.: Eisenbrauns. 417–436.

———. 1991. *From Tradition to Commentary: Torah and Its Interpretation in the Midrash Sifre to Deuteronomy*. Albany: State University of New York Press.

———. 1992. "Rabbinic Views on the Practice of Targum, and Multilingualism in the Jewish Galilee of the Third-Sixth Centuries." In *The Galilee in Late Antiquity*, ed. L. I. Levine. New York and Jerusalem: Ben Zvi Institute. 253–286.

Fraenkel, David son of Naphtali. 1922. *Qorban ha-Edah*. Published in the Vilna: Romm edition of the Palestinian Talmud.

Fraenkel, Jonah. 1978. "Hermeneutical Problems in the Study of the Aggadic Narrative." *Tarbiz* 47:140–172. Hebrew.

———. 1981. *Studies in the Spiritual World of the Homiletical Story*. Israel: Hakibbutz Hameuchad. Hebrew.

———. 1991. *The Ways of Aggadah and Midrash*. Israel: Yad la-Talmud. Hebrew.

Fridrichsen, Anton. 1916. *Hagios-Qados: Ein Beitrag zu den Voruntersuchungen zur Christlichen Begriffsgeschichte*. Kristiania: J. Dybwad.

Friedland, Roger, and Richard D. Hecht. 1991. "The Politics of Sacred Space: Jerusalem's Temple Mount/al-haram al sharif." In *Sacred and Profane Spaces: Essays in the Geographics of Judaism, Christianity, and Islam*, ed. J. Scott and P. Simpson-Housley. New York: Greenwood Press. 21–61.

Friedman, F. D. 1989. *Beyond the Pharoahs: Egypt and the Copts in the 2nd–7th Centuries A.D.* Rhode Island: Rhode Island Institute of Design.

Friedman, Mordecai. 1976. "The Minimum Mohar Payment as Reflected in the Geniza Documents: Marriage Gift or Endowment Pledge." *Proceedings of the American Academy of Jewish Research* 43:15–47.

———. 1980–1981. *Jewish Marriage in Palestine*. Tel Aviv: Tel Aviv University and New York: Jewish Theological Seminary.

———. 1983 "Ono- New Insights from the Writings of the Cairo Genizah." In *Between Yarkon and Ayalon*, ed. D. Grossman. Ramat Gan: Bar Ilan University. 73–85. Hebrew.

Friedman, Shamma. 1993. "The Holy Scriptures Defile the Hands—The Transformation of a Biblical Concept in Rabbinic Theology." In *Minhah le-Nahum: Biblical and Other Studies Presented to Nahum M. Sarna in Honour of his 70th Birthday*, ed. M. Brettler and M. Fishbane. Sheffield: Sheffield University Press. 117–132.

Gartner, Bertil E. 1965. *The Temple and the Community in Qumran and the New Testament*. Cambridge: Cambridge University Press.

Gafni Isaiah. 1987. "Synagogues in Talmudic Babylonia: Traditions and Reality." In *Synagogues in Antiquity*, ed. A. Kasher, A. Oppenheimer, and U. Rappaport. Jerusalem: Ben Zvi Institute. 155–164. Hebrew.

———. 1990. *The Jews of Babylonia in the Talmudic Era*. Jerusalem: Zalman Shazar Institute. Hebrew.

———. 1990. "Expressions and Types of 'Local Patriotism' among the Jews of the Sasanian Empire." In *Irano-Judaica* 2:63–71.

———. 1995. "Synagogues in Babylonia in the Talmudic Period." In *Ancient Synagogues: Historical Analysis and Archaeological Discovery*, ed. D. Urman and P. V. M. Flesher. Leiden: E. J. Brill. 1:221–231.

Gager, John. 1973. "The Dialogue of Paganism with Judaism: Bar Cochba to Julian." *Hebrew Union College Annual* 44:89–118.

Gal, Zvi. 1995. "Ancient Synagogues in the Eastern Lower Galilee." In *Ancient Synagogues: Historical Analysis and Archaeological Discovery*, ed. D. Urman and P. V. M. Flesher. Leiden: E. J. Brill. 1:167–173.

Gammie, John G. 1989. *Holiness in Israel*. Minneapolis: Fortress Press.

Gärtner, Bertil. 1965. *The Temple and the Community in Qumran and the New Testament*. Cambridge: Cambridge University Press.

Gayet, Al. 1889. *Les Monuments Coptes du Musee Boulaq*. Paris: E. Leroux.

Geiger, Bernhard. 1956. "The Middle Iranian Texts." In *The Synagogue. The Excavations of Dura Europos, Final Report VIII, Part 1*, ed. C. H. Kraeling. New Haven. 283–317.

Gibson, John C. J. 1982. *Textbook of Syrian Semitic Inscriptions, 3: Phoenician Inscriptions*. Oxford: Oxford University Press.

Ginzberg, Louis. 1901. "Antoninus in the Talmud." *Jewish Encyclopedia* 1:656–657.

———. 1928–1929. *Genizah Studies in Memory of Doctor Solomon Schechter*. New York: Jewish Theological Seminary. Hebrew.

———. 1938 "Beiträge zur Lexikographie des Juedisch Aramäischen III." In *Essays and Studies in Memory of Linda R. Miller*, ed. I. Davidson. New York: Jewish Theological Seminary. 57–108.

———. 1941–1961. *A Commentary on the Palestinian Talmud*. New York: Jewish Theological Seminary.

———. 1954. *Legends of the Jews*. Philadelphia: Jewish Publication Society.

———. 1968. *Geonica*. 2nd ed. New York: Jewish Theological Seminary.
———. 1976. *An Unknown Jewish Sect*. New York: Jewish Theological Seminary.
Glatzer, Nahum N. 1933. *Untersuchungen zur Geschichtslehre der Tannaiten*. Berlin: Schocken.
———. 1978. "The Attitude Toward Rome in Third-Century Judaism." In *Essays in Jewish Thought*. Alabama: University of Alabama Press. 1–15.
Goitein, S. D. 1960. "Ambol—The Raised Platform in the Synagogue." *Eretz-Israel* 6:162–167. Hebrew.
———. 1964. "The Synagogue Building and Its Furnishings According to the Records of the Cairo Geniza." *Eretz-Israel* 7:81-97. Hebrew. English summary, 169*–172*.
———. 1971. *A Mediterranean Society*. 2. Berkeley, Los Angeles and London: University of California Press.
———. 1974. "Religion in Everyday Life as Reflected in the Documents of the Cairo Geniza." In *Religion in a Secular Age*, ed. S. D. Goitein. Cambridge, Mass. and London: Harvard University Press.
Goldenberg, Robert. 1977. "The Broken Axis: Rabbinic Judaism and the Fall of Jerusalem." *Journal of the American Academy of Religion* 45 (3):849–882.
———. 1985–1986. "The Synagogue as Sacred Space." *Conservative Judaism* 38 (2):19–22.
Goldin, Judah. 1956. "The Thinking of the Rabbis." *Judaism* 5 (1):3–12.
Goldman, Bernard. 1966. *The Sacred Portal*. Detroit: Wayne State University Press.
Goodblatt, David. 1975. *Rabbinic Instruction in Sassanian Babylonia*. Leiden: E. J. Brill.
———. 1980. "Towards the Rehabilitation of Talmudic History." In *History of Judaism: The Next Ten Years*, ed. B. Bokser. Chino: Scholars Press.
Goodenough, Erwin R. 1954–1968. *Jewish Symbols in the Greco-Roman Period*. New York: Pantheon.
Goodman, Martin. 1983. *State and Society in Roman Galilee, 132–212 C.E.* Totowa, N.J.: Rowman and Allanheld.
———. 1990. "Sacred Scripture and "Defiling the Hands." *Journal of Theological Studies* 41:99–107.
———. 1996. "Sacred Space in Diaspora Judaism." In *Studies on the Jewish Diaspora in the Hellenistic and Roman Periods* (= *Te'uda* 12), ed. B. Isaac and A. Oppenheimer. Tel Aviv: Tel Aviv University Press. 1–16.
Gordis, Robert. 1955. *Koheleth: The Man and His World*. New York: Bloch.
Gordon, Hirsch Loeb. 1931. "The Basilica and the Stoa in Early Rabbinical Literature." *Art Bulletin* 13:353–375.
Gordon, Leonard D. 1987. "Becoming a Rabbi in First-Century Palestine." *Proceedings of the Eastern Great Lakes Biblical Society* 7:105–115.
Grabar, André. 1943–1946. *Martyrium: Recherches sur le culte des reliques et l'art cretien antique*. Paris: College de France.
Grabbe, Lester L. "Synagogues in Pre-70 Palestine: A Reassessment." In *Ancient Synagogues: Historical Analysis and Archaeological Discovery*, ed. D. Urman and P. V. M. Flesher. Leiden: E. J. Brill. 1:17–26.
Green, Arthur. 1997. *Keter: The Crown of Glory in Early Jewish Mysticism*. Princeton: Princeton University Press.

Green, William Scott. 1978. "Whats in a Name? The Problematic of Rabbinic Biography." In *Approaches to Ancient Judaism: Theory and Practice*. Missoula: Scholars Press. 1: 77–96.

———. 1979. "Palestinian Holy Men: Charismatic Leadership and Rabbinic Tradition." In *Aufstieg und Niedergang der Römische Welt*. Berlin and New York: Walther de Gruyter. 2 19.2:619-647.

———. 1987. "Romancing the Tome: Rabbinic Hermeneutics and the Theory of Literature." *Semeia* 40:147–168.

Greenberg, Moshe. 1983. *The Anchor Bible: Ezekiel 1–20*. Garden City: Doubleday.

Greenberg, Simon. 1990. "Coherence and Change in the Rabbinic Universe of Discourse: Kadushin's Theory of the Value Concept." In *Understanding The Rabbinic Mind: Studies in the Hermeneutic of Max Kadushin*, ed. P. Ochs. Atlanta: Scholars Press. 19–44.

Greenfield, Jonas. 1978. "The Languages of Palestine, 200 B.C.E.–200 C.E." In *Jewish Languages: Theme and Variation*, ed. H. H. Paper. Cambridge, Mass.: Association for Jewish Studies. 143–154.

Greenfield, J. C., and M. Sokoloff. 1989. "Astrological and Related Omen Texts in Jewish Palestinian Aramaic." *Journal of Near Eastern Studies* 48 (3):201–214.

Gressmann, Hugo. 1927. "Jewish Life in Ancient Rome." In *Jewish Studies—In Memory of Israel Abrahams*. New York: Jewish Institute of Religion. 170–191.

Griffiths, J. Gwyn. 1995. "Egypt and the Rise of the Synagogue." In *Ancient Synagogues: Historical Analysis and Archaeological Discovery*, ed. D. Urman and P. V. M. Flesher. Leiden: E. J. Brill. 1:3–16.

Gruenwald, Ithamar. 1980. "The Song of the Angels, the Qedushah and the Composition of the Hekhalot Literature." In *Jerusalem in the Second Temple Period: Abraham Schalit Memorial Volume*, ed. A. Oppenheimer et al. Jerusalem: Ben Zvi Institute. 459–481. Hebrew.

Gutman, S. 1981. "The Synagogue at Gamla." In *Ancient Synagogues Revealed*, ed. L. I. Levine. Jerusalem: Israel Exploration Society. 30–34.

Gutman, S., Z. Yeivin, and E. Netzer. 1981. "Excavations in the Synagogue of Horvat Susiya." In *Ancient Synagogues Revealed*, ed. L. I. Levine. Jerusalem: Israel Exploration Society. 123–128.

Gutmann, Joseph. 1970. "How Traditional Are Our Traditions?" In *Beauty in Holiness*, ed. J. Gutmann. New York: Ktav. 417–418.

———. "The Illustrated Jewish Manuscript in Antiquity: The Present State of the Question." In *No Graven Images: Studies in Art and the Hebrew Bible*, ed. J. Gutmann. New York: Ktav. 232–248.

———. 1972. "The Origin of the Synagogue." *Archaeologischer Anzeiger* 87:36–40.

———. 1973. "Programmatic Painting in the Dura Synagogue." In *The Dura Europos Synagogue*, ed. J. Gutmann. Missoula: Scholars Press. 137–154.

———. 1984. "Early Synagogue and Jewish Catacomb Art and Its Relation to Christian Art." In *Aufstieg und Niedergang der Römische Welt*. Berlin and New York: Walther de Gruyter. 2.21.2:1313–1342.

———. 1989. "The Sacrifice of Isaac: Variations on a Theme in Early Jewish and Christian Art." In *Sacred Images: Studies in Jewish Art from Antiquity to the Middle Ages*. Northampton: Variorum Reprints.

———. "Revisiting the Binding of Isaac Mosaic at Beth Alpha." *Bulletin of the Asia Institute* 6:79–85.

Hachlili, Rachel. 1976. "The Niche and the Ark in Ancient Synagogues." *Bulletin of the American Schools for Oriental Research* 222:43–53.

———. 1977. "The Zodiac in Ancient Jewish Art: Representation and Significance." *Bulletin of the American Schools for Oriental Research* 228:62–77.

———. 1987. *Jewish Art in the Golan*. Haifa: Hecht Museum.

———. 1988. *Ancient Jewish Art and Archaeology in the Land of Israel*. Leiden: E. J. Brill.

———. 1996. "Synagogues in the Land of Israel: Art and Archaeology." In *Sacred Realm: The Emergence of the Synagogue in the Ancient World*, ed. S. Fine. New York: Oxford University Press. 96–129.

Hacohen, Mordecai. 1975. *Miqdash Me'at*. Jerusalem. Hebrew.

Halivni, David. 1975. *Sources and Traditions*. New York: Jewish Theological Seminary of America. Hebrew.

Hallamish, Moshe. 1985. "The Struggle against Profane Talk in the Synagogue." In *Milet: Everyman's University Studies in Jewish History and Culture*, ed. S. Ettinger et al. Tel Aviv. 2:225–251. Hebrew.

Ḥananel son of Ḥushiel. 1884. *Commentary to the Babylonian Talmud*. Accompanying the Vilna: Romm edition of the Babylonian Talmud.

Hanfmann, George M. 1967. "The Ninth Campaign at Sardis." *Bulletin of the American Schools for Oriental Research* 187:9–62.

———. 1980. "The Continuity of Classical Art: Culture, Myth and Faith." In *The Age of Spirituality: A Symposium*, ed. K. Weitzmann. New York: Metropolitan Museum of Art. 75–99.

Haran, Menahem. 1985. "Bible Scrolls in Eastern and Western Jewish Communities from Qumran to the High Middle Ages." *Hebrew Union College Annual* 56:21–62.

———. 1985. *Temples and Temple-Service in Ancient Israel*. Winona Lake, Ind.: Eisenbrauns.

———. 1986. "Torah and Bible Scrolls in the First Centuries of the Christian Era." *Shnaton: An Annual for Biblical and Ancient Near Eastern Studies* 10:93–106. Hebrew.

Harper, George Mc Lean, Jr. 1928. "Village Administration in the Roman Province of Syria." *Yale Classical Studies* 1:105–170.

Harrison, Martin. 1989. *A Temple for Byzantium: The Discovery and Excavaton of Anicia Juliana's Palace-Church in Istanbul*. Austin: University of Texas Press.

Hauptman, Judith. 1992. "Review of *Chattel of Person? The Status of Women in the Mishnah* by Judith Romney Wegner, New York and Oxford, Oxford University Press, 1988." *Religious Studies Review* 18 (1):13–14.

Heilman, Samuel C. 1976. *Synagogue Life: A Study in Symbolic Interaction*. Chicago and London: University of Chicago Press.

Heinemann, Joseph. 1973. "Review of Peter Schäfer, *Die Vorstellung vom heiligen Geist in der rabbinischen Literatur*, Munichen, 1972, 185, [1] p. (Studien zum A u. N.T., xxviii)." *Kirjath Sepher* 48:434–437. Hebrew.

———. 1977. *Prayer in the Talmud*. Tr. R. S. Sarason. Berlin and New York: Walther de Gruyter.

———. 1981. *Studies in Jewish Liturgy*. Ed. A. Shinan. Jerusalem: Magnes Press. Hebrew.

Heinemann, Joseph, and J. J. Petuchowski. 1975. *Literature of the Synagogue*. New York: Behrman House.

Heisig, James W. 1987. "Symbolism." *Encyclopedia of Religion*, ed. M. Eliade. New York and London: Macmillan. 14:198–208.

Hellemo, Gier. 1989. *Adventus Domini: Escathological Thought in 4th-Century Apses and Catecheses*. Leiden: E. J. Brill.

Hengel, Martin. 1966. "Die Synagogeninschrift von Stobi." *Zeitschrift für die neutestamentliche Wissenschaft* 57:145–183.

———. 1971. "Proseusche und Synagoge: Jüdische Gemeinde, Gotteshaus und Gottesdienst in der Diaspora und in Palaestina." In *Tradition und Glaube. Das fruehe Christentum in seiner Umwelt, Festgabe für Karl Georg Kuhn zum 65 Geburtstag*, ed. G. Jeremias et al. Göttingen: Vanderhoeck and Ruprecht.

Hengel, Martin, and Roland Deines. 1995. "E. P. Sanders' 'Common Judaism', Jesus, and the Pharisees." *Journal of Theological Studies*, New Series, 46 (1):1–70.

Hirschfeld, Yizhar. 1987. *Dwelling Houses in Roman and Byzantine Palestine*. Jerusalem: Ben Zvi Institute. Hebrew.

Hirshman, Marc. 1983. *Midrash Qohelet Rabbah (Ch. 1–4)*. Doctoral dissertation, Jewish Theological Seminary of America. New York.

———. 1988. "The Greek Fathers and the Aggada on Ecclesiastes: Formats of Exegesis in Late Antiquity." *Hebrew Union College Annual*. 59:137–165.

Hoenig, Sidney B. 1963–1964. "The Supposititious Temple Synagogue." *Jewish Quarterly Review* 54:115–131.

———. 1979. "The Ancient City Square: The Forerunner of the Synagogue." In *Aufstieg und Niedergang der Römische Welt*. Berlin and New York: Walther de Gruyter. 2.1:448–476.

Hoffman, Jeffrey. "The Ancient Torah Service in Light of the Realia of the Talmudic Era." *Conservative Judaism* 42 (2):41–48.

Hoffman, Lawrence A. 1979. *The Canonization of the Synagogue Service*. Notre Dame, Ind., and London: University of Notre Dame Press.

———. 1989. *Beyond the Text*. Bloomington and Indianapolis: University of Indiana Press.

———. 1996. *Covenant of Blood: Circumcision and Gender in Rabbinic Judaism*. Chicago: University of Chicago Press.

Hoffmann, David Zvi. 1967. *Das Buch Leviticus*. Tr. Z. Har Shepper and A. Lieberman. Jerusalem: Rav Kook Institute. Hebrew.

Holtz, Avraham. 1978. *Rabbinic Thought: An Introduction to the Works of M. Kadushin*. Tel Aviv: Sifriyat Poalim. Hebrew.

Hüttenmeister, Frowald G. 1978. "The Aramaic Inscription from the Synagogue at H. Ha-Amudim." *Israel Exploration Journal* 28:108–112.
———. 1981. "The Synagogue and the Beth Ha-Midrash and Their Relationship." *Cathedra* 18:38–44. Hebrew.
Hüttenmeister, Frowald G., and Gottfried Reeg. 1977. *Die antiken Synagogen in Israel*. Wiesbaden: Ludwig Reichert.
Hunt, E. D. 1982. *Holy Land Pilgrimage in the Later Roman Empire* A.D. 312–460. Oxford: Oxford University Press.
Ilan, Zvi. 1991. *Ancient Synagogues in Israel*. Israel: Ministry of Defense. Hebrew.
———. 1995. "The Synagogue and Study House at Meroth." In *Ancient Synagogues: Historical Analysis and Archaeological Discovery*, ed. D. Urman and P. V. M. Flesher. Leiden: E. J. Brill. 1:256–288.
Ilan, Zvi, and Emmanuel Damati. 1987. *Meroth: The Ancient Jewish Village*. Tel Aviv: Society for the Preservation of Nature in Israel. Hebrew.
Itzchaky, Efraim. 1982. *The Halacha in Targum Jerushalmi I (Pseudo-Jonathan Ben-Uziel and its Exegetic Methods)*. Doctoral dissertation, Bar Ilan University. Hebrew.
Jacobs, Louis. 1971. "Are There Fictitious Baraitot in the Babylonian Talmud?" *Hebrew Union College Annual* 42:185–196.
Jacoby, Ruth. 1987. *Jerusalem Index of Jewish Art: The Synagogues of Bar'am, Jewish Ossuaries*. Jerusalem: Center for Jewish Art of the Hebrew University.
Jacoby, Ruth, and Rina Talgam. 1988. *Ancient Jewish Synagogues: Architectural Glossary*. Jerusalem: Center for Jewish Art of the Hebrew University.
Jaffee, Martin S. 1990. "The *Taqqanah* in Tannaitic Literature: Jurisprudence and the Construction of Rabbinic Memory." *Journal of Jewish Studies* 41 (2):204–225.
James, Simon. 1985. "Dura-Europos and the Chronology of Syria in the 250s AD." *Chiron* 15: 111–124.
Jastrow, Marcus. 1982. *Dictionary of the Targumim, the Talmud Babli, and Yerushalmi, and the Midrashic Literature*. New York: Traditional Press.
Jensen, Robin. 1994. "The Offering of Isaac in Jewish and Christian Tradition: Image and Text." *Biblical Interpretation* 11 (1):85–110.
Jenson, Phillip Peter. 1992. *Graded Holiness: A Key to the Priestly Conception of the World*. Sheffield: Sheffield University Press.
Kadushin, Max. 1952. *The Rabbinic Mind*. New York: Jewish Theological Seminary.
———. 1964. *Worship and Ethics*. Chicago: University of Chicago Press.
Kahane, Menachem. 1985. 1988. "Pages of the Deuteronomy *Mekhilta* on Ha'azinu and Wezot Ha-berakha." *Tarbiz* 57:165–201. Hebrew.
Karo, Joseph. n.d. *Shulhan Arukh*. Rpt. Jerusalem.
Kasher, Aryeh. 1985. *The Jews in Hellenistic and Roman Egypt*. Tubingen: J. C. B. Mohr.
———. 1995. "Synagogues as 'Houses of Prayer' and 'Holy Places' in the Jewish Communities of Hellenistic and Roman Egypt." In *Ancient Synagogues: Historical Analysis and Archaeological Discovery*, ed. D. Urman and P. V. M. Flesher. Leiden: E. J. Brill. 1:205–220.

Kasher, Rimon. 1990. "The Interpretation of Scripture in Rabbinic Judaism." In *Mikra*, ed. M. J. Mulder. Assen/Maastricht: Van Gorgum and Philadelphia: Fortress Press. 547–594.

Kaufmann, Carl Maria. 1922. *Handbuch der christlichen Archaeologie*. Paderhorn: F. Schoningh.

Kautzsch, E., ed. 1910. *Gesenius' Hebrew Grammar*. Tr. A. E. Cowley. Oxford: Oxford University Press.

Kee, Howard Clark. 1990. "The Transformation of the Synagogue after 70 C.E.: Its Import for Early Christianity." *New Testament Studies* 36:1–24.

———. 1994. "The Changing Meaning of Synagogue: A Response to Richard Oster." *New Testament Studies* 40:281–283.

———. 1995. "Defining the First-Century CE Synagogue: Problems and Progress." *New Testament Studies* 41:481–500.

Kennedy, Hugh. 1985. "From Polis to Madina: Urban Change in Late Antique and Early Islamic Syria." *Past and Present* 106:3–27.

Kessler, Herbert L. 1994. "Through the Veil: The Holy Image in Judaism and Christianity." In *Studies in Pictorial Narrative*. London: Pindar. 49–73.

Killebrew, Ann, and Steven Fine. 1991. "Qatzrin—Reconstructing Village Life in Talmudic Times." *Biblical Archaeology Review* 27 (3):44–56.

Kimelman, Reuven. 1988–1989. "The Daily Amidah and the Rhetoric of Redemption." *Jewish Quarterly Review* 79 (2–3):165–197.

Kindler, Arie. 1989. "Donation and Taxes in the Society of Jewish Villages in Eretz Israel during the 3rd to 6th Centuries CE." In *Ancient Synagogues in Israel*, ed. R. Hachlili. London: BAR International. 55–60.

Kinzig, Wolfram. 1991. "'Non-Separation': Closeness and Co-operation between Jews and Christians in the Fourth Century." *Vigiliae Christianae* 45:27–53.

Kirch, G. P. 1930. "Pitture Inedite di un Arcosolio del Cimitero dei SS. Pietro e Marcellino." *Rivista di Archeologia Cristiana* 7:31–46.

Kirk, George Eden, and C. Bradford Welles. 1962. "Inscriptions." In *Excavations at Nessana*, ed. H. D. Colt. London: British School of Archaeology in Jerusalem. 1:131–197.

Kirschner, Robert. 1984. "The Vocation of Holiness in Late Antiquity." *Vigiliae Christianae* 37:105–127.

Kitzinger, Ernst. 1965. *Israel Mosaics*. New York: New American Library.

Klawans, Jonathan. 1995. "Gentile Impurity in Ancient Judaism." *AJS Review* 20 (2): 288–292.

Klein, Michael. 1980. "Palestinian Targum and Synagogue Mosaics." *Immanuel* 11:33–45.

Klein, Samuel. 1925. "Inscriptions from Ancient Synagogues in the Land of Israel." *Bulletin of the Institute for Jewish Studies* 2:23–48. Hebrew.

———. 1939. *Sefer ha-Yishuv*. 1. Jerusalem: Bialik Institute and Dvir. Hebrew.

———. 1940. "Notes on an Early Lament on the Destruction of Communities in the Land of Israel." *Bulletin of the Jewish Palestine Exploration Society* 7:107–109. Hebrew.

Kleinbauer, W. Eugene. 1994. *Modern Perspectives in Art History*. Toronto: University of Toronto.

Kloner, Amos. 1989. "The Synagogues of Horvat Rimmon." In *Ancient Synagogues in Israel*, ed. R. Hachlili. London: BAR International. 43–48.

Kohl, Heinrich, and Carl Watzinger. 1916. *Antike Synagogen in Galilaea*. Leipzig: J. C. Heinrich.

Kohut, Alexander. 1955. *Aruch Completum*. New York: Pardes. Hebrew.

Koranda, Christian. 1988–1989. "Menora Darstellungen auf Spätantiken mosaikpavimenten." *Kairos* 30-31:218–228.

Kraabel, Alf Thomas. 1979. "The Diaspora Synagogue: Archaeological and Epigraphic Evidence since Sukenik." In *Aufstieg und Niedergang der Römische Welt*. Berlin and New York: Walther de Gruyter. 19.1:479–510.

Kraeling, Carl H. 1956. *The Synagogue. The Excavations of Dura Europos, Final Report VIII, Part 1*. New Haven: Yale University Press.

Krauss, Samuel. 1894. "The Jews in the Works of the Church Fathers." *Jewish Quarterly Review*, Old Series, 7:225–261.

———. 1898–1899. *Griechische und lateinische Lehnwörter im Talmud, Midrasch und Targum*. Berlin: S. Calvary and Co.

———. 1921. "Die Galilaeischen Synagogenruinen und die Halakha." *Monatsschrift für Geschichte und Wissenschaft des Judentums* 65:211–220.

———. 1922. *Synagogale Altertümer*. Berlin and Vienna: B. Harz.

———. 1923–1929. *Qadmoniot ha-Talmud*. Berlin and Tel Aviv. Hebrew.

Krautheimer, Richard. 1953. "Review of Andre Grabar, *Martyrium: Recherches sur le culte des reliques et l'art antique*, Paris, 1943–1946." *Art Bulletin* 35:57–61.

———. 1967. "The Constantinian Basilica." *Dumbarton Oaks Papers* 21:117–140.

———. 1979. *Early Christian and Byzantine Archaeology*. 3rd ed. Baltimore: Penguin.

Krinsky, Carol Herselle. 1985. *Synagogues of Europe: Architecture, History, Meaning*. New York and Cambridge, Mass.: M.I.T. Press.

Kühnel, Bianca. 1987. *From the Earthly to the Heavenly Jerusalem: Representations of the Holy City in Christian Art of the First Millenium*. Rome, Freiberg, and Vienna: Herder.

Kutscher, E. Y. 1967. "Jewish Palestinian Aramaic." In *An Aramaic Handbook*, ed. F. Rosenthal. Wiesbaden: Harrassowitz. Pt I, 1:51–70.

———. 1972. "Tannaitic Hebrew." In *Anthology of Articles in Rabbinic Hebrew*, ed. M. Bar-Asher. Jerusalem: Akadamon. 1:1–35. Rpt. from *Sefer Hanoch Yellin*, Jerusalem, 1963, 246–280. Hebrew.

Lampe, G. W. H. 1961. *A Patristic Greek Dictionary*. Oxford: Oxford University Press.

Landsberger, Franz. 1957. "The Sacred Direction in Synagogue and Church." *Hebrew Union College Annual* 28:181–203.

———. 1970. "Old Hanukkah Lamps." In *Beauty in Holiness*, ed. J. Gutmann. New York: Ktav. 283–309.

Le Goff, Jacques. 1992. *History and Memory*. Tr. S. Rendall, E. Claman. New York: Columbia University Press.

Lehmann, Karl. 1945. "The Dome of Heaven." *Art Bulletin* 27:1–27.

Leiman, Sid Z. 1976. *The Canonization of Hebrew Scripture: The Talmudic and Midrashic Evidence.* Hamden, Conn.: Connecticut Academy of Arts and Sciences by Archon Books.

Leon, Harry J. 1960. *The Jews of Ancient Rome.* Philadelphia: Jewish Publication Society.

Lerner, M. B. 1987 "The External Tractates." In *Literature of the Sages*, pt. 1, ed. S. Safrai. Assen/Maastricht: Van Gorgum and Philadelphia: Fortress Press. 367–403.

Levi, Eliezer. 1963. *Foundations of the Liturgy.* Tel Aviv: Avraham Ziony. Hebrew.

Levine, Baruch A. 1987a. "Biblical Temple." *Encyclopedia of Religion*, ed. M. Eliade. New York and London. 2.202–217.

———. 1987b. "The Language of Holiness: Perceptions of the Sacred in the Hebrew Bible." In *Backgrounds for the Bible*, ed. M. P. O'Connor and D. N. Freedman. Winona Lake, Ind.: Eisenbrauns. 241–255.

Levine, Etan. 1971. "Some Characteristics of Pseudo-Jonathan Targum to Genesis." *Augustinianum* 11:89–103.

Levine, Lee I. 1975. "R. Abbahu of Caesarea." In *Christianity, Judaism, and other Greco-Roman Cults*, ed. J. Neusner. Leiden: E. J. Brill. 4:56–76.

———. 1981. "Excavations at Horvat ha-Amudim." In *Ancient Synagogues Revealed*, ed. L. I. Levine. Jerusalem: Israel Exploration Society. 78–81.

———. 1987. "The Second Temple Synagogue: The Formative Years." In *The Synagogue in Late Antiquity*, ed. L. I. Levine. Philadelphia: American Schools for Oriental Research. 7–32.

———. 1989. *The Rabbinic Class of Roman Palestine.* Jerusalem: Ben Zvi Institute, New York: Jewish Theological Seminary.

———. 1991. "From Community Center to Small Temple: The Furnishings and Interior Design of Ancient Synagogues." *Cathedra* 60:36-84. Hebrew.

———. 1992a. "Judaism from the Destruction of Jerusalem to the End of the Second Revolt." In *Rabbinic Judaism and Christianity: A Parallel History of Their Origins and Early Development*, ed. H. Shanks. Washington, D.C.: Biblical Archaeological Society. 125–149.

———. 1992b. "The Sages and the Synagogue in Late Antiquity: The Evidence of the Galilee." In *The Galilee in Late Antiquity*, ed. L. I. Levine. New York and Jerusalem. 201–222.

———. 1996. "The Nature and Origin of the Palestinian Synagogue Reconsidered." *Journal of Biblical Literature* 115 (3):447.

Lewy, Yohanan (Hans). 1983. "Julian the Apostate and the Building of the Temple." *The Jerusalem Cathedra* 3:70–96.

Licht, Chaim. 1989. *Tradition and Innovation: Studies in Rabbinic Literature.* Givat-Haviva: Givat-Haviva Press. Hebrew.

———. 1991. *Ten Legends of the Sages: The Image of the Sage in Rabbinic Literature.* Hoboken: Ktav.

Liddell, Henry G., and Robert Scott. 1940. *A Greek-English Lexicon.* 9th ed. Oxford: Oxford University Press.

Lieberman, Saul. 1935. "Mekilta de-Rabbi Ishmael, ed. J. Z. Lauterbach." *Kirjath Sepher* 12:54–65. Hebrew.

———. 1938. "Tractate *Sofrim*, ed. M. Higger." *Kirjath Sepher* 15:56–60. Hebrew.
———. 1939. "Ḥazanut Yannai." *Sinai* 4:221–250. Hebrew.
———. 1942. *Greek in Roman Palestine*. New York: Jewish Theological Seminary.
———. 1955–1988. *Tosefta Kifshuto*. New York: Jewish Theological Seminary. Hebrew.
———. 1962. *Hellenism in Jewish Palestine*. New York: Jewish Theological Seminary.
———. 1965. "Some Aspects of the Afterlife in Early Rabbinic Literature." In *Harry Austryn Wolfson Jubilee Volume*. Jerusalem: American Academy for Jewish Research. 2:495–532.
———. 1970a. *Sheki'in*. 2nd ed. Jerusalem: Wahrmann. Hebrew.
———. 1970b. *Yemenite Midrashim*. 2nd ed. Jerusalem: Wahrmann. Hebrew.
———. 1980. "The Knowledge of the Halakha by the Author (or Authors) of the Heikhaloth." In *Apocalyptic and Merkavah Mysticism*, ed. I. Gruenwald. Leiden and Cologne: E. J. Brill. 241–244.
Lightstone, Jack N. 1984. *The Commerce of the Sacred: Mediation of the Divine among Jews in the Greco-Roman Diaspora*. Chico: Scholars Press.
Litvin, Baruch. 1987. *The Sanctity of the Synagogue*. Hoboken: Ktav.
Lowenthal, David. 1990. *The Past is a Foreign Country*. Cambridge: Cambridge University Press.
Mac Cormack, Sabine. 1981. *Art and Ceremony in Late Antiquity*. Berkeley and Los Angeles: University of California Press.
MacDonald, David. 1986. "Dating the Fall of Dura-Europos." *Historia* 35 (1):45–68.
Magen, Itzhak. 1990. "Mount Gerizim—A Temple City." *Qadmoniot* 23 (3–4):70–96. Hebrew.
———. 1992. "Samaritan Synagogues." *Qadmoniot* 25 (3–4):66–90. Hebrew.
Magness, Jodi. 1997. "Synagogue Typology and Earthquake Chronology at Khirbet Shema'." *Journal of Field Archaeology* 27:211–220.
Maguire, Eunice Dauterman, and Henry P. Maguire. 1989. *Art and Holy Powers in the Early Christian House*. Urbana and Chicago: University of Illinois Press.
Maimonides, Moses son of Maimon. 1862. *Mishneh Torah*. Berlin.
———. 1967. *Mishnah with the Commentary of Our Teacher Moses b. Maimon*. Tr. and ed. D. Kapah. Jerusalem: Rav Kook Institute. Hebrew.
Mango, Marlia Mundell. 1986. *Silver from Early Byzantium*. Baltimore: Walters Art Gallery.
Mann, Jacob. 1919. "Anan's Liturgy and His Half-Yearly Cycle for the Reading of the Law." *Journal of Jewish Lore and Philosophy* 1 (1–4):329–353.
———. 1920–1922. *The Jews in Egypt and in Palestine under the Fatamid Caliphs*. London: Oxford University Press.
———. 1921–1922. "A Tract by an Early Karaite Settler in Jerusalem." *Jewish Quarterly Review* 12:257–298.
Mann, Jacob, and Isaiah Sonne. 1966. *The Bible as Read and Preached in the Old Synagogue*. 2. Cincinnati: Hebrew Union College Press.
Maori, Yeshayahu. 1983. "The Relationship of Targum Pseudo-Jonathan to Halakhic Sources." *Te'uda: Studies in Talmudic Literature, in Post Biblical Hebrew and in Biblical Exegesis* 3:235–250. Hebrew.

Ma'oz, Zvi. 1981. "The Synagogue of Gamla and the Typology of Second-Temple Synagogues." In *Ancient Synagogues Revealed*, ed. L. I. Levine. Jerusalem: Israel Exploration Society. 35–41.

———. 1988. "Ancient Synagogues of the Golan." *Biblical Archaeologist* 51 (2): 116–128.

———. 1992. "The Synagogue in the Second Temple Period—Architectural and Social Interpretation." *Eretz-Israel* 23:331–341. Hebrew.

Markus, R. A. 1994. "How on Earth Could Places Become Holy? Origins of the Christian Idea of Holy Places." *Journal of Early Christian Studies* 2 (3):257–271.

Margaliot, Reuven. 1962. "The Death of R. Judah the Prince." *Sinai* 50:257–258. Hebrew.

Margalioth, Mordecai, ed. 1987. *Encyclopedia of Talmudic and Gaonic Literature*. Tel Aviv. Hebrew.

Margoliot, Moshe son of Simeon. 1922. *Pnei Moshe*. Published in the Vilna: Romm edition of the Palestinian Talmud.

Marmorstein, Arthur. 1968. *The Doctrine of Merits in Old Rabbinic Literature and The Old Rabbinic Doctrine of God*. New York: Ktav.

Martin, Malachi. 1958. *The Scribal Character of the Dead Sea Scrolls*. Louvain: Publications Universitaires.

Mathews, Thomas F. 1971. *The Early Churches of Constantinople: Architecture and Liturgy*. University Park, Penn: Pennsylvania State University Press.

———. 1993. *The Clash of the Gods: A Reinterpretation of Early Christian Art*. Princeton: Princeton University Press.

Mayer, Leo Ary. 1958. "Broadhouses in Jewish Religious Art." *Eretz-Israel* 5:238–239. Hebrew.

Mayer, Leo Ary, and A. Reifenberg. 1933. "A Samaritan Lamp." *Journal of the Palestine Oriental Society* 16:44–45.

———. 1937 "Three Ancient Jewish Reliefs." *Palestine Exploration Quarterly* 136-139.

Mazar, Benjamin. 1970. "The Inscription on the Pavement of the Synagogue of Ein Gedi." *Tarbiz* 40:18–23. Hebrew.

———. 1973. *Beth She'arim*. 1. New Brunswick: Rutgers University Press.

McKay, Heather A. 1994. *Sabbath and Synagogue: The Question of Sabbath Worship in Ancient Judaism*. Leiden: E. J. Brill.

McVey, Kathleen E. 1983. "The Domed Church as Microcosm: Literary Roots of an Architectual Symbol." *Dumbarton Oaks Papers* 37:91–121.

Meeks, Wayne A. 1983. *The First Urban Christians: The Social World of the Apostle Paul*. New Haven and London: Yale University Press.

Meeks, Wayne A., and Robert L. Wilken. 1978. *Jews and Christians in Antioch*. Missoula: Scholars Press.

Meer, Fredrik van der. 1967. *Early Christian Art*. Tr. P. and F. Brown. Chicago: University of Chicago Press.

Meimaris, Yiannis E. 1986. *Sacred Names, Saints, Martyrs and Church Officials in the Greek Inscriptions and Papyri Pertaining to the Christian Church of Palestine*. Athens: Kentron

Hellenikeskai Romaikes Archaiotetos Ethnik Hydryma Ereunon, Paris: Diffusion de Boccard.

Melamed, E. Z. 1988. *Halachic Midrashim of the Tannaim in the Babylonian Talmud*. Jerusalem: Magnes Press. Hebrew.

Merkelbach, Reinhold. 1976. *Die Inschriften von Assos*. Bonn: Habelt.

Meshorer, Yaakov. 1982. *Ancient Jewish Coinage*. Dix Hills: Amphora.

Metropolitan Museum of Art. 1986. *Treasures of the Holy Land: Ancient Art from the Israel Museum*. New York: Metropolitan Museum of Art.

Meyers, Carol. 1976. *The Tabernacle Menorah: A Synthetic Study of a Symbol from the Biblical Cult*. Missoula: Scholars Press.

Meyers, Carol L., and Eric M. Meyers. 1982. "A Ceramic Rendering of the Torah Shrine from Nabatrein." *Eretz-Israel* 16:176*–185*.

Meyers, Eric M. 1971. *Jewish Ossuaries: Reburial and Rebirth. Secondary Burials in Their Near Eastern Setting*. Rome: Biblical Institute.

———. 1973. "The Ancient Synagogue of Khirbet Shema." *Perspectives in Jewish Learning* 5:28–40.

———. 1976. "Galilean Regionalism as a Factor in Historical Reconstruction." *Bulletin of the American Schools for Oriental Research* 220–221:93–103.

———. 1979. "The Cultural Setting of Galilee: The Case of Regionalism and Early Judaism" In *Aufstieg und Niedergang der Römische Welt*. Berlin and New York: Walther de Gruyter. 2.686–702.

———. 1980. "Excavations at En-Nabratein, Upper Galilee: The 1980 Season." *American Schools for Oriental Research Newsletter* 2:3–11.

Meyers, Eric M., A. Thomas Kraabel, and James F. Strange. 1976. *Ancient Synagogue Excavations at Khirbet Shema', Upper Galilee, Israel, 1970–1972*. Durham: Duke University Press.

Meyers, Eric M., and Carol L. Meyers. 1981. "Finders of the Lost Ark." *Biblical Archaeology Review* 7 (4):24–39.

Meyers, Eric M., Carol L. Meyers, and James F. Strange. 1990. *Excavations at the Ancient Synagogue of Gush Halav*. Winona Lake, Ind.: Eisenbrauns.

Meyers, Eric M., James F. Strange, and Carol L. Meyers. 1981a. "The Ark of Nabratein: A First Glance." *Biblical Archaeologist* 44 (4):237–243.

———. 1981b. *Excavations at Ancient Meiron, Upper Galilee, Israel, 1971–72, 1974–75, 1977*. Cambridge, Mass: American Schools for Oriental Research.

Milgrom, Jacob. 1970. *Studies in Levitical Terminology*. Berkeley: University of California Press.

Millar, Fergus. 1992. "The Jews of the Greco-Roman Diaspora between Paganism and Christianity." In *The Jews among Pagans and Christians*, ed. J. Lieu, J. North, and T. Rajak. London and New York: Routledge. 97–123.

Miller, Patricia Cox. 1986. "In Praise of Nonsense." In *Classical Mediterranean Spirituality*, ed. A. H. Armstrong. New York: Crossroad. 481–505.

Miller, Stuart S. 1984. *Studies in the History and Traditions of Sepphoris*. Leiden: E. J. Brill.

Mirsky, Aharon. 1970. "Aquarius and Aries in the Ein Gedi Inscription and in Early Piyyutim." *Tarbiz* 40:376–384. Hebrew.
Moore, George Foot. 1927–30. *Judaism in the First Centuries of the Common Era*. Cambridge, Mass.: Harvard University Press.
Moreton, M. J. 1982. "*Eis Anatolas Blepsate*: Orientation as Liturgical Principle." *Studia Patristica* 18 (2):575–590.
Narkiss, Bezalel. 1992. "The Hekhal, Bimah and Teivah in Sephardi Synagogues." *Jewish Art* 18:31–47.
Narkiss, Mordecai. 1935. "The Snuff-Shovel as a Jewish Symbol." *Journal of the Palestine Oriental Society* 15:14–28.
———. 1939. *The Hanukkah Lamp*. Jerusalem: Beney Bezalel. Hebrew.
———. 1939–1940. "The Zodiac in Jewish Art." *Kirjath Sepher* 16:513–519. Hebrew.
Neaman, Pinchas. 1971. *Encyclopedia of Talmudical Geography*. Tel Aviv: Joshua Chachik Publishing House. Hebrew.
Netter, Solomon Zalman. 1859. "Commentary on Targum Jonathan." Printed in *Miqra'ot Gedolot*, ed. Vienna. Rpt. Jerusalem. 1976. Hebrew.
Netzer, Ehud. 1991. *Masada III, The Yigael Yadin Excavations 1963–1965, Final Reports, The Buildings: Stratigraphy and Architecture*. Jerusalem: Israel Exploration Society.
Neubauer, Adolphe. 1868. *La Géographie du Talmud*. Paris: M. Levy.
Neusner, Jacob. 1970. *Development of a Legend*. Leiden: E. J. Brill.
———. 1971. *Aphrahat and Judaism*. Leiden: E. J. Brill.
———. 1973. *The Idea of Purity in Ancient Judaism*. Leiden: E. J. Brill.
———. 1983a. *A History of Mishnaic Law of Appointed Times*. Part 5. Leiden: E. J. Brill.
———. 1983b. *Judaism in Society: The Evidence of the Yerushalmi*. Chicago: University of Chicago Press.
———. 1986. *Ancient Judaism and Modern Category-Formation*. Lanham, New York, and London: University Press of America.
———. 1990. *The Canonical History of Ideas*. Atlanta: Scholars Press.
Newsom, Carol. 1985. *Songs of the Sabbath Sacrifice: A Critical Edition*. Atlanta: Scholars Press.
———. 1990. "'He Has Established for Himself Priests': Human and Angelic Priesthood in the Qumran Sabbath Shirot." *Archaeology and History in the Dead Sea Scrolls*, ed. L. H. Schiffman. Sheffield: Sheffield University Press. 101–120.
Newsom, Carol, and Yigael Yadin. 1984. "The Masada Fragment of the Qumran Songs of the Sabbath." *Israel Exploration Journal* 34:77-88.
Nibley, Hugh. 1959–1960. "Christian Envy of the Temple." *Jewish Quarterly Review* 50: 97–122, 229-240.
Nissim son of Reuven Gerondi. 1884. *Commentary to Tractate Megillah*. Published accompanying *Hilkhot Alfasi* in the Vilna: Romm edition of the Babylonian Talmud.
Noy, David. 1992. "A Jewish Place of Prayer in Roman Egypt." *Journal of Theological Studies*, New Series, 43 (1):118–122.
Noy, Dov. 1964. "Twelve Constellations and Twelve Tribes." *Mahanayim* 4:128–133. Hebrew.

Obermann, Julian. 1931. "The Sepulchre of the Maccabean Martyrs." *Journal of Biblical Literature* 50:250–265.
Ochs, Peter, ed. 1991. *Understanding the Rabbinic Mind: Essays in the Hermeneutics of Max Kadushin*. Atlanta: Scholars Press.
Onn, Alexander. 1994. "The Ancient Synagogue of Kafr Misr." '*Atiqot* 26:117–134.
Oppenheimer, Aharon. 1980. "Benevolent Societies in Jerusalem." In *Jerusalem in the Second Temple Period: Abraham Schalit Memorial Volume*, ed. A. Oppenheimer et al. Jerusalem: Ben Zvi Institute. 178–190. Hebrew.
———. 1983. *Babylonia Judaica in the Talmudic Period*. In collaboration with B. Isaac and M. Lecker. Wiesbaden: L. Reichert.
———. 1995. "Babylonian Synagogues with Historical Associations." In *Ancient Synagogues: Historical Analysis and Archaeological Discovery*, ed. D. Urman and P. V. M. Flesher. Leiden: E. J. Brill. 1:40–48.
Oster, Richard E., Jr. 1993. "Supposed Anachronism in Luke-Acts' Use of *Sunagoge*: A Rejoinder to H. C. Kee." *New Testament Studies* 39:178–208.
Otto, Rudolf. 1917. *Das Heilige*. Breslau: Trewenot und Granier.
Ovadiah, Asher. 1969. "Excavations in the Area of the Ancient Synagogue at Gaza (Preliminary Report)." *Israel Exploration Journal* 19 (4):193–198.
———. 1977. "The Reciprocal Relationship between Synagogues and Churches in the Byzantine Period." In *Between and Sinai: Memorial to Amnon*. Ed. M. Broshi, Jerusalem: Yedidim. 163–170. Hebrew.
———. 1982. "The Synagogue at Gaza." In *Ancient Synagogues Revealed*, ed. L. I. Levine. Jerusalem: Israel Exploration Society. 29–32.
———. 1987. "Mosaic Art in Ancient Synagogues of Eretz-Israel." In *Synagogues in Antiquity*, ed. A. Kasher, A. Oppenheimer, and U. Rappaport. Jerusalem: Ben Zvi Institute. 185–203.
———. 1995. "The Mosaic Workshop of Gaza in Christian Antiquity." In *Ancient Synagogues: Historical Analysis and Archaeological Discovery*, ed. D. Urman and P. V. M. Flesher. Leiden: E. J. Brill. 2:367–372.
Ovadiah, Asher, and Talila Michaeli. 1987. "Observations of the Origin of the Architectural Plan of Ancient Synagogues." *Journal of Jewish Studies* 38 (2):234–241.
Ovadiah, Ruth, and Asher Ovadiah. 1987. *Hellenistic, Roman and Early Byzantine Mosaic Pavements in Israel*. Rome: "L'Erma" de Bretschneider.
Oxtoby, Willard G. 1987. "The Idea of the Holy." *Encyclopedia of Religion*, ed. M. Eliade. New York and London: Macmillan. 431–438.
Panofsky, Erwin. 1955. *Meaning in the Visual Arts*. Garden City: Doubleday.
Piccirillo, Michele. 1987. *Mount Nebo*. Jerusalem: Custodia Terra Sancta.
———. 1989. "Recenti Scoperte d' Archeologia Cristiana in Giordania." *Actes du XIe Congres International d' Archeologie Chretienne*. 2. Rome. 1697–1736.
Price, Martin J., and Bluma L. Trell. 1977. *Coins and Their Cities*. London: Vecci and Detroit: Wayne State University.
Pummer, Reinhard. 1989. "Samaritan Material Remains and Archaeology." In *The Samaritans*, ed. A. D. Crown. Tubingen: J. C. B. Mohr. 135–177.

Rabin, Chaim. 1957. *Qumran Studies*. London: Oxford University Press.
———. 1981. "The Linguistic Investigation of the Language of Jewish Prayer." In *Studies in Aggadah, Targum and Jewish Liturgy in Memory of Joseph Heinemann*, ed. J. J. Petuchowski and E. Fleischer. Jerusalem: Magnes Press. 163–171. Hebrew.
Rabinowitz, Louis Isaac. 1970. "Hakhel." *Encyclopedia Judaica* 7:1148–1149.
Rahmani, L. Y. 1960. "The Ancient Synagogue of Maon (Nirim): The Small Finds and Coins." *Louis M. Rabinowitz Fund for the Exploration of Ancient Synagogues Bulletin* 3:14–19.
———. 1964. "Mirror-Plaques from a Fifth-Century A.D. Tomb." *Israel Exploration Journal* 14:50–55.
———. 1990. "Stone Synagogue Chairs: Their Identification, Use and Significance." *Israel Exploration Journal* 40 (2–3):192–214.
———. 1994. *A Catalogue of Jewish Ossuaries in the Collections of the State of Israel*. Jerusalem: Israel Antiquities Authority.
Rajak, Tessa. 1992. "The Jewish Community and Its Boundaries." In *The Jews among Pagans and Christians*, ed. J. Lieu, J. North, and T. Rajak. London and New York: Routledge. 9–28.
Rashi, Shlomo son of Isaac. 1866. *Commentary on the Prophets and Hagiographa*. In *Miqra'ot Gedolot*, ed. Warsaw. Hebrew.
———. 1884. *Commentary to the Babylonian Talmud*. Published in the Vilna: Romm edition of the Babylonian Talmud.
———. 1969. *Raschi: Der Kommentar des Salomo b. Isaac Über Der Pentateuch*. Ed. A. Berliner; 2nd ed. by H. D. Chavel. Jerusalem: Rav Kook Institute. Hebrew.
Ratner, Dov Baer. 1901–1916. *Ahavat Zion ve-Yerushalem*. Vilna: Romm. Hebrew.
Reif, Stefan C. 1991. "The Early History of Jewish Worship." In *The Making of Jewish and Christian Worship*, ed. P. F. Bradshaw and L. A. Hoffman. Notre Dame, Ind.: University of Notre Dame Press. 109–136.
———. 1993. *Judaism and Hebrew Prayer*. Cambridge: Cambridge University Press.
Riesner, Rainer. 1995. "Synagogues in Jerusalem." In *The Book of Acts in Its Palestinian Setting*, ed. R. Bauckham. Grand Rapids: Eerdmans, and Carlisle: Paternoster Press. 179–210.
Renov, Israel. 1955. "The Seat of Moses." *Israel Exploration Journal* 5:262–267.
Revel-Neher, Elisabeth. 1984. *L'Arche d'Alliance dans l'Art Juif et Chrétien du Second au Dixième Siècles*. Paris: Association des Amis des Études Archaéologiques Byzantino-Slaves et du Christianisme Oriental.
Rivkin, Ellis. 1969. "Prolegomenon." In *Judaism and Christianity*, ed. W. O. E. Oesterley. New York: Ktav. vii–lxx.
Roberts, C. H., and T. C. Skeat. 1987. *The Birth of the Codex*. London: Oxford University Press.
Rostovtzeff, M. 1941. *Social and Economic History of the Hellenistic World*. Oxford: Oxford University Press.
Roth, Cecil. 1949. "The 'Throne of Moses' and Its Survivals." *Palestine Exploration Quarterly* 81:100–267.

———. 1953. "Jewish Antecedents of Christian Art." *Journal of the Warburg and Courtland Institutes* 16 (1–2):24–44.

———, ed. 1971. *Jewish Art*. 2nd ed. London: Vallentine, Mitchell.

Roth-Gerson Lea. 1987a. *Greek Inscriptions in the Synagogues in Eretz-Israel*. Jerusalem: Ben Zvi Institute. Hebrew.

———. 1987b. "Similarities and Differences in Greek Synagogue Inscriptions of Eretz-Israel and the Diaspora." In *Synagogues in Antiquity*, ed. A. Kasher, A. Oppenheimer, and U. Rappaport. Jerusalem: Ben Zvi Institute. 133–146. Hebrew.

Rubinstein, Jeffrey L. 1995. *The History of Sukkot in the Second Temple and Rabbinic Periods*. Atlanta: Scholars Press.

Rudolph, Kurt. 1989. "Mircea Eliade and the 'History' of Religions." Tr. G. D. Alles. *Religion* 19:101–127.

Rutgers, Leonard V. 1990. "The Jewish Catacombs of Rome Reconsidered." *Proceedings of the Tenth World Congress in Jewish Studies*, Division B. 2:29–36.

———. 1995. *The Jews of Late Ancient Rome: An Archaeological and Historical Study on the Interaction of Jews and non-Jews in the Roman-Diaspora*. Leiden: E. J. Brill.

Sabar, Shalom. 1990. *Ketubbah: Jewish Marriage Contracts of the Hebrew Union College Skirball Museum and Klau Library*. Philadelphia and New York: Jewish Publication Society.

Safrai, Shmuel. 1967. "The Jewish City in Eretz Israel during the Period of the Mishna and the Talmud." *Town and Country: Lectures Delivered at the Twelfth Convention of the Historical Society of Israel*, December 1966, Jerusalem. 227–236. Hebrew.

———. 1974. "Synagogues South of Mt. Judah." *Immanuel* 3:44–50.

———. 1983. "The Holy Community of Jerusalem." In *Eretz Israel and Its Sages during the Period of the Mishnah and the Talmud*. Israel: Hakibbutz Hameuchad. 43–56. Hebrew.

———. 1987. "The Temple and the Synagogue." In *Synagogues in Antiquity*, ed. A. Kasher, A. Oppenheimer, and U. Rappaport. Jerusalem: Ben Zvi Institute. 31–52.

Safrai, Ze'ev. 1984. "Sacred Tombs and Holy Sites in the Jewish Tradition." In *Zev Vilnay's Jubilee Volume*, ed. E. Schiller. Jerusalem: Ariel. 2:303–313. Hebrew.

———. 1986. "Samaritan Synagogues in the Roman-Byzantine Period." In *The Ancient Synagogue*, ed. Z. Safrai. 157–186. Rpt. from *Cathedra* 4 (1977):84–112. Hebrew.

———. 1987a. "Financing Synagogue Construction in the Period of the Mishna and the Talmud." In *Synagogues in Antiquity*, ed. A. Kasher, A. Oppenheimer, and U. Rappaport. Jerusalem: Ben Zvi Institute. 77–96.

———. 1987b. "Post-Talmudic Halakhic Literature in the Land of Israel." In *Literature of the Sages*, pt. 1, ed. S. Safrai. Assen/Maastricht: Van Gorgum and Philadelphia: Fortress Press. 404–409.

———. 1989. "Dukhan, Aron and Teva: How Was the Ancient Synagogue Furnished?" In *Ancient Synagogues in Israel*, ed. R. Hachlili. London: BAR International. 69–83.

———. 1990a. "From Synagogue to Little Temple." *Proceedings of the Tenth World Congress in Jewish Studies*, Division B. 2:23–28.

———. 1990b. "When Was Gender Segregation Introduced in the Synagogue?" *Moment* 15 (2):6–9.

———. 1990–1993. "From Synagogue to 'Lesser Temple'." *Israel People and Land* 6–7: 149–158. Hebrew.

———. 1994. *The Economy of Roman Palestine*. London and New York: Routledge.

———. 1995. "The Communal Functions of the Synagogue in the Land of Israel in the Rabbinic Period." In *Ancient Synagogues: Historical Analysis and Archaeological Discovery*, ed. D. Urman and P. V. M. Flesher. Leiden: E. J. Brill. 1:181–204.

St. Clair, Archer. 1985. "God's House of Peace in Paradise: The Feast of Tabernacles on a Jewish Gold Glass." *Jewish Art* 11:6–15.

Saller, Sylvester, and Bellarmino Bagatti. 1949. *The Town of Nebo (Khirbet El-Mekhayyat)*. Jerusalem: Franciscan.

Samson son of Abraham of Sens. 1884. *Commentary on Order Taharot*. Published accompanying tractate Niddah in the Vilna: Romm edition of the Babylonian Talmud.

Sanders, E. P. 1977. *Paul and Palestinian Judaism*. London and Philadelphia: Fortress Press.

———. 1990. *Jewish Law from Jesus to the Mishnah*. London and Philadelphia: Trinity International.

———. 1992. *Judaism: Practice and Belief 63 BCE–66 CE*. London and Philadelphia: Trinity International.

Sanders, James A. 1972. *Torah and Canon*. Philadelphia: Fortress Press.

Sarason, Richard S. 1986. "The Significance of the Land of Israel in the Mishnah." In *The Land of Israel: Jewish Perspectives*, ed. L. A. Hoffman. Notre Dame, Ind.: University of Notre Dame Press. 110–136.

Sarfatti, Gad Ben Ami. 1965. "Introduction to the Baraita of Constellations." *Bar Ilan* 3:56–83. Hebrew.

———. 1978. "I Segni Dello Zodiaco Nell' Iconografia Ebraica." In *Scritti in Memoria di Umberto Nahon*. Jerusalem: Mosad Shelomoh Meir, Mosad Refael Kantoni. 180–195.

Sarna, Jonathan D. 1987. "The Debate over Mixed Seating in the American Synagogue." In *The American Synagogue: A Sanctuary Transformed*, ed. J. Wertheimer. New York: Cambridge University Press. 363–394.

Sarna, Nahum M. 1970. "Bible." *Encyclopedia Judaica* 4:816–836.

Schäfer, Peter. 1972. *Die Vorstellung vom heiligen Geist in der rabbinischen Literatur*. Munich: Kosel-Verlag.

———. 1990. "Jewish Magic Literature in Late Antiquity and in the Early Middle Ages." *Journal of Jewish Studies* 41:75-91.

Schatkin, Margaret. 1974. "The Maccabean Martyrs." *Vigilae Christianae* 28:97–133.

Schechter, Solomon. 1891. "Jewish Literature in 1890." *Jewish Quarterly Review*, Old Series, 3:314–342.

———. 1909. *Aspects of Rabbinic Theology*. New York: Macmillan.

———. "Lovingkindness and Truth." In *Seminary Addresses and Other Papers*. New York: Arno Press and The New York Times. 245–253.

Schiffman, Lawrence H. 1983. *Sectarian Law in the Dead Sea Scrolls*. Chico: Scholars Press.

———. 1987a. "The Conversion of the Royal House of Adiabene in Josephus and in Rabbinic Sources." In *Josephus, Judaism and Christianity*, ed. L. H. Feldman and G. Hata. Detroit: Wayne State University Press. 213–214.

———. 1987b. "The Dead Sea Scrolls and the Early History of Jewish Liturgy." In *The Synagogue in Late Antiquity*, ed. L. I. Levine. Philadelphia: American Schools for Oriental Research. 33–48.

———. 1991. *From Text to Tradition: A History of Second Temple and Rabbinic Judaism*. Hoboken: Ktav.

Schiffman, Lawrence H., and Michael D. Swartz. 1992. *Hebrew and Aramaic Incantation Texts from the Cairo Genizah*. Sheffield: Sheffield University Press.

Scholem, Gershom. 1960. *Jewish Gnosticism, Merkabah Mysticism, and Talmudic Tradition*. New York: Jewish Theological Seminary.

Schubert, Kurt. 1981. "'Sacra Sinagoga'-zur Heiligkeit der Synagoge in der Spätantike." *Bibel und Liturgie* 54:27–34.

———. 1992. "The Holiness of the Synagogue and Its Figurative Decoration." In *Jewish Historiography and Iconography in Early and Medieval Christianity*, ed. Heinz Schreckenberg and Kurt Schubert. Assen/Maastricht: Van Gorgum and Minneapolis: Fortress Press. 161–170.

Schürer, Emil. 1973–1986. *The History of the Jewish People in the Age of Jesus Christ*. Rev. and ed. G. Vermes et al. Edinburgh: T. & T. Clark.

Schwabe, Moshe, and Baruch Lifshitz. 1974. *Beth She'arim*. 2. New Brunswick, N.J.

Schwartz, Joshua. 1986. *Jewish Settlement in Judaea*. Jerusalem: Magnes Press. Hebrew.

Seager, Andrew R. 1972. "The Building History of the Sardis Synagogue." *American Journal of Archaeology* 76:425–435.

———. 1981. "The Synagogue at Sardis." In *Ancient Synagogues Revealed*, ed. L. I. Levine. Jerusalem: Israel Exploration Society. 178–184.

———. 1989. "The Recent Historiography of Ancient Synagogue Architecture." In *Ancient Synagogues in Israel*, ed. R. Hachlili. London: BAR International. 82–92.

Shanks, Hershel. 1979. *Judaism in Stone*. New York: Harper and Row.

Shapiro, Menachem R., ed. 1976. *Otzar Ha-She'eloth U-Teshuvoth (Compendium Responsarum)*. Jerusalem. 1. Hebrew.

Shilo, Yigal. 1968. "Torah Scrolls and the Menorah Plaque from Sardis." *Israel Exploration Journal* 18:54–57.

Shinan, Avigdor. 1976. "*Lishon Beit Kudsha* in the Aramaic Targumim to the Pentateuch." *Beth Mikra* 3 (66):472–474.

———. 1991. "Targumic Additions in Targum Pseudo-Jonathan." *Textus* 16:139–155.

———. 1992a. "The Aramaic Targum as a Mirror of Galilean Jewry." In *The Galilee in Late Antiquity*, ed. L. I. Levine. New York and Jerusalem: Jewish Theological Seminary. 241–251.

———. 1992b. *The Embroidered Targum: The Aggadah in Targum Pseudo-Jonathan of the Pentateuch*. Jerusalem: Magnes Press. Hebrew.

Simon, Marcel. 1986. *Versus Israel*. Tr. H. McKeating. Oxford: Oxford University Press.

Sinding-Larsen, S. 1984. *Iconography and Ritual: A Study of Analytical Perspectives.* Oslo: Universitetsforlaget As.

Slomovic, Elieser. 1988. "Patterns of Midrashic Impact on the Rabbinic Midrashic Tale." *Journal for the Study of Judaism* 19 (1):61–90.

Slouschz, Nahum. 1921. "Hamath-by-Tiberias." *Journal of the Jewish Palestine Exploration Society* 1:5–37. Hebrew.

———. 1942. *Thesaurus of Phoenician Inscriptions.* Tel Aviv: Bialik Institute, Devir. Hebrew.

Smith, Alison Moore. 1922. "The Iconography of the Sacrifice of Isaac in Early Christian Art." *American Journal of Archaeology* 26:159–173.

Smith, Jonathan Z. 1978. *Map Is Not Territory: Studies in the History of Religions.* Leiden: E. J. Brill.

———. 1987. *To Take Place: Toward Theory in Ritual.* Chicago: University of Chicago Press.

Smith, Morton. 1957. "Review of *The Synagogue*, by Carl H. Kraeling, with contributions by C. C. Torrey, C. B. Welles, and B. Geiger. ('The Excavations at Dura-Europos, Final Report VIII, Part I,' ed. A. Bellinger, F. Brown, A. Perkins, C. Welles.) New Haven: Yale University Press, 1956." *Journal of Biblical Literature* 76:324–327.

———. 1967. "Goodenough's Jewish Symbols in Retrospect." *Journal of Biblical Literature* 86:53–68.

———. 1982. "Helios in Palestine." *Eretz-Israel* 20:199*–214*.

Sokoloff, Michael. 1972. "The Hebrew of Genesis Rabba, Manuscript Vatican 30." In *Anthology of Articles in Rabbinic Hebrew*, ed. M. Bar-Asher. Jerusalem: Akadamon. 1:257–301. Rpt. from *Leshonanu* 33 (25–42):135–149, 270–279. Hebrew.

———. 1980. "Epigraphical Notes on the Palestinian Talmud." *Bar Ilan* 18–19:218–220. Hebrew.

———. 1990. *A Dictionary of Jewish Palestinian Aramaic.* Ramat Gan: Bar Ilan University Press.

Sokoloff, Michael, and Joseph Yahalom. 1985. "Aramaic Piyyutim from the Byzantine Period." *Jewish Quarterly Review* 75:309–321.

Sonne, Isaiah. 1958. "Secondary Names for the Synagogue." *Tarbiz* 27:557–559. Hebrew.

———. 1962. "Synagogue." *The Interpreter's Dictionary of the Bible*, 4:476–491.

Sperber, Daniel. 1982. "On the Unfortunate Adventures of Rav Kahana: A Passage of Saboraic Polemic from Sasanian Persia." *Irano-Judaica* 1:83–100.

———. 1984. *Greek and Latin Legal Terms in Rabbinic Literature.* Ramat Gan: Bar Ilan University Press.

———. 1993. *Material Culture in Eretz-Israel during the Talmudic Period.* Jerusalem: Ben Zvi Institute and Ramat Gan: Bar Ilan University Press. Hebrew.

Spiegel, Shalom. 1965. "Regarding the Polemic of Pirkoi ben Baboi." In *Harry Austyn Wolfson Jubilee Volume*, Hebrew Section. Jerusalem: American Academy for Jewish Research. 243–274.

Stambaugh, John E. 1978. "The Functions of Roman Temples." In *Aufstieg und Niedergang der Römische Welt*. Berlin and New York: Walther de Gruyter. 2.16.1.554–608.

———. 1988. *The Ancient Roman City*. Baltimore and London: Johns Hopkins University Press.

Stern, Joseph. 1985. "The Contemporary Synagogue." *The Journal of Halacha and Contemporary Society* 10:30–56.

Stone, Michael E. 1980. *Scriptures, Sects and Visions: A Profile of Judaism from Ezra to the Jewish Revolts*. Philadelphia: Fortress Press.

Strack, Hermann L., and Paul Billerbeck. 1928. *Kommentar Zum Neuen Testament*. Munich: C. H. Beck.

Strack, Hermann L., and Gunther Stemberger. 1991. *Introduction to the Talmud and Midrash*. Tr. M. Bockmuehl. Edinburgh: T & T Clarke.

Strauss, Heinrich. 1960. "Jewish Art as a Minority Problem." *Journal of Jewish Sociology* 2:147-171.

Steudel, Annette. 1993. "The House of Prostration, CD XI, 21–XII, 1— Duplicates of the Temple (1)." *Revue de Qumran* 16 (1):49–68.

Stroumsa, Gedaliahu G. 1989. "Religious Contacts in Byzantine Palestine." *Numen* 36 (1):16–42.

Sukenik, Eleazar L. 1930. "The Throne of Moses in Ancient Synagogues." *Tarbiz* 1:145–151. Hebrew.

———. 1932. *The Ancient Synagogue of Beth Alpha*. Jerusalem: Hebrew University.

———. 1934. *Ancient Synagogues in Palestine and Greece*. London: Oxford University Press.

———. 1935. *The Ancient Synagogue of El-Hammeh (Hammath-by-Gadera)*. Jerusalem: R. Mass.

———. 1942. *The Synagogue of Dura Europos and Its Frescoes*. Jerusalem: Bialik Institute. Hebrew.

———. 1950–1951. "The Mosaic Inscriptions in the Synagogue at Apamea on the Orontes." *Hebrew Union College Annual* 28, pt. 2. 541–551.

Sussman, Jacob. 1973–74, 1974–75. "A Halakhic Inscription from the Beth-Shean Valley." *Tarbiz* 43: 88–158, 44:193–195. Hebrew.

———. 1981. "The Inscription in the Synagogue at Rehob." In *Ancient Synagogues Revealed*, ed. L. I. Levine. Jerusalem: Israel Exploration Society. 146–151.

Sussman, Varda. 1982. *Ornamented Jewish Oil-Lamps: From the Destruction of the Second Temple Period through the Bar Kokhba Revolt*. Jerusalem: Israel Exploration Society.

Swartz, Michael D. 1990. "Scribal Magic and Its Rhetoric: Formal Patterns in Medieval Hebrew and Aramaic Incantation Texts from the Cairo Genizah." *Harvard Theological Review* 83 (2):163–180.

———. 1992. *Mystical Prayer in Ancient Judaism: An Analysis of Ma'aseh Merkavah*. Tübingen: J. C. B. Mohr.

Talmon, S. 1989a. "Fragments of Scrolls from Masada." *Eretz-Israel* 20:278–286. Hebrew.

———. 1989b. *The World of Qumran from Within.* Jerusalem: Magnes Press and Leiden: E. J. Brill.

Tchalenko, Georges, and E. Baccache. 1979–1980. *Eglises de villages de la Syrie du Nord.* Paris: Librairie Orientaliste P. Guethner.

Tcherikover, Victor. 1959. *Hellenistic Civilization and the Jews.* Philadelphia: Jewish Publication Society of America.

Teicher, J. L. 1963. "Ancient Eucharistic Prayers in Hebrew." *Jewish Quarterly Review* 54 (2):99–109.

Torrey, Charles C. 1956. "The Aramaic Texts." In *The Synagogue. The Excavations of Dura Europos, Final Report VIII, Part 1,* ed. C. H. Kraeling. New Haven: Yale University Press. 261–276.

Tosafot on the Babylonian Talmud. 1884. Published in the Vilna: Romm edition of the Babylonian Talmud.

Tov, Emanuel. 1992. *Textual Criticism of the Hebrew Bible.* Minneapolis: Fortress Press, and Assen/Maastricht: Van Gorgum.

Trachtenberg, Joshua. 1961. *Jewish Magic and Superstition: A Study in Folk Magic.* Cleveland, New York, and Philadelphia: Jewish Publication Society.

Trell, Bluma L. 1964. "The Cult-image on Temple-Type Coins." *Numismatic Chronicle* 4:241–246.

Trifon, Dalia. 1989–1990. "Did the Priestly Courses (*Mishmarot*) Transfer from Judaea to the Galilee after the Bar Kokhba Revolt?" *Tarbiz* 59 (1–2):77–93. Hebrew.

Trowbridge, Mary Luella. 1930. *Philological Studies in Ancient Glass.* Urbana: University of Illinois Press.

Tsafrir, Yoram. 1984. *Eretz Israel from the Destruction of the Second Temple to the Muslim Conquest, Art and Archaeology.* Jerusalem: Ben Zvi Institute. Hebrew.

———. 1987. "The Byzantine Setting and Its Influence on Ancient Synagogues." In *The Synagogue in Late Antiquity,* ed. L. I. Levine. Philadelphia: American Schools for Oriental Research. 147–156.

———. 1989. "The Synagogues of Merot and Capernaum and the Dating of Galilean Synagogues—A Reappraisal." *Eretz-Israel* 20:337–344. Hebrew.

Turner, Harold W. 1979. *From Temple to Meeting Place: The Phenomenology and Theology of Places of Worship.* The Hague: Mouton.

Tzaferis, Vassilios. 1982. "The Ancient Synagogue at Ma'oz Hayyim." *Israel Exploration Journal* 32:215–244.

Urbach, Ephraim E. 1959. "The Rabbinical Laws of Idolatry in the Second and Third Centuries in Light of Archaeological and Historical Facts." *Israel Exploration Journal* 9 (3–4):149–165, 229–245.

———. 1975. *The Sages—Their Concepts and Beliefs.* Tr. I. Abrahams. Jerusalem: Magnes Press.

———. 1990. "The Role of the Ten Commandments in Jewish Worship." In *The Ten Commandments in History and Tradition,* ed. B. Segal and G. Levi, tr. G. Levi. Jerusalem: Magnes Press. 161–189.

Urman, Dan. 1995. "The House of Assembly and the House of Study: Are They One and the Same?" In *Ancient Synagogues: Historical Analysis and Archaeological Discovery*, ed. D. Urman and P. V. M. Flesher. Leiden: E. J. Brill. 1:232–255.

van der Horst, Pieter. Forthcoming. "Was the Ancient Synagogue a Place of Sabbath Worship?" In *Jews, Christians and Polytheists in the Ancient Synagogue: Cultural Interaction During the Greco-Roman Period*, ed. S. Fine. London and New York: Routledge.

Van Woerden, Isabel Speyart. 1961. "The Iconography of the Sacrifice of Isaac." *Vigiliae Christianae* 15:214–255.

Villa Hügel. 1963. *Koptische Kunst: Christentum m Nil*. Essen: Villa Hügel.

Vilnay, Zev. 1971. *The Guide to Israel*. Jerusalem: Ahiever.

Vitto, Fanny. 1981. "The Synagogue at Rehob." In *Ancient Synagogues Revealed*, ed. L. I. Levine. Jerusalem: Israel Exploration Society. 90–94.

———. 1982. "Decor mural des anciennes synagogues a la lumiere de nouvelles decouvertes." *XVI Internationaler Byzantinstenkongress Akten* (= *Jahrbuch der Österreichischen Byzantinistik* 32.5). 366–367.

Viviano, Benedict Thomas. 1978. *Study as Worship: Aboth and the New Testament*. Leiden: E. J. Brill.

Wacholder, Ben Zion. 1968. "The Date of the Mekilta De-Rabbi Ishmael." *Hebrew Union College Annual* 39:117–144.

———. 1978. *Messianism and Mishnah: Time and Place in the Early Halakhah*. Cincinnati: Hebrew Union College Press.

Walker, P. W. L. 1990. *Holy City, Holy Places?* Oxford: Oxford University Press.

Wegner, Judith Romney. 1988. *Chattel of Person? The Status of Women in the Mishnah*. New York and Oxford: Oxford University Press.

Weiss, Ze'ev. 1988. "Ancient Synagogues in Tiberias and in Hamat." *Idan* 11:34–48. Hebrew.

———. 1990. "The Location of the Sheliah Tsibbur during Prayer." *Cathedra* 55:9–21. Hebrew.

———. 1992. "The Synagogue at Hamat Tiberias (Stratum II)." *Eretz-Israel* 23:320–326. Hebrew.

Weiss, Ze'ev, and Ehud Netzer. 1996. *Promise and Redemption: A Synagogue Mosaic from Sepphoris*. Jerusalem: Israel Museum.

Weitzmann, Kurt. 1971a. "The Illustration of the Septuagint." In *No Graven Images: Studies in Art and the Hebrew Bible*, ed. J. Gutmann. New York: Ktav. 201–231.

———. 1971b. "The Question of the Influence of Jewish Pictorial Sources on Old Testament Illustration." In *No Graven Images: Studies in Art and the Hebrew Bible*, ed. J. Gutmann. New York: Ktav. 309–328.

———. ed. 1979. *Age of Spirituality*. New York: Metropolitan Museum of Art, and Princeton: Princeton University Press.

Weitzmann, Kurt, and Herbert L. Kessler. 1990. *The Frescoes of the Dura Synagogue and Christian Art*. Washington, D.C.: Dumbarton Oaks.

Wertheimer, Jack, ed. 1987. *The American Synagogue: A Sanctuary Transformed*. New York: Cambridge University Press.

Wharton, Annabel Jane. 1994. "Good and Bad Images from the Synagogue of Dura Europos: Contexts, Subtexts, Intertexts." *Art History* 17 (1):1–25.

White, Michael. 1990. *Building God's House in the Roman World*. Baltimore and London: Johns Hopkins University Press.

Wieder, Naphtali. 1946. "Islamic Influences on the Hebrew Cultus." *Melilah* 2:37–120. Hebrew.

———. 1957. "'Sanctuary' as a Metaphor for Scripture." *Journal of Jewish Studies* 7 (3–4): 165–175.

Wilken, Robert L. 1983. *John Chrysostom and the Jews: Rhetoric and Reality in the Late Fourth Century*. Berkeley and Los Angeles: University of California Press.

———. 1993. *The Land Called Holy: Palestine in Christian History and Thought*. New Haven: Yale University Press.

Wilkinson, John. 1981. *Egeria's Travels to the Holy Land*. Jerusalem: Ariel, and London: Aris and Phillips.

———. 1984. "Orientation, Jewish and Christian." *Palestine Exploration Quarterly* 116 (1):16–30.

———. 1993. "Christian Worship in Byzantine Palestine." In *Ancient Churches Revealed*, ed. Y. Tsafrir. Jerusalem: Israel Exploration Society. 17–27.

Wiseman, J., and D. Mano-Zissi. 1971. "Excavations at Stobi, 1970." *American Journal of Archaeology* 75:395–411.

Wright, David P. 1987. *The Disposal of Impurity: Elimination Rites in the Bible and in Hittite and Mesopotamian Religion*. Atlanta: Scholars Press.

———. 1991. "Review of Gammie, John G. *Holiness in Israel*. Overtures to Biblical Theology Series. Minneapolis: Augsburg Fortress, 1989, 215." *Journal of Religion* 71 (3): 428–429.

———. 1992. "Holiness, Old Testament." In *Anchor Bible Dictionary*, ed. D. N. Freedman. New York: Doubleday. 3:237–249.

Yaari, Abraham. 1957–1958. "The Mi' Sheberakh Prayers: History and Texts." *Kirjath Sepher* 33 (1–2):118–130, 233–251. Hebrew.

———. 1964. *The History of the Festival of Simhat Torah*. Jerusalem: Rav Kook Institute. Hebrew.

Yadin, Yigael. 1965. "The Excavation of Masada 1963/64 Preliminary Report." *Israel Exploration Journal, Jerusalem* 15 (1–2):1–120.

———. 1981. "The Synagogue at Masada." In *Ancient Synagogues Revealed*, ed. L. I. Levine. Jerusalem: Israel Exploration Society. 19–23.

Yahalom, Joseph. 1980. "Synagogue Inscriptions in Palestine—A Stylistic Classification." *Immanuel* 10:47–57.

———. 1986. "The Zodiac Wheel in Early Piyyut in Eretz-Israel." *Jerusalem Studies in Hebrew Literature*. 9:313–322. Hebrew.

———. 1987. "Piyyut as Poetry." In *The Synagogue in Late Antiquity*, ed. L. I. Levine. Philadelphia: American Schools for Oriental Research. 111–126.

Yeivin, Shmuel. 1946. "Notes on the Excavation at Beth She'arim." *Bulletin of the Jewish Palestine Exploration Society* 2:69–76. Hebrew.

Yeivin, Ze'ev. 1981. "The Synagogue of Eshtemoa." In *Ancient Synagogues Revealed*, ed. L. I. Levine. Jerusalem: Israel Exploration Society. 120–122.

———. 1985. "Reconstruction of the Southern Interior Wall of the Khorazin Synagogue." *Eretz-Israel* 18:268–276. Hebrew.

———. 1987. "Ancient Chorazin Comes Back to Life." *Biblical Archaeology Review* 13 (5):22–36.

———. 1989. "Khirbet Susiya, the Bima, and Synagogue Ornamentation." In *Ancient Synagogues in Israel*, ed. R. Hachlili. London: BAR International. 93–100.

Yellin, Aryeh Lev. 1884. *Yafeh Anayim*. Published accompanying the Vilna: Romm edition of the Babylonian Talmud. Hebrew.

Yerushalmi, Yosef Hayim. 1982. *Zakhor: Jewish History and Jewish Memory*. Seattle and London: University of Washington Press.

York, Anthony D. 1979. "The Targum in the Synagogue and School." *Journal for the Study of Judaism* 10 (1):74–86.

Yosef, Ovadyah. 1980. *Sefer She'elot u-Tshuvot Yeḥaveh Da'at*. Jerusalem. 3. Hebrew.

Zahavy, Tzvee. 1987. *The Mishnaic Law of Blessings and Prayers*. Atlanta: Scholars Press.

———. 1990. *Studies in Jewish Prayer*. Lanham: University Press of America.

Zeitlin, Solomon. 1950. "Introduction" *The First Book of Maccabees*. Tr. S. Tedesche. New York: Harper. 1–66.

———. 1962–1963. "There Was No Synagogue in the Temple." *Jewish Quarterly Review* 53:168–169.

———. 1963–1964. "Tefillah, the Shemoneh Esreh: An Historical Study of the First Canonization of the Hebrew Liturgy." *Jewish Quarterly Review* 54:210–249.

Zevi, F. 1972. "La Sinagoga di Ostia." *Rassegna mensile di Israel*. 38:131–145.

Zevulun, Uza. 1979. *Form and Function in the Talmudic Period*. Tel Aviv: Haaretz Museum.

Zimmerli, Walther. 1979. *Ezekiel 1*. Tr. R. E. Clemens. Philadelphia: Fortress Press.

Zori, N. 1966. "The House of Kyrios Leontis at Beth Shean." *Israel Exploration Journal* 16:123–134.

——— 1967. "The Ancient Synagogue at Beth-Shean." *Eretz-Israel* 8:149–167. Hebrew.

Zucker, Moses. 1959. *Rav Saadya Gaon's Translation of the Torah*. New York. Hebrew.

———. 1963. "Responses to the Karaite 'Mourners of Zion' Movement in Rabbinical Literature." *Chanoch Albeck Jubilee Volume*. Jerusalem: Rav Kook Institute. 378–401. Hebrew.

Zuri, Jacob Samuel. 1931. *The Rule of the Patriarchate and the Council*. 1. Paris. Hebrew.

Photo Credits

Page 2, courtesy of Leonard S. Berkowitz; page 142, from E. L. Sukenik, *The Synagogue of Dura Europos and Its Frescos* (Jerusalem: Bialik Institute, 1949); page 147, A. Refenberg, *Ancient Hebrew Arts* (New York: Schocken, 1950), 141; page 117, from M. Fendri, *Basiliques Cretiennes de la Skhira* (Paris: Presses Universitaires de France, 1961); pages 83, 85, 100, 110, 148 (upper), Steven Fine; page 107, courtesy of Glenda Friend; page viii, courtesy of Barry Gittlen; pages 119, 123, courtesy of the Hebrew University of Jerusalem, Institute of Archaeology, Archaeological Excavation at Sepphoris; pages 89, 120, 122, courtesy of the Israel Exploration Society; pages 154, 155, from *The Jewish Encyclopedia* (New York: Funk and Wagnalls, 1901); page 75, courtesy of Joseph Naveh and the Magnes Press; pages 106, 114, courtesy of Eric M. and Carole Meyers; page 102, courtesy of the Musée Royale de Mariemont, Belgium; page 150, courtesy of Leonard V. Rutgers; page 31, courtesy of Herbert Scher; page 152, courtesy of the Soprintendenza Archeologica di Ostia; pages 91, 104, 113, 116, from E. L. Sukenik, *The Ancient Synagogue of Beth Alpha* (Jerusalem: Hebrew University, 1932); pages 141, 143, 145, courtesy of the Yale University Art Gallery, Dura Collection; pages 96, 109, 128, 148 (lower), 151, courtesy of the Yeshiva University Museum.

Index of Ancient Literary Sources Cited

Hebrew Scriptures

Genesis
- 9:18 — 17
- 18 — 124

Exodus
- 3:5 — 209 n. 42
- 15:3 — 78
- 20:20 — 47, 56
- 20:21 — 54
- 25:31–40 — 118, 188 n. 110, 217 n. 155
- 25:31 — 49
- 37:17–24 — 118, 188 n. 110, 217 n. 155
- 37:17 — 49

Leviticus
- 6:19–20 — 209 n. 41
- 7:6 — 209 n. 42
- 10:10 — 11, 169 n. 60
- 10:13 — 209 n. 42
- 11:43–44 — 18–19
- 12:4 — 84
- 16:24 — 209 n. 42
- 19:2 — 18
- 19:30 — 82
- 24:2 — 84
- 24:9 — 209 n. 42
- 26:1 — 90–92
- 26:2 — 82
- 26:31 — 42–43

Numbers
- 8:2 — 115
- 22:5 — 115

Deuteronomy
- 4:44 — 79
- 6:4 — 78
- 31:26 — 90

Judges
- 13:15 — 65

1 Samuel
- 1:10 — 192 n. 13
- 1:13 — 64

1 Kings
- 8:30 — 52
- 9:3 — 81
- 18:39 — 78

2 Kings
- 4:9 — 19
- 8:4 — 163 n. 4
- 25:9 — 68

Isaiah
- 6:3 — 17, 53
- 50:2 — 66
- 55:6 — 63
- 56:7 — 82
- 60:13 — 209 n. 42

Jeremiah
- 32:14 — 132

Ezekiel
- 3:12 — 53
- 11:16 — 81, 82
- 42:13 — 209 n. 42

Hosea
- 14:3 — 86

Habakkuk
- 2:20 — 81

Psalms
- 12:9 — 62, 63
- 29:1 — 52
- 40:2 — 65
- 71:19 — 78
- 82:1 — 54, 63, 64
- 84:6 — 66
- 118 — 87
- 125:5 — 104

Proverbs
- 1:21 — 93, 132

Ecclesiastes
- 8:10 — 66, 67

Canticles
- 2:9 — 65

Daniel
- 6:11 — 58

Ezra
- 9:9 — 132

Nehemiah
- 7:65 — 13
- 8:1–8 — 13
- 8:3–6 — 44
- 8:5 — 77, 79

1 Chronicles
- 3:1 — 226 n. 77

2 Chronicles
- 6:32 — 52
- 6:34 — 52
- 6:38 — 51
- 24 — 88

Apocrypha and Pseudepigrapha

1 Maccabees
- 12:9 — 13

3 Maccabees
- 2:28 — 178 n. 32

Assumption of Moses
- 1:16–17 — 171 n. 89

Josephus

Jewish War
- 2:229 — 170 n. 184
- 2:289–92 — 179 n. 37
- 4:400 — 178 n. 27
- 4:408 — 178 n. 32
- 5:190 — 186 n. 71
- 5:190–193 — 206 n. 238
- 7:44–45 — 29, 178 n. 33, 186 n. 77
- 7:144 — 178 n. 32

Antiquities of the Jews
- 14:260 — 178 n. 30
- 15:396 — 186 n. 71
- 15:411–416 — 186 n. 71
- 16:164 — 170 n. 84
- 20:115 — 170 n. 84

Against Apion
- 1:209 — 178 n. 32
- 2:175 — 176 n. 3

Life
- 54:276–282 — 180 n. 55

Index of Ancient Literary Sources Cited | 283

Philo of Alexandria

Flaccus
46   27, 178 n. 22
48–49   27, 178 nn. 23, 24

Embassy to Gaius
132   178 n. 29
133   27, 178 n. 34, 186 n. 77
137   27, 178 n. 25

Every Good Man Is Free
81–82   31, 180 n. 50

Life of Moses
2:216   28, 178 n. 29

On Dreams
2:127   28, 178 n. 28

Qumran Literature

Damascus Covenant
4Q271, 11:21–22   32, 181 n. 58
4Q464   172 n. 107

4Q Mishmerot HaKohanim
60–118   204 n. 210

Rabbinic Literature, Liturgy, Targum, and Gaonic Sources

Mishnah

Berakhot
4:1   189 n. 135
7:3   181 n. 4, 189 n. 131
9:5   43, 82, 185 n. 56, 200 n. 138

Terumot
11:10   185 n. 53

Maaser Sheni
1:15   176 n. 163
3:13–14   176 n. 163
5:7   176 n. 163

Pesahim
4:4   185 n. 53, 202 n. 174

Sheqalim
6:4   39, 183 n. 28

Yoma
1:7   185 n. 68
7:1   188 n. 115

Sukkah
3:1   186 n. 82
3:12   188 n. 117
3:13   50, 181 n. 4, 189 n. 123
4:6   199 n. 110
5:2   47

Rosh ha-Shanah
2:7   169 n. 69
3:7   181 n. 4, 189 n. 124

Ta'anit
2:5   58

Megillah
1:5–11   170 n. 70
1:8   182 n. 10, 183 n. 25
2:2   183 n. 25
2:4   181 n. 4
3:1   38, 39, 40, 68, 91, 131–132, 183 n. 29, 204 n. 204
3:2–3   40, 224 n. 25
3:2   41
3:3   41–42, 43, 69, 132
3:4–6   181 n. 3
4:2   169 n. 68
4:3   181 n. 3
4:6   181 n. 4
4:7   57
4:10   181 n. 4

Nedarim		*Tosefta* (Ed. Lieberman through tractate	
5:5	183 n. 24	*Baba Bathra*. Ed. Zuckermandel to end)	
Sotah		*Berakhot*	
7:7–8	185 n. 70	1:9	53
7:7	188 n. 115	2:4	189 n. 131
7:8	185 nn. 66, 67	2:20	184 n. 41
Qiddushin		3:1	189 nn. 127, 135
2:1	169 n. 69	3:3	86, 189 n. 135
Eduyot		3:6	189 n. 133
5:3	171 n. 97	3:15, 16	51–52, 187 n. 90
Avodah Zarah		3:25	52
3:4	184 n. 41	*Terumot*	
Avot		1:10	181 n. 4
1:2	170 n. 77	*Bikkurim*	
3:6	54	2:8	185 n. 69
Horayot		*Shabbat*	
3:10	173 n. 127	16:22	181 n. 4
Menahot		*Kippurim*	
13:10	191 n. 177	2:3	187 n. 95
Hullin		3:18	181 n. 4, 187
1:7	169 n. 67	4:18	188 n. 116
Bekorot		*Sukkah*	
5:5	181 n. 4	2:10	50, 181 n. 4
Tamid		4:1	185 n. 57
3:4	206 n. 238	4:5	43, 57, 188 n. 127
7:4	189 n. 141, 204 n. 197	4:6	37, 43, 44, 185 n. 64
		4:8	185 n. 68
Middot		4:11–12	185 n. 68
1:6	206 nn. 236, 238	*Taanit*	
Kelim		1:13	185 n. 57, 192 n. 188
1:6–9	12–13, 46, 51	*Megillah*	
1:6	170 n. 75	2:1	36
1:9	170 n. 73	2:12	40–41, 184 n. 40
11:7	48	2:13	55, 182 n. 16
16:7	39, 182 n. 19, 194 n. 40	2:14	47, 182 nn. 14, 15, 184 nn. 38, 43, 187 n. 91, 200 n. 137, 207 n. 5, 210 n. 65
28:6	182 n. 20	2:16	55, 56, 182 nn. 14, 16, 207 n. 5
Zavim			
3:2	181 n. 4	2:18	36–37, 43, 69, 181 n. 4, 223
Yadaim			
2:19	171 n. 97	2:19	185 n. 59
3:5	171 n. 98	3:20	183 nn. 25, 30
4:5	183 n. 25		

3:21–23	45–46, 49	Baba Bathra	
3:21	37, 72, 180 n. 48, 185 n. 69	8:4	181 n. 4
		Zebahim	
3:23	132, 206 n. 24	13:1	176 n. 163
Nedarim		Bekhorot	
5:5	183 n. 24	3:2	176 n. 163
Sotah		Arakhin	
9:15	174 n. 135	2:7	176 n. 163
Sanhedrin		Kelim	
3:6	176 n. 163	B. Mes. 1:13	182 n. 21
4:4	184 n. 41	Yadaim	
4:8	184 n. 41	2:12	39, 183 n. 33, 194 n. 40
Baba Mesia		2:14	171 n. 98
11:2	208 n. 13	2:19	171 n. 97

Palestinian *Talmud*

Berakhot		Yoma	
1:1, 2c	86	3:8, 41a	187 n. 96, 200 n. 133
2:7, 5a–b	182 n. 7	6:3, 43c–d	191 n. 177
2:7, 5b	19	7:1, 44b	199 n. 130
3:1, 6a	58, 191 n. 184	Sukkah	
3:5, 6d	70–71, 80	5:1, 55a–b	185 n. 64
4:4, 8b	86, 203 n. 185	Taanit	
4:6, 8c	86	2:1, 65a	80, 199 n. 127
5:1, 8d–9a	62, 65, 86, 219 n. 195	3:11, 66d	186 n. 71
9:1, 13a	64	Megillah	
Terumot		1:1, 72b	174 n. 142
4:4, 42a	21	3:1–3, 73d–74a	67–68
Maaser Sheni		3:1, 73d	69–71, 79, 93, 130, 163 n. 4, 194 n. 39, 212 n. 95, 215 n. 125, 223 n. 20
5:5, 56b	173 n. 129		
Bikkurim			
3:2, 65c	195 n. 61		
3:3, 65d	81, 200 n. 141	3:2, 74a	80, 207 n. 6, 211 n. 66
3:7, 65d	184 n. 36	3:3, 74a	199 n. 131
Shabbat		3:4, 74a	193 n. 35
1:5, 3c	174 n. 135	4:1, 74d	72, 171 n. 102, 195 n. 59
15:1, 15b	171 n. 99		
Sheqalim		4:1, 75a	176 n. 3, 181 n. 3
2:7, 47a	186 n. 83	4:5, 75b	199 n. 130

MoedQatan
3:1, 81d   15, 71–72, 171 n. 103, 195 n. 56

Yebamot
2:4, 3d   175 n. 146

Nedarim
6:13, 40a   175 n. 156

Sotah
8:6, 22a   199 n. 130

Sanhedrin
1, 19a   175 n. 156
10:2, 29b   19–20, 174 n. 145
10:5, 29c   174 n. 142

Shevuot
4:10, 35c   193 n. 19, 219 n. 195

Avodah Zarah
3:1, 42c   174 n. 142
4:1, 43d   192 n. 191, 205 n. 230

Babylonian *Talmud*

Berakhot
6a   190 n. 159
8a   64, 192 n. 6, 224 n. 38
8b   171 n. 103, 195 n. 56
9b   174 n. 136
10b   174 n. 145
30b   64
33a   190 n. 150
33b   186 n. 72
54a   193 n. 33
62b   81, 176 n. 165

Shabbat
11a   223 n. 11
14a   15, 171 n. 100
32a–32b   223 n. 17
32a   133
115a   196 n. 78
118b   174 n. 142

Pesahim
13b   186 n. 72
44a   15, 171 n. 100
72b   176 n. 165
104a   11, 174 n. 142
113b   174 n. 142

Sukkah
51a   186 n. 82

Besa
27a   174 n. 136

Yoma
39a   18
69a   174 n. 136

Rosh ha-Shanah
19b   174 n. 136
24a–b   48
24b   224 n. 34
30a   189 n. 122
31b   191 n. 182

Taanit
14b   176 n. 165

Megillah
2a   176 n. 165
6b   192 n. 5
10a   191 n. 177
21b   217 n. 156
22b   192 n. 191, 205 n. 230
26a   184 n. 35
26b   70, 120, 171 n. 104
26b–27a   193 n. 29
27a   184 n. 36
28a   185 n. 36
28b   182 n. 6
28a–29a   134–137
29a   81
32a   171 n. 100

Yebamot
47a–b   176 n. 163

Sotah
*38b   191 n. 184
*39b   77

Gittin
36a   176 n. 163

Baba Bathra
3b   132–133

Avodah Zarah
20b   174 n. 135
43a   188 n. 99
43b   224 n. 34
50a   174 n. 142

Menahot
28b   188 n. 99
29a   218 n. 177
98b   217 n. 156
109a–110a   191 n. 177

Arakhin
6b   200 n. 134

Tamid
27b   174 n. 136

Niddah
13a   224 n. 34

Aramaic Poetry of the Byzantine Period from Eretz-Israel (Ed. M. Sokoloff and J. Yahalom)

43   77, 196 n. 80

Baraita de-Masseknet Niddah (version 1)

1:2   84, 202 n. 168
3:4   84, 202 n. 166

"An Early Lament on the Destruction of Communities in the Land of Israel" (Ed. S. Assaf)

204 n. 198

Differences in Religious Customs between Babylonian and Palestinian Jewries (Ed. B. M. Lewin)

36   73, 195 n. 62
49   77, 198 n. 107

Genizah Studies in Memory of Doctor Solomon Schechter (L. Ginzberg)

77   84, 202 n. 170
152–153   82, 200 n. 149

Megillat Ta'anit and Scolion (Ed. H. Lichtenstein)

339–340   191 n. 176

Mekilta of Rabbi Ishmael (Ed. H. S. Horowitz and I. A. Rabin)

Bo 1(2)   218 n. 77
Ba-Hodesh 2   173 n. 134, 190 n. 155
Ba Hodesh 10   56, 191 n. 168

Genesis Rabba (Ed. J. Theodor and C. Albeck)

49:23   203 n. 185
54:4   198 n. 105
63:6   193 n. 33
100:7   174 n. 141

Leviticus Rabba (Ed. M. Margulies)

24:4   174 n. 134
24:6   174 n. 145

Numbers Rabba

4:20	197 n. 89
15:4	218 n. 177

Deuteronomy Rabba

7:1	65–66

Canticles Rabba

2:5	76, 88, 197 n. 89

Ecclesiastes Rabba

2:8	176 n. 168
8:10	66

Hilkhot Eretz-Israel min ha-Geniza (Ed. M. Margoliot)

131–132	82, 200 n. 150
132	203 n. 188

Liturgical Poetry of Rabbi Yannai

1.105–106	17, 173 n. 123
1.170–71	17–18, 173 n. 124

Midrash Samuel

7:10	200 n. 141

Midrash Tanhuma (1833)

Va-yakel	90, 205 n. 224
Behukotai 3	93, 206 n. 240

Midrash Tanhuma (Ed. S. Buber)

Va-yakel	90, 205 n. 224
Behukotai 3	93, 206 n. 240

Midrash Tehillim

16:2	20, 175 n. 150
84:3	193 n. 20

Pereq Mashiah (Ed. S. Hopkins)

12–14	110–111

Pesiqta de-Rav Kahana (Ed. B. Mandelbaum)

1:7	195 n. 58
5:8	65, 190 n. 159, 192 n. 14
10:10	173 n. 129
24:18	203 n. 183
26:2	176 n. 168
28:8	65, 192 nn. 15, 16

Sefer Pitron Torah

18–19	202 n. 171
23	202 n. 172
23–24	202 nn. 173–174

Sifra

Aharei 13:9	173 n. 132
Qedoshim 9:2	173 n. 132
Behar 9:5	192 n. 191, 206 n. 235
Behukotai 6	42, 184 n. 46

Sifre Numbers

39	189
61	218 n. 177

Sifre Deuteronomy

85	173 n. 132
258	184 n. 41, 185 n. 36

Sifre Zutta

Ba'alotkha 255	115, 217 n. 156

Targumn Neofiti

Ex. 25:31	49, 188 n. 111
Ex. 37:17	49, 188 n. 111

Targum Onkelos

Ex. 30:28	188 n. 111

Targum Pseudo-Jonathan

Ex. 25:31	49, 188 n. 111
Ex. 37:17	45, 188 n. 111
Lev. 26:1	90–92

Targum to Psalms

84:8	193 n. 20

Targum to Proverbs

1:21	187 n. 87

Tractate Sofrim

14:4–11	78–79, 199 nn. 110–119
18:1–2	204 n. 197
18:12	181 n. 4

Yalkut Shimoni

Isa. 55:6	192 n. 8

Yose ben Yose Poems

127–203	204 n. 206
210–217	204 n. 206
222–239	204 n. 206

Greek and Latin Authors

Tacitus, *Histories*

5.4.41	178 n. 35

Vitruvius, *On Architecture*

1.7.1	187 n. 87

The Jews in Roman Imperial Legislation (Ed. A. Linder)

161–163	225 n. 54

Christian Authors

New Testament
Matthew

6:2	181 n. 4
23:2	195 n. 58

Luke

1:5	204 n. 210
1:8	204 n. 210

Acts

15:21	176 n. 3

Apostolic Constitutions

4	190 n. 150
12:84–85	190 n. 150

John Chrysostom, *Against the Jews*

1	138, 225 n. 44	6:5	138, 225 n. 50
1:3	137, 224 n. 41	6:7	137, 138, 224 n. 41, 225 n. 47
1:5	137, 224 n. 41		
6	138, 225 n. 44		

www.ingramcontent.com/pod-product-compliance
Lightning Source LLC
Chambersburg PA
CBHW070235230426
43664CB00014B/2311